Women and Education

Second Edition

Editors

Jane S. Gaskell
Arlene Tigar McLaren

Detselig Enterprises Limited
Calgary, Alberta

Jane S. Gaskell
The University of British Columbia

Arlene Tigar McLaren
Simon Fraser University

Canadian Cataloguing in Publication Data
Main entry under title:

Women and education

Includes bibliographical references.
ISBN 1-55059-038-3

1. Women – Education – Canada.   2. Women's studies
– Canada.   3. Feminism – Canada.   I. Gaskell, Jane S.
(Jane Stobo)   II. McLaren, Arlene Tigar.
LC1762.W65 1991   376'.971   C91-091594-6

© 1991 by Detselig Enterprises Limited
P.O. Box G 399
Calgary, Alberta, Canada T3A 2G3

Printed in Canada   SAN 115-0324   ISBN 1-55059-038-3

Preface

This is the second edition of *Women and Education: A Canadian Perspective.* The project was undertaken when all copies of the first edition had been sold, a gratifying phenomenon for both of us, because of the interest it signals in feminist work in educational circles. In 1987, when the first edition was published, some felt there was no market for such a lengthy and academic text in Canada, for there were few courses for which it could be adopted, and few faculty members who were interested. The steady if not dramatic sales are reassuring. Looking back at our first editon, we feel it marked an important provision of readings where there had been very little easily available.

We decided not to simply reissue the 1987 edition, because so much interesting new feminist scholarship on Canadian education has appeared in the past several years. The process of reconstituting a volume, without exceeding the page limits our publisher can live with, has been intriguing and difficult. We are left with material we would like to include but have no place for, and issues we would like to discuss but have had to exclude. What is included, however, is a selection of articles that will allow readers to explore a wide range of perspectives on education offered by Canadian feminist scholars in 1991.

The biggest change since 1987 has been in the section on curriculum. As we noted in the first edition, questions about whose knowledge gets transmitted in educational institutions is at the heart of the feminist critique. Ways of thinking about this question have become more sophisticated, more various and more politically informed. Postmodern theory and a burgeoning scholarship by women of color have particularly informed the debate.

Postmodern theory has had a major influence on all forms of academic work in the past few years. Feminist scholarship and educational scholarship have both been informed by its attention to language, text and voice, by its "deconstruction" of the taken-for-granted, and by its critique of essentialism and science. Both feminist scholarship and educational scholarship are also filled with reservations about the potential relativism which some postmodern theorists invite. The debate is a productive one, clarifying the assumptions about politics and epistemology which underlie all of our work.

The views of those who are not white and middle class have also been increasingly, if still too faintly, heard in feminist and educational writing. The women's movement has long been linked with struggles for the democratic rights of other groups, but it has often given the loudest hearing to relatively privileged women, and it has sometimes defended racism and class privilege. An understanding of what women's experience is, and how education works, must never take the experience of the privileged few to stand for the experience of all. While scholarship is unlikely to come equally from all places in society, the voices of non-white women are helping to produce a more comprehensive, non-racist and accurate feminist educational scholarship.

Jeanette Armstrong (1990) celebrates and reclaims her First Nations heritage in her poem, "From the Landscape of Grandmother." Her words serve to introduce the feminist project as we see it growing in its impact and understanding.

out of the landscape of grandmother
the sharing
in what we select
to remember
the physical power in thought
carried inside silently
pushing forward in each breathing
meaning wished onto tongues
transforming with each utterance
the stuff of our lives. (p. 164)

References

Armstrong, Jeanette. (1990). From the Landscape of Grandmother. In The Telling It Book Collective (Eds.), *Telling It: Women and Language Across Cultures.* Vancouver, BC: Press Gang Publishers. To be included also in Jeanette Armstrong's *Breathtracks*, forthcoming from Theytus Books and Williams/Wallace (co-publishers).

Contents

Acknowledgments

The idea for the first edition of this book originated from a conference funded primarily by a grant from the Social Sciences and Humanities Research Council through its Women and Work Strategic Grants Program.

We would like to thank a variety of people who have helped us along the way. The authors in this collection deserve our thanks for their contributions and for their patience. We appreciate the support of Jo-Ann Hannah, Betty Reid, the women in the Word Processing Services in the Faculty of Education at U.B.C., Celia Haig-Brown, and Lorna Weir. For this second edition we are indebted to Robin Van Heck for her editorial assistance. And to Angus and Jim, special thanks for their continuing support.

The following journals have kindly granted us permission to reprint particular articles new to the second edition: *Alberta Journal of Educational Research* (Patricia Valentine and Gordon McIntosh, "Food for Thought: Realities of a Women-Dominated Organization"); *Harvard Educational Review* (Magda Lewis and Roger I. Simon, "A Discourse Not Intended for Her: Learning and Teaching Within Patriarchy"); and *Gender and Education* (Helen Lenskyj, "Beyond Plumbing and Prevention: Feminist Approaches to Sex Education").

Contributors

Lesley Andres Bellamy is a Ed.D. candidate from the University of British Columbia. Her dissertation is a study of the transition of students from high school to post-high school destinations. Her research and teaching focuses on accessibility issues in higher education, women and higher education, and issues of research design and measurement.

Betty Collis received a B.A. in mathematics from the University of Michigan, an M.A. in mathematics education from Stanford University, and a Ph.D. in measurement, evaluation and computer applications from the University of Victoria (Canada). She was a member of the Faculty of Education at the University of Victoria in British Columbia for 12 years. In 1988 she took up residency in The Netherlands, where she is a faculty member at the University of Twente. She has written over 140 articles and reports on different aspects of computer use in education, including a book, *Computers, Curriculum, and Whole-Class Instruction: Issues and Ideas*, published by Wadsworth in California (1988). Currently she is co-chair of a research project supported by UNESCO involving approximately 15 countries and investigating the impact of computer use in education on children's cognitive development, from a cross-cultural perspective.

Marta Danylewycz was an Assistant Professor of History at Atkinson College, York University, when her life was tragically cut short in March 1985. The author of articles on the history of teachers and of religious women, she was revising her doctoral thesis on the latter for publication at the time of her death. In this study, *Taking the Veil: An Alternative to Marriage, Motherhood and Spinsterhood in Quebec, 1840-1920* (Toronto: McClelland and Stewart, 1987), the lives of teaching sisters are compared with those of the lay-women who taught, as part of the larger story of two of Quebec's most interesting female religious orders, the Sisters of Miséricorde and the Congregation of Notre Dame.

Linda Eyre is a doctoral candidate in the Department of Social and Educational Studies at the University of British Columbia. She did undergraduate work in education in England and graduate work at Michigan State University and Mount Saint Vincent University, Nova Scotia. She taught at the secondary level for 19 years. Her research interests concern gender, race and class inequalities and schooling. Her doctoral dissertation deals with how gender is socially constructed in the "Practical Arts."

Jo-Anne Fiske earned her M.A. and Ph.D. in Anthropology at the University of British Columbia. She is an Assistant Professor in the Sociology Department at Saint Mary's University, Halifax, Nova Scotia. She is currently engaged in research on sexual asymmetry in stratified lineage societies and on the gender implications of aboriginal justice systems. Her work has appeared in several anthologies and journals.

Jane Gaskell is a Professor in the Department of Social and Educational Studies at the University of British Columbia. She grew up in Toronto and received her Ed.D. from Harvard in Sociology of Education in 1973. She taught in the Faculty of Education at Queen's University before coming to UBC in 1974. She has been president of the Canadian Society for the Study of Education and vice-president of the Social Science Federation of Canada. Her research interests include vocational education, and feminist approaches to curriculum. Her forthcoming book is called *Gender Matters from School to Work*, published by the Open University Press.

Alison I. Griffith received her B.A. at Simon Fraser University, her M.A. at the University of British Columbia, and her Ph.D. from the University of Toronto. She is an Assistant Professor in the Department of Educational Leadership and Foundations at the University of New Orleans, where she teaches qualitative research and sociology of education. Her research concerns the gender text of organizational culture in schooling.

Neil Guppy is an Associate Professor in the Department of Anthropology and Sociology at the University of British Columbia. His research and teaching interests focus on social inequality, gender relations, labor markets and environmental practices. He has published recent articles on social mobility in Canada, pay equity in universities, and mandatory retirement policies.

Nancy Jackson is an Assistant Professor in the Faculty of Education, McGill University where she teaches qualitative research methodology and serves as the Associate Director of the Centre for Research on Instruction. Her recent research is concerned with the formulation of a more worker-centred standpoint for conceptualizing women's work and skill, and the development of a critical pedagogy for vocational learning.

Seema Kalia immigrated to Canada in 1970. She attended Carleton University and received a B.A. in Sociology and Anthropology. She is currently attending Law School at Queen's University, Kingston.

Roberta Lamb received her doctorate from Teachers College, Columbia University, after having taught music for several years in Oregon public schools. She has lived in Canada since 1985, when she took a position at the Brandon University School of Music in Manitoba. Currently she is an Assistant Professor in Music Education at the School of Music, Queen's University, Kingston, Ontario. She also teaches in the Women's Studies Program. Her research interests revolve around feminist critiques of music, women in music, and race, class and gender issues in music education.

Helen Lenskyj is a feminist researcher, teacher and activist living in Toronto. She teaches in the Department of Adult Education, Ontario Institute for Studies in Education. She is the author of *Out of Bounds: Women, Sport and Sexuality* (Women's Press, 1986), and *Women, Sport and Physical Activity: Research and Bibliography* (Ottawa: Fitness and Amateur Sport, 1988; 2nd ed., 1991).

Magda Lewis is Assistant Professor in the Faculty of Education at Queen's University, Kingston, where she also teaches in the Department of Sociology and Women's Studies. She attended the University of Waterloo and the University of Toronto, where she earned her Ph.D. She has been active in issues concerning women since the early 1970s. Her current work is in the area of feminist pedagogy and gender bias in education. She has published numerous articles and is presently preparing a manuscript for a book on the subject.

Beth Light is an independent researcher and historian. She is the co-author of a bibliography and four documentary studies in Canadian women's history. With five other feminists, she wrote *Canadian Women: A History* and most recently, with Ruth Pierson, edited *No Easy Road: Women in Canada, 1920s to 1960s.*

Gordon McIntosh is a Professor and Associate Chair in the Department of Educational Administration, University of Alberta. He did his undergraduate work at the University of Saskatchewan and his graduate work at the University of Saskatchewan (M.Sc.) and Harvard University (Ed.M., Ed.D.). His principal academic interests are organizational behavior (especially the study of leadership) and the use of case and simulation methods in the preparation of administrators. A specific area of current interest is the development of distance education programs in the area of organizational behavior.

Arlene Tigar McLaren is an Associate Professor in the Department of Sociology and Anthropology at Simon Fraser University. She was born in Vancouver, educated at the University of British Columbia, University of Iowa, and the London School of Economics. Since the late 1960s, when she helped establish the first abortion referral clinic in Calgary, she has been involved with feminist issues. She has written and edited several books on various subjects which include women and education, the history and politics of birth control in Canada, and feminist sociology in Canada. She is currently working on a study of gender, math and science in B.C. high schools.

Roxanna Ng teaches sociology at the Ontario Institute for Studies in Education. She teaches and writes about immigrant women; gender, race and class relations; community-state relations; and pedagogical issues from a critical perspective.

Alison Prentice teaches history at the Ontario Institute for Studies in Education. She has written books and articles on the origins of modern schooling and the history of women and education and is engaged in an ongoing project to study the changing experience of women in teaching. A member of the Canadian women's history group at OISE, she has also worked to promote the teaching of women's history in Canada through the creation of documentary studies, essay collections, and, more recently, a textbook on the history of Canadian women.

Kathleen Rockhill received her Ph.D. from the University of California, Berkeley, in 1972. After teaching at Rutgers University in New Jersey for three years, she returned, this time as a single parent with two sons, to the west coast, where she taught in the Department of Education at the University of California, Los Angeles. It was during this time that she undertook the research on immigrants and literacy. In 1983 she joined the faculty in the Department of Adult Education at the Ontario Institute for the Study of Education, where she teaches courses on feminist theory, education and interpretive approaches to research. She is currently working on questions of gendered subjectivity, violence, sexuality and comparative approaches to feminist politics.

Roger I. Simon teaches at the Ontario Institute for Studies in Education in the area of critical pedagogy and cultural studies. He has recently co-authored *Learning Work*, a book on the practical implications of critical pedagogy for work education.

Dorothy E. Smith was born in England. She obtained her bachelor's degree at the London School of Economics after some years in the workforce (mainly as a secretary). She completed her doctorate in Sociology at the University of California at Berkeley, taught briefly in England, and in 1968 came to Canada to teach at the University of British Columbia. She is now in the Department of Sociology of Education at the Ontario Institute for Studies in Education. She has been active in the women's movement in the university and the community and in her writing, recently focusing on the epistemological implications of feminism for the social sciences. She has published three books in this area: *The Everyday World as Problematic: A Feminist Sociology* (Toronto, 1987); *The Conceptual Practices of Power: A Feminist Sociology of Knowledge* (Toronto, 1990); *Texts, Facts and Femininity: Explaining the Relations of Ruling* (Routledge, 1990).

Patricia E. B. Valentine holds a B.Sc. (Nursing) from the University of British Columbia; M.A. (Sociology), University of Calgary; Ph.D. (Educational Administration), University of Alberta. She is currently an Associate Professor, Faculty of Nursing, University of Alberta. She has worked in community health, as a counsellor for alcoholics, taught in a hospital diploma program, and been a professor in nursing at two Canadian universities. She was Associate Dean of the Undergraduate Program at the University of Alberta from January 1987 through December 1989. She is interested in administration and the idea that women bring to organizations a different perspective that needs to be acknowledged and integrated into the organizational and administrative literature so that this literature is truly representative of both women and men.

Introduction

Fewer than four years have passed since the first edition of this book but much has happened in the analysis of women and education in Canada. Concern for this area of study has been heightened by the massacre of fourteen women on December 6, 1989 at the École Polytechnique, the Engineering School of the University of Montreal. This tragedy stunned the country. Commentators continue to wrestle with many of the questions that arose from this event. It signifies many things for many different people. For us, it reveals amongst other things the centrality of education in people's lives. Education can be life-giving, but it can also be life-threatening. The very excitement and value that education represents makes it a site for struggle and conflict among classes, races and religions, and between the sexes. The tragedy also reveals the country's deeply felt ambivalence towards feminism. Some commentators chose to vilify feminism as the cause of the murders. If only women were not so pushy, they reasoned, the tragedy would not have occurred. But we would argue the opposite. Because anti-woman and anti-feminist sentiments are legitimized in our culture, the murders were conceivable. Marc Lepine enacted the thinkable.

As did the earlier edition, this book takes as its central focus the relationship between feminist research and education. Given the ambivalence that exists in this country towards feminism, we feel this focus is all the more urgent. What unites the contributors to this volume is their insistence on the importance of female experiences, and their commitment to changes in education that will further women's equality with men.

Ideally, education and feminism should have much in common — both aim to empower all people, and to provide opportunities for the full expression of human potential. In reality, the practice of schooling and the multifaceted expressions of the women's movement have often come into conflict. For many decades feminists have challenged the existing organization of education in Canada and elsewhere. This book examines that challenge and indicates how feminist thought can help illuminate the fundamental issues around schooling. In contrast to standard works on education, which regularly exclude women, this book argues that female experiences are central to the educational enterprise. By exploring questions raised by feminist educational scholarship, it introduces new approaches to thinking about education in general, ways to understand better the complex relations between education and the host society.

Women and Education is intended for both researchers and students in education in the hope that they will be sensitized to and interested in the issues raised by the women's movement. The book will also be of interest to teachers and students of women's studies, social sciences and humanities, areas in which material on education is hard to locate and synthesize.

This book draws on the work of Canadian scholars and addresses issues in Canadian education. While Canadian scholarship flourishes in the context of international debate and research, it also continues to develop in particularly Canadian directions, reflecting the nation's particular organization of education and particular development of feminism. Yet national debates on education have been lacking in Canada. Although the federal government funds much of higher education and controls many job training programs, Canadian education is under provincial jurisdiction. National debates about education are at best irregular and large-scale funding of educational research remains episodic. In the United States, evaluation of federal sexual equity legislation, demonstration projects and major research grants have produced a wealth of policy findings (Klein et al., 1985) and critical scholarship (Belenky et al., 1986; Weiler, 1988). In Britain, too, the publication of policy-related and theoretical scholarship on women and education has been substantial (Arnot & Weiner, 1987; David, 1980; Deem, 1980; Weiner & Arnot, 1987; Whyte et al., 1985). In 1989 the British journal *Gender and Education* was established. By contrast, Canadians have only begun to produce full-length collections and studies on women and education (Dagg & Thompson, 1988; Forman et al., 1990; Gaskell & McLaren, 1987; Gaskell, McLaren, & Novogrodsky, 1989).

Feminist thought has a long history in Canada, and feminism has meant different things to different people at different times. But common themes also emerge. Above all, feminism insists on the importance of gender. Gender is fundamental to the ways we interact with each other, to the ways our public and private lives are organized. Its significance is evident almost everywhere we look — in the wages of men and women, in the structuring of friendships, in the persistence of Cinderella myths, and in the organization of domestic tasks. Feminism insists that the difference that gender makes is historically constructed and that gender is a major form of stratification that gives most men authority and power over most women. The forms of gender inequality past and present are diverse. They are not simply a reflection of biological differences but are an integral part of the complex social arrangements that constitute a society. Gender inequality is intertwined with other forms of socially constructed inequality based on class, race, ethnicity, religion and sexual orientation.

Feminism attempts to redress gender inequality. It is directed toward change. These essays are not the result of a disinterested academic enterprise. Rather, they form part of an action-oriented agenda that can help to eliminate gender-based imbalances in education. Education has always played an important part in the feminist political agenda, partly because women have had social responsibility for children; partly because teaching has offered opportunities to so many educated women, including many of the early feminists; partly because education offers hope for change in a new generation.

Sex Roles and Sex Role Stereotyping

Despite the commonalities among those who would call themselves feminists, there are also many differences. Feminism has changed over time and at any one time there have been and still are disagreements and controversies. The first stage in the re-emergence of feminism in Canada was marked by the publication in 1970 of the report of the Royal Commission on the Status of Women. The report paid a great deal of attention to education, stating that "Changes in education could bring dramatic improvements in the social economic position of women in an astonishingly short time. Equal opportunity for education is fundamental. Education opens the door to almost every goal. Wherever women are denied access to education they cannot be said to have equality."

The section on education in the report reflects the emphasis in the 1960s and early 1970s on the way young children were socialized into "sex roles" in the school as well as in the family. Boys got blue blankets in the hospital; girls got pink ones. Little girls were given dolls; little boys were given trucks. In school boys worked the projector, girls cleaned the brushes.

Before the advent of feminist social science, psychologists had been studying the process of sex role socialization for years. They argued that roles were biologically based. They claimed further that learning "appropriate" behaviors and traits in childhood was one of the prerequisites for adult mental health and smooth social functioning (Kagan, 1964; Parsons, 1942). They assumed that sex differences were important, that boys should be clear they were boys and girls should be clear they were girls. Boys were strong, independent and ambitious; girls were soft, kind and nurturant. By communicating and reinforcing the differences, schooling would contribute to the individual and the society. If there was a problem, it concerned boys, not girls. Commentators were preoccupied with the difficulty boys had with reading, blaming it on what came to be called the "feminized" classroom (Sexton, 1969). Teachers were encouraged to use books which represented the world of little boys in an attempt to cater to their needs in the classroom.

In the early 1970s, feminists began to question whether "sex-appropriate" behaviors were such a boon to the individual or to the society. As Greenglass (1973) wrote in the first collection of research articles on women in Canada:

Intensive differential socialization programs for male and female result in members of the two sexes seeking and valuing quite different experiences and attributes within themselves. While attributes such as independence, aggressiveness and competitiveness are rewarded and encouraged in males because these are the characteristics perceived as essential for success in traditionally male-dominated fields, dependence, passivity, and compliance are rewarded in females. Hardly those traits making for success. . . . If male and female teachers think that females are intellectually inferior to males . . . female students are less likely to have original intellectual contribution to make, and they are less likely to be logical. (pp. 112-113)

Feminists wanted to eliminate the emphasis on sex differences, to make education blind to gender, and to replace sex roles with androgyny. "Sex-appropriate roles" could also be called stereotypes; "sex role socialization" could be called discrimination, and "sex differences" could be called inequalities. Feminists documented gender stereotypes in many jurisdictions and in various ways. Their research became an assault on the notion that the sexes were separate but equal, and an assertion that "sex roles," rather than serving everyone's interest, inhibited achievement among women and the full development of both sexes. The female stereotype, feminist research showed, had negative consequences. Sexism was defined not just as a system of difference, but as a system of oppression.

Feminist researchers were particularly concerned about the books used in early grades in school. The Royal Commission's study on sex role imagery in the textbooks used to teach reading, social studies, science, mathematics and guidance courses in Canadian schools concluded that "a woman's creative and intellectual potential is either underplayed or ignored in the education of children from their earliest years. The sex roles described in these textbooks provide few challenging models for young girls, and they fail to create a sense of community between men and women as fellow human beings." The many studies that followed confirmed their verdict. (Batcher et al., 1975; Cullin, 1972; Fisher & Cheyne, 1977; Gaskell, 1977; Pascoe, 1975; Pyke, 1975; Women in Teaching, 1975).

These studies revealed that women were underrepresented in school books, and that when they were represented, they were stereotyped. Boys were stereotyped in more powerful and active roles. Little girls in elementary school played with dolls while their brothers played baseball; mothers wore aprons and baked cookies, while fathers drove off to work; adult women were princesses and witches, while men were doctors and farmers.

The critique of sex role socialization also focussed on the more intangible social relations of sex role stereotyping by teachers, parents and school practices (Shack, 1976; Spinks, 1970). This stereotyping was harder to document, but it was a question ripe for scholarly work and feminist critique. Feminist scholars documented and questioned practices such as having separate playgrounds and line-ups for girls and boys, allocating different chores for boys and for girls, and having girls and boys compete against each other. Teachers' expectations about the capacities and interests of males and females were revealed to be stereotyped (Eichler, 1979; Ricks & Pyke, 1973; Russell, 1979). Studies showed that boys received more attention from teachers than girls did. The results amounted to a well documented assault on stereotyping in its various guises in the school (Wilkinson & Marrett, 1985).

The research, in combination with political lobbying, had an effect. Under pressure from women's groups, publishers and ministries of education across the country appointed advisory groups on sexism and began to issue guidelines for non-sexist materials. In B.C. in 1974, for example, the ministry of education, which had appointed a provincial advisory committee and a special advisor on sex discrimination, issued a directive "On the Equal Treatment of the Sexes: Guidelines for Educational Materials." The guidelines were to make educators aware of the ways in which males and females have been "stereotyped" and "to assist educators and others who seek to provide equal treatment of the sexes in textbooks." The same year, the Ontario Status of Women Council published *About Face: Towards a Positive Image of Women in Textbooks,* and in 1976, the Quebec government published *L'École sexiste c'est quoi?*

Alternative materials were developed and published. The B.C. Teachers Federation published *Breaking the Mould: Non Sexist Curricula Materials for B.C. Elementary Schools* in 1975. In 1977 the B.C. ministry issued a *Resource Guide for Teachers in Women's Studies,* and an annotated bibliography of materials that might be used in courses. In 1976, the Ontario ministry of education published a resource guide entitled *Sex-Role Stereotyping and Women's Studies* "to assist educators in the on-going task of developing a learning environment that is free from sex role stereotyping of males and females and curriculum that accurately depicts the roles of women."

By the early 1980s a dramatic change had occurred in the primary readers that were being issued. More females were represented. The stereotypes began to disappear. The new readers had boys playing with girls, and represented adult women as police officers and doctors. Old books continue to be used in schools because of the cost of replacing materials as well as because some teachers prefer them (Galloway, 1980), and the implementation of non-sexist guidelines is more difficult than their promulgation (National Film Board, 1986). But significant victories were won and progress was made. Girls no longer had to take home economics while boys took industrial education. Teachers had been exposed to discussions of the issues of sex discrimination. Segregated staffrooms and playgrounds became less common.

This attention to sex role stereotyping in its various guises dominated the study of gender and education well into the mid-1970s. The approach was basically derived from psychology, from the child development literature and the study of sex differences. The aim was equal treatment in order to provide equal opportunity in the school. Few could disagree with the goal or the research. It produced a near-consensus among feminists about the problems of and solutions to gender inequality in schools.

By the late 1970s, other issues — excellence, multiculturalism and vocational preparation — were, however, replacing the issue of gender inequality on the agenda of school boards. There was some sense that battles had been won, making it less urgent to continue the attack on gender inequality. As well, a resurgence of conservative thought questioned whether the attack should be taken on at all. The voice of the new right was heard increasingly, calling for a return to traditional family structures, and objecting to affirmative action and day care. The media hailed the demise of the feminist movement, portraying women as moving into professional positions in increasing numbers, dressing for success and hiring nannies. But women's inequality persisted. Women continued to earn about 60 percent of what men earned, girls still aspired to traditionally female jobs and decent child care remained hard to find.

Revaluing the Female

In academic circles the concern for adding women into research nevertheless continued to gain momentum. It was supported by the emergence of journals devoted to the study of women, the appearance of women's studies programs and the increase in the number of women academics who brought their own experiences and questions to their research. In 1972, a journal now called *Resources for Feminist Research* was founded in order to provide reviews, bibliographies and a comprehensive periodical and resources guide to materials being published on women. *Atlantis,* a journal of women's studies, was founded in 1976 in Atlantic Canada. University women's studies courses appeared at Concordia in 1971, at the University of Toronto in 1972, at the University of British Columbia in 1973 and at Simon Fraser University in 1975 (Strong-Boag, 1983). The Social Sciences and Humanities Research Council of Canada initiated a program of funding research on "Women and Work," broadly construed to "foster and encourage research and scholarship which is non-sexist in language and methodology and which will contribute to an integrated understanding of women's paid and unpaid work." The Canadian Research Institute for the Advancement of Women was begun in 1976, and the Canadian Women's Studies Association was founded in 1982. Five regional permanent chairs in women's studies were funded by the Secretary of State from 1983 to 1985.

This infrastructure has allowed a multifaceted and complex scholarship on women to develop. Feminist scholarship has had an impact on academic work in every discipline and field of study, although the progress remains slow and far from even (Dubois et al., 1985; Langland & Gove, 1983). In part, this has meant an explosion of knowledge about women's experiences. Where women were invisible in academic texts, they are beginning to have a presence. Where questions about women were never asked, they are now being pursued. The enormous gaps in our knowledge about how women live, think and feel are providing opportunities for new research and innovative scholarship.

This constituted a second phase in feminist scholarship, a phase of revaluing the female, instead of dismissing gender differences. Feminists became increasingly critical of studies which assumed that gender was understood by the "add women and stir" approach. They insisted that gender had to be examined from a female-centred, not male-centred perspective.

Where the female stereotype had been criticized for inhibiting women's achievement, it was reassessed for its positive aspects. Nurturance, sociability and interdependence, feminists argued, can foster learning, can be important in schools, and have been too often devalued by those who care only for achievement in its narrowest sense. As Jeri Wine (1982) points out,

> the large literature on psychological sex differences is highly problematic from a feminist perspective because of its apparent demonstration of the inferiority of the female. In this work, the guiding assumptions are that any characteristic that males have more of than do females is an essential characteristic, a mark of superiority, while any characteristic that females have more of is a sign of weakness, of inferiority. Women's investment in the interpersonal realm has been consistently devalued in psychology, our connectedness with others seen as pathological dependency needs, nurturance and interpersonal sensitivity defined as weakness. (p. 70)

Instead of centring our analysis on how we can make women less defective, how we can get rid of sex roles, and how we can make women more like men, Wine argues, we must value the female, and build on it. Women do not have to be like men to deserve equal respect, and power. If women did have more power, they would be able to make the world a safer and more pleasant place for everyone. As Finn and Miles (1982) put it,

> female characteristics, concerns, and abilities marginalized in industrial society, are necessarily central to the building of a new more fully human society. The holistic, collective, intuitive, co-operative, emotional, nurturing, democratic, integrated, internal, and natural are affirmed against the over-valuation of the competitive, analytical, rational, hierarchical, fragmented, external and artificial. (p. 13)

There are many ways this approach can suggest a re-examination of educational issues. For example, Martin (1985) has argued that those who debate the purposes of education have misconstrued the arguments of such philosophers as Rousseau and Plato by dismissing their discussions of the education of women as unimportant. The ideals they held out for men's education — the rational and productive ideals we now apply to the education of both sexes — omit, even while they depend upon, the existence of a different kind of education, one concerned with caring and reproduction in its broadest sense, including the rearing of children. This education has been relegated to second-class status; Rousseau assigned it to Sophie, Plato assigned it to the lower classes. Both recognized its necessity, and how the education of the dominant group depended on it. Martin argues we must reincorporate "female" education into the education we give everyone. To revalue the female, we must reevaluate the totality of education.

Rethinking the Whole

As Martin's work shows, the process of revaluing the feminine has led to a third stage of feminist thought, where feminist scholarship means more than adding women onto existing lines of inquiry and more than revaluing the female as femaleness has been formed in a male-dominated society. By itself, revaluing the female falls prey to condoning characteristics that women have developed in response to male domination, and to denigrating automatically characteristics that are male. More recent feminist thought suggests that a new synthesis needs to be created for everyone, a synthesis that allows both male and female experiences to be seen, to be valued, and most importantly, to be rethought.

For scholarship, this third stage of feminism has meant an alteration in the questions that are asked, in the theoretical stances that are adopted, and in the methods that are used to create new knowledge. The main question is not so much how we are made into male and female, or how we are valued as gendered beings; rather it is how our knowledge of the world has been shaped by gender, and more particularly, by male domination. "Malestream" thought, as Mary O'Brien (1981) has dubbed traditional scholarship, is revealed as partial, based in male experience, and therefore inadequate. Seemingly objective and value-free inquiry is revealed to be based on unexamined assumptions about male and female. As Eichler and Lapointe (1985) have pointed out,

> As long as women were de facto excluded from academic work and higher education, sex related bias in research was not widely recognized as a problem for the social sciences and humanities. Culture and our way of thinking were shaped by a male perspective which applied even when the life, identity and thoughts of women were considered. There was little or no awareness that such an androcentic perspective generates serious intellectual problems. (p. 5)

Exposing these intellectual problems has been grist for the mill of feminist scholarship. Rethinking any number of problems to incorporate women's experience has led to new questions, new models and new methods. To take an example: Much of the research on the relationship between schooling and experience in the work force was done on males because males moved more predictably from school to work and stayed at work for long periods of time and because the work force experience of men (not women) was considered fundamental to family stability and income distribution in the society. The research was done by correlating the number of years of schooling a man had with his income and the status of his job. There was a strong relationship and this research tradition, known as status attainment research, grew in sophistication and importance, pointing always to the role of education in labor force attainment (Blau & Duncan, 1967; Jencks, 1972; Porter, Porter, & Blishen, 1982).

When they attempted to add women in, researchers confronted new methodological problems. They had to decide how to treat "housewife" as an (unpaid) occupation, and how to add in new variables like "sex role attitude" to explain some of the new variance (Porter, Porter, & Blishen, 1982). Moreover, a series of new questions about the research paradigm itself emerged. Women's education is correlated with their occupational attainment and income, but the same education gets a woman much less income than it gets a man. Status attainment models cannot account for the difference. Explaining the result requires taking a look at the ways jobs are organized and segregated by sex, and at the history and sociology of work. It requires breaking down education by type of schooling, not just by amount, and asking how different jobs come to require different types and amounts of formal educational preparation. It requires asking questions about the relationship between domestic and paid labor, questions which had been ignored when only men were included in the analysis. Incorporating gender makes clear the taken-for-granted and male assumptions underlying the research model, and leads to a renewed dialogue about the adequacy of the models, their limitations and their uses (Gaskell, 1981; O'Donnell, 1984; Sokoloff, 1980).

This same process can be illustrated in many areas of study from moral development (Gilligan, 1982) to the fur trade (Van Kirk, 1980) to achievement motivation (Kaufman & Richardson, 1982) to "ways of knowing" (Belenky et al., 1986). Our scholarship is richer for the questions that are posed by scholarship that takes women's experience seriously and tries to rethink the whole by reincorporating both men's and women's experiences.

Difference and the Female

But revaluing the female experience and rethinking the whole is still not enough. The question remains, "What female experience?" This question has led to a fourth stage of feminist thought and marks a major change between the first and second edition of this collection. Women who feel left out of characterizations of "the" female experience are increasingly challenging feminist thought to incorporate greater diversity of experiences. Scholarship suffers not only from male bias but also from other biases, such as race, class and sexual orientation (Nicholson, 1990; Ramazanoglu, 1989; Spelman, 1988). Eurocentric course offerings of Canadian universities, which magnify whiteness, leave people of color almost illiterate when it comes to what they have had to say about the world (Mukherjee, 1989). Feminist scholarship is not immune to such criticism. It has tended to reflect the interests of white, middle-class women and has failed to examine how gender is intertwined with class, race and so on. As Mukherjee (1990) points out, most feminist literary critics not only exclude non-white literary texts but ignore the racist aspects of the texts of their chosen authors.

In Canada, the recognition of diversity has been fairly strong for some time because of the well-developed perspective of socialist feminists (Hamilton & Barrett, 1986). This perspective has led to a great deal of debate (see, for example, Burstyn & Smith, 1985) and to research on the relationship between class and gender. Russell (1986), for example, studied the ways in which students' behavior and aspirations, and school personnel's channelling of students are shaped by the intricate interrelations between gender and class. But, as many women of color have argued, feminists, including socialist feminists, have been color-blind. They have ignored the significance of race and ethnicity and the relation of these to other forms of oppression. They have also been blind to other ways in which the female experience has been divided, such as disablement, age and sexual orientation.

An understanding of the diversity of the female experience does not, however, simply mean looking at double or triple forms of oppression. It does not mean an "add race or class (or whatever) and stir" approach to an analysis of gender. It does not mean starting from the experiences of the white, middle-class female as the norm and finding out how the experiences of "others" differ. As Roxana Ng (1989) notes, the unique experiences of women of color are frequently overlooked in discussions about women's oppression:

> At best, we are tokenized; at worst, we are told that our concerns, seen to be less advanced, have to do with a patriarchy characteristic of our indigenous cultures. There is something missing in the women's movement which gives us an increasing sense of discomfort as we continue to participate in struggles in which only a part of our experiences as women of colour is or can be taken up. (p. 10)

Women of different classes and racial and ethnic groups do not necessarily share the same political interests. Women can oppress and exploit other women and can benefit from the subordination of others (male and female). As bell hooks (1984) suggests, a "woman-centred" approach alienates many women from the feminist movement (p. 27). Despite sexist discrimination, exploitation or oppression, many women feel their lives are important and valuable and that the significance of this is not recognized by a feminist movement dominated by white, middle-class women.

An understanding of the diversity of the female experience means deconstructing the unified category of female. It means listening to the voices of Native women, girls, older women (not just "thirty-something" women), disabled women, immigrant women, poor women, lesbians. It does not mean a simple celebration of difference (Nicholson, 1990). It means valuing difference based on structured divisions in society, placing difference rather than commonality at the centre of feminism and rethinking the whole based on those differences. It means building alliances between feminism and other democratic struggles. In education, it means transforming the curriculum and pedagogy to ensure that all people give voice to their experience, to analyze and understand it, and to connect it to the experience of others.

Feminism and Educational Scholarship

The academy has provided a setting within which feminist scholarship has grown and has developed its own institutions. But the academy has not always welcomed the change. The resistance could be illustrated in many stories, as it has been in many reports on the status of women in universities across Canada (Franklin, Bertrand, & Gordon, 1986; McIntyre, 1987). Perhaps most relevant to this book are the notes taken down by a graduate student who was distributing notices for the conference on which the first edition of this book was based. As she put the brochures, prominently labelled "Women and Education," in the mail boxes of faculty members, she recorded the following comments:

> "Women and education. Christ! There wouldn't be much to say about that, would there?"

> [addressed to mailroom clerk] "Women and education — geez! Is that the best you can do for me?"

> "Women and education — isn't that a contradiction in terms? Ha, ha, ha!"

> "Women and education. Oh, women's lib stuff, eh?"

Despite the opposition and skepticism, the conference did receive university support, as well as support from the Social Sciences and Humanities Research Council. The conference and the two editions of this book demonstrate that there is a good deal to say, not just about women in education but about its implications for the way we study and think about the entire process of education.

Until recently, scholars in education, like scholars in other fields, largely ignored the study of women. They have considered learning and teaching to be quite independent of gender issues. They have examined the governance and organization of education, the curriculum, even issues of access and equality, without mention of male and female.

But there are several ways in which education stands out as an important field of study for feminists, and a field that might be particularly receptive to feminism. First, education has had a higher proportion of female students and faculty than most other areas on Canadian university campuses. In Canadian faculties of education in 1988/89, women constituted 74.9% of the undergraduate enrollment, 61% of the graduate enrollment, and 24% of the faculty members (Labour Canada, 1990). This is well above the average across campus.

Education is also a field that consciously links theory to practice. Research in education is carried out, in one way or another, to improve the ways we educate students. Educational research is not a disinterested exercise, but rather is directed towards practical and ultimately political ends. Like feminist scholarship, it is directed towards changing practice, towards producing conditions where all students learn more, have more control over their lives. Like feminist scholarship, it ultimately involves judgements about what is a desirable outcome for others.

Finally, education is an interdisciplinary field, drawing on a variety of modes of inquiry to understand a social phenomenon. In this way it is like women's studies. Psychologists with a concern for sex role stereotypes no longer dominate the study of gender in education. Historians, sociologists, economists and political scientists debate what constitutes feminist pedagogy, how women's experience has shaped schooling, how the organization of educational institutions excludes women, and what counts as education, as knowledge, as achievement. In its interdisciplinary approach to real-world problems, then, educational scholarship and feminist scholarship take parallel paths.

Ironically, however, this has not led to greater attention to gender issues in education, relative to other fields. The Social Sciences Federation of Canada's report on sexism indicated that education was less likely than other fields to show concern about the place and role of women in professional and scientific activity (Christiansen-Ruffman et al., 1986). The *Canadian Journal of Education* published fewer articles on women during a five-year period than the leading Canadian journals in such related academic fields as history, sociology and psychology, all which have a lower representation of women (Maciejko, 1987). In 1992 this journal is, however, devoting an entire issue to feminist pedagogy.

The dominance of men in positions of authority in education, along with a concern that the large number of females in the field is somehow linked to the field's inferiority and low status, seem to have led to an avoidance of academic work about, or for, women. While the similarities between educational research and feminist research are important, the very political nature of education can make educators particularly wary of those with a "political axe to grind," and anxious to adopt a research stance that places them outside the political arena.

But the relation between thought, research and political action is under intense scrutiny throughout the academy. Even in the traditional disciplines, commentators have become increasingly sensitive to the role of subjectivity, and the importance of the researcher in shaping academic questions, choosing sources of data, and determining appropriate analyses and standards of proof (Alexander, 1982; Allender, 1986; Atkinson, 1990; Fiske & Schweder, 1986; Gergen, 1982). It is increasingly accepted that all research is socially located and value laden, rather than disinterested and objective. No discourse exists without a subject speaking, a subject who speaks in a particular voice, reflecting particular values and assumptions. The study of women in education illustrates the links between the content of scholarly work and its social context. It has grown with the feminist movement and reflects the issues and experiences that arise there.

This book does not aim to be a disinterested academic enterprise. It is linked to a concern for gender equity. Just what this would look like can be debated. But the fact that feminist scholarship is concerned with social change as well as with academic inquiry is central to our work.

Diversity and the Organization of This Book

As the "sex role" paradigm breaks down, some of the political divisions within feminism become clearer. There are a variety of ways to describe the differences (Dubois et al., 1985; Eisenstein, 1984; Tong, 1989), and each topic and each historical period generates its own controversies as the various sections in this book will demonstrate. In each section, we describe a variety of feminist approaches that are relevant to the subject of that section. The categories we use vary, depending on what the issues are in traditional scholarship as well as on what kind of feminist debates are relevant.

In an overview of feminist thought, it is customary to divide the ideas along the traditional political lines of liberal, radical and socialist. Put briefly, liberal feminists are concerned with providing equal opportunities for women to participate in the social and economic institutions that exist. Both socialist and radical feminists are concerned with changing those institutions so that they create less gender inequality in power, status and income. Radical feminists locate the causes of gender oppression in patriarchy, that is, in male ownership and control of social, ideological and economic processes. They want more space, power and attention to women's concerns. Socialist feminists locate the causes of gender oppression in economic structures that benefit the few. They examine the way capitalism shapes gender relations in modern industrial societies. They want to transform the structures in their entirety. Such political orientations are useful to keep in mind in a general way. They alert us to an author's assumptions and the implications of his/her ideas. In many cases, however, the distinctions are not clear: changing opportunities for women means changing social structures; changing patriarchy means changing economic processes, and changing capitalism can involve challenging male power. Indeed, few feminist writers can be placed easily into one political camp as opposed to another.

There are no easy goals, much less victories, in feminist educational thought. But the questions are exciting and the struggle invigorating. The purpose of this book is to introduce the new feminist debate, and to show the varied forms that the study of women in education can take and is taking.

This book is divided into four sections, charting four ways in which feminist work has forced us to see major issues in education differently. The first section examines the study of teachers, child care workers and mothers, the women who in various ways are responsible for much of the education that goes on. The fact that these people are women makes a difference. It has led to the invisibility and devaluing of the work that is done. It has had an impact on the organization of schools and families. Those studying education must take into account the segregation of work into "men's work" and "women's work." They must also take into account the racial segregation of work. When all teachers and students are white, their race, with its attendant privileges, goes unnoticed. When teachers are non-white, women's problems of devaluation are exacerbated.

The second section examines differences in the educational attainment of men and women. The research explores how schools are involved in producing gender, class and race inequality through regulating access to skills, credentials and ultimately the labor market. When these inequalities are examined, we see that some of the traditional models for explaining how inequality in schools is produced and how it is linked to inequality in the labor force need to be rethought. Contrary to existing myths, getting a "good" education has not improved women's position in the labor force in relation to men.

The third section looks at what counts as important knowledge to be taught to students. The "taken-for-granted" curriculum has for decades excluded and/or misrepresented women's experiences, in all their variety. To understand how, why and what to do about it demands rethinking what the curriculum represents, how it is arrived at, and how it can be changed. It involves bringing a critical perspective and the tools of the sociology of knowledge and social history to bear on discussions about what is and what should be taught.

The final section of the book looks at education that takes place outside the traditional arena of schooling, and calls our attention to the fact that we learn most of what we know outside schools. To understand what women know and what they need to know, we are drawn to places which have been relatively ignored in the study of education, but which are increasingly important. By looking at a variety of institutional arrangements for learning, we come to better understand the peculiarities of what we commonly take for granted as "school" and the variations of what constitutes "students."

We have tried to illustrate and explore diverse strands of feminist scholarship in the selections in this book, by including a variety of methodologies and disciplines. But these articles do not cover all the topics or modes of inquiry that are part of Canadian feminist scholarship on education. There are gaps in our selection of articles, for our selection reflects the emphases of scholarship of the moment. But gaps could be filled by a more extensive collection of work. We hope this book will encourage our readers to look further at topics we have not been able to examine here — such as the wide variety of experiences of women from different racial, ethnic and class groups, the involvement of women in policy processes, the conditions of women's teaching and mothering work, the relationship of day care to teaching and mothering, the experiences of girls in math and science, and so on — and to carry forward their own research and teaching with feminist questions in mind. The references at the end of section introductions and chapters will serve as a guide to further reading and research.

References

Alexander, J. (1982). *Theoretical logic in sociology: Positivism, presuppositions and current controversies.* Berkeley: University of California Press.

Allender, J.S. (1986). Educational research: A personal and social process. *Review of Educational Research 56*(2), 173-193.

Arnot, M., & Weiner, G. (Eds.). (1987). *Gender and the politics of schooling.* London: Hutchinson/The Open University.

Atkinson, P. (1990). *The ethnographic imagination: Textual constructions of reality.* New York: Routledge.

Batcher, E., Brackstone, D., Winter, A., & Wright, V. (1975). *And then there were none . . . A report commissioned by the Status of Women Committee.* Toronto: F.W.T.A.O.

Belenky, M.F., Clinchy, B.M., Goldberger, N.R., & Tarule, J.M. (1986). *Women's ways of knowing: The development of self, voice and mind.* New York: Basic Books.

Blau, P., & Duncan, O.D. (1967). *The American occupational structure.* New York: John Wiley.

Burstyn, V., & Smith, D. (1985). *Women, class, and the state.* Toronto: Garamond Press.

Christiansen-Ruffman, L., Murphy, A., Stark-Alance, C., & Davidson, R. (1986). *Report of the task force on the elimination of sexist bias in research to the Social Science Federation of Canada.* Ottawa: SSFC.

Cullin, L. (1972). *A study into sex stereotyping in Alberta elementary text books.* Mimeo.

Dagg, A.I., & Thompson, P.J. (1988). *MisEducation: Women and Canadian universities.* Toronto: Ontario Institute for Studies in Education.

David, M. (1980). *The state, the family and education.* London: Routledge and Kegan Paul.

Deem, R. (1980). *Education for women's work.* London: Routledge and Kegan Paul.

Dubois, E.C., Kelly, G.P., Kennedy, E.L., Korsmeyer, C.W., & Robinson, L.S. (1985). *Feminist scholarship: Kindling in the groves of academe.* Urbana: University of Illinois Press.

Eichler, M. (1979). Sex role attitude of male and female teachers in Toronto. *Interchange 10*(2), 2-14.

Eichler, M., & Lapointe, J. (1985). *On the treatment of the sexes in research.* Ottawa: Social Sciences and Humanities Research Council.

Eisenstein, H. (1984). *Contemporary feminist thought.* London: Unwin Paperbacks.

Finn, G., & Miles, A. (1982). *Feminism in Canada.* Montreal: Black Rose Books.

Fisher, L., & Cheyne, J.A. (1977). *Sex roles: Biological and cultural interactions as found in social science research and Ontario educational media.* Toronto: Ontario Ministry of Education.

Fiske, D.W., & Schweder, R.A. (1986). *Metatheory in social science.* Chicago: University of Chicago Press.

Forman, F., O'Brien, M., Haddad, J., Hallman, D., & Masters, P. (Eds.). (1990). *Feminism and education: A Canadian perspective.* Toronto: Centre for Women's Studies in Education, Ontario Institute for Studies in Education.

Franklin, U., Bertrand, M., & Gordon, J. (1986, November). Women in the university: Who are we? *CAUT Bulletin.*

Galloway, P. (1980). *What's wrong with high school English? It's sexist . . . un-Canadian . . . outdated.* Toronto: OISE Press.

Gaskell, J. (1977). Stereotyping and discrimination in the curriculum. In Hugh A. Stevenson & J. Donald Wilson (Eds.), *Precepts, policy and process: Perspectives on Canadian education.* London, ON: Alexander, Blake Associates.

Gaskell, J. (1981). Education and women's work: Some new research directions. *Alberta Journal of Educational Research 29,* 224-241.

Gaskell, J.S., & McLaren, A.T. (Eds.) (1987). *Women and education: A Canadian perspective.* Calgary: Detselig.

Gaskell, J., McLaren, A., & Novogrodsky, M. (1989). *Claiming an education: Feminism and Canadian schools.* Toronto: Our Schools/Our Selves Education Foundation.

Gergen, K. (1982). *Toward transformation in social knowledge.* New York: Springer Verlag.

Gilligan, C. (1982). *In a different voice.* Cambridge: Harvard University Press.

Greenglass, E. (1973). The psychology of women, or, The high cost of achievement. In M. Stephenson (Ed.), *Women in Canada.* Toronto: New Press.

Hamilton, R., & Barrett, M. (Eds.). (1986). *The politics of diversity: Feminism, Marxism and nationalism.* Montreal: Book Center Inc.

hooks, bell. (1984). *Feminist theory: From margin to center.* Boston: South End Press.

Jencks, C. (1972). *Inequality.* New York: Basic Books.

Kagan, J. (1964). Acquisition and significance of sex typing and sex role identity. In M.C. Hoffman & L.W. Hoffman (Eds.), *Child development research.* New York: Russell Sage Foundation.

Kaufman, D., & Richardson, B. (1982). *Achievement and women.* New York: The Free Press.

Keller, E.F. (1985). *Reflections on gender and science.* New Haven: Yale University Press.

Klein, S.S., et al. (1985). *Handbook for achieving sex equality through education.* Baltimore: Johns Hopkins University Press.

Labour Canada. (1990). *Women in the labour force, 1990-91.* Ottawa: Labour Canada, Women's Bureau.

Langland, E., & Gove, W. (1983). *A feminist perspective in the academy: The difference it makes.* Chicago: University of Chicago Press.

McDonald, M. (1981). *Class, gender and education.* Milton Keynes: Open University Press.

McIntyre, S. (1987, January). Gender bias within a Canadian law school. *CAUT Bulletin,* 7-11.

Maciejko, B. (1987). *Feminism in Canadian academic journals: A sample survey.* Mimeo. Vancouver: University of British Columbia, Department of Social and Educational Studies.

Martin, J.R. (1985). *Reclaiming a conversation: The ideal of the educated woman.* New Haven: Yale University Press.

Mukherjee, A. (1989). *Equity and access: A forum for black, Asian and Native women at York University.* Unpublished paper.

Mukherjee, A. (1990). *A house divided: Women of colour and American feminist theory.* Unpublished manuscript.

National Film Board. (1986). *Report of the National Film Board/Educators Forum on Women's Studies in Secondary School.* Ottawa: Author.

Ng, R. (1989). Sexism, racism, and Canadian nationalism. In Jesse Vorst (Ed.), *Race, class, gender: Bonds and barriers.* Toronto: Between the Lines and Society for Socialist Studies.

Nicholson, L.J. (Ed.) (1990). *Feminism/Postmodernism.* London: Routledge.

O'Brien, M. (1981). *The politics of reproduction.* London: Routledge and Kegan Paul.

O'Donnell, C. (1984). The relationship between women's education and their allocation to the labour market. *Studies in Higher Education, 9*(1), 59-72.

Parsons, T. (1942). Age and sex in the social structure of the U.S. *American Sociological Review 7,* 604-612.

Pascoe, C.D. (1975). *Sex stereotyping study.* Mimeo. Halifax.

Porter, J., Porter, M., & Blishen, B. (1982). *Stations and callings: Making it through the school system.* Toronto: Methuen.

Pyke, S. (1975). Children's literature: Conceptions of sex roles. In E. Zureik & R. Pike (Eds.), *Socialization and values in Canadian society.* Toronto: McClelland and Stewart.

Ramazanoglu, C. (1989). *Feminism and the contradictions of oppression.* London: Routledge.

Ricks, F., & Pyke, S. (1973). Teacher perceptions and attitudes that foster or maintain sex role differences. *Interchange 4*(1), 26-33.

Royal Commission on the Status of Women. (1970). *Status of women in Canada.* Ottawa: Information Canada.

Russell, S. (1979). Learning sex roles in the high school. *Interchange 10*(2), 57-66.

Russell, S. (1986). The hidden curriculum of school: Reproducing gender and class hierarchies. In R. Hamilton & M. Barrett (Eds.), *The politics of diversity: Feminism, Marxism and nationalism.* Montreal: Book Center Inc.

Saskatchewan Human Rights Commission. (1974). *Sex Bias in Primary Readers.* Saskatoon: Author.

Sexton, P. (1969). *The feminized male.* New York: Random House.

Shack, S. (1966). How equal is equal in education? *Quest 3*(4), 14-15.

Sokoloff, N. (1980). *Between money and love: The dialectics of women's home and market work.* New York: Praeger.

Spelman, E.V. (1988). *Inessential woman: Problems of exclusion in feminist thought.* Boston: Beacon Press.

Spinks, S. (1970). Sugar 'n' spice. In S. Repo (Ed.), *This book is about schools.* New York: Pantheon Books.

Strong-Boag, V. (1983). Mapping women's studies in Canada: Some signposts. *Journal of Educational Thought 17*(2), 94-111.

Tong, R. (1989). *Feminist thought: A comprehensive introduction.* Boulder: Westview Press.

Van Kirk, S. (1980). *Many tender ties: Women in fur trade society in western Canada, 1750-1850.* Winnipeg: Watson and Dwyer.

Weiler, K. (1988). *Women teaching for change.* Massachussets: Bergin and Garvey Inc.

Weiner, G., & Arnot, M. (Eds.). (1987). *Gender under scrutiny: New enquiries in education.* London: Hutchinson/The Open University.

Whyte, J., Deem, R., Kant, L., & Cruickshank, M. (1985). *Girl friendly schooling.* London: Methuen.

Wilkinson, C., & Marrett, C.B. (1985). *Gender influences in classroom interaction.* Orlando: Academic Press.

Wine, J. (1982). Gynocentric values and feminist psychology. In G. Finn & A. Miles (Eds.), *Feminism in Canada.* Montreal: Black Rose Books.

Women in Teaching. (1975). *Text book study.* Vancouver, BC: Distributed by the B.C. Teachers Federation.

Part One:

Women as Mothers, Women as Teachers

This section examines the interrelated activities of three groups of persons involved in education: school teachers, child care providers and mothers. In most books on education, only teachers would be discussed. Alhough child care providers and mothers teach children, commentators do not usually consider them as educators. Feminists, on the other hand, have stressed that much can be learned by examining the commonalities of educational activities within and outside schools, most of which are the responsibility of women.

As O'Brien (1983, p. 10) notes, a primary problem for women in education is the public-realm definition of the educational process. From Durkheim (1956) onward, sociologists have assumed that with industrialization the family lost its major functions to economic production and education. Families were no longer adequate for teaching children specialized skills and the moral values of society. Children needed to be taken out of their families and taught the ways of the wider society in publicly controlled schools (Durkheim, 1956; Parsons, 1959). The family was perceived to be a residual institution, the place of women, and of little importance to wage labor or to educational activity.

With the separation of the role of the family and the role of public institutions, the story goes, the work of women and men also became clearly separated. Women stayed in the family in the private world of the home. Men went out to the increasingly important public spheres of the economy, politics, religion, medicine, education and so forth. Men were to carry out instrumental roles as breadwinners outside the home, to work and take responsibility for linking the family to the wider social system. Women were to carry out expressive roles as housewives and mothers inside the home; they were to be responsible for the emotional and physical care of family members. This separation of roles was elevated to the status of myth, of an official ideology which insists that women's place is in the home and men are the providers.

This ideology rests on the premise that men and women are naturally suited for different activities, by virtue of their biology. In 1856 in his lecture at the YMCA in Halifax, Reverend Robert Sedgewick expressed this view:

> As to the idea that woman has a self evident and inalienable right to assist in the government of the race, I reply she does assist in that government now, and would to heaven she would exercise a still larger share in its administration. But this great work, like all others, is naturally divided between the sexes, the nobler government of children belonging to women, the less noble government of adults to man. (Sedgewick, 1856/1976, p. 13)

The view proclaimed the importance of both male and female spheres, but rhetoric notwithstanding, granted power to the male. The belief in separate spheres became an ideology about the inherent differences between the sexes and the superiority of masculinity over femininity.

In fact, this myth misrepresented women's work then, as it does now. No clear line divides the "public" and "private" realms. Women work both inside and outside the home. They work in the "public realm"; many, for example, are employed as teachers. Their work in the home is laborious and complex, a result of social learning, not biological impulse. Taking care of others is taxing and requires skills. Household tasks are not naturally and inevitably the responsibilities of women; men can also do them. The allocation of household labor to women is a social and patriarchal construction (Gittens, 1985; Mandell & Duffy, 1988; Rich, 1977; Thorne & Yalom, 1982). Further, rather than being separate spheres, the so-called public realm of waged labor and the so-called private realm of unpaid labor in the home each affect the performance of the other (Jaggar & McBride, 1985; Maroney, 1985).

By examining teachers, child care workers and mothers as groups, we can begin to explore their differences and similarities and their relationships to one another. Women's work in each sphere has a different history and has developed different structures and meanings. But because they are all concerned with the well-being of children and are carried out largely by women, they are alike in some ways and are interrelated. They also affect one another. Three of these similarities will be pointed out here. First, they are all sexually segregated forms of work; second, they are undervalued by society; third, they are perceived in ways that emphasize the gendered nature of the work and ignore its working conditions.

The Sexual Division of Labor

That women and men carry out different kinds of work is easy to take for granted. But the sexual division of labor is a shifting and historically specific social product, not a result of biological givens. It is important to ask why women "mother" and men "work." And it is important to ask why women who work outside the home are more likely to be teachers than engineers, secretaries than plumbers.

In the Canadian/U.S. home, a clear division of labor has developed, especially since the nineteenth century. Even though fathers are usually present and involved with children, mothers remain the primary caregivers. When a child is born, a mother is more likely than a father to leave the workforce in order to stay at home to look after the child. If a mother is employed outside the home, she is more likely than a father to be largely responsible for child care (Armstrong & Armstrong, 1984; Kome, 1982; Luxton, 1980). If parents separate, mothers are more likely than fathers to gain primary custody of their child(ren). In 1986, 13% of all Canadian families were composed of only one parent and their child(ren); in the vast majority of cases, this parent was female (Moore, 1987).

The fact that child care is considered women's work influences the public educational system. Very few men look after other people's young children. As we move up the age ladder from pre-schools to universities, the proportion of female teachers in Canada drops dramatically. Women constitute about 95% of child care providers and 72% of elementary teachers, but only 35% of secondary teachers and 17% of university teachers (Statistics Canada, 1986; Statistics Canada, 1987).[1]

Though women teachers are dominant in numbers at lower levels of the educational system, they are not dominant in the exercise of authority. Women teach, but men manage (Strober & Tyack, 1980). In 1985-86, women made up just 15% of principals and vice-principals in public schools (elementary and secondary). Only 6% of secondary principals were women (Cusson, 1990).

Because the division of labor is so strong, we cannot possibly understand educational work without considering it as a gendered experience (Apple, 1983; Lather, 1986). Yet discussions of teachers usually ignore the fact that teaching is organized by gender divisions. A recent sociological text, *Canadian Education* (Martin & Macdonell, 1982), mentions only in passing (p. 109) that Canada has more female than male full-time teachers. The authors provide little commentary on how women and men are distributed within the educational system, why their access to jobs is so different, and what such differences imply.

Devaluation of Women's Work

One implication of the sexual division of labor in Canada and the U.S. is the devaluation of "women's work." The devaluation of women's educational work can be seen most simply in wage differentials; it can also be seen through the prestige that is accorded the work.

Women's educational work is considered private, of no economic value unless it is done by a babysitter, a teacher or a child care provider. As "personal dependents" of male partners, women are economically, socially, and/or legally tied to another person who has authority over them (Eichler, 1973, p. 52). Research on wage sharing inside families is sparse, but shows women often do not have access to their partners' wages (Comer, 1982, p. 185; Luxton, 1980, p. 165). Because a mother does not receive a wage, her work is invisible in economic terms.

> If a mother is not in the labour force, she is not working; she is caring for her children. Only if the mother is replaced in looking after her children does this work enter into economic calculations. And the wages paid to babysitters indicate the market value of this work. In 1980, according to unpublished census data, the average yearly income for female babysitters working year-round and mainly full-time was $5,683. (Armstrong & Armstrong, 1984, p. 92)

It is no wonder, then, that many mothers do earn wages by working outside the home. As of 1984, 52% of mothers with a child under three, 57% of mothers with their youngest child aged three to five, and 64% of women with school-aged children were in the labor force. These figures represent, since 1976, increases of 62%, 39% and 29%, respectively (Task Force on Child Care, 1986, p. 8). These trends are not abating. By 1988, 58% of mothers with a child under three were in the labor force (Wilson, 1991).

Women are increasingly working outside the home, mostly in jobs which offer little remuneration. Child care workers in licensed centres, almost all of whom are women, are paid much less than the average weekly industrial wage. They earn even less than workers who look after animals (Townson, 1986, p. 17). The earnings of family home caregivers are even lower (Task Force on Child Care, 1986). The absence of monetary recognition for child care in a society that places so much value on money provides glaring evidence of the devaluation of women's work.

Due to a long struggle to gain pay equity, women who teach in elementary and secondary schools fare a lot better in their earning power than mothers or child care providers. In the early twentieth century, young women in teaching earned less than secretaries. They were paid on a different scale from men, who, after all, had to "keep a family." After the second war, woman teachers finally earned the right to be paid at a rate equal to men; elementary teachers' pay scales became equal to those of secondary teachers and the wages for teachers increased. Today, differences in the salaries of female and male elementary and secondary teachers rest not on their gender per se, but on their training and seniority. Women still have lower qualifications than men, on the average, and as noted above, they are much less likely to be in administrative positions.

In universities, comparison of the salaries of men and women with similar degrees, academic rank, age and fields of study show that women continue to earn less than their male counterparts (Symons & Page, 1984, p. 194). Recent figures indicate that full-time female faculty earn, on average, 82 cents for every dollar earned by full-time male faculty (Status of Women, December 1986, p. 10). This is only partly because women are in lower ranks and in lower-paying faculties than men; partly it is because women still earn less than men in similar positions.

The question of the prestige of these three kinds of educational workers — teachers, child care workers and mothers — is complex. On prestige scales, the occupation of housewife is in a lower category than registered nurse or teacher, but higher than most leading female occupations, such as typist or sales clerk. Being a housewife accords women some independent status, despite the negative association in capitalist societies of being labelled "just a housewife." A housewife's prestige is, however, also tied to the status of her husband. The wife of a physician is accorded a much higher status than the wife of a plumber. In nearly all cases, nevertheless, such wives are seen to have a lower status than their husbands (Eichler, 1978).

The status of child care workers is related to that of mothers. Both suffer from the public disdain for those who spend the day with young children

(Biklen, 1985, p. 215). This disdain is reflected in the lower prestige of elementary teachers relative to secondary teachers. Educational work that is largely carried out by women is caught up in the contradictory rhetoric of a child-centred society which devalues and underpays the care and raising of children (Lather, 1986). This work suffers from the cultural assumption that it is the proven and natural duty of women which, because it comes naturally to women, needs only minimal rewards.

Job Models Versus Gender Models

Because of the assumptions about women's work being naturally in the home while children and men's activities lie outside, the work experiences of men and women are interpreted differently by researchers. Women's functions are explained by their biology and their family, men's by their responsibilities, wages and working conditions.

In their review of the sociological literature on work, Feldberg and Glenn (1982) claim that "job models" are generally applied to understanding the behavior of male workers, while "gender models" are applied to female workers. Studies of male workers examine such job conditions as standardization, mechanization and repetitiveness to explain low motivation or alienation. Studies examining female workers stress personality and family-related factors instead. For example, in a study of factory workers, Beynon and Blackburn (1972) assume that women's "low motivation" is related to their primary commitment to family roles, whereas men's "sociability" (which seems to be another term for low commitment) is related to alienating job conditions and lack of opportunities for mobility.

This double standard can also be seen in analyses of teachers. To explain the low status of female relative to male teachers, researchers have implicitly adopted a "gender model." For example:

A woman's primary attachment is to the family role; women are therefore less intrinsically committed to work than men and less likely to maintain a high level of specialized knowledge. Because their work motives are more utilitarian and less intrinsically task-oriented than those of men, they may require more control. (Simpson & Simpson, 1969, p. 199)

Such an analysis blames women for their low status in the profession as well as for the low status of the profession as a whole. As Acker (1983) puts it, women teachers are portrayed as "damaging, deficient, distracted and sometimes dim" (p. 124).

These analyses ignore the possibility that women are confined to the devalued jobs of teaching younger rather than older children and that they may have a different, but as strong, commitment to teaching as have men. In her study of elementary school teachers, Biklen (1985) found that the women had a strong idealistic commitment to their work. They were more concerned about its content and their performance than with its usefulness to them for their personal upward mobility. Current conceptualization of teaching as a career, Biklen concludes, tends to be based on "the clockwork of male careers."

Feldberg and Glenn's (1982) analysis also suggests the importance of looking at the job conditions of mothers. Oakley (1974) found that most of the housewives she talked to experience more monotony, fragmentation and speed in their work than do factory workers. The average working week of the women in her sample was 72 hours — almost twice as long as an average industrial working week. With the development of such professions as medicine, psychology and, indeed, teaching, professional standards for child development techniques have increasingly been applied to mothering (Eichler, 1988; Mandell, 1988). One mother in Flin Flon eloquently summed up the contradictions of parenting: "I love them more than life itself and I wish they'd go away forever" (Luxton, 1980, p. 87). The complex rewards and responsibilities of mothering have only begun to interest researchers (Armstrong & Armstrong, 1984; Jackson, 1982; Luxton, 1980; Luxton, Rosenberg, & Arat-Koc, 1990; Storr, 1974).

The Interpenetration of Spheres

Teachers, child care workers and mothers share a concern for the well-being of children, but their relationships to each other are not characterized by simple cooperation. These are complex, shifting and strongly shaped by social class and race as well as by gender. Researchers have just begun to see these relationships from the point of view of women themselves, rather than through the eyes of the dominant institutions.

Research on the relationships between child care and mothers has been preoccupied with the conseqûences of child care for "culturally deprived" children, on the assumption that child care workers make up for the inadequacies of mothers, especially of poor mothers. Poor Canadian parents have used day care to help them look after their children from at least the 1850s. Most day care then was managed by voluntary philanthropic women's organizations. These nurseries not only provided child care but usually served also as employment agencies for mothers who sought domestic work. The nurseries offered children minimum physical, emotional and cognitive care and were primarily custodial rather than educational (Schulz, 1978). Today, child care is still associated with charity and welfare.

The state subsidizes care for only a small percentage of very-low-income families (Schulz, 1982, p. 125). But as Pence (1985) notes, higher maternal employment rates and a decline in the number of two-parent families have increased the demand for day care. Central to these transformations, he writes, is "the extension of the daycare issue from its traditional child welfare focus on the need-of-the-few, to the 'Well Fare' of the majority of Canadian families with young children" (p. 236). Child care, however, is far from attaining the status of public schooling, in which all children have the right to education.

As an issue, child care is fraught with debate over fundamental values, conceptions of family life, motherhood, childhood and the role of the state. Many advocates of child care who approach it from the perspective of women and their relationship to their children are concerned about the direction in which current provision is heading. Pupo (1988) is critical of the state's piecemeal approach to developing a child care policy; its objective, she claims, is "to preserve the family as a privatized unit without incurring substantial public costs or obstacles to private profit-making" (p. 224). Prentice (1988) is fearful that the increased provision of day care spaces has led to "mainstreaming" of the child care movement and to "commodification" of child care. Demands for non-commodified care such as community-based care — which struggles to challenge the social relations between women and men, children and adults/parents, and the relationship of individuals to the community/state — are now "barely a whisper."

Alternatively, many critics of child care pit the liberation of women against the welfare of children (e.g., Suransky, 1982, p. 191). If women go to work outside the home, they assume, children will suffer in substitute child care. There is no evidence for this; children sometimes gain, sometimes suffer, depending on the quality of care at home and in day care centres. We must rid ourselves of, as O'Connor (1984) puts it, "the always hovering ghost of 'mother', who continues to reappear as the inevitable right answer" (p. 163). The 'war' is not between women and their children but rather between women and children on the one hand and social and economic structures that do not support quality child care at home or outside it, on the other. While the debate about government versus parental responsibility persists, the provision of child care suffers.

In reference to Britain, but also applicable to North America, David and New (1985) argue that public policy is too often directed toward the "revitalization" of the traditional and private family. They suggest that a major "renegotiation of work and family" should be the goal of government policy and they recommend a wide range of changes, including the incorporation of men into child care at home and elsewhere; and the use of educational facilities as "community centres" that would combine nursery and primary schools.

Several European countries have already developed comprehensive child care policies based on the assumption of the shared responsibility of parents and society for children (Kamerman, 1979). The recent Report of the Task Force on Child Care (1986) suggests that substantial support exists in Canada for a system of child care and parental leave that recognizes the interrelationship of paid work outside the home and unpaid work with children within the home.

As the above suggests, the relationship between child care workers and mothers are complex. Though they may have similar interests, because of the ways the dominant institutions are organized, cooperation is difficult. The relationship between mothers and teachers also may be antagonistic. As with child care, teaching has often been perceived as making up for inadequacies of the home — read "mother," especially "poor mother." Research on the home-school relationship focuses on how families either facilitate or hinder their children's educational progress. The studies examine how the cultures of specific types of families (e.g., working-class, immigrant, Native) deprive children of advantages that are taken for granted by the educational system (Craft, 1970; Keddie, 1974; Manicom, 1984). In its abstract reference to "families" this research gives little recognition to the work of mothers. It is primarily concerned with a one-way relationship — how families affect the educational achievement of children. It blames mothers for any failures in their children, but takes their work for granted. It neglects to question how schools affect families, and more specifically, how they affect the work of mothers in the home.

This traditional examination of the family-school linkage is taken from the point of view of educators. It is approached from the standpoint of those who work within the educational system, not from that of mothers. It does not ask how women's work is shaped by schools; how child rearing is related to educational pedagogy; how both teaching and mothering are affected by changing educational resources; or how gender affects the work of teachers and mothers.

These are the kinds of questions that some feminists are beginning to ask (see, for example, David, 1980, 1986; David & New, 1985; Grumet, 1981; Jackson, 1982; Lather, 1986). Jackson (1982), for example, argues that as the school changes its practices and policies, and resources are cut back, new demands are placed on teachers and parents (in particular the mother). She writes:

> Two familiar developments in the school are noteworthy here. One is the movement toward more standardization of curriculum and evaluation and increased accountability for classroom practices. The second is the reduction in the level of support services as a result of cutbacks in educational spending . . . both of these policies result in increased demands on teachers. They also result in intensification, both directly and indirectly, of the demands on parents. (p. 23)

Mothers, child care workers and teachers are too often pitted against each other and blamed for each other's failings. Instead, we need to look at the structures that marginalize and devalue them all, making it difficult for them to care for children. Though children are often touted to be society's most valuable resource, the actual work of raising them is trivialized and poorly paid. But we also need to look at the rewards and opportunities these positions provide. Although teaching, child care and mothering are devalued and subjected to the authority of men in a variety of ways within the present economic and cultural climate, they also offer opportunities for women.

In the first edition of this book we included a chapter on the education and training, earnings and working conditions, and rights and obligations of child care providers, taken from the Report of the Task Force on Child Care

(1986). Since this report is readily available, we did not repeat the chapter in this edition. We can only hope that in the future more research will be done on child care and its commonalities, differences and interrelationships with teaching and mothering.

The four contributors to this section examine the educational work of teachers and/or mothers and address some of the issues mentioned above concerning the sexual division of labor, the devaluation (and revaluation) of women's work, women's work experiences, and the interpenetration of public and private spheres. Danylewycz, Light and Prentice are concerned with trying to understand how the "feminization of teaching" emerged historically. As Prentice (1977) notes in an earlier article, the idea of a predominantly female elementary teaching force only gradually gained acceptance in British North America. Carefully analyzing the provinces of Ontario and Quebec during the formative period of public schooling from 1851 to 1881, these authors tease out the most important factors (e.g., rural poverty, the presence of a resource frontier, the traditional roles of women in the family, and the legacy of nuns in teaching) that explain how teaching became women's work.

Teaching is women's work not only at the elementary level of education, but also in some university faculties such as nursing. Valentine and McIntosh are largely concerned with the ways in which female educators may bring distinct views of the world to the workplace and how this might influence the organizational culture. They argue that nursing has evolved in tandem with the idea of the "female world," which is based on the ideology of women's sphere and has given rise to a "gemeinschaft" orientation and a love-and/or-duty ethos. Rather than women learning to fit into male-oriented organizations, these authors suggest that organizations need to change to reflect the aspirations and values of the female world. Such changes will ultimately improve the "health" of organizations as a whole.

Mothering, the ultimate "women's work" in western capitalist societies, is examined by Griffith and Smith as a work process. They consider the way that mothering is structured by schooling. In addition, they contribute to an ongoing debate concerning the development of feminist research methodologies. By developing the crucial insights of Smith's earlier works (1974, 1975, 1979), they aim to provide a sociology not of, but for women. They are critical of traditional, positivistic research that assumes that subjects can be treated as objects and that researchers do not have a relationship with their subjects. Their concern is to understand mothering from the standpoint of the mothers themselves and to take into account the social relations within which their work is embedded.

While the majority of educational workers are women, in some settings, such as most university faculties, women are a minority. Ng discusses the difficulties of being not only a minority woman, but also a racial minority in a white, male-dominated society. She focusses particularly on the contradictions minority teachers experience in implementing critical teaching.

Critical teaching which aims to democratize the classroom has largely been concerned with the unequal relationship between all-powerful teachers and powerless students. But, Ng notes, the minority teacher experiences a variety of contradictions in the classroom, because of the pervasiveness of common-sense sexism and racism in society.

Note
[1]The percentages of female elementary and secondary teachers are based on our computations and on figures from 6 provinces (see Statistics Canada, 1987, p. 22).

References

Acker, S. (1983). Women and teaching: A semi-detached sociology of a semi-profession. In Stephen Walker & Len Barton (Eds.), *Gender, class and Education.* Sussex: Falmer Press.

Apple, M.W. (1983). Work, class and teaching. In Stephen Walker & Len Barton (Eds.), *Gender, class and education.* Sussex: Falmer Press.

Armstrong, P., & Armstrong, H. (1984). *The double ghetto: Canadian women and their segregated work* (Rev. ed.). Toronto: McClelland and Stewart.

Beynon, R., & Blackburn, R.M. (1972). *Perceptions of work.* London: Cambridge University Press.

Biklen, S.K. (1985). Can elementary school teaching be a career? A search for new ways of understanding women's work. *Issues in Education, 3*(3), 215-231.

Comer, L. (1982). Monogamy, marriage and economic dependence. In Elizabeth Whitelegg et al. (Eds.), *The changing experience of women.* Oxford: Martin Robertson.

Craft, M. (Ed.). (1970). *Family, class and education: A reader.* London: Longman.

Cusson, S. (1990, Autumn). Women in school administration. *Canadian Social Trends,* pp. 24-25.

David, M. (1980). *The state, the family and education.* London: Routledge and Kegan Paul.

David, M. (1986). *Morality and maternity: Towards a reconciliation.* Paper presented at the Women and Education Conference, University of British Columbia, Vancouver, B.C.

David, M., with New, C. (1985). *A feminist perspective on child care policy.* Revised unpublished paper. (Original prepared for the EOC Day Workshop on Child Care Services for Working Parents, Connaught Hall, London)

Durkheim, E. (1956). *Education and sociology.* Glencoe, IL: The Free Press.

Eichler, M. (1973). Women as personal dependents. In Marylee Stephenson (Ed.), *Women in Canada.* Toronto: New Press.

Eichler, M. (1978). The prestige of the occupation housewife. In Patricia Marchak (Ed.), *The working sexes.* Vancouver, BC: University of British Columbia, Institute of Industrial Relations.

Eichler, M. (1988). *Families in Canada today* (2nd. ed.). Toronto: Gage.

Feldberg, R.L., & Glenn, E.N. (1982). Male and female: Job versus gender models in the sociology of work. In Rachel Kahn-Hut, Arlene Kaplan Daniels, & Richard Colvard (Eds.), *Women and work: Problems and perspectives.* New York: Oxford University Press.

Gittens, D. (1985). *The family in question: Changing households and familiar ideologies.* London: Macmillan.

Grumet, M. (1981). Pedagogy for patriarchy: The feminization of teaching. *Interchange, 12* (2-3), 165-184.

Jackson, N.S. (1982). *Between home and school: The crisis in educational resources.* Paper prepared for the Canadian Teachers' Federation, Professional Development Services.

Jaggar, A.M., & McBride, W.L. (1985). 'Reproduction' as male ideology. *Women's Studies International Forum, 8*(3), 185-196.

Kamerman, S.B. (1979). Work and family in industrialized societies. *SIGNS: Journal of Women in Culture and Society, 4,* 632-650.

Keddie, N. (1974). *Tinker, tailor: The myth of cultural deprivation.* Harmondsworth: Penquin.

Kome, P. (1982). *Somebody has to do it: Whose work is housework?* Toronto: McClelland and Stewart.

Lather, P. (1986). *The absent presence: Patriarchy, capitalism and the nature of teachers' work.* Paper presented at Theoretical and Empirical Issues in Gender Research: So You Want to Talk about Theory? symposium, San Francisco.

Luxton, M. (1980). *More than a labour of love: Three generations of women's work in the home.* Toronto: The Women's Press.

Luxton, M., Rosenberg, H., & Arat-Koc, S. (1990). *Through the kitchen window: The politics of home and family.* Toronto: Garamond Press.

Mandell, N. (1988). The child question: Links between women and children in the family. In Nancy Mandell & Ann Duffy (Eds.), *Reconstructing the Canadian family: Feminist perspectives.* Toronto: Butterworths.

Mandell, N., & Duffy, A (Eds.). (1988). *Reconstructing the Canadian family: Feminist perspectives.* Toronto: Butterworths.

Manicom, A. (1984). Feminist frameworks and teacher education. *Journal of Education, 166*(1), 77-87.

Maroney, H.J. (1985). Embracing motherhood: New feminist theory. In Marilouise Kroker, Arthur Kroker, Pamela McCallum, & Mair Verthuy (Eds.), *Feminism now: Theory and practice.* Montreal: New World Perspectives.

Martin, W.B.W., & Macdonell, AJ. (1982). *Canadian education: A sociological analysis* (2nd ed.). Scarborough, ON: Prentice-Hall Canada.

Moore, M. (1987, Winter). Women parenting alone. *Canadian Social Trends,* pp. 31-35.

Oakley, A. (1974). *The sociology of housework.* London: Martin Robertson.

O'Brien, M. (1983). Feminism and education: A critical review essay. *Resources for Feminist Research, 12*(3), 3-16.

O'Connor, S.M. (1984). Review of day care: Scientific and social policy issues and the erosion of childhood. *SIGNS: Journal of Women in Culture and Society, 9,* 161-163.

Parsons, Talcott. (1959). The school class as a social system: Some of its functions in American society. *Harvard Educational Review, 29,* 297-318.

Pence, A.R. (1985). Day care in Canada. In Kenneth L. Levitt & Brian Wharf (Eds.), *The challenge of child welfare.* Vancouver: University of British Columbia Press.

Prentice, A. (1977). The feminization of teaching. In Susan Mann Trofimenkoff & Alison Prentice (Eds.), *The neglected majority: Essays in Canadian women's history.* Toronto: The Women's Press.

Prentice, S. (1988). The 'mainstreaming' of day care. *Resources for Feminist Research, 17*(3), 59-63.

Pupo, N. (1988). Preserving patriarchy: Women, the family and the state. In Nancy Mandell & Ann Duffy (Eds.), *Reconstructing the Canadian family: Feminist perspectives.* Toronto: Butterworths.

Rich, A. (1977). *Of woman born: Motherhood as experience and institution.* New York: W.W. Norton.

Schulz, P.V. (1978). Day care in Canada: 1850-1962. In K.G. Ross (Ed.), *Good day care.* Toronto: The Women's Press.

Schulz, P. (1982). Minding the children. In Maureen Fitzgerald, Connie Guberman, & Margie Wolfe (Eds.), *Still ain't satisfied: Canadian feminism today.* Toronto: The Women's Press.

Sedgewick, R. (1976). Woman's sphere. In Ramsey Cook & Wendy Mitchinson (Eds.), *The proper sphere: Woman's place in Canadian society.* Toronto: Oxford University Press. (Original published 1856)

Simpson, R.L., & Simpson, I.H. (1969). Women and bureaucracy in the semi-professions. In A. Etzioni (Ed.), *The semi-professions and their organization.* New York: The Free Press.

Smith, D.E. (1974). Women's perspective as a radical critique of sociology. *Sociological Inquiry, 4*(1), 7-13.

Smith, D.E. (1975). An analysis of ideological structures and how women are excluded: Considerations for academic women. *Canadian Review of Sociology and Anthropology, 12,* 353-369. (Reprinted in this volume as chapter 8)

Smith, D.E. (1979). A sociology for women. In Julia A. Sherman & Evelyn Torion Beck (Eds.), *The prism of sex: Essays in the sociology of knowledge.* Madison: University of Wisconsin Press.

Statistics Canada. (1986). *Teachers in universities 1984-85.* Ottawa: Minister of Supply and Services.

Statistics Canada. (1987). *Characteristics of teachers in public elementary and secondary schools 1985-86.* Ottawa: Minister of Supply and Services.

Status of Women. (1986, December 10). Pay equity. *CAUT Bulletin.*

Storr, C. (1974). Freud and the concept of parental guilt. In Arlene S. Skolnick & Jerome H. Skolnick (Eds.), *Intimacy, family and society.* Boston: Little, Brown.

Strober, M.H., & Tyack, D. (1980). Why do women teach and men manage? A report on research on schools. *SIGNS: Journal of Women in Culture and Society, 5,* 494-503.

Suransky, V.P. (1982). *The erosion of childhood.* Chicago: University of Chicago Press.

Symons, T.H.B., & Page J.E. (1984). *To know ourselves: The report of the Commission on Canadian Studies: Vol. 2. Some questions of balance: Human resources, higher education and Canadian studies.* Ottawa: Association of Universities and Colleges of Canada.

Task Force on Child Care. (1986). *Report of the Task Force on Child Care.* Ottawa: Minister of Supply and Services.

Thorne, B., & Yalom, M. (Eds.). (1982). *Rethinking the family: Some feminist questions.* New York: Longman.

Townson, M. (1986). The costs and benefits of a national child care system in Canada. *Women's Education des Femmes, 4*(4) 16-21.

Wilson, S.J. (1991). *Women, families, and work* (3rd ed.). Toronto: McGraw-Hill Ryerson.

1

The Evolution of the Sexual Division of Labor in Teaching: Nineteenth Century Ontario and Quebec Case Study[1]

Maria Danylewycz, Beth Light and Alison Prentice

Shortly after her marriage to a widower with four children in December of 1916, country school teacher Leila V. Middleton recorded the wedding and her hopes as a stepmother in her diary.

> I was married Wed. Dec. 27 and came to my new home Sat. evening after spending a few days in Toronto. I feel that I am taking on a big responsibility with four young step children. I hope my teaching experience of 5 years may be of help to me in doing for each what is best . . .[2]

In seeing teaching as appropriate preparation for her new role, Leila Middleton was expressing a commonly held view. It was a view that had developed out of the experience of thousands of North American women who, since the early decades of the nineteenth century, had spent the years between the end of their own schooling and marriage as mistresses of rural schools. It was a view that had been put forward by early promoters of women teachers, such as Catherine Beecher, and was also carefully nurtured by hundreds of school administrators, those makers of educational ideology for whom it was convenient that a labor pool of idealistic and uncomplaining young women should continue to fill poorly paid teaching posts in thousands of rural schools. The belief that teaching was an ideal preparation for motherhood was of course meant to apply to all female teachers, not just those living in the country. Urban women, persuaded that their role was to teach the youngest children in the graded schools of towns and cities, were also subject to such domestically oriented ideology.

For the many women teachers who did not marry, the mystique of the teacher-in-training for motherhood must have had a hollow ring and, because of them, there was another twist to the tale. To schoolmistresses of the nineteenth century who remained celibate, the mission of the school was less a preparation than a substitute for woman's divine calling in the home. For these women, teaching was held up as a vocation and was in fact often a lifetime career (Burstyn, 1974; Melder, 1972; Riley, 1969; Sklar, 1973).

If women were seen to be either preparing for or playing a mothering role in the school room, the implied ideal role for the male teacher was that of the patriarchal father. Often a young man would use school teaching as a stepping stone to another more lucrative profession; if he stayed in teaching it was usually in the hope of exerting his natural authority as a principal, as a model school or high school teacher, or as an inspector or superintendent of schools.

Historians investigating the history of teaching have been impressed with the extent to which these ideal constructs reflected reality. The vast majority of nineteenth- and even twentieth-century women teachers, like women employed in other occupations, have tended to leave their schools to become wives and mothers. On the other side of the coin, the proportionally fewer men who have been teachers since the development of public school systems have had better than average chances of progressing from the classroom to administrative jobs. School teaching has thus presented a classic case of the sexual division of educational occupational ladders and men have been favored at the top (Katz, 1968; Prentice, 1975; Strober and Tyack, 1980; Tyack, 1967; Tyack and Strober, 1981).

But to make such general statements is to talk only about the tip of the iceberg. Investigations of the movement into public school teaching have begun to reveal that there is a great deal hidden beneath the surface. Segregation by gender in school teaching, it turns out, is a far from simple or static fact. It is, rather, a complex phenomenon which has not only undergone important changes over time, but has manifested major regional and national variations as well.

A striking area of complexity and the one most thoroughly examined to date is the comparison between urban and rural teachers in the past. Focusing largely on the nineteenth century, studies of school systems have revealed that the larger schools of cities tended to spawn occupational hierarchies in teaching. In these schools, women teachers were segregated in lower paying positions as the instructors of the junior grades and men were slotted into higher paying positions as senior teachers, principals and superintendents. Where such urban hierarchies developed, the proportion of women teachers tended to be higher than average for the region or period in question (Graph 1). At the same time, the gap between male and female salaries tended to grow wider (Prentice, 1975: 12-13; Strober and Best, 1979).

In contrast, historians have noted, rural areas were generally slower to develop a segmented labor market in teaching. Although women teachers gradually became the majority in rural schools, male teachers held their own in the one-room rural school house well into the later years of the nineteenth century. Rural authorities worried about the ability of women teachers, particularly if they were young, to manage schools attended by young men and about the ability of women to "govern" children in general (Strober and Tyack, 1980: 497-98). In some rural regions young women may have been less available for school teaching because of the demand for domestic labor on the typical family farm (Strober and Tyack, 1980: 497).[4] Finally, it has been argued, rural society presented fewer alternative opportunities to young men and therefore teaching was likely to seem more attractive to rural males than it might have to their urban contemporaries (Strober and Tyack, 1980: 497). Whatever the reasons for the generally more equal numbers of male and female teachers in rural areas over a longer period in the nineteenth century than was the case for urban North America, this greater general equality in numbers was reflected both in wages and conditions. The gap between female and male salaries tended to be narrower than that found in cities. And because the job generally consisted in the management of a one-room school, the work experience of women and men who taught rural schools was more comparable than the contrasting roles usually played by male and female teachers in hierarchically organized urban schools (Strober and Best, 1979; Strober and Tyack, 1980; Tyack and Strober, 1981).

Graph 1

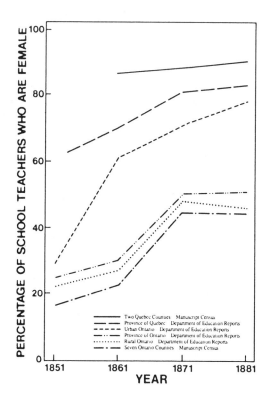

Percentages of Female Teachers in Ontario and Quebec 1851-1881

This situation of relative equality did not last, however. Broad statistical studies, in this case dealing exclusively with the United States, are beginning to demonstrate how measures of formalization, such as a longer school year

or a larger number of teachers per school, correlated with growing proportions of women teachers almost everywhere. Men, who had once combined
teaching with farming in economies where women teachers were able to take
the schools in the summer, appear to have been forced out of the occupation
by the lengthening school year. In the late nineteenth and early twentieth
centuries, continuing urbanization signalled increasing hierarchy, widening
gaps between female and male wages, and more women in the occupation,
presumably filling the lower ranks even in village schools where there were
now three or four teachers instead of one. By the early twentieth century
there was a clear sexual division of labor in rural as well as urban schools
(Day and O'Connor, 1978; Strober and Landford, 1981).

Whether urban or rural, both nineteenth- and early twentieth-century
female teachers emerge in most of the studies that have been done to date as
malleable, commandable beings. Young and socialized to obedience in a
patriarchal family setting, they were the ideal people to fill the growing
number of jobs in schools that were increasingly governed by rules and
regulations emanating from above, whether from immediate superiors such
as principals and trustees, or from more distant authorities such as state or
provincial departments of education. Male teachers, on the other hand, are
portrayed as either the seekers of such authority for themselves or, in one
case, as the only sex capable of fighting against bureaucratic authority and
of promoting the professional status of their occupation (Labarree-Paulé,
1965; Strober and Tyack, 1980: 500; c.f. Tyack and Strober, 1981).[5]

If these are the stereotypes, it is also true that several studies stress the
potential for development and affirmation of self that teaching offered for
many nineteenth-century North American women. As well, they stress the
occasional connections that can be traced between teacher activism and
nineteenth- and early twentieth-century feminism (Clifford, 1981). An examination of the relations between male and female teachers in France,
moreover, has uncovered government legislation favoring the advancement
of women over that of men teachers in the 1890s and the eventual emergence
of a significant alliance between schoolmasters and schoolmistresses against
what those allied saw as the enemy of correct republican education, the
Roman Catholic Church (Bryans, 1974; Meyers, 1980).

Such studies clearly illustrate the importance of local or regional contexts in any examination of the evolution of sexual divisions of labor in
teaching. They also suggest that if the historian looks at the sexual division
of labor in schools from the perspective of the women teachers themselves,
a complex picture, one that is neither completely positive nor completely
negative, is likely to emerge.

The present study explores the evolution of a predominantly female
workforce in teaching in the context of two regional political economies;
those of the provinces of Ontario and Quebec, during the period from 1851
to 1881. While the two Canadas[6] shared many characteristics with each other
and with parts of the United States in the nineteenth century, they were also

in some ways sharply contrasting societies. With its French population dating back to the beginnings of New France, Quebec was an established rural society, but a rural society with a difference. Wheat production insufficient to feed the growing population and a serious land shortage in the older colonized parishes and counties produced, by mid-century, a great migration of Quebec families to new lands in the north of the province and in eastern Ontario and, most noticeably perhaps, to the industrializing cities of New England. Quebec's largest city, Montreal, was also experiencing industrial development and the influx of large numbers of migrants, first from Ireland and then from its own rural hinterland. Last but not least, resource industries such as lumbering played an increasingly important role in the Quebec economy (McCallum, 1980; Paquet and Wallot, 1975; Séguin. 1977).

Ontario, by contrast, was a relatively new rural society. Indigenous populations in this province had first been joined by American landseekers and Loyalists following the American revolution; these were followed by those from the British Isles. Most immigrants lived primarily by farming, but lumbering also flourished in Ontario, especially in the Ottawa Valley, while commercial and some industrial development was making an important centre of the city of Toronto. Indeed, and apparently because of its later development and the marketing needs of its wheat economy, Ontario boasted quite a number of smaller urban centres, in contrast to Quebec where small towns were proportionally less numerous (McCallum, 1980). Materially, then, the two provinces differed in that Ontario had a more evenly spread urban network, that Quebec had a longer history of farming and greater rural overcrowding, and, possibly, that the French province suffered greater rural poverty during much of the nineteenth century. The greatest cultural contrast between the two provinces, aside from the obvious difference in dominant languages, was the Roman Catholic character of Quebec by the third quarter of the nineteenth century compared with the increasingly Protestant identity of Ontario (Linteau, et al., 1979: 232-39, 517-25; Wallot, 1971). All these contrasts lead to the first question addressed by this chapter: How did the different economic, social and cultural settings of education in Quebec and Ontario affect the evolution of the sexual division of labor in teaching in the two provinces?

A second goal of the present study was to look more closely at rural patterns of development, for rural teaching patterns have been insufficiently studied. Like researchers elsewhere, we were convinced that the development of urban bureaucracies did not fully explain the eventual feminization of the occupation in the predominantly agricultural societies of North America. In addition to these concerns, we also realized that the province of Quebec and at least some Ontario counties did not fit very well into the general North American picture of shifting male/female ratios in teaching.

Indeed, the most cursory look at central Canadian educational statistics for the nineteenth century reveals two startling facts. The first is that in Ontario, although women teachers were clearly a minority overall until the

1870s, certain counties in the eastern part of the province favored them much earlier. Prescott, Stormont, Dundas, Russell and Grenville began to report female majorities to the Department of Education during the odd year in the early 1850s and by the early 1960s, quite a few of the eastern counties were consistently reporting a majority of women teachers (Map 1). The second and more obvious fact is that Quebec women teachers outnumbered men in the province as a whole by mid-century. Moreover, one of the first complete sets of school inspectors' reports revealed that men in rural settings were no more likely than their counterparts living in urban centres like Montreal, Quebec City, and Sherbrooke to take up teaching as an occupation. Contrary to what historians have found to be the case in the United States at that time, the work of teaching in Quebec belonged to country as much as city women (Graph 1 and Table 1).

The point at which women became the majority of the teaching force in Quebec remains a mystery. Some historical accounts suggest they outnumbered men as early as the 1930s (Labarrer-Paulé, 1965: 93). Given the possibility that women in late eighteenth- and early nineteenth-century Lower Canada may have been more literate than men, that at the time of the Conquest and following the banishment of male religious orders, girls' schools run by religious women or by laywomen trained in convent schools were more abundant than educational institutions for boys, women teachers may have been in the majority during much of French Canada's early history.[7] Whatever the early history of the sexual division of labor in Quebec, it is clear that by the beginning of the second half of the nineteenth century self-conscious school promoters, who shared the educational philosophies of men like Ontario's Egerton Ryerson and Massachusett's Horace Mann, were concerned about what they thought was a new trend. Who taught school, how male and female teachers conducted themselves in the classroom, and what roles women and men were to play in the developing school systems were questions much pondered by the architects of public schooling in Quebec.

In this context, the growing presence of women teachers was noted and its causes and consequences studied. School inspectors and educational administrators remarked that the rapid multiplication of schools in the 1860s and 1870s, the ratepayers' opposition to high educational costs, and the school commissioners' policy of hiring the least expensive teachers ensured the dominance and eventual monopoly of teaching by women. Understanding the connection between the influx of women into teaching and the money-saving policies of local school commissioners, school promoters realized that as long as custom and prescription dictated a lower pay scale for women and a qualitatively higher one for men, the flow of women could not be stemmed. They lamented the loss of male teachers, yet too few were prepared (or even able) to change that situation by equalizing the salaries of men and women.[8]

Table 1
Percentages of Female Teachers in
Inspectoral Districts of Quebec, 1853

Inspector	District	Female Teachers	Male Teachers	% Female
M. Lanctot	Huntingdon, Beauharnois	84	48	63.6
M. Child	Stanstead, Sherbrooke, Drummond	185	48	79.4
F. Hubert	St. Maurice, Champlain	53	36	59.6
W.A. Adamson	City of Quebec (Protestant)	2	2	50.0
J.H. Morin	Saguenay	2	1	66.7
J.G. Lespérance	Gaspé	2	1	66.7
J. Crepault	Bellechasse, L'Islet	88	23	79.3
C. Germain	Terrebonne, Two Mountains	70	47	59.8
G. Tanguay	Kamouraska, Rimouski	107	28	79.3
J.N.A. Archambault	Chamably, Vercheres, Richilieu	83	45	64.8
R. Parmelee	Missisquoi, Rouville, Shefford, Stanstead	117	56	67.6
F.X. Valade	Montreal, Vaudreuil	67	57	54.0
P.M. Bardy	Portneuf, Quebec, Montmorency	57	56	50.4
A.P.J. Consigny	St. Hyacinth, Rouville	82	40	67.2
B. Maurault	Yamaska, Nicolet	73	14	83.9
P.F. Béland	Dorchester, Lotbiniere	166	37	81.8
G.A. Bourgeois	Drummond	8	6	57.1
J. Bruce	Beauharnois, Two Mountains	52	82	38.8
C. Chagnon	Leinster, Berthier	54	68	44.3
C. Cimon	Saguenay	12	15	44.5
W. Hume	Dorchester, Bellechasse, Mégantic	11	19	36.7
B.F. Painchaud	Gaspé	0	4	0.0
P. Winter	Bonaventure, Gaspé	4	34	10.5
J.J. Roney	Ottawa	25	41	31.8
Totals		1 404	808	63.5

Source: Report of the Superintendent of Education for Lower Canada for 1853.

If the low price at which women teachers sold their services led to the virtual elimination of the schoolmaster, the popular practice among the agricultural and working classes of removing boys from school at a younger age than girls also favored the proportional increase of women in teaching. Girls were allowed to remain in school longer, inspectors noted, because parents and employers placed a higher value on the work of young men. Sons were expected to set books aside and to help with the intensive work of farming and lumbering. Girls presumably could spend many of their days in school and still help with the household chores in the late afternoons and evenings. One school inspector contrasted the practice of withdrawing sons from school to the encouragement given by parents to their daughters as follows: "Nothing," he wrote, "is neglected as far as the girls are concerned; they are even sent to the superior schools. . . ."[9]

While our second concern, then, was to explore this very early development of predominantly female teaching forces in eastern Ontario and in Quebec, our third goal evolved from the decision to use the manuscript census as a source. Scrutinized for the years 1851 to 1881 for Ontario, and 1861 to 1881 for Quebec, the manuscript census permitted us to examine such variables as the ethnicity of Canadian female and male teachers, their ages, and their household and marital statuses over time. We wanted to know how these variables affected the evolution of the sexual division of labor in the schools.[10]

Before examining these questions, it is important to recognize that statistical information on Ontario and Quebec before the middle of the nineteenth century is minimal. The result is that we are left somewhat in the dark about divisions of labor in teaching prior to the full-scale emergence of state-supported school systems, a situation that makes it easy to blur the origins of the phenomenon we are studying. It would be of considerable interest to know more about male/female ratios in the traditional, "non-public" schools that existed before the development of a sexual division of labor in state-supported schools. Of equal interest is the extent of formalization that was to be found in the common and parish schools of mid-century. Were the high proportions of women teachers in Quebec or the counties of eastern Ontario related to longer school years and larger schools, as suggested in American studies, or were the causes more likely to be found in a tradition of women in teaching and the particular exigencies of regional economies, as school inspectors of the time seemed to believe?

Certainly, in central Canada, as in other parts of North America, state involvement in schooling altered the character of the schools. Although this involvement began early in the nineteenth century in both Ontario and Quebec, government financial assistance to schools was minimal until the 1840s and it is unclear how effective or uniform early attempts at government intervention in the conduct of schools may have been. Ontario studies have suggested, in fact, that even in the 1840s and 1850s government controls were slow to take hold (Gidney and Lawr, 1978; esp. 178-79). And, if in Ontario a tax-supported system of public, primary schooling had by 1871 largely replaced the voluntaristic and predominantly domestic schooling that had prevailed earlier, in Quebec the move from private and locally oriented education to genuinely state-controlled schools seems to have proceeded more slowly (Audet, 1971). Considerable resistance to government interference in education existed in both provinces.

The resistance produced a wave of rural school burnings and riots at mid-century in Quebec.[11] In eastern Ontario the protest was less violent but not necessarily less pervasive. Take, for example, the county of Prescott where women teachers early became a majority. Stretched along the Ottawa River and settled by British immigrants who at mid-century were being joined by migrants from Quebec, Prescott was far removed both physically and psychologically from the centre of Ontario's educational power in Toronto. The length of the school year in Prescott seems to have been average for Ontario, wavering between 9 months and 8 days and 9 months and 29 days, in the early 1850s. Therefore, a long school year preventing men from combining teaching with farming cannot be the explanation for early feminization of teaching in Prescott. Nor did the other counties, where 45 % or more of the teachers in any given year were women, deviate greatly from the Ontario average in the length of their school years. Their significant common characteristic seems simply to have been distance from the metropolis, rather than any high level of formalization in the conduct or organization of their schools.[12]

It is more fruitful to look for common features uniting these counties of eastern Ontario with rural Quebec. Immediately apparent is the fact that in both regions there was considerable rural poverty. If farm families were having to leave many parts of Quebec at mid-century, settlers were just beginning to come into many parts of eastern Ontario. Surplus cash to pay school taxes and hence to supplement provincial funds to remunerate teachers was not readily available. Eastern Ontario school superintendents reported that the bush was just being cleared, that both people and schools were widely scattered and, finally, that trustees were simply "unwilling" to pay salaries sufficient to attract a "better" class of teachers into the schools. In 1855 the problems of poverty and lack of interest were outlined with particular clarity in the report on the Prescott township of Alfred.

> All the teachers in the township are young girls under eighteen years of age, as none other would teach for the salaries that the trustees are able to pay them, on account of the difficulty of collecting, or rather the disinclination of paying, local rates.[13]

The disinclination was clearly shared by the rioting farmers and school burners of Quebec.

In 1850, a teacher from Russell County analyzed the problems of poverty and poor salaries in the Canadas in an irate letter to Ontario's Chief Superintendent of Schools. No wonder there were riots in Lower Canada, James Breakenridge complained. The government grants to teachers were paltry and local trustees endured endless trouble to procure them, including journeys of up to sixty miles. Far from assisting local teachers to do better, the new "school machinery," it would appear from Breakenridge's account, was little more than an irritant in poor and thinly settled regions.[14]

Evidence that poverty was at the root of such troubles and the cause of many cases of hiring women school teachers is to be found in Education Department statistics on school building materials. The relative prosperity of some Ontario counties was made manifest in these statistics by the high proportions of schools that were of frame construction or were built of brick or stone. With the single exception of Lennox, the eastern counties showing high proportions of female teachers in the early 1850s indicated their poverty by reporting higher than average proportions of log school houses, compared to the province as a whole.[15]

If poverty was the major characteristic shared by many eastern Ontario counties and parts of the province of Quebec, another was the presence of the "resource frontier." As John Abbott and Charles Gaffield have argued for turn of the century Algoma and mid-nineteenth-century Prescott County, respectively, resource frontier economies were similar in their attitudes to schooling (Abbot, 1983; Gaffield, 1978). In places like Prescott, Russell or Stormont and in many Quebec counties, especially in the northeast, lumbering was an important industry attracting large numbers of young men into the bush during the winter season, when in other places they might have been available to teach. Thus, it seems male unavailability was, at least in part, responsible for female predominance in teaching in these regions.

What we are proposing essentially is a third and possibly a fourth model of the sexual division of labor in teaching. To the early urban pattern, in which women teachers quickly filled the lower ranks of expanding city school systems, and the later rural pattern, where high proportions of women teachers were related to a gradually increasing formalization and to the repetition of urban patterns on a smaller scale, we would add an early rural model of the sexual division of labor in teaching, which was characteristic of troubled agricultural regions and the resource frontier. In this model, poverty and the presence of industries such as lumbering, calling young men into the bush rather than the school, combined to produce a majority of women teachers almost from the beginning of the introduction of public schooling.

Our fourth model is suggested by the special characteristics of Quebec. We would argue that a factor that affected the early sexual division of labor in teaching in French Canada, and may also have had an impact elsewhere, was the presence of an important tradition of women in teaching prior to the emergence of government-supported schooling. This tradition dates back to the involvement of nuns in education since the founding of New France; it may also have been related to the sexual division of labor in the rural household economies, as described by the nineteenth-century school inspectors. The rapid growth of women's teaching religious orders in the second half of the nineteenth century merely strengthened the female presence in education (Danlewycz, 1981).

In Ontario, the counties of Northumberland, Ontario and Oxford, Dundas and Essex, and Prescott and Grey were chosen for intensive study using the manuscript census.[16] The growing proportion of female teachers[17] recorded in the census for the seven counties follows the basic pattern for Ontario, but at a slower pace (Graph 1). From the Department of Public Instruction annual reports, we see in 1851 a higher proportion of women teachers for the province as a whole (25.2%) and for rural Ontario (21.8%) compared to the average for the seven counties of 16.1% derived from the manuscript census. But this is to be expected given the apparent underenumeration of female teachers in the early census reports, a phenomenon probably resulting from the fact that the 1851 and 1861 censuses were taken in the wintertime, a season during which fewer women taught.[18] In 1861, the Ontario rural average indicated by the Department of Public Instruction annual reports was still generally higher than the seven counties' average derived from the manuscript census, but the two averages were much closer to each other. If we examine the counties individually, the education records for 1861 also reveal the diversity of the seven counties, with Prescott reporting, as it had several times in the 1850s, a majority of female teachers; Dundas, Northumberland and Essex repeated the pattern of the early 1850s of between 25% and 49.9% women; by contrast, Oxford and Ontario actually dropped to join Grey County with fewer than 25% of all teachers female (Map 1).

What does the manuscript census reveal about teachers in the seven counties considered as a group? Certainly one of the most significant revelations is the important difference between male and female teachers, between 1851 and 1881, in terms of age (Table 2). While in every decade there were some adolescent males teaching in the seven counties, they never comprised more than 12% of all male teachers and, in the first three census years studied, fewer than 10% of the male teachers were under 20 years of age. Most schoolmasters were between 20 and 29, especially in 1871 and 1881, but male teachers who were 30 and over were also an important category.

Women, in contrast, were young. Indeed, 52.4% of the women were under 25 years of age in 1851, compared to only 27.2% of the men. Although male teachers in the under 25 age group increased to 35.4% in the following decade, the women in this group had by then jumped to 67.4% of all women teachers. The percentages for women under 25 stabilized at approximately 70% during the next two census years; but by 1881, although their numbers and proportion had increased, men under 25 were still only 46.4% of all male teachers. The shift, then, for both men and women teaching in the seven counties, was towards a younger age. But in all census decades, the women were on the average much younger than the men.

Table 2
Cases of Common School Teachers
Seven Ontario Counties, 1851-1881

		Female Teachers		Male Teachers	
		No.	%	No.	%
1851	19 & under	5	11.9	10	4.6
	20-24	17	40.5	50	23.1
	25-29	11	26.2	47	21.8
	30 & over	9	21.4	109	50.5
	Total	42	100.0	216	100.0
1861	19 & under	34	27.6	33	7.7
	20-24	49	39.8	119	27.7
	25-29	13	10.6	101	23.5
	30 & over	27	22.0	177	41.2
	Total	123	100.0	430	100.1
1871	19 & under	74	24.3	28	7.5
	20-24	144	47.4	107	28.6
	25-29	39	12.8	77	20.6
	30 & over	47	15.5	162	43.3
	Total	304	100.0	374	100.0
1881	19 & under	116	25.1	70	12.0
	20-24	204	44.2	201	34.4
	25-29	78	16.9	102	17.5
	30 & over	64	13.9	211	36.1
	Total	462	100.1	584	100.0

This seems an important contrast, given the greater equality between nineteenth-century female and male rural teachers in terms of numbers, conditions of employment and wages that has been emphasized in existing studies. If the four decades are averaged, over half of all male teachers were 25 and older between 1851 and 1881, whereas only about 37% of the women were in this older group. Still, the very presence of older women in teaching is important. Although both their numbers and relative proportions in the seven counties were much smaller than those for men, there clearly were some "career" teachers among the rural women in the four census decades. At least a few of the women teachers in the 25 and older category had avoided the typical pattern of only three or four years of school teaching followed by marriage and withdrawal from the public labor force. Such women occasionally surface in literary records as well. Catherine Carter, née Plantz, of Dundas County, taught from the age of 14 (or 15) to the age of 35 before she withdrew from teaching in 1872 to marry (Carter, 1905: 128; Harkness, 1946).[19]

If female teachers tended to be younger than male teachers in the seven counties, they also tended to be more often Ontario-born than their male counterparts (Table 3). It is true that this was largely a reflection of their age. The younger the teacher of either sex in Ontario during the third quarter of the nineteenth century, the more likely she or he was to have been born in the province. Or, to put it another way, the tendency of male teachers to be non-Ontario born was related to their greater average age. Yet a glance at the proportions of Ontario- and non-Ontario-born among male and female teachers in 1881 suggests that the situation gradually shifted. Whereas in previous census decades, the proportions of Ontario-born women teachers approximated their proportions in the general seven counties' population, in 1881 fully 86.1% of the school mistresses had been born in Ontario, compared to only 75.8% of the population at large.[20] By this time, male teachers were slightly younger than in previous census decades and were still clearly a good deal older on the average than the women, but were now very close, as far as birth place was concerned, to the seven counties' average. It may thus be that the age of the male teachers was now more typical of the general population.Whatever the relationship between age and place of birth, the over-representation of the non-Ontario-born among male teachers is suggestive. It seems entirely possible that the existence of a pool of older, immigrant men, who were willing and able to teach, may well have played an important role in rural Ontario's resistance to the trend towards predominantly female teaching forces. As immigrants, they probably had special needs for cash to subsidize the purchase of farms or to supplement farm incomes, and/or fewer opportunities or skills for employment in other fields, so they may have been available for teaching when their Ontario-born counterparts were not.

Statistics on the marital status of teachers support the picture we have alrady drawn of a rural teaching force in which women tended to be younger than men. Women teachers in the seven counties, predominantly single in 1851 (78%), were overwhelmingly so by 1881 (95%). The percentages for male teachers show a slight movement away from the married state, especially between 1871 and 1881 (from 46% to 36%), when the downward shift in age was also clearly in evidence. But overall, rural schoolmasters tended to be married far more often than rural schoolmistresses.

Table 3
Place of Birth of Common School Teachers
Seven Ontario Counties, 1851-1881

		Female Teachers		Male Teachers		County	
		No.	%	No.	%	No.	%
1851	Ontario	25	59.5	59	26.9	80 995	54.4
	Quebec	1	2.4	4	1.8	10 261	6.9
	England	2	4.8	43	19.6	13 890	9.3
	Scotland	1	2.4	31	14.2	13 718	9.2
	Ireland	6	14.3	58	26.5	19 387	13.0
	Other	7	16.7	24	11.0	10 524	7.1
	Total	42	100.1	219	100.0	148 775	99.9
1861	Ontario	78	62.9	168	38.7	139 261	61.7
	Quebec	2	1.6	8	1.8	11 119	4.9
	England	9	7.3	51	11.8	19 362	8.6
	Scotland	7	5.6	89	20.5	17 860	7.9
	Ireland	17	13.7	91	21.0	23 016	10.2
	Other	11	8.9	27	6.2	15 041	6.7
	Total	124	100.0	434	100.0	225 659	100.0
1871	Ontario	221	72.5	178	47.8	185 250	70.8
	Quebec	10	3.3	9	2.4	8 806	3.4
	England	19	6.2	41	11.0	18 968	7.2
	Scotland	18	5.9	57	15.3	16 264	6.2
	Ireland	20	6.6	60	16.3	19 184	7.3
	Other	17	5.6	27	7.3	13 257	5.1
	Total	305	100.1	372	100.1	261 729	100.0
1881	Ontario	398	86.1	419	71.7	229 451	5.8
	Quebec	17	3.7	19	3.3	11 251	3.7
	England	10	2.2	47	8.0	19 420	6.4
	Scotland	14	3.0	41	7.0	13 574	4.5
	Ireland	10	2.2	39	6.7	16 045	5.3
	Other	13	2.8	19	3.3	12 991	4.3
	Total	462	100.0	584	100.0	302 732	100.0

Naturally enough, the household status of the teachers in the seven counties reflected these facts (Table 4). Not all married male teachers were heads of households,[21] but most were, the proportions fluctuating between 36% and 44 % of all male teachers over the period. Female household heads corresponded fairly closely to the number of widows in each census decade, although the correspondence is not exact, suggesting that a few single women teachers were also heads of their own households in these rural counties during the second half of the nineteenth century.

Even more interesting than the findings on heads of households is the fact that the number of teachers identifiable as boarders, relatives, or children was far from stable, proportional to all teachers, in the period between 1851 and 1881. For both sexes, the boarder/relative category[22] was reduced by almost one half; a corresponding increase took place in the proportion of teachers who were children living in their parents' households. This shift was especially pronounced among women teachers because so many of them were young. By 1881, over 70% of all female teachers in the seven counties were daughters living at home with their parents.

This trend may have reflected a shift away from boarding among young people generally. Certainly such a change has been noted for Hamilton, Ontario, during the same census decades (Katz, 1975: 276, 280). But it is also true that a vigorous campaign was conducted by mid-nineteenth-century education authorities against teachers boarding out in the homes of others. Anxious to promote an image of teachers as stable and settled members of their communities, Department of Public Instruction officials and professional-oriented teachers heaped scorn on the boarding teacher who moved "from house to house like a beggar."[23] What they put forward as the ideal, however, were mature schoolmasters with household of their own, not the youthful daughters, or even the sons, of local farmers (Prentice, 1975: 7-11).

What was happening is revealed even more clearly when household heads, sons, daughters and boarders or relatives are considered as percentages of all teachers. If the proportion of heads of household remained stable as far as male teachers as a group were concerned, they declined sharply from 35.7 to 20.6 percent of all teachers by 1881, while sons increased from 13.2 to 23.4 percent. But it was daughters who made the larger leap, from a mere 5 to 31 percent of the total teaching force by the end of our period. Interestingly, the major part of the decline in boarding took place among the men teachers. In sum, women (and to some extent men) living at home with their parents were replacing both male household heads and male boarders among rural Ontario teachers. Looking at age in terms of all teachers is equally revealing. Women were increasing in all categories, but the women teachers who were under 30 years of age grew from 12.8 to 38.1 percent of all teachers. At the same time, schoolmasters who were 30 and older declined from almost one half (42.3 percent) to one fifth (20.2 percent) of the teaching force in the seven counties between 1851 and 1881.

Table 4
Household Status of Common School Teachers 1851-1881

		Female Teachers		Male Teachers	
		No.	%	No.	%
1851	Head	5	12.2	92	42.4
	Boarder or Relative	17	41.5	91	41.9
	Child	13	31.7	34	15.7
	Other	6	14.6	0	0.0
	Total	41	100.0	217	100.0
1861	Head	8	6.6	159	36.6
	Boarder or Relative	70	57.8	191	44.0
	Child	33	27.3	74	17.1
	Other	10	8.3	10	2.3
	Total	121	100.0	434	100.0
1871	Head	13	4.2	164	44.3
	Boarder or Relative	79	25.8	81	21.9
	Child	207	67.6	124	33.5
	Other	7	2.3	1	0.3
	Total	306	99.9	370	100.0
1881	Head	15	3.2	216	37.1
	Boarder or Relative	118	25.5	121	20.8
	Child	325	70.2	245	42.1
	Other	5	1.1	0	0.0
	Total	463	100.0	582	100.0

If in Ontario important shifts in the age structure, ethnicity and household status of teachers accompanied the change in elementary school teaching from a male to an increasingly female occupation, in Quebec the combined effect of elementary school expansion and preferential hiring, the availability of other work for men, and the greater tendency of boys to leave school at a very early age had already created an essentially female teaching force by the middle of the nineteenth century. The disappearance of the schoolmaster in Quebec, however, proceeded at an uneven pace. In the period studied, some regions never had more than one or two male teachers, in others 30 to 40 percent of the teaching force was male, and in still others the numbers of men teachers fluctuated between a handful to a significant minority of the educating corps. In order to explore these variations, we selected two rural counties, Montmagny and Terrebonne, for detailed study for the years 1861, 1871 and 1881.[24]

The inspectoral districts in which the counties of Montmagny and Terrebonne were located registered a majority of women teachers in 1853 (Table 1). In fact, the percentages of schoolmistresses in these two districts in 1853 and in the two counties over the three census decades were slightly higher than the provincial average. By 1881, 84 and 99 percent of the teachers in Terrebonne and Montmagny, respectively, were women. Provincially, men had a slightly better showing; they were 16.7 percent of the teaching force in the province during that year. Even more striking is that of the few men who were teaching in the two rural counties, a great many were members of religious orders (Table 5). The lack of interest in teaching among laymen in rural Quebec is clearly illustrated, as in Ontario, by the substantial proportion of the male teachers who were foreign born. Of the laymen engaged in teaching in Terrebonne and Montmagny in 1861, 1871 and 1881, nearly one third, or 31 percent, had migrated from either Scotland or Ireland to Quebec, most probably during the great migrations of the 1840s and 1850s.[25]

Although Terrebonne and Montmagny were similar in having few male teachers and a high proportion of foreign born among males, the differences between the two counties in the proportions of male and female teachers suggest the usefulness of examining them more closely. What factors could account for the more rapid feminization of Montmagny, compared to Terrebonne, and by 1881, the almost complete absence of male teachers in the former?

Enclosed by the St. Lawrence River on one side and the State of Maine on the other, Montmagny borders L'Islet County which leads to the Gaspé peninsula. To the east, the county of Bellechase stands between Montmagny and Quebec City. Although the land in Montmagny is exceptionally fertile and was plentiful in the period studied, farming was not necessarily the major and only occupation of its male inhabitants. Large numbers of men travelled annually to the Gaspé or across the river to Saguenay and Lac St. Jean where the likelihood of finding adventure and making money was much greater than in the sedentary and low-paying occupation of teaching.[26] Terrebonne, on the other hand, is in the plain of Montreal north of the city. But unlike most of the counties surrounding the city of Montreal, it did not suffer economic stagnation and population loss during the second half of the nineteenth century. With the extension of the railway, Terrebonne became a way station for pioneering men and women hoping to establish themselves in the uncolonized land of the Laurentians. At the same time, the prospering saw and grist mills in several of the county's villages attracted new settlers and further development. Most important was St. Jerome. In the late 1870s developers and entrepreneurs enticed by the promise of government subsidies and tax cuts flocked to this village and transformed it into a booming industrial town (Auclair, 1934; Blanchard, 1953).

Table 5
Teachers by Gender and Vocational Identity, 1861-1881

	Lay Teachers	Teaching Brothers	Male Teachers Total	% of all Teachers	Lay Teacher	Teaching Sisters	Total	Female Teachers % of all Teachers
1861:								
Montmagny	3	4	7	8.1	34	7	41	91.9
Terrebonne	10	0	10	15.4	55	9	64	84.6
1871:								
Montmagny	3	5	8	6.3	45	6	51	93.7
Terrebonne	8	0	8	13.6	51	17	68	86.4
1881:								
Montmagny	1	0	1	1.8	55	9	64	98.2
Terrebonne	9	6	15	12.3	64	17	81	87.7

In Montmagny, the presence of the resource frontier likely helped to deflect men from school teaching and to reinforce the traditional female involvement in popular education. Men in Terrebonne, on the other hand, were less prone to leave the farm and less likely to spend long periods in the bush or at sea fishing and for that reason were more likely than in Montmagny to be engaged in teaching.[27]

Of equal interest are the differences between the two counties in terms of religious and lay teachers, and, specifically, in the context of the growing numbers of people from religious orders engaged in teaching in the province

179, 300), and in Terrebonne the percentage of religious teachers grew from 12 to 24 percent between 1861 and 1881. In Montmagny, however, the exact opposite occurred. Religious men and women declined in strength in the twenty-year period from 23 to 14 percent, a shift indicating that lay women were solely responsible for the rise in the number of teachers in the county (Table 5).

The decreasing importance of the religious teacher in Montmagny is significant and suggestive. It makes clear yet another peculiarity in the evolution of the teaching force in late-nineteenth-century Quebec. While the number of religious teachers increased with each decade, the presence of the teaching brothers and sisters was not equally felt in the province. As the figures in the aggregate census and the histories of the Catholic church show, the most rapid expansion in religiously run schools and the most impressive rise in the number of religious teachers took place in the Montreal region during the third quarter of the nineteenth century (Denault, 1975: 77-78). At that time counties outside the Montreal plain and especially those further in the hinterland remained almost immune to the expansion of religiously administered schooling.

In addition to representing the varying degrees of religious involvement in education, the differences between Terrebonne and Montmagny bring to light an important variation in the evolution of occupational hierarchies during the middle decades of the nineteenth century. If in many places in North America the proportion of women teachers tended to be higher where the teaching force was hierarchically structured, in Quebec the number of women was the greatest in the areas *least* likely to take on the appearance of a bureaucratized and industrialized society. Furthermore, the category that grew most vigorously in strength and size in the centres where urban-type hierarchies were taking form was that of the religious teacher.

The clustering of religious men and women in the most advanced and centrally located regions of the province shows clearly in the location and structure of educational institutions in Montmagny and Terrebonne. Religious brothers and sisters taught only in villages that were easily accessible by train or ferry and showed promise of economic prosperity. In function and structure, their schools were the predecessors of modern educational institutions: two to three storeys high, built of brick, graded and serving a student body of about two hundred. Teaching in the one-room schools that were scattered throughout Terrebonne and Montmagny was not the fate of nuns, but of lay school mistresses.[28] They were the missionaries of public schooling to the rural hinterland and, like most missionaries, were subjected to harsh and often unbearable conditions of work. The lowest paid category of the teaching force, rural schoolmistresses (for whom the school often doubled as a home) found little material or psychological compensation for the work they performed. Yet their numbers continued to grow and, ironically enough, the more of them there were the less able they seemed to better their conditions of work (Dorion, 1979: 229-70; Douville-Veillet, 1973).

The rise of the one-room school and the increasing tendency of teachers to reside in their place of work are reflected in the changing household status of women teachers. As in the seven Ontario counties, the number of teachers who boarded with strangers or relatives outside the nuclear family dropped between 1861 and 1881 from 29 to 13 percent in Montmagny and from 27 to 11 percent in Terrebonne. But in contrast to Ontario where with the passing of each decade increasing numbers of men and women teachers remained with their parents while working, the gradual disappearance of the boarding teacher went hand in hand with an impressive rise in the percentage of teaching women living alone as heads of households in schoolhouses. Indeed, by 1881 in Terrebonne and Montmagny 44 and 33 percent of the women teachers, respectively, belonged to this category (Table 6).

It may be that the persistence of the linear mode of land settlement, a pattern dating from the earliest days of colonization, played an important role in the proliferation of one-room schools (Deffontaines, 1964: 3-19). Contrary to the hopes of school inspectors and other high ranking educational officials, who called for greater centralization, the French Canadian pattern of rural settlement dictated that the one-room school would be an enduring feature of the rural educational landscape. And an enduring feature of this school was that it was not only taught but often inhabited by its schoolmistress.

The shift from the teacher as boarder to the teacher as occupant of a schoolhouse took place at the same time as the running of schools became more the work of the "professional" teacher and less a family enterprise. In 1861 in Montmagny and Terrebonne 27% of the teachers worked in pairs with a brother or sister. Twenty years later only 14% taught with one of their siblings. The formalization of teaching, the "intervention" of boards of examiners and normal schools in the process of educating educators, raised the standards in the profession and the schools. By the same token, this process lowered the level of family input in the preparation of teachers. No doubt the family unit still played an important role in influencing the career choices of its members. Its involvement, however, was no longer as direct as it might have been earlier in the passing along of classroom management skills (Katz, 1976).

If indeed the formalization of teacher training was responsible for the lower rate of members of the same family pursuing the same trade, this might also help to explain the evident aging of the teaching force in Terrebonne and Montmagny. Schoolmistresses in these two counties were actually older by the end of the third quarter of the century,[29] resembling by 1881 the average age of female teachers in the seven counties of Ontario (Tables 7 and 2).

Table 6
Household Status of Lay Teachers, 1861-1881

	Montmagny				Terrebonne			
	Female Teachers		Male Teachers		Female Teachers		Male Teachers	
	No.	%	No.	%	No.	%	No.	%
1861:								
Head[1]	2	5.9	1	33.3	0	0.0	2	20.0
Schoolhouse Occupant[2]	3	8.8	1	33.3	14	25.5	5	50.0
Spouse	0	0.0	0	0.0	2	3.6	0	0.0
Child	12	35.3	0	0.0	19	34.5	2	20.0
Relative[3]	7	20.6	0	0.0	5	9.1	1	10.0
Boarder	10	29.4	1	33.3	15	27.3	0	0.0f
Total	34	100.0	3	99.9	55	100.0	10	100.0
1871:								
Head	1	2.2	1	33.3	2	3.9	0	0.0
Schoolhouse Occupant	20	44.4	1	33.3	27	52.9	5	62.5
Spouse	2	4.4	0	0.0	1	2.0	0	0.0F
Child	16	35.6	0	0.0	11	21.6	1	12.5
Relative	3	6.7	1	33.3	3	5.9	0	0.0
Boarder	3	6.7	0	0.0	7	13.7	2	25.0
Total	45	100.0	3	99.9	51	100.0	8	100.0
1881:								
Head	0	0.0	1	100.0	0	0.0	0	0.0
Schoolhouse Occupant	18	32.7	0	0.0	28	43.8	5	55.6
Spouse	3	5.5	0	0.0	3	4.7	0	0.0
Child	14	25.5	0	0.0	24	37.5	1	11.1
Relative	13	23.6	0	0.0	2	3.1	0	0.0
Boarder	7	12.7	0	0.0	7	10.9	3	33.3
Total	55	100.0	1	100.0	64	100.0	9	100.0

[1]Head designates head of household and family.

[2]Schoolhouse occupant includes teachers living in the household and residing alone or with a dependent (younger sibling, or assistant teacher). In most cases, however, the teacher was listed in the census as the only resident.

[3]Relative indicates sibling or grandchild.

The changes we have noted in the gender, age, ethnicity, household status, and lay or religious identity of Ontario and Quebec teachers make clear the inadequacy of existing models of the sexual division of labor in nineteenth-century teaching. Not only must these models be refined in order to explain the manifold short-term and regional variations lying beneath the surface or even on the periphery of long-term trends, alternate ones must also be developed that are appropriate to the peculiar evolution of the teaching force in Quebec and parts of Ontario.

In most regions of central Canada, urban hierarchies among teachers and many other aspects of formalization were hardly to be found in the third quarter of the nineteenth century. Instead, in some of these regions, factors such as poverty, the presence of a resource frontier, the traditional roles of women in the family and the legacy of nuns in teaching, appear to have encouraged a remarkably early sexual division of labor in rural schools.

In some regions of the two provinces, the sexual division of labor in rural teaching occurred side by side with other developments which must have had a profound effect on this transformation. In Ontario, rural teachers were slightly younger as the decades wore on and tended increasingly to be single women. Teachers who were boarders tended to be replaced during the third quarter of the nineteenth century by the daughters of local farmers who lived at home with their parents. In both provinces, a disproportionate number of male rural teachers were foreign born, suggesting that, to the extent that school authorities found men who were willing to teach, they were able to do so only because of a pool of potential candidates among immigrants. In Quebec, the increasing feminization of an already predominantly female rural teaching force was accompanied by the gradual clericalization of that teaching force. Religious teachers favored the wealthier, more densely settled regions of the province, leaving the one-room school houses in the poorer and more remote parishes to lay teachers. More and more often, in fact, the lay women teachers of the counties of Terrebonne and Montmagny were not only teaching but living in the school houses of their villages. If fewer siblings were to be found teaching in 1881 than was the case in 1861, when several female teachers to a family were not uncommon, it is also true that the average age of women teachers in Montmagny and Terrebonne was increasing.

It is difficult to generalize about what this may have meant to the women whose work rural school teaching became. For many, teaching may have provided an opportunity for relative independence and self-development. Certainly those teachers whose careers spanned a decade or more and the average ages of women teachers and biographical data suggest that these women were far from rare and must have become figures of some authority in their local communities. For the Leila Middletons who married after several years in the school room, teaching evidently provided useful experience in child management, as well as a period of relative autonomy between their own schooling and the beginning of married life.

But rural teaching also had its dark side. Many young women who taught school for a few years were making vital contributions to the support of their families and controlled little or nothing of their meagre wages. From Quebec sources documenting the lives of individuals who both taught and lived in remote and isolated school houses, we learn that teaching could be not only an impoverished existence, but a lonely and even frightening one (Dorion, 1979; Douville-Veillet, 1973). For such women, the burden of their position may well have outweighed the potential for growth described above. Poor pay was clearly common to all rural women teachers. Low status, dependency and isolation were also the lot of many of those who presided over rural school rooms during the period when country teaching was "women's work."

Notes

*The article is reprinted with permission from *Historie Sociale/Social History.*

[1]We wish to thank Chad Gaffield, Bob Gidney, Michael Katz and Paul Mattingly for probing criticisms of earlier Prentice papers on the history of teachers, and Mary Katzenstein, Karen Skold and Myra Strober for helpful discussions of an early draft of the present study. We are also grateful to Geraldine Jonçich Clifford, Jo-Ann Day, Audri Gordon Lanford, James O'Connor, Myra Strober and David Tyack for generously making unpublished materials available. Rosalie Fox, Liz Good Menard, Lise Kreps and Louise Ledoux, who assisted with the gathering and entry of the quantitative data, lent much enthusiasm and support to the project. Finally, we thank the Ontario Institute for Studies in Education and the Social Science and Humanities Research Council, for their generous financial support, and the Center for Research on Women, Stanford University, California, which provided one of the authors with space and a stimulating environment while part of the paper was being written.

[2]Leila V. Middleton Diary, kindly lent to one of the authors by her granddaughter, Sharon Trewartha, 1974-75.

[3]See Alexander Forrester's comments about the importance of reserving headmasterships and the more advanced classes for male teachers in *The Teachers' Text-Book* (Halifax, Nova Scotia, 1867), pp. 565-66. In the case of Quebec, see the remarks of school inspector Jean Crepault printed in *The Report of the Minister of Public Instruction for the Province of Quebec* (1872-73, pp. 51-52) in which he insists that the model schools be reserved for male teachers.

[4]In much of rural North America, there is evidence that women were heavily involved in domestic textile production until at least the 1840s, and consequently spent long hours spinning and weaving. Even after the wide-spread adoption of factory made textiles, much clothing was made at home in rural households until the advent of ready-made garments and catalog shopping at the turn of the 20th century. Finally, girls and women had year round work in the preparation of food and care of dairy and poultry yards, not to mention seasonal work as well, if they were responsible for vegetables or fruit grown on the farm.

[5]A study of at least one set of Ontario rural trustee records confirms this finding. The minute books for S.S. No. 11, Norwich North, in Oxford County, indicate the firm intention of the trustees of this two-storey village school to hire a male

headmaster and female assistants, during the period covered by the books, when the school expanded from a staff of two to four teachers. Record Group 51, 108 61, No. 2, Public Archives of Ontario.

[6]Ontario and Quebec underwent constitutional changes in 1840 and 1867 and both resulted in changes in their official names. For the sake of simplicity, we have sacrificed minute historical accuracy and referred to Lower Canada/Canada East and Upper Canada/Canada West as Quebec and Ontario, respectively, throughout the paper.

[7]For a discussion of literacy in Quebec as well as an overview of the literature on the topic, see Allen Greer, "The Pattern of Literacy in Quebec, 1745-1899," *Social History/Histoire Sociale* 11, 22 (Nov. 1978): 293-335. The author argues quite convincingly that "the 1842-61 and 1862-71 female educational cohorts in Quebec have proportionately more semi-literates and more literates than the male cohorts" (p. 61). The observation is also made that in Ontario, in contrast to Quebec in this period, men were more literate.

[8]One need only skim the reports of the school inspectors to see how keenly interested they were in the feminine takeover of schooling. It is especially worth nothing the following in Quebec (Province), *Report of the Superintendent of Public Instruction* (1871, p. 34; 1872, pp. 51-52; 1873, pp. 54-55).

[9]Remarks made by inspector Maurault and recorded in Quebec (Province), *Report of the Superintendent of Public Instruction for Lower Canada* (1861, p. 188).

[10]The 1851 manuscript census was not used for the Quebec case study because many county boundaries were changed in the 1850s. Montmagny, one of the counties in which we were interested, did not exist in 1851.

[11]For instance, one school inspector, J.N.A. Archambault, reported to the superintendent that parishes in his district were teaming with "firebrands" hostile to educational legislation. See *The Report of the Superintendent of Public Instruction* (1853, p. 72). In 1853 a similar report was submitted by Inspector Maurault for the county of Yamaska; see p. 113.

[12]Annual Reports of the Ontario Department of Education for the 1850s.

[13]Ibid, for the years 1851 (p. 69), 1852 and 1856 (p. 216).

[14]James W. Breakenridge to Egerton Ryerson, 23 May 1850, RG 2 C-6-C, Public Archives of Ontario.

[15]Annual Reports of the Ontario Department of Education for the 1850s.

[16]Public Archives of Canada (hereafter PAC), Statistics Canada, RG31, Census Records, 1851-1881 (microfilms). For exact references to the microfilms of the censuses that have been used, see Thomas H. Hillman, *Catalogue of Census Returns on Microfilm/Catalogue de recensements sur microfilm, 1661-1881* (Ottawa: Public Archives of Canada, Federal Archives Division, 1981).

[17]For the purposes of the Ontario study, a number of teacher categories listed in the manuscript census returns, such as "governess," "music teacher" and "professor" were eliminated. Those counted as school teachers were the individuals listed as "teacher," "common school teacher," "school teacher," "school mistress" and "school master." This was because we wished to focus on teachers in the "public" (in the sense of "non-domestic") schools and also to eliminate colleges from the study.

[18]When census statistics were compared to the numbers collected by departments of education for the years 1851 and 1861, we discovered that the numbers

did not match, with female teachers tending to be more prominent in the latter than the former. We suspect that this was not only because the census failed to reflect the widespread sexual division of labor that occurred in rural schools where men taught in the winter and women in the summer, but also because census enumerators were more likely to take note of male than female employment.

[19]See also, manuscript Census for Dundas County, 1871. The fact that Catharine Carter was not listed in either 1851 or 1861 confirms our belief that female teachers were underenumerated in those census years, since both of the other sources indicate a teaching career spanning the years between 1851 and 1872. Since she appears on the 1871 census return as Plantz, her marriage must have taken place in 1872 or later, and therefore does appear to have ended her teaching career.

[20]Information on place of birth for the population at large was found in the *Census of Canada, 1881.*

[21]The designation "head of household" does not appear on the census returns, and the instructions to the enumerators refer only to "heads of families occupying lands, whether male or female" under the heading "Agricultural Census" in 1861. The designation is an historical convention which presumably corresponds to 19th-century views on the nature of the family and the household. The head is taken to be the first person listed in each household group on the census returns. The person listed first is invariably the husband in the case of a married couple, or the oldest husband in the case of two married couple. Widows and widowers are listed first in households with no married children; but when living with married children, they are usually found as relatives. In the Ontario census, young teachers were rarely found living in non-family situations.

[22]Because there were those who were not children of the head of household, it was difficult to distinguish between boarders, relatives and visitors on the manuscript census. We decided to incorporate these categories into a single group in the Ontario research, labelled "boarder/relative," for the sake of simplicity and also because visitors would likely have been a very small group in any case. For the present analysis, the important point is that the main distinction to be made was between children of household heads and persons whose relationships to household heads were more distant.

[23]"Resolutions of the School Association of the Eastern District" in D.P. McDonald to Egerton Ryerson, 9 July, 1850, RG 2 C-6-C, Public Archives of Ontario. See also "The Superintendent of Schools for the London District on the Working of the School Act of 1846, February, 1848," in J.G. Hodgins, ed., *Documentary History of Education in Upper Canada* (Toronto, 1894-1910), Vol 7, p. 130; Superintendent, Scott Township, to Ryerson, 22 February 1851, RG 2 C-6-C and Ryerson to John Hendry, 7 November 1846, RG 2 C I, Letterbook C, p. 160, Public Archives of Ontario.

[24]Montmagny and Terrebonne were chosen for this study because they represent different types of economies, the former sending men to the Gaspé where they worked in fishing or lumbering and the latter providing work on the homestead. The location of Terrebonne in the Montreal Plain, north of the city, and of Montmagny on the St. Lawrence River, close to Quebec City, also provided interesting points of contrast. It should be noted as well that in the process of coding, the following were recorded: music teacher, English teacher, teacher, master, mistress, brother and sister. All religious men and women listed as living in a convent or monastery were included. From the manuscript census it is impossible to tell which of the nuns

and brothers were not teaching, but it is unlikely that more than two or three of the entire sample were engaged in work outside the classroom.

[25]The 31 percent represents the average for the three census years. Because the number of male lay teachers was so small, providing a table on the place of origin of male teachers did not seem useful.

[26]The census taker in 1861 for one of the villages in Montmagny provided details about the work of fishermen in the county. For a description see Manuscript Census of Canada, Montmagny County, St. Thomas, 1861. For a study of Montmagny and the counties surrounding it see Raoul Blanchard, *L'Est du Canada Français* (Montreal: Beauchemin, 1935).

[27]One school inspector put it quite succinctly: "Men prefer engaging as servants, or following some other vocation to that of teaching." *Report of the Superintendent of Public Instruction* (1853, pp. 93-94).

[28]The location of the schools and the names of the teachers who taught there can be traced through the manuscript census.

[29.]Legislation implemented in the 1850s demanding of prospective teachers a diploma from a normal school or the successful completion of a qualifying exam in the presence of a board of examiners or the school inspector may have had the effect of discouraging the very young from assuming the responsibilities of tending school.

References

Abbott, J.R. (1983). "Educational policy formation and implementation on the Ontario primary resource frontier: The case of the district of Algoma, 1903-1922." Ph.D. dissertation, University of Toronto.

Auclair, E.J. (1934). *Saint Jérome de Terrebonne*. St. Jérome: Imprimerie-photogravure Labelle.

Audet, L.P. (1971). *Histoire de l'enseignement au Québec*. Montréal: Holt, Rinehart and Winston.

Blanchard, R. (1953). *Le Centre du Canada Français: Montréal et sa region*. Montréal: Beauchemin (1935).

Blanchard, R. 1935 *L'Est du Canada Français*. Montreal: Beauchemin.

Bryans, W.E. (1974). "Virtuous women at half the price: The feminization of the teaching force and early women teacher organizations in Ontario." M.A. Thesis, University of Toronto.

Burstyn, J.N. (1974). "Catherine Beecher and the education of American women." *New England Quarterly* 47:386-403.

Carter, S. (1905). *The Story of Dundas*. Iroquois, Ontario: St. Lawrence News Publishing House.

Clifford, G.J. (1981). "Teaching as the seedbed of feminism." Read at the Fifth Berkshire Conference on Women's History, Vassar College, Poughkeepsie, New York, June 1981.

Danylewycz, M. (1981). "Taking the veil in Montréal, 1840-1920: An alternative to marriage, motherhood, and spinsterhoods." Ph.D. dissertation, University of Toronto.

Day, J.A., & O'Connor, J. (1978). "Urbanization, school system variables and the sex composition of teaching: An historical view." Read at the Annual Meeting of the American Education Research Association, Toronto, March 1978.

Deffontaines, P. (1964). "The Rang: Patterns of rural settlement in French Canada." In Marcel Rioux and Yves Martin, eds., *French Canadian Society.* Toronto: McClelland and Stewart.

Denault, B. (1975). "Sociographie général des communautés religieuses au Québec (1837-1970)." In Bernard Denault et Benoit Lévesque, *Elements pour une sociologie des communautés religieuses au Québec.* Montréal et Sherbrooke: Les Presses de l'Université de Montréal.

Dorion, J. (1979). *Les écoles de rang au Québec.* Montréal: Les Editions de l'homme.

Douville-Veillet, V. (1973). *Souvenirs d'une institutrice de petite école de rang.* Trois Rivieres: Imprimerie du Bien Public.

Gaffield, C.M. (1978). "Cultural challenge in eastern Ontario: Land, family and education in the nineteenth century." Ph.D. dissertation, University of Toronto.

Gidney, R. & Lawr D. (1978). "The development of an administrative system for the public schools: The first stage, 1841-50." In Neil McDonald and Alf Chaiton, eds., *Egerton Ryerson and His Times.* Toronto: Macmillan, pp. 160-183.

Greer, A. (1978). "The pattern of literacy in Québec, 1745-1899." *Histoire sociale/Social History* 11:293-335.

Harkness, J.G. (1946). *Stormont, Dundas and Glengarry: A History, 1784-1945.* Oshawa, Ontario. n.p.

Hillman, T.H. (1981) *Catalogue of Census Returns on Microfilm/Catalogue de recensements sur microfilm, 1661-1881.* Ottawa: Public Archives of Canada, Federal Archives Division.

Katz, M.B. (1968). "The emergence of bureaucracy in urban education: The Boston case." *History of Education Quarterly* 8, 3:319-357.

Katz, M.B. (1975) *The People of Hamilton, Canada West.* Cambridge, Mass.: Harvard University Press.

Katz, M.B. (1976). "The origins of public education: A reassessment." *History of Education Quarterly* 16 4:381-405.

Labarree-Paulé, A. (1965). *Les instituteurs laiques au Canada français, 1836-1900.* Québec: Les Presses de l'Université Laval.

Linteau, P.-A., Durocher R.,& Robert, J.C. (1979). *Histoire du Québec contemporain: De la Confédération à la crise.* Montréal: Boréal Express.

McCallum, J. (1980). *Unequal Beginnings: Agriculture and Economic Development in Quebec and Ontario Until 1820.* Toronto: University of Toronto Press.

Melder, K.E. (1972). "Woman's high calling: The teaching profession in America, 1830-1860." *American Studies* 13:19-32.

Meyers, P.V. (1980). "From conflict to cooperation: Men and women teachers." In David N. Baker and Patrick J. Harrigan, eds. *Belle Epoque.* Waterloo, Ontario: Historical Reflections Press.

Paquet, G., & Wallot, J.P. (1975). "The agricultural crisis in Lower Canada, 1802-1812: A response to T.J.A. LeGoff." *Canadian Historical Review* 56, 2:133-61.

Prentice, A. (1975). "The feminization of teaching in British North America and Canada, 1845-1875." *Histoire sociale/Social History* 8:5-20. Reprinted in Susan Mann Trofimenkoff and Alison Prentice, eds., *The Neglected Majority: Essays in Canadian Women's History.* Toronto: McLelland and Stewart, 1977, pp. 49-65.

Riley, G. (1969). "Origin of the argument for improved female education." *History of Education Quarterly* 9, 4:50-70.

Séguin, N. (1977). *La Conquête du sol au 19e siecle.* Québec: Boréal Express.

Sklar, K.K. (1973). *Catherine Beecher: A Study in American Domesticity.* New Haven: Yale University Press.

Strober, M.H., & Lanford, A.G.. (1981). "The percentages of women in public school teaching: A cross-section analysis, 1850-1880." Read at the Annual Meeting of the Social Science History Association, Nashville, Tennessee, October 1981.

Strober, M.H. & Tyack, D. (1980). "Why do women teach and men manage?" *Signs* 5, 3:494-503.

Tyack, D. (1967). "Bureaucracy and the common school: The example of Portland, Oregon, 1851-1913." *American Quarterly* 19, 3:475-98.

Tyack, D., & Strober, M.H. (1981). "Jobs and gender: A history of the structuring of educational employment by sex." In Patricia Schmuck and W.W. Charles, eds., *Educational Policy and Managment: Sex Differentials.* San Diego: Academic Press.

Wallot, J.P. (1971). "Religion and French Canadian mores in the early nineteenth century." *Canadian Historical Review* 52:51-94.

2

Food for Thought:
Realities of a Women-Dominated Organization[1]

Patricia Valentine and Gordon McIntosh

Would organizational behavior in an organization staffed largely by female professionals be different in significant ways from the typical, predominantly male, professional organization? In the past, most of the theorizing about organizations reflected an aspect of the social world that has been dominated largely by men. Research into the administration of organizations has generally been carried out by men, in settings where men are the majority of actors, using strategies which are meaningful from a male perspective.

Research into educational organizations has been no exception even though there are significant numbers of women in these organizations. The research indicates that the male perspective pervades most of the approaches to administration and organizational research in education.

Only recently in the organizational and administrative literature has the idea been acknowledged that women may bring distinctive views of the world to the workplace. The ways women's views might influence organizational culture have not been explored in research. A specific arena in which the influence of a female perspective might best be examined is in an organization staffed largely by women. Because 98% of nurses in Canada are female (Okrainec, 1986, p. 16), and nursing is one of the oldest and largest women-dominated professions, studying a nursing organization is ideal for exploring administrative aspects of a women-dominated organization. This article reports on a case study of a Canadian hospital school of nursing. It attempts to reappraise old administrative theories, to concentrate on aspects of administration that may have been ignored or taken for granted, and to encourage an alternative mode of thinking about organizations. It is hoped that the current work will contribute to a more inclusive understanding of the work of women in organizations in general and have implications for the study of educational organizations.

The Context of the Study

In the past, researchers have made little attempt to include females in their studies. Generally, males "have assumed implicitly a kind of sexual symmetry" (Bernard, 1981, p. 14), that is, that everything that exists for males also exists for females. For example, two instruments that in the past have been frequently used in educational administration research, the Leader

Behavior Description Questionnaire (LBDQ) and LBDQ-XII (Halpin & Winer, 1957), are both sexist in theory and construction. "Using the male pronoun throughout and validated with men, these instruments have been used to judge the performance of female administrators" (Shakeshaft, 1981, p. 22). There has been little attempt to adapt these instruments to female administrators.

Kohlberg (1981) assumed sexual symmetry in his cognitive development model of moral reasoning which is largely based on a study of 84 boys whose development was followed for 20 years. He assumed that his findings could be generalized to girls; however, Gilligan's (1982) and Lyons' (1983) research findings concluded there was a difference in the moral development of girls and boys. In referring to sociological investigation, Daniels (1975, p. 346) suggested that women were excluded from consideration in research studies because male scholars believed that what women did was trivial and therefore unworthy of scientific exploration. This point could also be made of administrative investigation. For example, most research in educational administration has either left females out of the sample but generalized the findings to both genders or has included females and attempted to account for the effects of gender (Shakeshaft, 1987, p. 162). However, the research results are biased by the androcentrism of the original research (Shakeshaft & Nowell, 1984, p. 200). Spender (1981) contended that, "the scale on which women have been omitted from educational consideration is massive" (p. 162). For example, in surveying the sociology of education literature in Britain in Acker in 1980 documented the absence of women (cited in Spender, 1981, pp. 162-163). Of 184 articles published since 1960, 58% purported to be studying both sexes, but 37% had exclusively male samples while only 5% had all-female samples. Often these female samples were used to study mothers' influence on their children.

For the most part, knowledge of females has been limited to how they impinge on males. The neglect of the study of women, including women in organizations (Gould, 1980, p. 459), imposes limits on our intellectual horizons. As Gould stated, "regrettably absent are descriptive case studies and interpretive analyses of roles women play as creators or innovators of organizations" (p. 459).

Conducting the Inquiry

In order to investigate the role women play in organizations, the faculty in a Canadian hospital school of nursing were selected for this study. This organization was selected because such educational institutions annually graduate the largest number of nurses. Also, hospital schools of nursing come closest to being a cloistered female world; they typically are run by females and predominantly populated by females.

The school of nursing consisted of 220 students and 40 female faculty members, all of whom had at least baccalaureate-level preparation. Three faculty members also had master's degrees. The ages of the instructors ranged from 30 to 50 years. The marital status was 21 married, three divorced, 12 single, and one who described her living arrangement as cohabiting. The curriculum was taught by three teaching teams. Most of the activity in the school revolved around these teams. Although the study included all faculty members of the school, six faculty members served as key participants. When faculty members were asked to volunteer to serve as key participants, five instructors responded. The investigator asked an additional faculty member to participate. She was a full-time member of one particular team, married with children, two aspects not fully represented in the self-selected sample.

The key participants varied in age from 30 to 43. One was married with two children; one was a single parent; one was divorced; and the other three were single. These participants represented all teams. One participant represented the faculty support services. The educational background of the six key participants was as follows: three hospital diploma graduates, two college diploma graduates, and one generic nursing baccalaureate degree graduate. Two participants had university education in other non-nursing disciplines. Five had worked for several years in a variety of hospital nursing units before returning for a post basic baccalaureate degree in nursing. Four were currently enrolled in university courses toward a master's degree. The role of the six key participants (Cecile, Janine, Martine, Odile, Simone and Thérèse) was crucial. They shared important information about the organization and administration of the school and helped the investigator focus on vital data.

During the 12-month period in which the investigator was collecting the data, she attended meetings of all three teaching teams, full faculty meetings, and other committee meetings and spent considerable time with faculty members in the faculty lounge during coffee breaks and lunches. Data mainly consisted of three types: copious documents distributed to faculty, transcribed audiotapes of interviews with key participants, and field notes. Two interviews lasting from 60 to 90 minutes were conducted with each of the six key participants, one during the first six months and the second during the last month of the study. The key participants either confirmed the results or noted exceptions to the themes tentatively proposed by the investigator. The grounded theory approach was used to analyze the field notes out of which were generated five categories that pertained to the organization and administration of the school. Four of the categories are discussed here. The fifth category was omitted because it was of a different order than the other categories.

The Findings

Food as a Facilitator of Relationships

Food was a category that liberally peppered the 254 pages of single-spaced typed field notes. This category was thoroughly discussed during the two interviews with the six key participants. The discussing, preparing, cooking and eating of food were strong elements of this culture, and such topics often dominated conversations over lunch, coffee breaks and during meetings. Food was seen as the panacea for many situations. It was used for celebrating births, birthdays and marriages, for dealing with stress, for celebrating the departure of staff and faculty members, for expressing appreciation to a team for supporting a new instructor, for thanking hospital staff for working with students, for introducing new students to the school faculty and the administrators of the hospital, for celebrating the end of the term, for celebrating various graduation events, for rewarding a student who participated in a school project, as Christmas gifts, as the impetus for exchanging recipes with colleagues, and as a reason for dieting.

Food was seen as a lubricant for facilitating smooth colleague-colleague or faculty-student relationships. Initially, the investigator was struck by the number of times she arrived in the lounge or the meeting room to find some kind of goodie on display. For example, at the coffee break of the first team meeting of the term, three homemade desserts were served to first-year team members.

Conversation often revolved around food. For example, the best buys in bulk food were discussed. Recipes were frequently talked about and exchanged among faculty members and staff and were often posted on the bulletin board in the faculty lounge. During one meeting two duplicated recipes were distributed to every member, and to the investigator. One team celebrated each team member's birthday with a cake.

Food became the reason for faculty getting together in groups after work. Some faculty members met during the summer to can peaches and prior to Christmas to prepare poppycock and antipasto for gifts. Baking for Christmas was discussed by several instructors, one of whom brought in a sample of Norwegian cake she had served at Christmas. One faculty member who was taking a course on bread-making brought in samples of bread for her colleagues to taste. During one lunch hour, there was considerable discussion about how to make cabbage rolls. At another break, one instructor talked about making 600 perogies over the weekend. At another time, the preparing of pastry from pig's fat from a colleague's farm, the making of both homemade pasta and yogurt, and the buying of fresh sausages from a local farmer were discussed by four different instructors.

During the interviews, when the investigator asked the participants about the meaning of this emphasis on food, they replied:

Odile: Like, it's a facilitator, almost communication, socializing, everything from the organizing of it to the eating of it.

Thérèse: Maybe work, and the people here [are] a large part of people's social life and so they don't see it as an imposition because they are bringing food for their friends.

Simone: I think that here it represents being social, bringing the group together, you eat together, you're friends, you break bread . . . we are all really good pals, we get along so well.

Martine: Well, I think [for] women . . . [it is a way of] establishing camaraderie.

Janine: As far as having any great significance, the food . . . it's a way of taking a few minutes out to do something that people enjoy and relax over. . . . It is a way of coping with stress.

Cecile: The underlying reason for suggesting a drink or lunch or a breakfast meeting. . . . It is more informal, and if everybody made the effort of going and sitting beside someone that they didn't spend much time with, [then] maybe they would feel a little bit more comfortable with that person and, therefore, be able to express some feelings about working with them or be comfortable in giving constructive feedback.

Social Events as Integrators

Food and social events blended together and complemented each other. From the time the investigator started her field work, she found that instructors were involved in many social events, some of which were informally considered mandatory while others seemed to be optional; some were directly related to the students while other events were faculty-related. For example, there were baby showers, a shower for an instructor who was getting married, parties for those faculty/staff who were leaving, a "roast" for an administrator who resigned, a coffee party for students who had worked there during the summer, and coffee parties for two other people who had resigned. Other events were potluck suppers for the various teams, a faculty-student barbecue, a volleyball tournament, a Halloween party, a Valentine's Day party, numerous student-faculty events leading up to graduation, several functions to celebrate the Christmas season, as well as coffee parties or teas for the hospital staff who helped with the nursing program and end-of-term parties for the entire faculty and staff as well as separate functions for each team.

During the 12-month period the investigator was in the school, there were some 55 social events. Although these events were not mandatory for all instructors, and some were limited to particular teams, nevertheless the faculty were expected to attend a large number of events, often after work hours.

Comments from three participants who attempted to explain the meaning of this category were:

Janine: The year I started . . . we had a potluck supper or some kind of a get-together among the first-year faculty. The stress level was really, really high . . . we had a social thing about once a month. It seemed to be a time when we could have a laugh, we tried to minimize the work or the shop talk . . . to appreciate people as people, not just as a teaching partner . . . it's a way of sharing something with other people in the group . . . I think it's a socialization . . . to help try and reduce the stress somewhat, to get to know each other better.

Cecile: Well . . . the social events that occur here bring the faculty closer together.

Odile: The reason that social events are planned is an attempt to help establish happy relationships amongst faculty . . . that socially doing things together is seen as a way . . . of being ourselves, getting to know people. . . . Certainly . . . that's one of the things on the agenda at the retreat every year and . . . from my perspective, that gets fostered.

Support Mechanisms as Essential

Food and social events acted as mechanisms for promoting social interaction, as did support mechanisms, the next category to be discussed. Support mechanisms evolved as another category that characterized the school. It was not unusual for a faculty member to ask for support from her colleagues. For example, during one team meeting, the coordinator, after talking about how the stress level of faculty increased as the year progressed, added, "We need each other's support." Another coordinator thanked all the team members for their "support and assistance" when the team was short one member. She also discussed methods for coping with the "minimal support" accorded instructors during the supervision of students on the hospital units. At one team meeting when a coordinator announced that she had agreed, at the request of the students, not to post certain examination results, she asked for team support on this decision. All new instructors were assigned a "buddy" — a supportive person who would help to orient them to the school. These buddies helped them prepare lectures, attended their classes, and aided them with any problems they experienced in the clinical areas. Also, senior students in the preceptorship experience were "buddied" with hospital nursing staff members.

The coordinators often demonstrated support by validating marks on papers, helping with evaluations, and generally aiding new instructors. A more seasoned instructor requested that the coordinator mark her papers to give her feedback (support) on her marking ability. A new instructor brought home-baked cookies in to thank the team for their support. Comments made to support an instructor when she was receiving feedback on her class were: "great examples"; "enjoyed the class"; "a capital job"; and, when one team was reviewing the year's progress, "I think we did well."

Support was given to mothers when their children were sick. On two occasions the teaching schedules were changed to allow mothers to attend to their sick children at home. The emphasis on support carried over to the students. For example, one faculty member contended that during a senior rotation when the students were relatively autonomous and received little faculty supervision, the students "mainly wanted support." The male nursing students were paired together for support.

When the investigator asked about the need for support in the work situation during interviews with the key participants, they all readily agreed that if they did not have at least one supportive colleague at work, they would feel "isolated." Simone told the investigator about a new faculty member who felt alienated from the other instructors on her team; this instructor "hasn't found very much of that support at all . . . and is finding it quite difficult. . . . I know she feels quite out of place in any social event or meeting where the whole group is together."

As Simone explained: "If you play the game [ask for help], then they support you too." However, there is evidence that she failed to follow this creed in her comment that she "[had] probably alienated the instructors from [her specialty area]; I really don't have any support at all." Because she had other school colleagues who were supportive, she did not find this situation devastating.

Janine commented that, "as a faculty we sort of strive to develop more than just working relationship[s], but, to a certain extent, personal [relationships] or friendships that . . . don't necessarily go beyond the work setting but at least at work people are friendly with each other." She added that "some people [get] their support from their students. I think that's an important aspect as well, but I don't think you can always rely solely on the students."

Martine described the small supportive groups that formed within the faculty as a "very informal thing." There were people that she felt close to philosophically: "I do rely on them for support, but I don't think it's a formal thing." Cecile said that when she joined the faculty, the "atmosphere was calm, relaxing and . . . people were very supportive." Odile agreed there was the "opportunity to build supportive relationships at all the social functions but she indicated there was a "fair amount of 'cliquishness' at these events." Thérèse reported that at meetings faculty needed supportive feedback about their teaching.

Meetings as Cohesion Builders

Just as supportive relationships were crucial for the nurse educators, meetings, the next category to be discussed, also acted as cohesion-building mechanisms. "Correlation" meetings were the major mechanism for getting the school's work done. Although these meetings were mainly used as mechanisms for sharing curriculum information, they also had other unwritten objectives. For all teams, correlation meetings were held twice a month and usually lasted between 90 minutes and two hours. The general format of these meetings consisted of instructors giving feedback on classes they had conducted the previous two weeks, highlighting areas well done and suggesting changes where appropriate. At this time, team members responded with comments, especially if they had attended these classes. It was common practice for faculty members to attend each others' classes. Often instructors brought verbal feedback from student groups. When instructors distributed written evaluation forms, these were reported in summary form.

Feedback sessions were followed by correlation. During this part of the meetings, the group of instructors who were presenting classes in the following two weeks would give a summary of their presentations. This summary included instructions for other faculty members who might be teaching some of this content in small groups, during laboratory exercises, or on the hospital units. Handouts, considerable in number, were circulated. These summary presentations always stimulated comments and questions by team members. The investigator's field notes indicated that the participation rate was high. For example, at one first-year meeting all but two instructors commented. At two third-year meetings, out of a total of nine team members, nine and seven instructors, respectively, made comments. At two separate second-year meetings, all but two of the 13 team members participated in the discussion.

When the investigator asked the five key participants whose duties called for attendance at correlation meetings to explain these events, they replied:

Martine: On the surface it is informing instructors who don't necessarily attend the classes themselves, what exactly is being taught . . . to make sure that we are all touting the same party line.

Thérèse: When we discuss what was taught last week and how did the class go, usually there are general comments — what did the students have to say, do we need to make changes in it for next year. . . . It is easier to do at the time because six months later . . . it is long forgotten, and so that kind of evaluation . . . is more meaningful, and then many of the faculty members go to some classes . . . so they will comment also.

Janine: It's done to keep everybody informed of what is being taught, different strategies that are being used in presenting that material to the students . . . what types of strategies have either worked well or are being planned to be used. . . . It was hoped that it would promote consistency among faculty. If you know what has been taught in class, then you can check to see how students are performing as compared to what was taught.

Cecile: We do that because we need the feedback from the past lecture that we have given as to how to improve and what the students need a bit more of, or we need some positive feedback, too, if we did a good job. . . . It allows the instructor, who doesn't necessarily attend the lecture, to decide whether they should attend the lecture or prepare themselves in some way for the content so that they can work with the students.

Simone: It was originally set up in order to get feedback on faculty to improve but I think now it's just disintegrating to giving information, because the comments made, usually someone will say "the class went well. I need more (or less) time."

Three key informants concurred when the investigator suggested that correlation meetings served as integrating mechanisms, along with food and social events. The other three informants were not queried about this phenomenon. Do the above data suggest that in a women-dominated organization a distinct view of the world emerges in the workplace? How does this relate to the research literature?

Conceptualizing the Female World

Because women, for the most part, have been ignored in the research literature, conceptualizing the female world is difficult. One term that attempts to conceptualize the female world is "women's sphere." This term can be traced back at least as far as 1792 when Wollstonecroft (1891, p. vii) suggested this was a "separate" sphere that had about it a sense of "roundness," an enclosure that was "cozy, protected, safe" (Bernard, 1981, pp. 80-81).

The ideology of women's sphere helped to support the belief that women were not intrinsically inferior to men but their sphere had to be kept in a subordinate position in the interests of the national welfare (Bernard, 1981, p. 91). The work carried on in women's sphere also had a major contribution to make to society in the running of households and the raising of children. Women's sphere was a place for nurturance against the outside world and was responsible for transmitting moral standards to society. It was believed that the home, along with moral and charitable activities, was "the natural, normal and only concern of women's sphere" (Bernard, 1981, p. 91).

In the 1830s, "nursing was seen as an innate and loving responsibility of women and mothers"(O'Brien, 1987, p. 12). Home was supposed to be a place of cheer and comfort with women as the major comforters:

One of the most important functions of woman as comforter was her role as nurse. . . . The sickroom called for the exercise of higher qualities of patience, mercy and gentleness as well as for her housewifely arts. She could thus fulfil her dual feminine function — beauty and usefulness. (Welter, 1966, p. 163)

Nursing, a women-dominated profession, clearly reflects this conceptualization of women's sphere. According to O'Brien (1987):

> Nursing was still very much a domestic art in the mid-nineteenth century. To practice it in the home was to fulfil the calling of "true womanhood." To practice it for a wage kept one within the domestic sphere, a world where the only pertinent analogy was to the "chambermaids." (p. 14)

Around this time (1860s), the "new" profession of nursing was established in England by Florence Nightingale who insisted that women from the upper classes could make a respectable career out of nursing. In order to fit the Victorian era's expectations of women, Nightingale "encouraged the myth that women's [nurses'] work outside the home was not considered 'real work' but merely an extension of home work" (Seymer, cited in Coburn, 1974, p. 156). This image of nursing was transmitted to North America (O'Brien, 1987, p. 16).

The ideology of women's sphere was not easy to put into practice for women or nurses. Although this ideology was based on a "realm of the heart," "women had to foster the 'bonds of womanhood,' the sisterhood, the support systems that were its essence and made it bearable in a world not always congenial or supportable to women" (Bernard, 1981, p. 91). Because women were prohibited from any significant involvement in the polity or the economy and were excluded from equal partnership with men, women survived by giving emotional sustenance to each other (Bernard, 1981, p. 91).

Participation in women's voluntary organizations was one way of providing this sustenance. According to historians, 19th-century women in Canada and the United States had a strong propensity for cooperating with each other in voluntary organizations (Armeny, 1983, p. 14; Coburn, 1974, p. 133; Shaw, 1957, pp. 37-75). "One reason for [the] proliferation of women's groups was the sense of a special female identity, created, or at least intensified, by the gap between men's and women's experiences and responsibilities in an increasingly specialized urban and industrial economy" (Armeny, 1983, p. 14). A common female heritage led to alliances between Canadian nurses and philanthropic women that flourished during the latter half of the 19th century and the early part of the 20th century. One such alliance occurred in the National Council of Women of Canada (National Council), the most important Canadian national women's organization, which was established in 1893 (Cook & Mitchinson, 1976). The Council "staunchly support[ed] the interests of Canadian nurses in war service, as in peacetime" (Shaw, 1957, p. 157). Nurses' alliance with such women's groups was based mainly on the precepts of "a sense of women's solidarity in good works" (Armeny, 1983, p. 33).

As indicated above, nursing developed in concert with the female world. The ideology of women's sphere influenced the development of nursing. In order to try to bridge the gap between the "cult of true womenhood" and the work world of nursing, the fit between nursing and women's special sphere was developed. Nursing was portrayed as merely an extension of women's nurturing role at home along with the passive attributes associated with it.

Characterizing the Female World

A starting point for characterizing the female world is provided by polarities used by male social thinkers to explain the transition from the rural, preindustrial world to the urban, industrial world in the 19th and 20th centuries. These polarities were not based on gender differences and predated the female world conceptualization. Bernard (1981) is able to relate these polarities to both the female and male worlds. For example, in 1861, Maine (Bernard, 1981, p. 24) contrasted societies by distinguishing between those in which relationships were based on status and those in which relationships were based on contract. Relationships that are based on status are characterized by ascription and affectivity. Duties, obligations and privileges are assigned to certain positions in society. Everybody's needs are taken care of to the best extent possible. Relationships based on contract, however, involve duties, obligations and privileges that are specified and agreed to by the involved parties (Bernard, 1981, p. 24). The former describes the female world, the latter the male one.

Tönnies (1940, pp. 37-38) described two forms of human will as the basis of all social relationships. The first is "natural will" which is the basis for *Gemeinschaft*. Natural will spontaneously expresses the human's inner wishes and demands and sees affiliation with others as an end in itself. Rational will, the second one and the foundation of *Gesellschaft,* denotes deliberation or calculation of both means and ends, viewing both these conditions as separate. Women's relationships are generally based on natural will while men's relationships are more closely associated with rational will.

Boulding (1969) contrasted the economy with the "integry." The economy is described as a world in which monetary exchange acts as an intermediary in human relationships, a description more akin to the male world. The integry, strongly associated with the female world, is defined as "that part of the social system which deals with concepts and relationships such as status, identity, community, legitimacy, loyalty, love, trust" (p. 4). Boulding defined the integry as a "distinctive segment of the social system with a dynamics of its own, and strong interactions with other elements of the social system" (p. 4).

Aspects of the Female World

Gemeinschaft. Out of these polarities, Bernard (1981, p. 28) developed two primary characteristics of the female world. The first is the kinship- and locale-based or *Gemeinschaft* nature of the structure of the female world — "the realm of life and work in *Gemeinschaft* is particularly befitting to women: indeed it is even necessary for them" (Tönnies, 1940, p. 186). In 1899, Veblen (1953, p. 21) discussed the gender-related aspects of society by indicating that women still maintained an "archaic view of things" that prevented them from having a direct relation to the industrial society of that time. Seventy-five years later, Scheppele's research supported Veblen's observation by pointing out that the transition from *Gemeinschaft* to *Gesellschaft* generally bypassed women (Scheppele, cited in Bernard, 1981, p. 28). In the movement from the rural to the urban areas, women lost the productive duties they had performed on the farm. This was replaced by a division of labor where the wife became a housewife responsible for the house and children while the husband went out to the world of work. They did not establish relationships with groups of people who were unknown to each other. Instead they lived predominantly in *Gemeinschaft*, where women have always maintained a pivotal role in sustaining relationships among relatives and upholding family traditions that have been the mainstay of *Gemeinschaft* (Scheppele, cited in Bernard, 1981, p. 28). Bernard pointed out that the portrayal of the female world as *Gemeinschaft* rests on "evidence from a respectable research literature which documents . . . that the world of women has indeed been a kin- and locale-based world — a world of *Blut-und-Boden* [blood and soil] that performs an integrating function" (p. 28).

The roots of nursing derive from the *Gemeinschaft* orientation. Several authors have indicated that nurses' roles have been strongly associated with the roles of mothers (Apple, 1988, p. 47; Delamonthe, 1988, p. 345; Fagin & Diers, 1984, p. 16; Fitzpatrick, 1977, p. 821; Glass & Brand, 1979, pp. 38-39; MacPhail, 1988, p. 48):

> During the nineteenth century, health institutions borrowed their model from the bourgeois family where the father dominated and performed the role of decision-maker (doctors, administrators), while the mother's expected role consisted of "serving" activities, carrying out the wishes of the father (i.e., nurses)

and patients were relegated to the role of children (Colliere, 1986, p. 103). During the 20th century, Ashley (1977) described the role of hospital nurses as one of caring for the "hospital family": "Like mothers in a household, nurses were responsible for meeting the needs of all members of the hospital family — from patients to physicians" (p. 17). O'Brien (1987) maintained that historically nurses' ability to "link home and hospital" (p. 16) was the main source of status and prestige of the profession. Coburn (1974) stated that "the 'ideal lady' transplanted from home to hospital was to show wifely obedience to the doctor [husband] and motherly self-devotion to the patient [child]" (p. 155) while Colliere (1986) contended that nurses' "subordination to others' thought and knowledge, and the duties toward everyone, were the appropriate rules to follow" (p. 102).

Nurses have traditionally been the integrators in the hospital culture. Just as housewives usually occupy the pivotal position around which other family members revolve, nurses are the professionals who remain on the hospital units while other health care personnel move about freely. This results in other health care professionals ascribing to nurses the role of coordinators who are responsible for integrating the various components on health care.

Love-and/or-duty ethos. The second characterizing aspect developed by Bernard to describe the female world is the love-and/or-duty ethos. The integry as described by Boulding (1969, p. 4) is characterized by the love-and/or-duty ethos. Sorokin (1969, p. 21) in his studies of altruistic love in American society found the integry inhabited almost exclusively by women. Because women are expected to display altruism and compassion in their traditional roles as wives and mothers, choosing a helping profession such as nursing fits the stereotype of the appropriateness of nursing as women's work (Lewin, 1977, p. 88).

The role of mother is based on the love-and/or-duty ethos and plays an important part in shaping the female character (Bernard, 1981, p. 164). The mother is expected to nurture her child out of love-and/or-duty. Another characteristic of the love-and/or-duty ethos is selflessness. Samuels' (1975) review of the literature on working-class women revealed that the predominant values of these women were "duty, sacrifice, repression, denial of self-interest, self-expression and self-gratification" (p. 9), all characteristics of a "good" mother.

"Nurturance, self-sacrifice and mothering" are characteristics commonly associated with nurses (MacPhail, 1988, p. 48). Nursing places great emphasis on "nurturing and mothering" (Wilson, 1971, p. 217). "Womanhood was equated with motherhood . . . and mother [was] equated with 'nurse'" (Church & Poirier, 1986, p. 104). According to Roberts and Group (1973, p. 318), nursing pioneers emphasized that hospital work required the "selfless devotion of mother" while Coburn (1974) stated that "nursing the ill . . . [was] 'esteemed' as [a] familial labour of love" (p. 155). Nursing was considered merely a supplement to the primary duties of housewife. Low wages and poor working conditions were accepted because nursing work was considered a public service or "labour of love" (Coburn, 1974, p. 155). "Nursing was to be, therefore, a woman's duty not her job. Obligation and love, not the need of work, were to bind the nurse to her patient. Caring was to be an unpaid labour of love" (Reverby, 1987, p. 6).

Although avant-garde women at the turn of the century recognized that the love-and/or-duty ethos was exacting a high price of women, attempting to change it has proved to be a difficult task. That is, a large proportion of women conform, or at least try to conform, to the requirements of this ethos at whatever the cost. The love-and/or-duty ethos is nonegalitarian, demands a serving role, and expects those following it to be compliant and constantly serving others. "Stroking" best describes the behavior called for in the love-and/or-duty ethos. Stroking refers to "giving, supportive, compliant" (Bernard, 1981, p. 374) behavior such as "showing solidarity, raising the status of others, giving help, rewarding, agreeing, concurring, complying, understanding [and] passively accepting" (p. 502). Nursing epitomizes these "expressive" traits (Coburn, 1974, p. 155; Fagin & Diers, 1984, p. 16; Johnson & Martin, 1958; Roberts, 1983, p. 27; Wilson, 1971, pp. 218-219).

Other aspects of the love-and/or-duty ethos relate to the manner in which women function in organizations. While men's peer relationships, for the most part, have emphasized competition and decision making based on a hierarchical structure (Kalisch & Kalisch, 1982, p. 23), women's relationships have largely been based on the love-and/or-duty ethos. Women in public service administration, according to Neuse's research (1978, p. 440), were less committed to formal hierarchy but instead were more willing to submerge their personal power in hierarchical ranking. Women "were more apt to develop lateral relationships and cross-relationships" than were men, according to Ortiz and Marshall (1988, p. 183). Fairholm and Fairholm's research findings (1984) concluded that female school administrators tended to favor tactics such as "coalition building, cooptation, and the use of their personalities" (p. 72) to get the work done. The data on nurse educators supported the Fairholms' findings. Food and social events were used to facilitate relationships among the nurse educators, to "bring faculty closer together" to foster common action.

Charters and Jovick (1981), Fishel and Pottker (1975), and Meskin (1974) found that female principals stressed cooperation in interpersonal relationships that resulted in a nonstructured, participatory style of decision making that encouraged inclusiveness rather than exclusiveness (Kanter, 1977). Women's consistent desire for consensus in decision making was supported by Dumas (1985, p. 98), a nurse.

According to Shakeshaft (1987), several studies have found that "women [were] perceived as being more democratic and participatory than [were] men" (p. 187). For example, Hemphill, Griffiths, and Frederiksen (1962, p. 333) found that female principals involved more teachers at all levels as well as outsiders in their in-basket problems while Hines and Grobman (1956, p. 100), in their self reports of principals, found female principals to be more democratic than male principals. One conclusion of Charters and Jovick's (1981) research was that "more participatory decision making appeared in female-managed schools" (p. 322). The data on the nurse educators indicated that in all three teaching teams, there was a high rate of participation by all team members and decisions were usually made by consensus. This is not to suggest that *all* women are more participatory in this approach to management than *all* men.

The administrative research literature does not identify a need for support or the need for at least one supportive relationship at work as the findings from the study of nurse educators indicated. However, Gilligan's (1982) and Miller's (1976) research suggested that women develop "in a context of attachment and affiliation with others" (p. 83). Therefore, supportive relationships among women may be an important part of the work environment.

Bernard's (1981) and other authors' depictions of the female world suggest that any attempt to characterize this world simply means that "the norms — legal, conventional, moral, whatever — prescribe, permit or at least tolerate this behaviour" in females (p. 30). It does not mean that all female members conform to every item described above because, to date, there are insufficient data from which to develop a comprehensive and unified portrait of the female world (p. 30). "Neither does it imply that all the women in it are angels or saints or loving, serving goddesses, or embodiments of the 'true womanhood' celebrated in women's sphere in the nineteenth century" (p. 504).

All the characteristics described above led Bernard (1981) to conclude that the female world is "an integrating system with as much conceptual validity as say the economy or the polity" (p. 29). Although this integrating system, like other aspects of the female (nursing) world, has not been carefully researched, it is apparent from the above description that it is recognized as a part, perhaps a somewhat invisible part, of society.

Summary, Conclusions and Implications

In summary, the nursing world has evolved in tandem with the female world exhibiting *Gemeinschaft* and the love-and/or-duty ethos. The four major categories generated from the data exemplified the *Gemeinschaft* nature of the school and the presence of the love-and/or-duty ethos. Nurses have traditionally given sustenance to others — patients, physicians and family members. The preceding data suggest that for the nurse educators, the categories of food and social events as integrators, support as essential, and meetings as cohesion builders exemplify the ways these women attempted to nourish each other. Food and social events served mainly as facilitators for interaction. Social events, usually accompanied by home-made food, were used to celebrate births, birthdays and marriages, to mark the beginning and end of the school term, and to express appreciation for assistance given to students.

Support was a word liberally used by all instructors and was readily acknowledged as a necessary ingredient in the school. Being supportive was considered an important aspect of course coordinators' roles. The six key participants agreed they needed at least one supportive colleague at work. These relationships were more than just working relationships; they strove to be friends. The nurse educators valued support and tried, for the most part, to be supportive of each other. Meetings as cohesion builders reflected the emphasis on facilitating the implementation of curriculum content. They also were opportunities for "co-relating." Meetings were used to dispense information, as a method for sharing teaching content and strategies, personal anecdotes, or food, and as a mechanism for supporting team members. One objective of team meetings was to meld the teams into smoothly functioning units.

In conclusion, the female nurse educators exhibited orientations unique to the organizational and administrative research literature. The school had a distinctive culture that contained features that could be attributed to both the nursing and the female worlds. Examples are the strong need for integration as expressed in constructs such as food and social events, the need for meetings, and the need for support. The case study method provided a rich data source on the world of nurse educators that is exemplified in the participant narratives.

There are several outcomes or recommendations that have implications for organizational and administrative researchers and administrators. Organizational and administrative researchers need to think differently about organizations. Because administrative theory currently reflects a male-oriented world, there is a need for the incorporation of a perspective consistent with the female world so that the theory is truly representative of both women and men.

There needs to be further refinement of the female-world concept and identification of other aspects of this world. This might be accomplished through more intensive studies of women-dominated organizations, for example, girls' schools; women's colleges; hospital, college and university nursing programs; organizations in which the composition results in a clash of male and female cultures such as elementary schools; and organizations where males dominate such as universities, and engineering faculties in particular.

Female culture should be carefully considered by administrators, especially administrators in women-dominated organizations such as nursing and elementary education. For example, administrators need to recognize the dilemmas women face when they have sick family members and to develop mechanisms to help them cope with this situation. The emphasis on developing camaraderie among faculty, facilitating effective relationships between faculty and students, and coping with stress through mechanisms such as food and social events need to be given special attention by administrators. Because this research indicated that it was crucial to have at least one supportive relationship at work, mechanisms need to be built into organizations to promote supportive relationships among women. Administrators generally need to recognize the importance accorded relationships by women and develop methods for facilitating relationships in organizations. They also need to recognize that supportive relationships that fail to recognize differences among women and competition may not necessarily be the best strategy for dealing with the realities of the work world.

Perhaps as a result of the better integration of the literature on female experiences in organizations, there may be less inclination to give female administrators courses and books on how to be more like male administrators but instead an increased emphasis on changing organizations to better fit the aspirations and values of the female world. In the longer term, the female perspective may be promoted by administrators as a way to improve the "health" of organizations.

Note

[1]This article first appeared in the *Alberta Journal of Educational Research, 36*(4), December 1990, 353-369.

References

Apple, R.D. (1988). Image or reality? Photographs in the history of nursing. In A. Jones (Ed.) *Images of nurses: Perspectives from history, art, and literature* (pp. 40-62). Philadelphia: University of Pennsylvania Press.

Armeny, S. (1983). Organized nurses, women philanthropists, and the intellectual bases for cooperation among women, 1898-1920. In E. Condliffe Langemann (Ed.), *Nursing history: New perspectives, new possibilities* (pp. 13-46). New York: Teachers College, Columbia University.

Ashley, J. (1977). *Hospitals, paternalism, and the role of the nurse.* New York: Teachers College, Columbia University.

Bernard, J. (1981). *The female world.* New York: Free Press.

Boulding, K. (1969). The grants economy. *The Michigan Academician, 1,* 3-11.

Charters, W.W., Jr., & Jovick, T.D. (1981). The gender principals and principal/teacher relations in elementary schools. In P.S. Schmuck, W.E. Charters, Jr., & R.O. Carlson (Eds.), *Educational policy and management: Sex differentials* (pp. 307-331). New York: Academic Press.

Church, O.M., & Poirier, S. (1986). From patient to consumer: From apprenticeship to professional to practitioner. *Nursing Clinics of North America, 21*(1), 99-108.

Coburn, J. (1974). I see and am silent: A short history of nursing in Ontario. In J. Acton, P. Goldsmith, & B. Shepard (Eds.), *Women at work: Ontario 1850-1930* (pp. 127-163). Toronto: Canadian Women's Education Press.

Colliere, M.F. (1986). Invisible care and invisible women as health care-providers. *International Journal of Nursing Studies, 23*(2), 95-109.

Cook, R., & Mitchinson, W. (1976). *The proper sphere: Women's place in Canadian society.* Toronto: Oxford University Press.

Daniels, A.K. (1975). Feminist perspectives in sociological research. In M. Millman & R.M. Kanter (Eds.), *Another voice* (pp. 340-380). New York: Anchor Books.

Delamonthe, T. (1988). Women's work. *British Medical Journal, 296,* 345-347.

Dumas, R.G. (1985). Women and power. In D. Mason & S.W. Talbot (Eds.), *Political action handbook for nurses: Changing the workplace, government, organization and community* (pp. 94-100). Don Mills, ON: Addison-Wesley.

Fagin, C., & Diers, D. (1984). Nursing as metaphor. *International Nursing Review, 31*(1), 16-17.

Fairholm, G., & Fairholm, B. (1984). Sixteen power tactics principals can use to improve management effectiveness. *NASSP Bulletin, 68*(472), 68-75.

Fishel, A., & Pottker, J. (1975, Spring). Performance of women principals: A review of behavioral and attitudinal studies. *Journal of National Association for Women Deans, Administrators and Counselors, 39,* 110-117.

Fitzpatrick, M.L. (1977). Nursing review essay. *SIGNS: Journal of Women in Culture and Society, 2,* 818-837.

Gilligan, C. (1982). *In a different voice.* Cambridge: Harvard University Press.

Glass, L., & Brand, K. (1979). The progress of women and nursing: Parallel or divergent? In D. Kjervik & I. Martinson (Eds.), *Women in stress: A nursing perspective* (pp. 38-50). New York: Appleton-Century-Crofts.

Gould, M. (1980). The new sociology. Review essay. *SIGNS: Journal of Women in Culture and Society, 5,* 459-467.

Halpin, A.W., & Winer, B.J. (1957). A factorial study of the leader behavior descriptions. In R.M. Stogill & A.E. Coons (Eds.), *Leader behavior: Its description and measurement* (pp. 39-51). Columbus: Ohio State University, Bureau of Business Research.

Hemphill, J.K., Griffiths, D.E., & Frederiksen, N. (1962). *Administrative performance and personality.* New York: Bureau of Publications, Columbia University.

Hines, V., & Grobman, H. (1956). The weaker sex is losing out. *The School Board Journal, 133,* 100-102.

Johnson, M.M., & Martin, H.W. (1958). A sociological analysis of the nurse role. *American Journal of Nursing, 58,* 373-377.

Kalisch, B., & Kalisch, P. (1982). *Politics of nursing.* Toronto: Lippincott.

Kanter, R.M. (1977). *Men and women of the corporation.* New York: Basic Books.

Kohlberg, L. (1981). *Essays on moral development: The philosophy of moral development.* San Francisco: Harper and Row.

Lewin, E. (1977, Summer). Feminist ideology and the meaning of work: The case of nursing. *Catalyst, 10/11,* 78-103.

Lyons, N. (1983). Two perspectives: On self, relationships, and morality. *Harvard Educational Review, 53*(2), 125-145.

MacPhail, J. (1988). The professional image: Impact and strategies for change. In J. Kerr & J. MacPhail (Eds.), *Canadian nursing: Issues and perspectives* (pp. 47-58). Toronto: McGraw-Hill, Ryerson.

Meskin, J.D. (1974). The performance of women school administrators: A review of the literature. *Administrator's Notebook, 23*(10), 1-4.

Miller, J.B. (1976). *Toward a new psychology of women.* Boston: Beacon Press.

Neuse, S. (1978). Professionalism and authority: Women in public service. *Public Administrative Review, 38,* 436-441.

O'Brien, P. (1987). All a woman's life can bring: The domestic roots of nursing in Philadelphia, 1830-1885. *Nursing Research, 36*(1), 12-17.

Okrainec, G.D. (1986). Men in nursing. *The Canadian Nurse, 82*(7), 16-18.

Ortiz, F.I., & Marshall, C. (1988). Women in educational administration. In N.J. Boyan (Ed.), *Handbook of research on educational administration: A project of the American Educational Research Association* (pp. 178-183). New York: Longman.

Reverby, S. (1987). A caring dilemma: Womanhood and nursing in historical perspective. *Nursing Research, 36*(1), 5-11.

Roberts, J.T., & Group, T.M. (1973). The women's movement and nursing. *Nursing Forum, 12*(3), 303-322.

Roberts, S. (1983). Oppressed group behavior: Implications for nursing. *Advances in Nursing Science, 5*(4), 21-30.

Samuels, V. (1975). *Nowhere to be found: A literature review and annotated bibliography on white working class women* (Working Paper #13). New York: Institute on Pluralism and Group Identity.

Shakeshaft, C. (1981). Women in educational administration: A descriptive analysis of dissertation research and a paradigm for future research. In P. Schmuck, W.W. Charters, & R.O. Carlson (Eds.), *Educational policy and management: Sex differentials* (pp. 9-31). Toronto: Academic Press.

Shakeshaft, C. (1987). *Women in educational administration.* Beverly Hills, CA: Sage Publications.

Shakeshaft, C., & Nowell, I. (1984). Research on theories, concepts, and models of organizational behavior: The influence of gender. *Issues in Education, 2*(3), 186-203.

Shaw, R. (1957). *Proud heritage: A history of the National Council of Women in Canada.* Toronto: Ryerson Press.

Sorokin, P.S. (1969). *Altruistic love: A study of American "good neighbours" and Christian saints.* New York: Kraus Reprint Company.

Spender, D. (1981). Education: The patriarchal paradigm and the response to feminism. In D. Spender (Ed.), *Men's studies modified: The impact of feminism on the academic disciplines* (pp. 155-173). Oxford: Paragon Press.

Tönnies, F. (1940). *Community and society* (C.P. Loomis, Trans. & Ed.). New York: American Book. (Original work published 1881)

Veblen, T. (1953). *Theory of the leisure class.* New York: Macmillan. (Original work published 1899)

Welter, B. (1966). The cult of true womanhood. *American Quarterly, 18*(2), 151-174.

Wilson, V. (1971). An analysis of femininity in nursing. *American Behavioral Scientist, 15*(2), 213-220.

Wollstonecroft, M. (1891). *A vindication of the rights of women.* London: Walter Scott.

3

Constructing Cultural Knowledge: Mothering as Discourse[1]

Alison I. Griffith and Dorothy E. Smith

Introduction

Mothering is usually thought of as an intimate relationship within which the well-being of a child is dependent on his or her biological mother. Much of our knowledge about mothering comes from our own experiences of mothering or of being mothered, and relies on an unexamined link between biology and social responsibility. Mothering is rarely investigated in terms of the work organization it produces or of the social organization which underpins and gives shape to our experience of it. When we begin to address mothering as a work process, it comes into view as a set of activities oriented to the child and to the institutional relations in which the family is embedded, for example, the compulsory mass education system.

The institutional order of the school requires particular activities to be accomplished within the home, a work organization usually managed and coordinated by mothers. At the primary educational level, an overtired or hungry child is unable to keep up with the morning's teaching program. In the later grades, a child living in a crowded space, who has limited times and resources, has difficulty completing homework assignments. Where mothering work does not conform to the generalized requirements of schooling, or to the particularities of the classroom, it appears as inadequate mothering due to incompetence, or social deprivation (Griffith, 1984).

In this paper, we address mothering as a personal and emotional experience but also as work. We attend to the work organization through which individual mothering experiences are linked to the social and institutional fabric, particularly the school. By taking up mothering as a work organization, we can explore the interaction between an institutional work order such as the school and the material organization of the family.

This paper also addresses issues raised by feminist research, issues that have arisen for us out of our research project. First, we have been concerned with the methodological practices required for a feminist sociology from the standpoint of women. Second, in attending to our experience as mothers and as researchers inquiring into the social organization of mothering work, we have discovered the presence of a discourse on mothering[2]; a discourse which is integral to both our mothering experience and to our research experience. And finally, the examination of the mothering discourse has led us to the discovery of the standardization of mothering produced in the institutional ordering of the family-school relation. The standardization of

through discourse brings into view the social organization of class: an integral feature of the discursive organization of mothering.

A Sociology for Women: Research Issues

The women's movement, confronting an intellectual and cultural world largely made and certainly dominated by men, had at first no language for the experience of oppression. Women learned how to name their common oppression and discover it as oppression by sharing experiences in what came to be called "consciousness raising" groups. This insistence of women on speaking from their experience and for themselves has also been significant in the formulation of a feminist critique of social scientific methods. As Smith has noted, the objectifying methodologies in sociology deny the speech of women's experience in two ways. First, they substitute the categories and interpretations of an impersonal discourse for those of women themselves. People's experience is the basis of sociology, but what they have to say of themselves is transposed into the objectified forms of meaning created by sociology (Smith, 1974). Second, the forms of meaning provided by sociology are constructed from an almost exclusively male standpoint, a standpoint within the institutional complex which rules the society (Smith, 1979). This standpoint is embedded in the sociological discourse, its objects, relevances and concepts — in part because sociology itself is a constituent of this institutional complex (Smith, 1974, 1979).

The feminist critique of social science has reinforced the ongoing critique of positivist sociology, insisting perhaps more forcefully and clearly than others on a sociology fully embedded in the social world.[3] As Hartsock describes it:

> a feminist standpoint emerges . . . out of the contradiction between the systematically differing structure of male and female life activity in western cultures. It expresses female experience at a particular time and place, located in a particular set of social relations. (Harsock, 1983:303)

Feminist sociologists have been actively questioning established methods and seeking alternatives. We have sought ways of giving women's experience a voice in sociological discourse. In doing so we have broadened the conception of what this might mean, begun to confront and hopefully to overcome the discursive and political problems of such speech. The standpoint of women insists on the validity of women's right to speak for themselves of their experience.

Remaining faithful to the original speech of women has been important in extending the range of women's voices that are heard in sociology, but it has limitations. If we function merely as a medium through which women can be heard, we remain tied to the microcosms of the everyday world, of personal experience, of feeling. We are unable then to make available to women what a sociological discourse makes possible, namely, a capacity to investigate and analyze not only the social matrices of experience but also how the everyday, the personal, the level of feeling are embedded in larger social, economic and political relations. Confinement to the everyday world is a severe limitation on what we can offer women. On the other hand, feminist theory and methods proposed as alternatives too often replicate the strategies of established social sciences.[4] We share Stanley and Wise's rejection of the mere substitution of feminist for male theorizing where feminist theory imposes its interpretations of women's experience (Stanley & Wise, 1983).

The relations between a generalizing discourse and those whose experience it proposes to represent are unequal. It is all too easy for us as feminist sociologists to fall into speaking for women in the terms, contexts and relevances of a sociological discourse, a discourse which the women we claim to speak for have no power to shape. It is all too easy for us to find ourselves replicating in new forms precisely the relations we had sought to escape.

In our research, we have attempted to do a sociology for women; that is, a sociology that will express women's experience and yet embed our experience as women in the generalizing relations of the society (Smith, 1979). The general aim is to explicate the social processes and practices organizing people's everyday experience. It means a sociology in which we do not transform people into objects but preserve their presence as subjects. It means taking seriously the notion of a sociology concerned with how phenomena are brought into being through the actual activities of individuals and of exploring how those activities are organized in social relations.[5] It means rejecting methods which begin with the categories of the discourse and which approach the social world with a view to discovering in the world the lineaments of the theoretical object. It means developing an inquiry that will disclose how activities are organized and articulated to the social relations of the larger social and economic processes.

It is our view that a sociology for women must be able to disclose for women how their own social situation is recognized. It must reveal to us how our everyday world is determined by social processes, which cannot be learned through the ordinary ways of discovering it. A sociology for women explores women's experience in the context of work organized by the complex of institutions through which power is exercised in our kind of society. Though the experience of individuals is unique, it is situated in social forms of relations that are, of their nature, generalized. Generalized social relations exist only as the forms in which people's activities are coordinated and concerted. Our concern is to explicate the social matrices of experience. We are particularly interested in the ways in which women enter into the concerting of the extended relations of the larger social, political and economic order; in the ways in which women's lives *shape and are shaped by* the social order.

Strategies such as these, however, leave an important problem unresolved. As we will see below, feminists have insisted on recognizing sociology's embeddedness in the society of which it speaks. Issues of the relation of sociology and of the feminist sociologist to the women with and for whom we do our research — and in particular to those women whose experience is a resource for our work as sociologists — remain unresolved. As we have seen in our own research, the practices of interviewing themselves produce the respondent's experience as object. Our analytic strategies have had no way of incorporating our own part in these processes into the study itself. In the following section, we will look at how these issues have been handled by other feminist researchers. Their work describes various strategies and solutions used to address the methodological problems described above.

Feminists have been sensitive to issues of the unequal relation between researcher and respondent. They have proposed solutions that seek to reconstruct the relationship. For example, Mies (1983) attempted to handle this problem by breaking down the relationship. Research, rather than being the specialized task of the researcher, was distributed among researcher and "subjects" who collectively undertook responsibility for the research task. This is an interesting strategy that provides an important model. But it has severe limitations if we are to be able to offer women a "sociology," i.e., a body of knowledge that accounts to them for the properties and organization of structures of power, of economy and of discourse shaping our everyday experience. This requires specialized methods and procedures; it requires expertise.

Oakley has taken another tack. Suggesting that we recognize the necessarily interactive character of the relationship, she criticizes the "predominantly masculine model of sociology and society," which is reflected in the separation of the interviewer from the data gathered through the interviews. This, she notes,

> had led to an unreal theoretical characterization of the interview as a means of gathering sociological data which cannot and does not work in practice. (Oakley, 1981:31)

Since the personal component cannot be excluded, it should be explicit. The objectifying criteria of social scientific research should be "replaced by the recognition that personal involvement is more than dangerous bias — it is the condition under which people come to know each other and to admit others into their lives" (Oakley, 1981:58). She proposes that the researcher freely engage with respondents, speaking personally, responding to their needs for advice and information as she can appropriately.

McRobbie (1982) has sharply criticized strategies such as these. She says the "the most sensitive issue" is:

> the nature of the relationship between the researcher and researched, a relationship paralleling in its unequal power that of social worker and client, or teacher and pupil. (McRobbie, 1982:51)

While in our view she exaggerates the power differences between researcher and respondent, there is no question that the institutional relations of discourse organize the relationship between interviewer and respondent, giving the interviewer a special authority. Whether she likes it or not, the researcher participates in that order and her interviews and their uses are embedded in its relations. Certainly in our encounters with those we interview, we are seen as representatives of "authority." The issues of method, of how to give speech to women's experience, do not address this problem.

Our experience as mothers is situated in a research discourse in which we play a subordinate part. By contrast, when we enter our role as researchers, we function on the other side — as representatives of the institutional order. The ironies with which we and others, such as McRobbie, have been concerned, are projected into the research context by the women's movement. We want to speak and function as researchers in ways that do not violate a level of knowledge[6] originating in individuals' actual, local experience: outside the modes of ruling. At the same time we are doing research and, though we wrench them into different forms, we still work within the canons and conventions of an academic discourse. If we are to advance our capacity to do feminist research, these ironies must be analyzed not as moral dilemmas but as experiences arising in the context of social relations and organization; that is, they must be analyzed as integral parts of the same relations we are concerned as feminists to explicate. In the next sections, we will describe some of the strategies we have used to address these ironies in the feminist research process.

Doing Research

In devising the project and in conducting it, we have consciously included ourselves and our experience as mothers. In developing the interview schedule, we "interviewed" each other, talking out everything we could recall for each other of the work we had done as mothers in relation to our children's schooling. Although the overall methodological strategies are a feminist innovation, the routine practices of our research, particularly the interview procedures are fairly standard.[7] Partly taking a consciously principled methodological approach adopted in recognition of our own historical presence in the research process, and partly relying on an unthought ordinary responsiveness, we have deployed our own experiences as mothers to establish "rapport" by indicating shared experiences and a common knowledge of typical situations, problems, etc. In the interviews, we used phrases such as: "When my children were small, I . . ."; or: "When the teacher called to discuss problems, I often felt . . ."; apart from these minor personal incursions, we have not attempted to modify the ways in which the interview is conducted in any radically innovative direction. We have not sought to give ourselves a more active and visible presence in the transcribed products of the interview process.

But feminist strategies of research tell us to attend to our experience and to be conscious of the research process as a relationship. Hence when we became aware of things going on in the interview situation with ourselves which did not register in the interviews as such, we decided to try to understand them as also part of the phenomena we were exploring. Some of these experiences, recounted below, correspond to those described by Oakley.

1. We found that occasionally mothers asked our advice. Here is an example from our notes:

> I had an interview with a working class mother whose child was having difficulty in school. Ms. Dexter had 3 other children but her talk and attention kept coming back to this one son who was having such a hard time. During the interview, she asked me whether I thought she should move her son to another classroom or whether she should let him stay there and work it out. Ms. Dexter insisted, in her own non-assertive way, that I engage with her in a discussion of strategies which might fix the problem.[8]

The mother's questions arose out of the discussion of her children's schooling and her work organization. Her insistence on the topic of her child's difficulties in the school was framed within the context of the interviewer as representative of an "expert" knowledge of the educational process. This became part of the mother's strategies for dealing with a school process she did not understand and did not know how to evaluate. Her questions revolved around issues of what to do that would *fix* the problem. She took for granted that there are things a mother can do to alleviate her child's problem and things she can do that will make it worse. Expert advice was sought as guidance in making the *right* choice of strategy. This was an uncomfortable situation for the interviewer, who felt no better equipped than the mother herself to know what should be done and certainly had no knowledge of the particular school. But even though this discomfort was expressed, advice was sought and, when cautiously and tentatively given, was added to the fund of knowledge Ms. Dexter was collecting.

How does an incident of this kind contribute to our understanding of the social organization of the relationship between mother and schooling? Clearly Ms. Dexter took for granted (as did we in the interview setting) that it was her responsibility to find a solution to her child's problem and that her responsibility was such that it was appropriate to discuss it with the researcher who appeared at the door. But her son's problem was in the classroom, not at home. Would she have consulted us about a behavioral problem in the home? That would have been unusual, quite outside our expectations. More importantly, her talk about her son's problem and her search for ways of fixing it assumed that her responsibility extended into a situation to which she had no direct access. This was clearly an understanding shared by both mother and teacher. In the interview, the mother described interactions with the school in which both the mother and the teacher expected that she would find some way to change the child's behavior and

therefore alleviate the classroom problem. In the interview context, responding to her request for advice, the interviewer also took this for granted. The
mother's absence from the classroom, her lack of control over the classroom
situation, her lack of direct knowledge of what the child was doing, sharply
limited her ability to intervene, but did not prevent the assigning of responsibility for the problem to her by the teacher, the interviewer and the mother
herself.

This instance shows us a complex of practices which cannot be ascribed
to purely particularistic relationships between mother and child. They belong
in a space in which interviewer, mother and teacher and the others Ms. Dexter
consulted (her husband, friends, kin) share assumptions about her responsibility for taking some action to solve the problem. This conception of
responsibility is clearly organized both within the personal interaction of Ms.
Dexter with her child, her husband, her friends, etc. It is also organized
externally to that local complex of relationship. It is organized extra-locally
in the assumptions of the teaching and administrative staff of the school and
in the work organization of a school system which relies on the work of
mothers to monitor the child's schooling and initiate repair sequences within
the home to alleviate a problem arising in the school (Griffith and Smith,
1985). We are talking about practices which are situated in an extra-local
institutional order, which any of us know how to pick up and work with in
appropriate contexts: mothers, teachers, researchers and other members of
the society.

2. In the interview, Ms. Dexter's almost obsessive preoccupation with
the merits of various strategies seemed generated by anxiety about what was
happening to her son, an anxiety produced in the dual context of a responsibility that extended to his behavior in the classroom while depriving her
of direct practicable means of intervention. Similar strong "personal" feelings of concern, of guilt and anxiety, organized by the practices of an
institutional order, appeared in other contexts of our interviewing. Among
them were those of our own personal experience.

We found sometimes that the work of interviewing mothers was more
than usually emotionally exhausting. As we have noted above, our project
came out of our experience as mothers in relation to our children's schooling.
Its topics revived those experiences for us. Sometimes we responded to what
they said with incidents from our own experience, trying, as we were, to
establish our shared experience as mothers as a common ground for the
interview. And of course, as we listened to women telling us about their own
work as mothers, we also silently reflected on our experiences in the light
of theirs. Sometimes this was painful. Sometimes our own practices as
mothers compared unfavorably with a mother's account of her work. Sometimes feelings of guilt were evoked with the feeling of having done our own
mothering inadequately. Talking with other mothers about their work as
mothers in relation to their children's schooling revived concerns about our

own mothering which had never fully subsided. Here is an account of one mother who created these kinds of feelings for Alison.

> Ms. Fisher has a child who is in the French Immersion Program at a school in a middle class area. The mother has an advanced degree and her husband works in an academic institution. She does not work outside the home. Her interview described the extensive time and energy she spends on her children; for the time being she considers them her job. She organizes car pools so that they are always supervised on their community activities. She takes them to Stratford to the Festival. The children, who are already familiar with some of Shakespeare's plays, help to choose the ones they will attend. She is active in the Home-School Association and any problems which arise in the classroom for her children are taken up without delay with the teacher and the principal.

This account of Ms. Fisher drawn from our field notes might make many mothers feel inadequate. Her experience is certainly in contrast to that of a sole-support parent living on an inadequate income. Both of us were single-parent mothers. Both of us have had the experience of ourselves and our children being treated in these terms. We learned to be aware of our essential defects as "single-parent"[9] arising from membership in that category rather than from any definite patterns of parenting. At the same time, the realities are that the work required of mothers by the school is difficult to do under conditions of sole-support mothering. This is made additionally problematic for the sole-support mother when she is working on an inadequate income.

In writing up the field notes from the interview later, Alison became aware of how her own experience was shaping the account (above) of Ms. Fisher. Indeed, the interview had precipitated strong feelings which began to appear in the notes themselves. As the fieldnote went on, Alison described her response to Ms. Fisher and to the comparison between Ms. Fisher's mothering work and her own:

> And where was I in all this? I was feeling that I hadn't done my own mothering *properly.* I had let my children watch T.V.; they'd never been taken to a Shakespearian play; when I was upset with the school, I had never managed to make things better for my children and indeed, at times made it worse; etc. In other words, my mothering, in relation to other women's mothering, appeared to be less than adequate on almost every count. As a consequence, I was finding the interview process very difficult emotionally.

We could see in this a familiar procedure. There were very good reasons why Alison's mothering practices had been different from Ms. Fisher's. She lacked Ms. Fisher's parenting facilities, time and opportunities. But characteristically, this did not excuse her, did not remove her sense of guilt. The ideals of mothering in the context of schooling and the mother's responsibility for realizing them are absolute. The practicalities of the contexts and conditions of mothering did not appear to modify the interpretation of a mother's responsibility for her child's schooling. Experiences of this kind, when we reflected on them, showed us a strongly moral dimension governing the relationship of mothers to the school, capable of generating an almost theological sense of guilt and anxiety. Our question then became as follows: Is mothering organized in relationship to schooling as the social relational matrix of such experiences?

3. Having made these observations of our strikingly emotional experiences, we returned to our interviews to see whether there were aspects of the same moral organization of mothering for schooling there. We found it appearing in how mothers described and reflected on their work in "apologetic" terms and phrases used to mark deviations from the paradigmatic mother. Notable again is that such an apologetic marking is appropriate even when the conditions of mothering are such as to make conformity to the paradigm impossible.

Ms. Apple is a nurse who works part-time at a hospital in her neighborhood. She works proportionally more night shifts than the full-time nurses and her shift work hours make child care and babysitters a constant juggling act. Having described how she tries to keep up with reading to the children, she mentions, apologetically, the ways in which her employment interferes with this:

> No, I'm really a basket case on nights. I just don't have the energy or whatever to read to them or do anything with them. . . .

In the context of the interview, Ms. Apple reflects on her inability in terms of standards of mothering which are consistently eroded by the demands of her nursing job. The standard includes reading to the children on a nightly basis. During her graveyard shifts, she is not able to manage this. She blames no one but herself: she is the guilty party. By implication, if she could only muster up more energy she'd still be able to meet the standards she ought to be realizing. The conditions of her paid employment, of the level of her husband's earnings, of the lack of adequate childcare facilities, etc. do not appear as relevant to or responsible for the situation.

On the basis of even these few examples, we can trace some aspects of the social organization of the relations we are exploring. We see the disparity of control and responsibility; the deference to standards taken to be held in common; the categorical character of the standards, taking no account of practicalities and conditions; the ways in which mothers compare their own practices with others' in relation to a moral or normative standard. These are practices in which we as researchers and as mothers have been implicated. The standards are organized extra-locally in a discourse on parenting and on child development, a discourse which sets up the parameters for "normal" child development and the parenting required to develop and maintain that normalcy (Chambouredon and Prevot, 1975; Griffith, 1984). It is an organization of relations beyond the local settings of our interviews, ourselves as interviewers and the particular women we talked to.

The Mothering Discourse: In Relation to Schooling

We suggest that these observations and experiences have their site in a "mothering" discourse. By discourse we mean an organization of relations among people participating in a conversation mediated by written and printed materials. A discourse has a social organization of authorities, sites, production processes, etc. It does not consist only of "statements" but of ongoing interchanges among "experts" doing research and developing theories in the context of universities and similar sites, the training of teachers in the theories and categories thus developed. The discourse provides the working language coordinating teachers' classroom experience with that of other educators and administrators; it provides material for the writing of newspaper stories and materials for women's magazines; it links the preparation of courses in high school and colleges to practices of reading and learning on the part of professional and lay practitioners (mothers), etc. As we are using it, the term does not just refer to the "texts" of this conversation and their production alone, but also to the ways in which people organize their activities in relationship to them.[10] As mothers orient towards the texts (whether in books, women's magazines, television, radio, or by participating in "second-hand" textually organized processes such as courses, church meetings, etc.) in how they do their work in relationship to their children's schooling, in how they measure what they do in terms of its standards, in how they interpret and orient to what other mothers do in its terms, etc., they are participating in this discursive process.

Thus, the paradigm of the ideal mother constructed in relation to her children's schooling, the operation of invidious comparisons among mothers, our own recognition of ourselves as defective mothers (by virtue of our being sole-support mothers), the curious moral structuring of responsibility for the child's behavior in the school unsupported by corresponding control, etc., are moments in the practice of a discourse through which the educational role of mothers has been and still is coordinated with that of school. The duality of our own experience, as representatives of the discourse to the mothers we interview and as mothers ourselves, becomes visible as a feature of the discursive organization of mothering.

The History of the Mothering Discourse

The discourse of mothering emerges distinctly towards the end of the nineteenth century (Davin, 1978; Lewis, 1980) and enlarges and develops with the advance of public schooling (David, 1980). It provides systematically developed knowledges, recommendations, systems of categories and concepts, which coordinate the division of labor of a universalized public educational system and the family, producing the kind of children needed in twentieth-century capitalism. Key to these distinctive properties of its organization is the standardization of parenting practices in the context of increasingly standardized educational organization.

The discourse of mothering supports a standard family organization: the complete nuclear family. No concessions are made to variations in the practical and material contexts of mothering work or to the realities of a mother's ability to control the school situation in which her child works during the day. Exposure to guilt, invidious comparisons, and anxiety: all are constant hazards for mothers participating in the discourse. The child who does not read on time, who does not behave in ways that fit the classroom order established by the teacher in conjunction with the particular groups of students, who does not fit in well with her peers, who is going through a difficult time for whatever reasons, invites — via the discourse — her mother to scrutinize her own mothering practices for what is wrong. A mother's knowledge of how to take responsibility is complemented by that of the teacher who knows as a matter of her professional membership in the same or an intersecting discourse how to allocate responsibility to her. We can see this at work in our earlier account of Ms. Dexter's experience when her son was having problems in the classroom. Both she and the teacher apparently shared a common understanding that the primary responsibility for modifying his behavior in the classroom was hers.

The notion of standardization, here, does not mean an obliteration of individuality but the production by the family of a standard level of functioning within the school, which is, or can be presupposed, in the work organization of the classroom.[11] The standardized curriculum, which it is the teacher's business to work with in the classroom, presupposes students who already have a background of competences of certain kinds. In the elementary classroom in particular, certain "basic" levels of functioning may not be met because "mothers have not done their job."

Discourse, in seeking to standardize parenting practices in relation to children's schooling, articulates to a class structure. Its recommendations do not recognize what mothers do as work, hence do not attend to the material and social conditions of that work as modifiers. It enables the standardization of curriculum in ways that ensure the reproduction of class differences in children. The discourse of mothering defines the boundaries of the school's responsibility for the child's education, concealing the parameters of the educational budget and its allocation. The paradigmatic mothering of the discourse matches middle-class, not working-class, resources. Our own sense of guilt, experienced in the interview setting and informing our analytic work, is in part situated in the practicalities of being a sole-support mother and unable therefore to function fully (try as we would) as full-time middle-class mothers.

The Organization of Classes

Our discussion of mothering as a discursively organized practice has returned us to the topic of class and how class differences are reproduced through the educational process. We can spell out the transgenerational reproduction of class in how career-structured occupations enable a man to earn enough to reserve his wife's labor from the labor force and to provide the material and social conditions under which her mothering can be exercised to its fullest effect. The middle-class parent can afford (or has in the past afforded) a suburban house with a social environment of those like themselves who maintain similar standards and styles of childrearing and in a school district in which appropriate kinds of schooling are available. And they are members of a class which, through its greater control over the political process, has been able to influence school policies and to ensure in general that a proportionately larger part of the state investment in education becomes an investment in the education of the middle classes. The significance for the overall process of the transgenerational continuity of the middle-class section of the dominant classes is less the effect of these work processes and their social organization on individual children *than on the general level at which the schooling process can go forward.* The work organization of the classroom and the extent to which the teacher can institute types of teaching activities producing middle-class levels of achievement depends greatly upon much of the prior and supplementary work of mothers. At the kindergarten and primary level, much of what the teacher can do depends upon the children in her charge being competent in such matters as the use of scissors, paint, paste, being able in general to discriminate colors, and hence to follow instructions in these terms, etc. (Manicom, 1981).

Situating the work organization of mothering for schooling in its material conditions directs us to differences in how this relation works in differing class contexts and hence is part of the social organization of class reproduction. Among the middle classes, privileged access to occupations with the possibilities of career advancement have come to substitute for inheritance in ensuring the transgenerational continuities of class. A family organization making it possible for mothers to invest considerable time and skills in the "development" of children in relation to education is an essential part of this process (with the occasional alternative of sufficient income to hire specialists for this purpose). Middle-class mothers' skills have been generally acquired through prior investment (both state and private) in advanced training, giving them access to the psychological and child-developmental knowledge facilitating the coordination of mothering and schooling. The career process and the accumulation of personal wealth ensures the material conditions, the settings, the equipment and other means as well as the choice of school in which teachers can function on the assumption that mothering in the school catchment area will enable the middle-class classroom to function as such.

For example, Ms. Evans and Ms. Fisher, both middle-class mothers, work in the home and consider their work in the family as their job. They are able to take their children to cultural and social events regularly and contribute some of their time while the children are in school to the organization of schooling — volunteering, helping out on school trips, organizing the Home and School Association as a pressure group reflecting parental concerns about the quality of education and the availability of particular educational programs, such as French Immersion. By contrast, a working-class mother is likely to have less available time. She will not be able to substitute paid domestic service for her own labor or, to a lesser extent, for labor embodied in commodities. She is more likely to have to take paid employment. Her mothering skills, particularly those articulated to systematic knowledge of child development, will represent a lower level of investment in education (both state and private). These are effects for the individual child, but perhaps more importantly, for the conditions under which classroom work can be organized. The working-class neighborhood creates different conditions for the work organization of the classroom as a whole and hence for the local school process (Manicom, 1981). Ms. Apple, Ms. Baker and Ms. Dexter all engage in mothering work that includes the immediate possibility of paid labor. Accordingly, they have to face ongoing scheduling problems that arise in coordinating the relation between paid labor and mothering work for schooling. Regardless of their skill at replicating the conditions of mothering described in the schooling discourse cited above, the work must be done within the material conditions of juggling paid labor, stretched finances and a relation to the school which is not collegially organized. If Ms. Evans or Ms. Fisher are unhappy with the classroom teacher or the way the school is being run, they speak to the administrative staff, organize lobbies and/or remove their child from the public school system. If Ms. Apple, Ms. Baker or Ms. Dexter encounter what appear to be insurmountable difficulties, the alternatives for education do not extend to the private school system and at times do not even extend to removing the child from a classroom within which they are unhappy.

Thus, the way in which the discourse on mothering enters into the organization of class and the reproduction of class through the educational process returns us to the problems posed at the outset as problems of methodology. The division of labor in socializing and educating children has come to be defined in ways that take for granted middle-class family knowledge, time and resources. What may properly be considered the work of parents (and mothers in particular) and the boundaries of school responsibility has been and continues to be negotiated within a discourse that presupposes middle-class resources and familial organization. The same division of labor between school and home applies also in contexts where the middle-class material and skill resources do not exist. Participation in discourse ensures that educational authorities, school, parents, and voters will see the problem of class differentiation in the school as the differential educational efficacy of families and in particular of mothers.

This is the consistent message of the extensive literature on the relationship between family and school achievement, which is fully a part of the discourse with which we are concerned. The findings of social scientists such as Coleman (1966) that family variations rather than schooling in itself account for differences in individual school achievement presupposes the division of labor that has been given textual presence as an ideology by the discourse of mothering. The objectifying practices of social science, taking this division of labor between school and home for granted, interpret the relationship between them as causal relations. As this is taken up as part of the practical discourse of mothering, it is interpreted as responsibility, concealing the operation of class.

Concluding Remarks

Doing research is a process of discovery, both substantive and methodological. Our interviews with mothers have provided the foundation for our school-based interviews as well as for our advances in refining the formulation of the research problematic: what it means to do a sociology for women. The interview process has also provided the ground for our discoveries of the moral or normative ordering of women's work as mothers. As we saw above, the mothering discourse informs and gives shape to the work of mothers in relation to the elementary school as well as to the memories and knowledge of the researchers. Including ourselves in the research process has provided us with knowledge about mothering that would not otherwise be available.

We have been exploring the dilemmas of feminist research as we have experienced them in our study: dilemmas that we have seen are, in part, embedded in the social organization of a discourse integral to educational institutions. Our experiences as researchers, as mothers — as our dialogues with the women we have interviewed show — no longer appear as isolated moral events, but as practices within the social organization of a discourse coordinating mothers' work in the home with the work of the school. Our work as feminists confronts the stable organization of power within that discourse, which subordinates women's work as mothers to the authority of educational experts. The feminist project works both from outside and within the discourse to reshape it. It seeks to give voice to a position within which it is suppressed. Whereas the objectified forms of knowledge produce representations of family and mothering from the standpoint of those who govern, our work as feminists seeks to build a knowledge of the institutional relations of power from the standpoint of those who are governed.

Our current study begins to show the direction of the research to be done. Our methodology reminds us that research is a political process that requires the development of an alternative knowledge: a feminist knowledge. Building an alternative knowledge is one step but one step only. Reshaping discourse so that those who are subjugated within it will have a voice entails a reorganization of power beyond the research enterprise.

Notes

[1]This is a revised version of a paper presented at the *Motherwork Conference,* Institut Simone de Beauvoir, Université Concordia, Montreal, Que., Oct. 4-6, 1985. The research project was funded by the Social Sciences and Humanities Research Council, Grant 410-84-0450.

[2]The term "discourse" draws on Foucault's usage to indicate a conversation in and between texts. We have expanded the term to describe a textually-mediated form of social organization embedded in and facilitating the work of managing, administering and ordering the everyday social world. For further discussion, see below, "The Mothering Discourse."

[3]See Mies' formulation (1983). She notes that feminist social science has been one of the major critical approaches eroding positivist claims to social scientific knowledge.

[4]See, for example, the articles by Jayaratne (1983) and Reinharz (1983) who, despite their methodological differences, remain tied to the conceptual strategies of the established social sciences. Both researchers suggest methodological refinements which would transform the concerns of women into those of social science. Our methodological strategy is one which brings into view those transformative processes as one aspect of the ways through which our society is managed and administered. Thus, their attempts to rethink methodology from a feminist perspective are flawed by the same conceptual procedures they criticize.

[5]Social relations are a complex coordination of actions beyond the scope of any one individual's experience but requiring the participation of individuals in those concerted activities for their accomplishment.

[6]Perhaps corresponding to Foucault's notion of subjugated knowledges.

[7]We are using open-ended interview methods guided by topics rather than specific questions. We have interviewed six women in one city and twelve in another. In the first set of interviews, we met with the women twice in most cases and in one three times: a total of 25 hours of interviewing. The second set of interviews were much more structured and gave us another 25 hours of tape to work with.

[8]The data gathered for the project consists of transcriptions of taped interviews plus fieldnotes made to capture some aspect of the interview not present on the tape recordings.

[9]As Griffith has shown, in the work organization of institutions constructing the ruling apparatus, the concept "single-parent" is an ideological category identifying families who are 'deficient' vis à vis the educational system because they do not have the full complement of family members (Griffith, 1984).

[10]See Alison Griffith (1984) for an analysis of the concept of "single parent" as constituent of an educational discourse with multiple sites — administration, school, newspapers, etc.

[11]An article in the *Toronto Star* (Tuesday, August 27, 1985:B1) is an example of the standardizing features of the mothering discourse which structures particular versions of mothering work in relation to the work organization of the school. The article cites teachers, health consultants, a principal and a school psychologist. The article makes specific recommendations which, if followed by all parents, would mean that the teacher in the kindergarten class would confront a more homogeneous work environment with children already prepared to engage directly with the

classroom work. It also orients parents (and they will for the most part be mothers) towards the discourse and its local representatives and authorities.

References

Chambouredon, J.C. & J. Prevot. (1975). "Changes in the social definition of early childhood and the new forms of symbolic violence." *Theory and Society,* 3:331-50.

Coleman, J.S. et al. (1966). *Equality of Educational Opportunity.* Washington, D.C.: U.S. Government Printing Office.

David, M.E. (1980). *The State, the Family and Education.* London: Routledge and Kegan Paul.

Davin, A. (1978). "Imperialism and motherhood." *History Workshop Journal,* 5:9-65.

Griffith, A.I. (1984). "Ideology, education and single parent families: The normative ordering of families through schooling." Unpublished Ph.D. dissertation, University of Toronto.

Griffith, A.I. & D.E. Smith. (1985, February). "The monitoring and repair sequence: Mother's work for school." Unpublished manuscript presented at the Women and the Invisible Economy Conference, Institute Simone de Beauvoir, Montreal, Quebec.

Hartsock, N. (1983). "The feminist standpoint: Developing the ground for a specifically feminist historical materialism." In S. Hardin and M.B. Hintikka, eds., *Discovering Reality: Feminist Perspectives on Epistemology, Metaphysics, Methodology and the Philosophy of Science. Dordrecht, Holland: D. Reidel Publ.*

Jayaratne, T.E. (1983). "The value of quantitative methodology for feminist research." In G. Bowles and R.D. Klein, eds., *Theories of Women's Studies.* London: Routledge and Kegan Paul.

Lewis, J. (1980). *The Politics of Motherhood.* London: Croom Helm.

Manicom, A. (1981). "The reproduction of class: The relations between two work processes." Paper presented at the Political Economy of Gender Relations in Education Conference, Toronto.

McRobbie, A. (1982). "The politics of feminist research: Between talk, text and action." *Feminist Review,* 12 (October): 46-57.

Mies, M. (1983). "Towards a methodology for feminist research." In G. Bowles and R.D. Klein, ed., *Theories of Women's Studies.* London: Routledge and Kegan Paul.

Oakley, A. (1981). "Interviewing women: A contradiction of terms." In H. Roberts, ed., *Doing Feminst Research.* London: Routledge and Kegan Paul.

Reinharz, S. (1983). "Experimental analysis: A contribution to feminist research." In G. Bowles and R.D. Klein, eds., *Theories of Women's Studies.* London: Routledge and Kegan Paul.

Smith, D.E. (1986). "Institutional ethnography: A feminist method." (Abridged). *Issues of the Decade: Feminists and State Power, Resources for Feminist Research,* 15, 1(March).

Smith, D.E. (1979). "A sociology for women." In J. Sherman and F. Beck, eds., *The Prism of Sex: Essays in the Sociology of Knowledge.* Madison: University of Wisconsin Press.

Smith, D.E. (1974). "The ideological practice of sociology." *Catalyst,* No. 8 (Winter):39-54.

Stanley, E. and S. Wise. (1983). *Breaking out: Feminist Consciousness and Feminist Research.* London: Routledge and Kegan Paul.

4

Teaching Against the Grain:
Contradictions for Minority Teachers[1]

Roxanna Ng

Introduction

This chapter is an exploration of the contradictions of critical teaching from the standpoint of the minority teacher. I use the term "minority" in its standard sociological sense; it refers to people who are relatively powerless in the hierarchy of power and authority. Thus, although women as a group and blacks in South Africa are numerically the majority, in power terms they are minorities. As I am both a woman and an ethnic minority (i.e., non-white, non-British in Canada), I use the term "minority teacher" to refer to both minority statuses. The term "minority," then, is applied broadly to members of subordinate groups vis-à-vis the dominant group, and includes women and ethnic and racial minorities.

I use the term "critical teaching" to include the discourses which question and challenge existing knowledge bases and power relations. These discourses include critical pedagogy, anti-racist education and feminist pedagogy. I make no claim here to provide a systematic review of these burgeoning bodies of work. Throughout this chapter, I draw on existing literature to throw light on and to guide my own pedagogical beliefs and practices.

Although it is true that each of these discourses is substantively different and riddled with internal debates, they have in common a concern with power and inequality. In the words of Peter McLaren (1989), a major proponent of critical pedagogy, critical theorists

> begin with the premise that men and women [and I would add people belonging to ethnic and racial minority groups] are essentially unfree and inhabit a world rife with contradictions and asymmetries of power and privilege. (p. 166)[2]

Barbara Thomas (1984), in spelling out the differences between multi-cultural and anti-racist education,[3] also points out that the recognition of unequal power between groups is the salient feature of anti-racist education. She writes:

> Anti-racist education posits that diversity (per se) is not the problem. . . . It is the significance that is attached to the differences, and more importantly, the way that differences are used to justify unequal treatment that is the

problem — i.e., racism. It is unequal power that limits the dimensions of one's culture which can be legitimately expressed. More significantly, it is unequal power that limits one's ability to earn a living, meet basic needs, make one's voice heard. It is unequal power that makes the struggle for self-respect ... a formidable task. (p. 105)

Certainly, feminist pedagogy, growing out of feminist theory and women's studies, begins with the premise that men and women are unequal and have differential access to power structures. This has led to a distortion in the construction of knowledge itself, so that what counts as knowledge and much of what we learn in the formal educational process is one-sided and biased.[4]

Thus, one of the major aims of these critical approaches to education, diverse though they are, is to develop critical consciousness among the students/learners and to empower them (for example, by reducing the power differential between teachers and students, or by involving students in curriculum development). The long-term goal implicit in these pedagogical approaches is the belief that democratizing the classroom and empowering students will lead to changes in structures of inequality. Jargon such as "emancipatory teaching," "student empowerment," "pedagogy for radical democracy," and so on are the leading principles of critical teaching.[5]

The assumption is that critical teaching is by definition subversive. The role of the critical teacher is to bring into sharp relief the historical inequalities which have been entrenched in social structures, and to facilitate the radicalization of students. With the exception of feminist pedagogy, the power differential between the teacher and students is rarely problematized. While the literature on feminist pedagogy is attentive to issues of power, there is a tendency to treat power differentials as existing merely between teachers and students.[6] There is little examination of power as a dynamic relation which permeates classroom interactions. In exploring the contradictions of critical teaching, I wish to examine the way in which power, embodied in and affecting all participants in educational settings, operates to sustain existing forms of inequality — in order to discover how to alter these relations.

In this chapter, "power" is not seen simply as a fixed property of social structures and social institutions (for example, police have the power and authority to charge and arrest people who are seen to be breaking the law). Rather, it is treated as a dynamic relation which is negotiated continuously in interactional settings. This notion of power is derived from the work of Max Weber (1969) and Berger and Luckman (1967) in the interpretive sociological tradition.[7] I am making a distinction between "authority" and "power." In the context of this chapter, *power,* however derived, is a more individual property which is subject to negotiation interactionally. *Authority,* on the other hand, is formal power granted to individuals through institutional structures and relations. Thus, police have legal authority to take certain courses of action. Teachers have authority over students as a consequence of their ascribed role in the educational system. But in an interactional setting, this authority can be challenged by those without formal power.

Furthermore, I wish to explicate how sexism and racism, as *relations* of domination and subordination which have developed over time, and which saturate all interactional contexts, are operative in educational settings.

On Common Sense Sexism and Racism

I use the term "common sense sexism and racism" to refer to those unintentional and unconscious acts which result in the silencing, exclusion, subordination and exploitation of minority group members — that is, what people generally refer to as sexist and racist attitudes. Gender, race and class are *relations*, not just analytical categories, which are sutured[8] into the development of Canada as a nation: the building of the railway for the colony's westward expansion, exploiting Chinese men through a system of indentured labor which forbade the immigration of Chinese women, is an example of the conjunction of race, gender and class in nation building (see Ng, 1989).

In the process of colonization and nation building we can see how racism and sexism become crystallized as systems of domination and subordination. In this chapter, I want to get away from the notion that sexism and racism are merely products of individuals' attitudes (although of course they cannot be separated from people's attitudes) by emphasizing that they are *systems* of oppression giving rise to structural inequality over time. Indeed, certain norms and forms of action are so entrenched that they have become the "normal" and taken-for-granted ways of doing things. For example, when men unconsciously and automatically control and direct topics of conversations in an interactional setting, it can be seen as one form of common sense sexism. The other side of the coin is that women, all too often, actively perpetuate their own subordination, not only by deferring to men, but actually doing the work of supporting conversations in which their centrality is minimized (see Fishman, 1978).

Himani Bannerji (1987) is among the first Canadian writers to introduce the concept of "common sense racism." The term "common sense," used in the everyday vernacular, denotes ordinary good sense. The present usage is derived from Gramsci's work, and refers to the incoherent and at times contradictory assumptions and beliefs held by the mass of population (see Sasson, 1982, p. 13). Common sense racism and sexism can refer to the norms and forms of action that have become ordinary ways of doing things, of which people have little consciousness about, so that certain things, to use Bannerji's (1987) term, "disappear from the social surface" (p. 11). Sexism and racism *are* normal ways of seeing, thinking and acting. In working toward an anti-racist feminist movement, this is how Bannerji (1987) puts it:

Racism becomes an everyday life and "normal" way of seeing. Its banality and invisibility is such that it is quite likely that there may be entirely "politically correct" white individuals who have a deeply racist perception of the world. It is entirely possible to be critical of racism at the level of ideology, politics and institutions . . . yet possess a great quantity of common sense racism. This may coexist, for example, with a passively racist aesthetic. Outside the area which is considered to be "political" or workplace . . . this same white activist (feminist or solidarity worker) probably associates mainly or solely with white middle class people. That fine line which divides pleasure and comfort from politics is constituted with the desire of being with "people like us." (p. 11)[9]

I want to add that if we treat sexism and racism as common sense features of the world (in the way in which I use the term following Gramsci and others), then we can see that none of us can be "immune" or separated from these features of society. Educationally, it is the responsibility of critical teachers to begin to explicate them so that we can begin to confront our own racism and sexism, and to work toward eradicating them in all spheres of social life.

Contradictions for the Minority Teacher

In addition to making use of secondary sources, this chapter includes my own teaching experience in a university setting over the past seven years. Putting my commitment to democratic pedagogy into practice, I have experimented with different unorthodox teaching techniques. Since I asked students to keep a journal on their own progress in an advanced level graduate seminar on "Feminist Theory and Methodology" in 1989, I began to record my own and the students' responses in this and other classes. These records enter in various ways into the writing of this chapter, as data, reflections and analytical remarks.

I also use anecdotes to explicate the taken-for-granted features of everyday life — to explicate common sense sexism and racism. These mundane, off-hand remarks illustrate how (a) power is enacted interactionally, and (b) common sense sexism and racism operate as part of the relations which constitute our educational experience. My assumption is that analyzing them will tell us something about the social organization in which these remarks are embedded. This is similar to the way in which Dorothy Smith treats individual experience:

If you've located an individual experience in the social relations which determine it, then although that individual experience might be idiosyncratic, the social relations are not idosyncratic. [All experiences] are generated out of, and are aspects of the social relations of our time, of corporate capitalism. These social relations are discernible, although not fully present or explicable in the experiences of people whose lives, by reason of their membership in a capitalist society, are organized by capitalism. (cited in Campbell, n.d., n.p.)[10]

I write as a teacher — a middle-class woman and a member of the intelligensia with some authority and privileges — , as a woman of color who is marginal in the overall system of authority and privilege, as a social scientist who is supposed to be rational, analytical and detached, and as a sensuous living individual (to borrow Marx's phrase) who has emotions and feelings. These positions and identities do not sit well together. They give rise to contradictions and dilemmas which I, and every human being in her/his multiple locations and subjectivities, experience and must deal with continuously. It is nevertheless in these contradictions that I exist, and therefore think, speak and write.

In my writing, then, I try to do away with the false notion that the knower/writer can be "objective," that she can occupy a position which transcends all viewpoints. I attempt to preserve the knower/writer as an active subject in the text, grappling with her own multiple locations and contradictions. I believe that it is in confronting these contradictions and dilemmas that all of us may come to grips with what haunts us and propels us to work toward a better world. As Cynthia Cockburn (1983) writes, "it is precisely out of the process of bringing such contradictions to consciousness and facing up to illogicality or inconsistency, that a person takes a grip on his or her own fate. Politically it is of vital importance that we understand how we change" (p. 13).

Although there has been an increasing willingness among progressive academics, including critical teachers, to assert the importance of gender, race and class in social analyses, the ways relations of gender, race and class operate in educational settings remain unexplicated. In this section, I will explore how common sense sexism and racism penetrate the power dynamics between minority teachers and students.

In the discourses of critical teaching, feminists are among the first educators to describe and analyze problems encountered by female teachers in the classroom. Friedman (1985) observed from her own teaching experience: "Any kind of authority is incompatible with the feminine" (p. 206). The way this sexist and patriarchal assumption operates in the classroom is to deny the woman teacher her right to speak as a figure of authority. "[T]o be 'woman,' she has no authority to think; to think, she has made herself 'masculine' at the cost of her womanhood" (Friedman, 1985, p. 206). The fact that female professors are sometimes addressed as "Mrs.," rather than "Professor" or "Dr." like their male counterparts, is an example of the denial of female teachers' authority at a superficial but telling level.[11]

As a woman and a university teacher, one's power and authority is undermined constantly by existing gender relations which operate in the society at large. If a teacher is female (or a member of a racial minority) and engages in critical teaching, she is in a position of double jeopardy. In examining ninety-four student evaluations she received from a sociology course, Susan Heald (1989) found that only three mentioned content about women and feminist issues as positive. Most students considered her approach problematic, and the issues she raised unwelcome digressions from the formal curriculum:

> A slightly opinionated personality emerged on feminist issues which is all right but sometimes took the topic under discussion astray.

> Perhaps a less biased approach to certain issues. I feel her feminist attitudes, at times, interfered with the understanding of some course content. (p. 23)

A feminist perspective, then, is seen to be biased knowledge, vis-à-vis pure knowledge. Teaching from this critical perspective further undermines the credibility of a female teacher. Interestingly, the positive qualities of her classroom, such as students having space to voice their opinions, small group discussions and co-operative learning, were not treated by the students as part of Heald's pedagogical approach. Rather, they were seen to be features of her personality.

Minimally, sexism manifests itself in the classroom in terms of students' challenge to the female teacher's authority and credibility. More endemically, women's presence in institutions of higher learning is met with overt hostility. This hostility manifests itself in minor incidents such as sexist jokes and graffiti, and traumatic events (for women) such as campus rapes, culminating in the shattering tragedy of the Montreal massacre in the fall of 1990.[12] The following illustration from the *Toronto Star* (8 September 1990) brings sexism as a systemic property in higher educational institutions into focus:

> An outgoing woman attending a big-city university is unaware that a male classmate has an abnormal interest in her. During a class, she expresses views counter to his idea of how she should feel about the issue being discussed. After class, in front of witnesses, he slams her against a wall, calls her names and verbally abuses her. She complains to the administration, asking that he be charged with assault, but is persuaded that the matter should be handled internally. A conviction, she is told, would perhaps destroy the future of a good student. It is suggested that she tone down her contribution to discussions. The university is to make arrangements for the man to continue his education under individual tuition. (p. G1)

While the above example concerns the experience of a female student, female professors' experiences are not drastically different. For example, Sheila McIntyre, a law professor at Queen's University, detailed in a memorandum to her faculty dated 26 July 1986, the hostile incidents directed at her by law students, especially male students. She received no support from her colleagues and the administration until she resigned and took her case to the press and Canadian Association of University Teachers (CAUT). Even though CAUT took up her case, with the final result that she was offered a tenure-track position at Queen's (as opposed to the two-year term appointment into which she was originally hired), some of her male colleagues both at Queen's and CAUT felt that she "had jumped the gun" and mishandled the whole situation.[13] The fact that these comments were made and received as perfectly sensible pinpoints precisely the embeddedness of sexism in our collective consciousness. Her experience is not unique; it is what female faculty face as part of their lives on campus.[14]

For a racial minority female teacher, the devaluation of her authority and credibility is compounded by her race and ethnicity. Her presumed inferiority has its roots in the historical colonization of Canada which resulted in the vertical mosaic (Porter, 1965), and in the inequality between the developed countries and the Third World as a result of imperialist expansion of the West. Speaking from my own experience as a Chinese woman, I have frequently been called "cute" by my students and occasionally by colleagues. (Yes, it is meant to be a compliment, but why do I think of Suzie Wong when people say that?)[15] Many comment on my accent, either as practically flawless or as needing improvement. In one university where I taught, a group of female students expressed the concern that my voice (with the accent) was too soft and therefore the other students laughed at me after class. They wondered whether I could increase my volume or behave more authoritatively (or both). Ironically, I once overheard a comment between two male professors regarding a woman in a sessional appointment who had applied for the tenure-track job in the department. They were not in favor of this candidate because her voice was too strident: "You can hear her all the way down the hall when she is lecturing."

To be a minority teacher in a higher educational institution is to be continually at risk. The risk increases when minority teachers attempt to instill critical consciousness among the students, as the experience of Susan Heald shows. Over the years of my teaching, I have had students complain both about the content of my courses as well as my teaching methods. On one occasion, when I taught a course on "Cross Cultural Education," a male student complained to the department chair half-way through the academic year. Although from the course outline it was clear that I had included gender relations as an integral part of cross-cultural education, he maintained that there was no reason why this should be part of the curriculum; he had come to the course wanting to learn about multicultural education and techniques of controlling a multi-racial classroom. Instead, he argued, he only received materials on how schooling produced and maintained social inequality. He conducted an analysis of the course content, and concluded that 35% of the materials dealt with gender (in addition to race) relations; if he added the number of times "women" were mentioned in the lectures, the percentage increased to 50%. He felt that he was being short-changed and demanded that I change the course content or be fired. The department chair supported the student, and requested that I change the course half-way through the year.

The kinds of experiences reported here are experiences that I, and other minority professors, encounter on a regular basis. Thus, even when minority teachers have been granted formal institutional power, other practices are at work in the university setting which strip minority teachers of their right to speak and act as figures of authority. The above examples illustrate how common sense sexism and racism operate to disempower minority professors of the legitimate power they may have earned.

In describing the sexist encounters of female and feminist teachers, I do not mean to suggest that men are the only instigators of these practices. Women—both students and university staff, including secretaries and peers — collude and participate in the denigration of female authority. In other words, women's presumed inferority and lack of authority is internalized by *both men and women.*

Because the gender and racial lines are so clearly drawn in the hierarchy of the academy in which the power holders and power brokers are primarily white men, minority professors are marginalized even when they have gained entry to the academy. It is no longer curious to me that in some universities where I have taught, female students interested in gender relations and women's studies asked white male professors to supervise their work while calling upon me to give them references and feedback on a regular basis, and to complain about their supervisors. Similarly, I am a member on several thesis committees of minority students who are working in race and ethnic relations (one of my specializations) chaired by my (white) male colleagues who may be working in other fields altogether. As Friedman (1985) observes, women are called upon to play "the role of the all-forgiving, nurturing mother whose approval is unconditional" (p. 206), but they cannot be granted intellectual leadership. And when indeed female professors act in their professorial role, as a number of my senior colleagues do, they are the recipients of intense resentment and hostility, ironically from feminist students.

In exploring the experience of feminist academics and how feminist pedagogical discourse informed their practice, Ilona Miner discovered that feminist faculty were subject to excessive criticism by female students. (She did not interview male students in her study.) For critical teachers, especially feminist teachers, attempts at critical teaching can be acutely painful experiences, as one informant revealed:

> If you are a feminist you are very exposed, particularly because you have to have this moral commitment to the women's movement, and to what feminists share. Therefore the criticisms that students make, they're often made very harshly, and they're often made as though as a teacher you have no insides and they can hurt you as much as they want, and you're not seen as someone who feels pain. It would be nice to see another version of feminist pedagogy that called on students to see that teachers are also human, are also women. . . . I think of one or two people here . . . who went through absolute fucking hell from groups of feminists, who if you heard them talking you think, yes, . . . wonderful, open, free, etc. And then you'd hear the other side of it. You'd see this person in awful pain and in tears, and I don't know how to put those two things together. I think there is some real problem with feminist pedagogy as an orthodoxy. (Miner, 1990, p. 16)

Ironically, Miner found that when male teachers incorporate feminist principles in their classrooms, they get more praise and a warmer reception from female students (Miner, 1990). This is another aspect of common sense sexism which manifests itself in the classroom.

Thus, a major contradiction for minority teachers implementing critical teaching is that as they attempt to humanize the classroom, as figures of authority their own humanity is taken away. There is a fundamental tension in the notion of empowerment: as they attempt to empower students, minority teachers are disempowered.

Institutional Power and Student Resistance

Minority status notwithstanding, professors do possess real authority over students conferred by the institutional structure(s) of which they are a part. One of the major criticisms by Elizabeth Ellsworth of theories of critical pedagogy is that they have left this fundamental power relation between teacher and student unproblematized (Ellsworth, 1989). While the literature on anti-racist education tells of the silencing of minority students, it does not address this power issue directly. Again, it is feminist teachers who have undertaken to explore this tension, perhaps because their own marginality in the power structure is such a poignant part of their work process. Thus, Barbara Roberts (1988) writes: "I personally think that such a relation [between professor and student] is inherently abusive, and that exercising this type of power over another person is by definition abusive, even if not [done] 'abusively'" (p. 3). In exploring the paradox of the feminist professor as a "bearded mother," Kathryn Morgan writes: "If the feminist teacher actively assumes any of the forms of power available to her — expert, reward, legitimate, maternal/referent — she eliminates the possibility of educational democracy in the feminist classroom" (quoted in Briskin, 1990, p. 11).[16]

Their views paint a pretty grim picture of the possibility of critical teaching; indeed, they suggest the impossibility of education as an empowering tool in a patriarchal and hierarchical society. Furthermore, in implying that the adoption of any form of authority by women professors is oppressive and potentially abusive to students, they unwittingly deny women the right to be experts and intellectual leaders, in much the same way that students deny minority teachers these rights (see Friedman, 1985). However, I do think that they point out an important issue for the critical teacher to explore, and that is that institutional authority *is* an embodied and oppressive feature in a pedagogical setting *regardless of the intention of the teacher*. These analysts point the way to examining how common sense sexism and racism enter our consciousness and practice in insidious ways. Here, I wish to explore two ways in which common sense sexism and racism operate in the classroom.

Firstly, professors do have control over the forms and content of knowledge, a control they take completely for granted irrespective of their own race and gender. This is part of the institutional relation into which we enter and over which we have some, but never total, control. We can be more or less open about student input, but we cannot go into the class without a course outline and have the students design it. This is especially true for those of us in marginal positions (e.g., part-time, sessional, untenured) in the university hierarchy.[17]

More fundamentally, the learning environment in post-secondary institutions is organized in such a way that the student must learn whatever the course offers, and "to *display* what she has learned, *that* she has learned" (Roberts, 1988, p. 5) to the teacher. Roberts points out correctly that this is the basic contradiction of feminist, and I would add other forms of critical, teaching. Again, I want to point out that this is an institutional feature of the work process of teaching, and not an attribute of individuals. The crucial point is not to deny the existence of such constraint(s) and assume that somehow, with good intentions and skills, the critical teacher can reverse this process and turn the classroom into a democratic place (as theorists of various forms of critical pedagogies, including Kathryn Morgan — see above — imply). The university classroom is, by definition, *not* a democratic place. To pretend it can be is to deny that the hierarchy and institutional power exist. It is to delude ourselves that democracy and empowerment can be achieved by good will alone.

Secondly and more insidiously, what we know how to do well, that is, to teach students how to construct rational arguments and conduct objective analyses, is also shot through with gender, racial and class subtexts. In her critique of critical pedagogy, Elizabeth Ellsworth (1989) insightfully points out that forms of rational thinking and arguing, which we develop and refine through the educational process, is already racist and sexist because they set up as opposite an irrational Other (p. 301; see also de Beauvoir, 1952).

Another realm in which people's taken-for-granted assumptions operate at a completely spontaneous level is through the routine accomplishment of classroom interactions. Similar to the way in which minority teachers' authority is routinely challenged in the classroom, teachers also enforce their authority by controlling topics and forms of discussion. It is in analyzing interactional, including conversational, strategies that we begin to unpack the depth of common sense sexism and racism.

Examining interactions between professors and students in a feminist classroom by means of conversational analysis, Stockwood (1990), writing from the position of a student, describes how feminist professors exercise their authority to control topics of discussion. In the case documented, the professor used interruptions and questioning, among other strategies, to curtail disagreements and re-direct the topic(s) of discussion. But this is not a game played by the professor alone. Students reinforce their own subordinate position by *allowing* themselves to be interrupted, or by using comments such as "I don't know" to soften potential confrontation and disagreement between themselves and the professor. Analyzing a segment of the dialogue between herself and the professor, Stockwood (1990) writes:

> What is interesting is that I was, in my mind, very clear about my position, a position that I would not have retreated from under different circumstances where I felt an equal in the discussion. I was, in effect, structuring talk in order to elicit agreement from the professor. What is also interesting is that I chose not to, or was unable to articulate my position. Somehow the location of the professor as judge, tutor, critic, and evaluator of the students' scholastic abilities set up a relationship between us that was not only locally produced through talk, but also extra-locally managed through the normative requirements regulating teacher-student interaction. (p. 11)

> While the professor is speaking, I chose not to self-select a turn to talk to rectify this understanding [between herself and the professor] even though I could have theoretically regained the floor by . . . an interruption, or by introducing a repair at the next available transition-relevancy place . . . I felt it was inappropriate to interrupt the professor. Given the public nature of the dialogue and my own preconceived notions that the professor's right to the floor ultimately takes precedence over mine, I did not attempt to interject at the next available transition-relevancy place, rather I waited until the professor clearly signalled turn completion. My waiting, based on my interpretation of appropriate student-teacher interaction, serves to illustrate how I effectively contributed to reinforcing dominant-subordinate relations. (pp. 12-13)

Stockwood's analysis shows clearly that power is a relation which in the classroom has to be continually negotiated between teacher and students. Professors, including feminist professors, use a number of dialogic strategies to assert their authority as conferred by the institution. Students participate by either co-operating with the professor, as the above example shows, or by refusing to grant her such authority by confrontational and other strategies.

Those of us who have taught undergraduate classes, especially first-year classes, are well aware of the tactics used to disrupt classroom dynamics and challenge teacher authority. These tactics include chattering among classmates, passing notes and creating other disturbances which disrupt the flow of the lesson, not to mention direct confrontation by questioning and forcefully disagreeing with the professor in charge. Ultimately, in most situations, the professor's authority prevails due to the position she occupies in the educational hierarchy vis-à-vis the student. While she has formal authority in the classroom, her *power* is subject to challenge. In the case of the minority teacher, her power is challenged more due to the marginal position occupied by minority groups in the society at large.

In addition to interactional strategies professors consciously employ to assert their authority in the classroom, sexism and racism operate at a more subliminal level. The work by Sara Michaels (1986) on a grade 1 classroom illustrates this. Michaels' (1986) study focuses on discursive patterns of a racially mixed grade 1 classroom with half white and half black students. By tape-recording an activity called "sharing time" and conducting class-room ethnography, Michaels discerned two distinct intonation patterns and discourse styles among the black and white students. She noticed that the white students' discourse style tended to be topic-centred. That is, the discourse was tightly organized, centring on a single topic or series of closely related topics "with thematic development accomplished through lexical cohesion, and a linear ordering of events, leading quickly to a punch line resolution" (p. 102). By contrast, black students tended to use a topic-associating style. That is, their narrative pattern consisted of a series of segments or episodes which were implicitly linked in highlighting some person or theme (p. 103). Michaels further noted that Mrs. Jones, the teacher who was presumably white, was much more successful at picking up on the white students' topics, and interjected at the right moment questions to help the student develop the theme of his/her narrative. She was less successful at picking up on the black students' stories. In fact, she often mistimed her question and interrupted the child in mid-clause.

> Moreover, the teacher appeared to have difficulty discerning the topic of discourse, and anticipating the direction of thematic development. As a result, her questions were often thematically inappropriate and seemed to throw the child off balance, interrupting his or her train of thought. In cases where the child continued to talk, undaunted, these turns were often cut short by the teacher, who jokingly referred to them as "filibusters" on occasion. (Michaels, 1986, p. 108)[18]

From a liberal perspective, this kind of situation can be interpreted as a problem in cross-cultural communication. From the vantage of critical teaching, we must recognize and acknowledge that this is how students are silenced in the classroom. This example shows how the teacher acts unconsciously to reinforce the subordination of black children, and as such constitutes an instance of how common sense racism operates interactionally.

With regard to my own teaching experiences, the following incident is telling. This story concerns a course on "Gender Stereotyping" I offered to a group of student teachers around 1985. In an attempt to show how gender hierarchy was routinely established, I used a study by Pamela Fishman (1978) of intimate heterosexual couples. The Fishman study is one of my favorite teaching pieces because it is both illuminating and provocative. Students' standard reaction is to discredit the study by saying, "It's not true." Women, they maintain, are the dominant ones because they talk more. I would then ask them to do some empirical research to determine whether indeed Fishman's observation could be corroborated or rejected.

Similar reactions occurred on this occasion among the eight female and two male students in the class. As the discussion and debate ensued, I noticed another dynamic going on in the classroom. The women started to make faces to each other and giggle. When I asked what was going on, they just giggled more, and started to write and pass each other notes. As the class progressed, I became increasingly frustrated and mystified. Finally, when the class concluded, one student, a young woman who was assertive, and maintained that she was definitely the dominant one in her marriage, came and talked to me.

She told me that the female students noticed, as the class proceeded, that I was giving the men more air space. Indeed, I was interrupting the women more than the men, and they felt I was sexist! I was completely stunned by this revelation, and took the next two classes to discuss, in more depth, the embeddedness of gender hierarhcy and sexism in our own consciousness. The group also made a pact that they would take responsibility to remind each other and me when such patterns occurred in the future so that we could change not only our ideas but our practice.

This example pinpoints precisely the insidiousness of racism and sexism, not only in institutional structures, but in our individual and collective consciousness as well. It throws light on the contradictions faced by critical teachers. In spite of our theoretical commitment to a pedagogy of empowerment, as human beings we, too, have internalized power relations which predominate in the society. In our everyday activities, the people to whom we defer and over whom we exercise our power and authority are all constitutive and reflective of the patriarchal and racist ordering of the society of which we are a part. We show, not so much through theory, but more significantly through practice, what critical teaching is all about. We, too, participate in the very systems of oppression of members of society we want to empower.

Summary

This chapter has been an attempt to explore some of the contradictions minority teachers experience in implementing critical teaching. These contradictions arise because of the contradictory location of minority teachers themselves in a white, patriarchal and hierarchical structure. Their minority statuses in society at large operate to undermine the authority granted to them as gatekeepers of higher education. Their credibility is also undermined by their own commitment to critical teaching, which challenges the norms and assumptions of the very institutions that grant them formal authority. I further began to explicate how common sense sexism and racism permeate most, if not all, interactions between teachers and students, which has further implications for critical teaching. While it is not the purpose of this chapter to explore the possibilities of critical teaching within the university hierarchy, I want to end by suggesting that explicating and confronting these contradictions is a step forward in testing and pushing the limits of critical teaching.

Notes

[1]This is an abbreviated version of a longer paper entitled, "Teaching Against the Grain: Contradictions and Possibilities," prepared for a Working Symposium on "Multicultural, Anti-Racist Education and Critical Pedagogy," Kempenfelt Conference Centre, Barrie, Ontario, 20-21 October 1990. I wish to thank members of the Working Symposium for their helpful comments on the earlier draft of this paper.

[2]Critical pedagogy is not a coherent or monolithic body of work with a single theory or viewpoint. It is derived from various critical theoretical perspectives, notably the critical theory of Habermas and the pedagogical theory of Paulo Freire. The major contemporary proponents of critical pedagogy include Henry Giroux, Roger Simon, Michael Apple and Peter McLaren, among others. For a good introductory overview of critical pedagogy, see McLaren, *Life in Schools* (1989).

[3]While multicultural education has been in vogue since the promulgation of the multiculturalism policy in 1971, anti-racist education is an emerging and relatively untheorized field of study in Canada. For various attempts to describe and analyze multicultural education, see Masemann (1978/79) and Young (1979). For an excellent comparison between multicultural and anti-racist education, see Thomas (1984).

[4]For a critique of knowledge making from a feminist perspective, see Dorothy E. Smith (1975). For one of the earliest collections of feminist pedagogy, see Culley and Portuges (1985).

[5]Elizabeth Ellsworth (1989) provides a convincing self-critique of the pitfalls of critical pedagogy in her article, "Why Doesn't This Feel Empowering? Working Through the Repressive Myths of Critical Pedagogy."

[6]Issues of power are posed in various ways by feminist teachers. Writing about their own experiences in the classroom, Sheila McIntyre (1986) and Susan Heald (1989) speak poignantly of the sexism directed toward them as teachers by students, especially male students. Barbara Roberts (1988) and Kathryn Morgan (1988), on the other hand, write of the power teachers, including feminist teachers, have over students in the classroom.

[7]Max Weber (1969) defines power as the ability and chances of an actor to impose his or her will on another in a social relationship. Berger and Luckman (1967) take this notion further to suggest that particular people have the power to construct and impose their definition of reality on others. More recently, researchers in ethnomethodology and social linguistics have begun to analyze how power is enacted microsociologically. For example, Thorne and Henley's work (1975) mapped how men dominate women through the use of language. Fishman's (1978) conversational analysis shows precisely how conversational patterns between intimate heterosexual couples maintain existing power relations between the sexes.

[8]I am indebted to Cameron McCarthy for the use of this word. He came up with it when members of the Working Symposium helped me to clarify my conceptualizations of gender, race, class, sexism and racism.

[9]Elsewhere, I have asserted that gender, race and class are equally important relations to understand and explicate in social analysis (see Ng, 1989). While I have focused on racism and sexism in this chapter, I want to emphasize that class inequality and oppression is equally pervasive and important for us to explicate and eradicate.

[10]This is recorded in a report entitled, "An Experimental Research Practicum based on the Wollstonecraft Research Group," conducted by Marie Campbell. See also Smith (1987).

[11]While this is not a universal phenomenon, I have observed this in more than one university where I have taught.

[12]The Montreal massacre involves the shooting death of fourteen female engineering students by a frustrated young man who felt that his denial of entry into engineering school was due to the admittance of female students. While his act could be interpreted as that of a madman, analyses of the event make it clear that his action, no matter how irrational, had targetted women whom he considered "feminist." This indicates the pervasiveness of sexism, including misogyny, in our culture.

Here, I did not distinguish between the experiences of female students and female teachers. Although female students, due to their relatively powerless position in the university hierarchy, experience special problems such as sexual harassment, women as a minority group are marginal to the academy in general. More to the point, their very presence upsets the status quo; it threatens male power and engenders hostility in the way I describe here. See D.E. Smith, 1990.

[13]Even though I know this statement is in some sense scandalous and verges on gossip, I decided to include it here because this is precisely the way in which sexism operates effectively as a silencing and disempowering instrument. I was party to some of these comments in a CAUT conference I attended in Toronto in March 1990.

[14]See, for example, Nielsen (1979).

[15]Suzie Wong was a movie and TV character in the 50s and 60s: a high-class prostitute of mixed Chinese and English parentage. As the protagonist of the film, she mesmerized the men she met, mostly Caucasian, by her grace and demure seductiveness, and they fought for the honor to protect and cherish her. At least in Hong Kong — a British colony — and Britain, the film and its sequels captured the hearts of western and Chinese audiences alike, and led to the stereotype of Chinese women as lovely creatures who are in need of protection and love, but who cannot be taken seriously.

[16]Whereas I make a clear distinction between the terms "power" and "authority," Morgan (1988) does not make such a distinction. Thus, I find her discussion problematic because it fails to examine power as a dynamic process in the way that I try to show in this chapter.

[17]Various theorists have reflected on changing the forms and content of education. See bell hooks (1988) and Russell (1981), for example. In her paper entitled "Interactive Phases of Curricular Re-vision: A Feminist Perspective," Peggy McIntosh (1983) describes a four-phase process of change. In the final phase, she envisions that the dichotomy between teacher and student would disappear, and everyone would participate in developing and shaping the curriculum. While this kind of vision is important, it is not entirely possible under existing structural constraints of universities.

[18]I am indebted to Sandra Ingram, who drew my attention to Michaels' work by sharing her own writing with me.

References

Bannerji, H. (1987). Introducing racism: Notes towards an anti-racist feminism. *Resources for Feminist Research, 16*(1), 10-13.

Berger, P., & Luckmann, T. (1967). *The social construction of reality.* New York: Anchor Books.

Briskin, L. (1990). *Feminist pedagogy: Teaching and learning liberation.* Ottawa: Canadian Research Institute for the Advancement of Women.

Campbell, M. (n.d.). *An experimental research practicum based on the Wollstonecraft Research Group.* Unpublished Report, Ontario Institute for Studies in Education, Department of Sociology, Toronto.

Cockburn, C. (1983). *Brothers: Male dominance and technological change.* London: Pluto Press.

Culley, M., & Portuges, C. (Eds). (1985). *Gendered subjects: The dynamics of feminist teaching.* Boston: Routledge and Kegan Paul.

de Beauvoir, S. (1952). *The second sex.* New York: Alfred A. Knopf.

Ellsworth, E. (1989). Why doesn't this feel empowering? Working through the repressive myths of critical pedagogy. *Harvard Educational Review, 59,* 287-324.

Fishman, P. (1978) Interaction: The work women do. *Social Problems, 25,* 397-406.

Friedman, S. S. (1985). Authority in the feminist classroom: A contradiction in terms? In M. Culley & C. Portuges (Eds.), *Gendered subjects: The dynamics of feminist teaching.* Boston: Routledge and Kegan Paul.

Heald, S. (1989). The madwoman out of the attic: Feminist teaching in the margins. *Resources for Feminist Research, 18*(4), 22-26.

hooks, bell. (1988). *Talking back: Thinking feminist, thinking black.* Toronto: Between The Lines.

McIntosh, P. (1983). *Interactive phases of curricular re-vision: A feminist perspective.* Wellesley College, Center for Research on Women.

McIntyre, S. (1986, July 28). Gender bias within the law school. Memorandum to Faculty Board, Faculty of Law, Queen's University.

McLaren, P. (1989). *Life in schools.* Toronto: Irwin Publishing.

Masemann, V. (1978/79). Multicultural programs in Toronto schools. *Interchange, 9*(1), 29-44.

Michaels, S. (1986). Narrative presentations: An oral preparation for literacy with first graders. In J. Cook-Grumperz (Ed.), *The social construction of literacy.* Cambridge: Cambridge University Press.

Miner, I. L. (1990). Women teaching women: A contradiction in terms. Unpublished manuscript, Ontario Institute for Studies in Education, Department of Sociology.

Morgan, K. P. (1988). *The paradox of the bearded mother: The role of authority in feminist pedagogy.* Unpublished manuscript, University of Toronto.

Nielsen, L. (1979). Sexism and self-healing in the university. *Harvard Educational Review, 49,* 467-476.

Ng, R. (1989). Sexism, racism, and Canadian nationalism. In Jesse Vorst (Ed.), *Race, class, gender: Bonds and barriers.* Toronto: Between the Lines and Society for Socialist Studies.

Porter, J. (1965). *The vertical mosaic: An analysis of social class and power in Canada.* Toronto: University of Toronto Press.

Roberts, B. (1988, June). *Canadian women's studies classrooms as learning sites: Dis-abling double messages.* Paper presented at the Canadian Women's Studies Association annual meeting, Windsor, Ontario.

Russell, M. (1981). An open letter to the academy. In *Building Feminist Theory: Essays from Quest.* New York: Longmans.

Sasson, A.S. (Ed.). (1982). *Approaches to Gramsci.* London: Writers and Readers.

Smith, D.E. (1975) An analysis of ideological structures and how women are excluded: Considerations for academic women. *Canadian Review of Sociology and Anthropology, 12,* 353-369. (Reprinted in this volume as chapter 8)

Smith, D. E. (1987) *The everyday world as problematic: A feminist sociology.* Toronto: University of Toronto Press.

Smith, D. E. (1990, May 28). *Whistling women: Reflections on objectivity, science and women's exclusion.* The Hawthorn lecture, Canadian Sociology and Anthropology Association annual meeting, Victoria, B.C.

Stockwood, P. (1990, March). *Out of the fat and into the fire: Confronting patriarchy in a graduate feminist seminar.* Paper presented at the Atlantic Association of Sociologists and Anthropologists annual meeting, St. John, N.B.

Thomas, B. (1984). Anti-racist education: A response to Manicom. In Jon Young (Ed.), *Breaking the mosaic: Ethnic identities in Canadian schooling.* Toronto: Garamond Press.

Thorne, B., & Henley, N. (1975). *Language and sex: Difference and dominance.* Rowley, MA: Newbury House.

Weber, M. (1969). *The theory of social and economic organization.* New York: Free Press.

Young, J. C. (1979). Education in a multicultural society: What sort of education? What sort of society? *Canadian Journal of Education, 4*(3), 5-21.

Part Two:

Unequal Access to Knowledge

"Educational opportunity" is a fundamental if controversial and shifting concept for educators. Few would disagree that all children should have an equal chance at an education. Few would agree on exactly what this implies (Fennema & Ayer, 1984; Houston, 1985; Marcil-Lacoste, 1984). Most of the research and debate about equal opportunity has taken place in relation to social class and, at least in the United States, race (Coleman, 1968; Levine & Bane, 1975; Oakes, 1985). Looking at it from the point of view of gender equality raises some new issues, while continuing some of the old debates.

Feminists have always demanded equality of opportunity for women. But the meanings of this have shifted over time, and continue to vary with the political assumptions of the analyst. For early feminists, equality of opportunity meant the right of any qualified woman to attend all educational institutions. Royce (1975) documents the arguments used in 1865 when Ontario's Superintendent of Education, Egerton Ryerson, tried to stop local school boards from admitting girls to grammar schools and the study of Latin. George Paxton Young, the inspector of grammar schools, argued that:

> There is a very considerable diversity between the mind of a girl and that of a boy; and it would be rash to conclude that, as a matter of course, the appliances which are best adapted for bringing the faculties of reflection and taste to their perfection in one must be the best also in the case of the other ... they are not studying Latin with any definite object. They have taken it up under pressure ... there is a danger of grown up girls suffering as respects the formation of their moral character, from attending school along with grown up boys. (cited in Prentice & Houston, 1975, pp. 253-255)

Young's arguments did not prevail over the economic interest of local school boards in coeducation. Recruiting more girls meant recruiting more pupils, and therefore getting more money for the grammar schools. In rural areas particularly, the main impetus for coeducation was not sexual equality, but financial stability (see also Rosenberg, 1982; Tyack & Hansot, 1991). Since sexual equality was not one of the aims of educators, the admission of women to higher education and professional training took a great deal of time and struggle (Gillett, 1981; Strong-Boag, 1979). Even admission to teacher training in the Toronto normal school was not granted without a fight. Universities at the turn of the century were considered "a male sphere, a place of serious learning that fitted men for positions in the public world. Women's entrance into the university was considered at best irrelevant, and more likely detrimental, to women's future roles as wives and mothers" (Marks & Gaffield, 1986). Women who finally won admittance to universities on an equal basis with men challenged the validity of the stereotypes of women and began an assault on male educational power.

When women won formal equality and were allowed entrance to all university programs, the fight for equal opportunity did not end. Since the public re-emergence of feminism in the late 1960s, women have argued that equal opportunity for women entails extensive social and educational changes in order to allow women to participate on equal terms with men. Equality of opportunity means a good deal more than formally equal access.

The Deficit Model

In the early sixties, the educational community was forced to reexamine the idea of equal educational opportunity. It was clear that children from poor families had a persistent disadvantage in schools. Large-scale research studies showed that family background predicted school success (Coleman, 1966; Jencks, 1972), and that school success predicted adult jobs (Blau & Duncan, 1967; Porter, 1965). Massive intervention projects were mounted to attack the educational deficits of disadvantaged children in the hope of eliminating, or at least reducing, poverty. These programs were designed to teach poor children the skills they needed at school but had not picked up in their homes, as had more materially privileged youngsters.

This model held appeal for feminists, who argued that girls too were disadvantaged in school. The evidence for women's disadvantage was twofold. First, they were less likely than men to go on to higher education. Second, they earned much less than men. In 1970, only a third of university students were women, and full-time woman wage earners earned only 50% of what men earned. By 1983, women were almost equally represented at university, but they still earned 59 cents for every dollar earned by their male counterparts. Feminists suggested that girls, like children from poor families, lacked some of the skills and personal attributes necessary for success, and that society, through the school, had a responsibility to deal with these problems in order to give girls an equal opportunity.

As a result of this deficit model, much of the research in the 1960s and 1970s focussed on pinpointing women's problems. A large literature on "sex differences" amounted to an attempt to explain what it was about women that led to their lack of achievement (Maccoby & Jacklin, 1974; Wine, 1990). The fear was that little girls who learned to be quiet, to be feminine and to put other people's needs first would not become intellectually aggressive enough to excel at school.

> Girls are discouraged from growing into intellectually inquisitive, independent and self-assured persons. They are inhibited with regard to the acquisition of qualities that are highly valued in our society, and therefore are prevented from mastering the skills and achieving the status that would allow them to participate in the power structure. (Henschel, 1973)

When in 1968 Horner published her research on the "fear of success" in high achieving college women, it was widely heralded. In her study, Horner gave students the following written cue: "At the end of first term finals, Anne was at the head of her medical school class" and she asked them to write about Anne. Horner observed that women described Anne as unfeminine, unattractive and unlikely to succeed. Some sample responses were: "Hard-working, devoted. Wears long skirts. Not feminine; tall, straight. Doesn't go out" or "Anne will deliberately lower her academic standing the next term while she does all she subtly can to help Carl (her boyfriend). His grades come up and Anne soon drops out of medical school. They marry and he goes on in school while she raises their family." Students who wrote about "John," who was at the head of his medical school class, described him as attractive, successful and very marriageable.

Horner (1970) concluded that femininity and achievement are in conflict:

> It is clear that a psychological barrier exists in otherwise achievement-motivated and able women that prevents them from exercising their rights and fulfilling their potential. Even when legal and educational barriers to achievement are removed, the motive to avoid success will continue to inhibit women from doing 'too well' — thereby risking the possibility of being socially rejected as 'unfeminine' or 'castrating.' (p. 72)

Any number of other characteristics of women could be held responsible for women's lack of attainment at school and work. Ability and aptitude, personality characteristics, family background and support, attitudes towards gender, and aspirations were all explored by researchers in the 1970s and 1980s. Research on achievement (Kaufman & Richardson, 1982), on sex role attitudes (Gaskell, 1977; Porter, Porter, & Blishen, 1982) and on brain lateralization and hormonal influence (Fischer & Cheyne, 1977) were all attempts to find out what it was that made women different from men, and what might explain their lower achievement.

The deficit model suggests remedial programs designed to make women more like men. It leads to assertiveness training programs, to remedial math and science programs, and to career counselling that points out that women too participate in the labor force, and must plan for careers. All of these innovations require resources, attention to the problems of women and a commitment to equality. They have been important to many women and girls.

But the deficit model has a variety of problems. It ignores social structures, it constructs a single model of being female, it devalues female achievement, and it misrepresents the connections between education and the gender segregated labor market. An increase in research and shifting political climate brought these concerns to the feminist research community. What became clear was that the dynamics of gender inequality are different from, as well as similar to, the dynamics of class and race inequality. Each has to be explored on its own terms, and then the intersection of gender and race and class must be refocussed.

Blaming the System: Rethinking the Deficit

The literature on the deficits in women ignores the impact of social and educational structures, assuming their constancy while concentrating instead on the differing characteristics of individuals. By locating the causes of women's inequality in women themselves, and documenting what is wrong with them rather than what is wrong with the world in which they must operate, this literature "blames the victim" (Ryan, 1971). By treating all women as subject to the same socialization pressures, it substitutes a stereotype of middle-class femininity for the diversity of women's lives.

An alternative is to look for problems in the "system," instead of in "the victim," to focus on the way the provision of education is stacked against girls and women. This implies policies aimed at eliminating gender bias in what goes into education, or even more radically, aimed at eliminating the gender bias in results.

The extensive research on sex stereotyping in texts, in teachers' attitudes, and in classroom practices, which was discussed in the Introduction to this book, constitutes a massive indictment of the sexism of the "inputs" in the educational system. This research reveals a "chilly climate for women" (Project on the Status and Education of Women, 1982) in many classrooms. The goal of this research and the political practice based on it has been to produce an education where differential treatment is eliminated and girls and boys are treated alike. This involves attitude change among teachers, but it also involves administrative restructuring, curriculum reform and widespread social change.

This research is concerned with the equality of what goes into the educational setting — texts, curriculum, teachers' attitudes and actions. But many would now argue that getting rid of overt discrimination and treating everyone the same is not enough (Houston, 1985). Educators need to be concerned with producing equal results, equal achievement for all children, and this entails being sensitive to difference and sometimes treating children differently. For example, exposing blind children to the same curriculum as seeing children does not give blind children an equal opportunity. In her important Royal Commission report on equal employment opportunity, Rosalie Abella (1984) argued that "to treat everyone the same way would be to offend the notion of equality . . . it is not fair to use the differences between people as an excuse to exclude them arbitrarily from equal participation . . . ignoring differences and refusing to accommodate them is a denial of equal access and opportunity."

Abella proposes an attack on "systemic" discrimination, arguing that institutions must adapt to women's needs and produce equal results for women, as well as for Native people, visible minorities and persons with disabilities. She suggests that all institutions collect statistics on the performance of individuals in all these groups, in order that problem areas can be seen and attacked. The institutions would then be held responsible for producing equity in whatever ways this could be accomplished. As the New Brunswick Advisory Council on the Status of Women (1984) states, "if equality of results is not occurring, then, quite simply, the system is failing" (p. 8). Accountability rests with educators, they must find ways to educate everyone.

Valuing the Female: Rethinking Achievement

Looking for ways to explain and improve women's levels of achievement assumes that women do achieve less than men. But it is not at all clear that they do. Concern for women's lack of educational attainment obscures the fact that women as a group perform as well if not better than men in school. It can also obscure problems that exist for particular groups of women, but do not exist for most women.

Early research emphasized university graduation, where women do less well than men, rather than high school graduation, where women outperform men. Debates about how poorly women perform in math and science depend partly on whether one looks at school grades, where girls do well, or at standardized test scores, where they do less well.

The educational attainment of men and women in Canada is now virtually equal. Men in 1981 had, on average, 11.9 years of schooling, while women, on average, had 11.8. In 1971, men had 10.5 years and women had 10.6. Girls tend to get better grades than boys in school, and to drop out of high school less often. This difference was much more pronounced in the past than it is today. In 1900 in British Columbia 63% of all secondary students were women. Only in 1950 did the number of males aged 15-19 catch up with the number of females aged 15-19 in school.

Whether women do or do not achieve as much as men depends partly on what counts as achievement. Feminists have increasingly mounted an assault on the male-oriented scales used to evaluate performance, arguing that they discount the skills and abilities women have. This applies to tests of math and science ability, where girls do better on school grades than on standardized tests, and better on items that include content from female areas of experience than on items that include content from male experience (Linn & Hyde, 1989). It also applies to tests of moral reasoning, where Gilligan (1982, 1990) argues that the schemes used to evaluate answers do not reflect the ways women tackle moral dilemmas.

Belenky et al. (1986) argue that women's "ways of knowing" are different from men's and are devalued by the educational institutions and measures that men have devised.

> Relatively little attention has been given to modes of learning, knowing and valuing that may be specific to, or at least common in, women. It is likely that the commonly accepted stereotype of women's thinking as emotional, intuitive and personalized has contributed to the devaluation of women's minds and contributions, particularly in Western technologically oriented cultures, which value rationalism and objectivity. (p. 6)

Arguments about the differences between males and females treat women as a group in order to make a point. But they are silent on differences among women and silent on the ways male/female differences vary among cultures and socioeconomic groups. While women achieve in school as well as do men, and immigrant women are as well educated as immigrant men, stressing achievement can deflect attention from important barriers to school achievement faced by First Nations women and some visible minorities and class groups. Abella (1984) shows that only 42% of First Nations women had a grade 9 education (and only 42% of First Nations men, also) and only 1.1% of First Nations women had a university education (and 1.6% of First Nations men). By contrast, Abella reports, 18.2% of Indo-Pakistani women and 6.2% of women from the British Isles had a university degree (compared to 29.7% of Indo-Pakistani men and 10.3% of men from the British Isles) (pp. 143-144).

Gilligan's work has been carried out primarily on privileged young women attending a private school on the East Coast of the United States. Belenky et al. have a more diverse sample, but they want to oversimplify to find a model that describes "female" development. Women who do not fit the model they propose can feel just as left out by *this* scholarship as by the old version of a single model of development. Nevertheless, such scholarship does sensitize educators and researchers to the possibility, indeed the inevitability, of variation in ways of approaching learning and thinking. Going beyond a single "male" and "female" model is the next step.

Men and women, girls and boys often do not compete against each other directly because they are segregated into "male" and "female" areas. One result is that achievement in female areas counts less than achievement in male areas. The extensive gender segregation of schools, and of the workplace, means that men and women study and work in different areas. Women achieve in the humanities; men in science. Women achieve in typing; men in woodworking. The areas in which men study and work have higher prestige than the areas in which women study and work. Graduates from engineering earn more than graduates from nursing. Wage rates are higher for plumbers than for secretaries. It is clear that people with credentials in "male" areas get paid more, and exercise more power as adults. For this reason feminists have emphasized the importance of women achieving in male domains, and of getting women into male areas of endeavor, especially into science and technology (Science Council of Canada, 1982).

Feminism calls for reassessment of the value of female achievement, and of the scales that are used to measure it. Feminists have argued that teachers' grades rather than standardized tests should be used to determine scholarship winners. They have argued that instead of urging young women to make nontraditional choices, we should appreciate the value of, and raise the wages in, women's traditional work areas. They argue not just for equal pay for women who do the same work, but for equal pay for men and women who do work that is of equal value (Gold, 1983; Treiman & Hartman, 1981).

Gender Segregation: Rethinking Connections to the Labor Market

The assumption that a better eduction will improve women's economic chances also needs rethinking. Researchers often turn to school achievement to explain differences in occupational attainment. They assume that an important role of education is to sort students out according to their abilities and allocate them to different positions in the labor market. Good students get A's, go on to university, and get professional jobs. Poor students get low marks, leave school early, and end up in poorly paid, less prestigious jobs. Or so the story goes. It suggests that if a group's achievement in school is improved, their achievement in the labor market will also improve.

Education does pay off at work. Those with more education are much less likely to be unemployed, much more likely to earn high salaries and have high status jobs, as Guppy and Bellamy show in table 1 in chapter 7. Although education does increase women's salaries, the increase is much less for women than it is for similarly educated men. The average woman with a university degree earns barely more than the average man with a high school diploma. Differences persist at every level of education (Devereaux & Rechnitzer, 1980). A study of 1982 post-secondary graduates showed that their average earnings in 1984 went up with the level of their degrees. The average salary was $15 000 for trade/vocational graduates, $18 000 for college graduates, $23 000 for those with bachelor's degrees, $32 000 for those with master's degrees and $34 000 for those with doctorates (Secretary of State, 1986). Ensuring that more women achieve in school is likely to increase their earnings, especially since some groups of women, particularly poor and Native women, still drop out of school early without the credentials they need for work. Education is correlated with an increase in women's salaries, a decrease in their unemployment rates, and an increase in their level of participation in the labor market, just as it is for men. But education does not bring about any reduction in the inequality men and women on average experience at work.

The issue of why education pays off at work — and why it doesn't — is a contentious and surprisingly under-examined issue. Human capital theory posits that better-educated workers are more valuable to the employer, and will be more productive, so they are paid more (Becker, 1964). "Screening" theorists argue that education simply acts like a filter, where more productive people are given credentials certifying their productivity and signalling to employers that these people should be hired into more demanding jobs (Spence, 1973). Credentialling theory argues that those who succeed in school have cultural attributes employers prefer for high status jobs (Collins, 1979). None of these models pays much attention to gender.

But sex-blind models of human capital, screening and credentialling cannot explain women's disadvantage in turning education into income. Women who participate in the labor force are more highly educated than those who do not, and women in the labor force in fact have, on average, slightly more education than men in the labor force. So education makes gender differences at work harder, not easier, to explain.

An important factor that needs to be taken into account is the segmented nature of labor markets. There is no single labor market where every job applicant is evaluated against every other job applicant on their merits. Instead, labor markets are segmented (Edwards, Reich, & Gordon, 1975). The labor markets in which women predominate are different from the labor markets in which men predominate. An emphasis on the gender segmentation labor markets reframes questions about education and the economy. It becomes important to ask how women are channelled into specifically female areas, and why the rewards available for achievement in these areas are smaller than they are in male areas.

Women's jobs are closely tied to their education, but these jobs are different from men's jobs, and have different kinds of educational requirements. Women's work is characterized by the requirement for extensive educational training prior to job entry. Teachers, librarians, clerical workers and nurses train at their own expense, and are qualified by their specialized credentials. Their jobs offer few opportunities for promotion; they have a 'flat' career structure. More frequently, men move into jobs where general credentials permit entry, while on-the-job training and promotion provide for upward mobility (Madden, 1973; Wolf & Rosenfeld, 1978). To understand the historical roots of gender segregated workplaces, their persistence, and their characteristics, we need to look at how employers make hiring decisions, at the impact of unions and their defense of apprenticeships, at the organization of job categories and assumptions about women's commitment to the labor force. This opens up a variety of new questions about the organization of education in relation to work, questions which could easily be ignored when only men's experiences were considered.

Looking at gender segregation entails looking at the way schooling is organized, particularly in relation to the labor market. It calls our attention to dimensions of schooling that have been relatively ignored in the literature on education. Why does vocational preparation take the form it does? Why is gender differentiation built into the structure of the curriculum in schools? How can the structure of the curriculum and the organization of the school be changed so that it is more "girl-friendly" (Whyte et al., 1985).

The 1970 Royal Commission on the Status of Women looked at gender segmentation. It began with statistics on women's enrollment patterns in high school courses. In 1969, one quarter of all high school girls were enrolled in commercial courses compared to only 5% of boys. Seventy percent of girls but only 65% of boys were in academic courses, while 7% of girls were in "other" courses (mainly industrial) compared to 30% of boys.

Today, differential patterns of enrollment persist. They are easiest to see at the community college and university levels, where statistics are collected on program enrollments. Men predominate in engineering, science and law. Women continue to enroll in programs of study different from and less prestigious than men's programs. In the high school, numbers are harder to come by, but there is no evidence that the gender segregation the Royal Commission pointed to has decreased (Gaskell, 1985).

These differential enrollment patterns tie women closely to a gender segregated labor market. Women are clustered in non-professional clerical, sales and service occupations. In 1984, women had 32% of managerial jobs, 79% of clerical jobs, 56% of service jobs and 43% of sales jobs (Statistics Canada, 1985-86). If occupational categories are broken down further, the differences are even clearer. Women are 75% of elementary school teachers, 88% of nurses and related workers, 99% of secretaries, but only 8% of sales supervisors, 5% of dentists and 12% of insurance salespeople (Boyd, 1982). Women do jobs different from and lower paying than the jobs most men do. School prepares them for it.

All the articles in this section define equal opportunity in ways that go beyond formal access. They assume that equal opportunity implies wide-ranging social and educational changes, but they concentrate on different aspects of the problem.

Fiske looks at the educational experiences of Native women who attended residential schools. Canadian educational policy in relation to First Nations people has a long and undistinguished history. Children of First Nations origins tend to leave school much earlier than children from other racial or ethnic groups. While a focus on the similarities of the experiences of all First Nations children has told us a great deal about racism and about education, a focus on gender allows us to see First Nations schooling from a different angle and to ask some new questions. The challenge for feminist scholarship is to keep issues of race, class and ethnicity in focus alongside issues of gender.

Collis looks at computer education, an area that has expanded dramatically, but with little attention to gender issues. She sets out the reason why she is concerned about girls' low participation in computer-oriented courses, and explores a variety of potential interventions that would increase it. She clearly puts the onus for providing equal opportunity on the school.

Guppy and Bellamy look at the changing patterns of women's participation in higher education, pointing to women's gains as well as to difficulties they still confront. The authors note that theories that do not take gender into account cannot explain changes in university enrollments over the past 20 years, claiming that explanations of enrollment changes must be based in an awareness of gender differences — and that these gender differences are substantial ones.

Linda Eyre's study of a grade 8 class where boys and girls have been brought together to study home economics takes us into the heart of gender relations inside the classroom. She demonstrates that coeducation does not produce gender equity; she provides some dramatic examples of how relations of domination and exclusion work in classroom practices; and she discusses the teachers' dilemmas as they confront the problem of changing their pedagogy.

References

Abella, R.S. (1984). *Report of the Commission on Equality in Employment.* Ottawa: Minister of Supply and Services.

Becker, G.S. (1964). *Human capital.* New York: Columbia University Press.

Belenky, M.F., Clinchy, E.M., Goldberger, N.R., & Tarule, J.M. (1986). *Women's ways of knowing: The development of self, voice and the mind.* New York: Basic Books.

Blau, P., & Duncan, O.D. (1967). *The American occupational structure.* New York: Wiley.

Boyd, M. (1982). Occupational segregation: A review. In Labour Canada, *Sexual Equality in the Workplace.* Ottawa: Minister of Supply and Services.

Coleman, J.A. (1966). *Equality of educational opportunity.* Washington, DC: U.S. Office of Education.

Coleman, J.A. (1968). The concept of equal educational opportunity. *Harvard Educational Review, 38,* 7-22.

Collins, R. (1979). *The credentials society.* New York: Academic Press.

Devereaux, M.S., & Rechnitzer, E. (1980). *Higher education: Hired? Sex differences in employment characteristics of 1976 post-secondary graduates.* Ottawa: Minister of Supply and Services.

Edwards, R., Reich, M., & Gordon, D. (Eds.). (1975). *Labour market segmentation.* Lexington, MA: D.C. Heath.

Fennema, E., & Ayer, M.J. (1984). *Women and education: Equity or equality?* Berkeley: McCutchan Publishing.

Fischer, L., & Cheyne, J.A. (1977). *Sex roles: Biological and cultural interactions as found in social science research and Ontario educational media.* Toronto: Ontario Ministry of Education.

Gaskell, J. (1977). Sex role ideology and the aspirations of high school girls. *Interchange, 8*(3), 43-53.

Gaskell, J. (1982). Education and job opportunities for women: Patterns of enrollment and economic returns. In D. Smith & N. Hersom (Eds.), *Women and the Canadian labour force.* Ottawa: Social Sciences and Humanities Research Council of Canada.

Gaskell, J. (1985). Women and education: Branching out. In *Towards Equity.* Ottawa: Economic Council of Canada.

Gillett, M. (1981). We walked warily: A history of women at McGill. Montreal: Eden Press.

Gilligan, C. (1982). *In a different voice.* Cambridge: Harvard University Press.

Gilligan, C., Lyons, N., & Hammer, T. (1990). *Making connections: The relational worlds of adolescent girls at Emma Willard School.* Cambridge: Harvard University Press.

Gold, Michael E. (1983). *A dialogue on comparable worth.* New York: Cornell University.

Henschel, A.M. (1973). *Sex structure.* Don Mills, ON: Longman Canada.

Horner, M. (1968). *Sex Differences in achievement motivation and performance in competitive and non-competitive situations.* Unpublished doctoral dissertation, University of Michigan.

Horner, M. (1970). Femininity and successful achievement: A basic inconsistency. In J. Bardwick, E. Durran, M.S. Horner, & D. Gutman (Eds.), *Feminine personality and conflict.* Belmont, CA: Brooks/Cole Publishing.

Houston, S. (1985). Should public education be gender-free? *Educational Theory, 35,* 4.

Jencks, C. (1972). *Inequality.* New York: Basic Books.

Kaufman, D., & Richardson, B. (1982). *Achievement and women.* New York: The Free Press.

Levine, D.M., & Bane, M.J. (1975). *The "inequality" controversy: Schooling and distributive justice.* New York: Basic Books.

Linn, M.C., & Hyde, J.S. (1989). Gender, mathematics and science. *Educational Researcher, 18*(8), 17-27.

Maccoby, E., & Jacklin, C. (1974). *The psychology of sex differences.* Stanford, CA: Stanford University Press.

Madden, J. (1973). *The economics of sex distribution.* Lexington, MA: Lexington Books.

Marcil-Lacoste, L. (1984). Cent quarante manières d'être égaux. *Philosophiques, 11*(1), 125-136.

Marks, L., & Gaffield, C. (1986). Women at Queen's University, 1895-1905: A little sphere of their own. *Ontario History, 78,* 331-346.

New Brunswick Advisory Council on the Status of Women. (1984). *Plan of action on the status of women in education.* Moncton, NB: Author.

Oakes, J. (1985). *Keeping track: How schools structure inequality.* New Haven: Yale University Press.

O'Donnel, C. (1984). The relationship between women's education and their allocation to the labour market. *Studies in Higher Education, 9*(1), 59-72.

Porter, J. (1965). *The vertical mosaic: An analysis of social class and power in Canada.* Toronto: University of Toronto Press.

Porter, J., Porter, M., & Blishen, B. (1982). *Stations and callings: Making it through the school system.* Toronto: Metheun.

Prentice, A.L., & Houston, S.E. (Eds.). (1975). *Family, school and society in nineteenth century Canada.* Toronto: Oxford University Press.

Project on the Status and Education of Women. (1982). *The classroom climate: A chilly one for women.* Washington, DC: Association of American Colleges.

Rosenberg, R. (1982). *Beyond separate spheres: Intellectual roots of modern feminism.* New Haven: Yale University Press.

Royal Commission on the Status of Women. (1970). *Status of women in Canada.* Ottawa: Information Canada.

Royce, M. (1975). Arguments over the education of girls: Their admission to grammar schools in this province. *Ontario History, 67,* 1-13.

Ryan, W. (1971). *Blaming the victim.* New York: Vintage Books.

Science Council of Canada. (1982). *Who turns the wheel? Proceedings of a workshop on the science education of women in Canada.* Ottawa: Author.

Secretary of State. (1986). *The class of '82: Summary report on the findings of the 1984 national survey of graduates of 1982.* Ottawa: Minister of Supply and Services.

Spence, M. (1973). Job market signalling. *Quarterly Journal of Economics, 87,* 355-374.

Statistics Canada. (1985-86). *Women in the labour force.* Ottawa: Minister of Supply and Services.

Statistics Canada. (1986). *Education in Canada 1984-85.* Ottawa: Minister of Supply and Services.

Strong-Boag, V. (1979). Canada's women doctors: Feminism constrained. In L. Kealey (Ed.), *A not unreasonable claim: Women and reform in Canada, 1880's-1920's.* Toronto: Women's Educational Press.

Trieman, D., & Hartman, H. (1981). *Women, work, and wages: Equal pay for jobs of equal value.* Washington, DC: National Academy Press.

Tyack D., & Hansot, E. (1991). *Learning together: A history of coeducation in American public schools.* New Haven: Yale University Press.

Whyte, J., Deem, R., Kant, L., & Cruikshank, M. (1985). *Girl friendly schooling.* London: Methuen.

Wine, J. (1990). The reproduction of female relationality. In F. Forman, M. O'Brien, J. Haddad, D. Hallman, & P. Masters (Eds.), *Feminism and education: Canadian perspectives.* Toronto: Centre for Women's Studies in Education.

Wolf, W.C., & Rosenfeld, R. (1978. Sex structure of occupations and job mobility. *Social Forces, 56*(3), 823-844.

5

Gender and the Paradox of Residential Education in Carrier Society[1]

Jo-Anne Fiske

Introduction

Studies of the colonial educational system imposed upon North American indigenous peoples have focussed on three issues: cultural conflict arising from the imposition of a "moral" education designed to "civilize" aboriginal peoples, the failure of schooling to assimilate aboriginal workers into the paid labor force, and the unintended development of political leadership among male graduates of mission schools (see, for example, Fisher, 1977; Iverson, 1978; Knight, 1978; Miller, 1987). At the same time, however, these studies have paid scant attention to the implications of formal schooling for women's social and economic placement in the home community. Significantly, they have neither explored the ramifications of gender differences in the educational process and its outcomes, nor charted the linkages between school attendance, on the one hand, and family and kinship organization, on the other.

In this paper I analyze the significance of residential schooling for Carrier women of central British Columbia who attended the Lejac Residential School, a facility financed by the Canadian state and operated by Catholic congregations. I trace the contradictory outcomes of formal schooling for students over the course of six decades, 1922-1984. I argue that the process of education subverted the social goals of the Catholic missionaries who ran the residential school. The aim of the federal government and the missionaries was to train female students to become farm wives, members of nuclear households resident in reserve communities. In consequence, their education primarily included "domestic sciences," reading, arithmetic and religious instruction. Since the missionaries clearly intended that the girls become "Catholic" wives and mothers, submissive to male authority, all school activities were subordinated to religious instruction and ritual. Today, however, Carrier women are employed in a variety of vocations and professions and are active in community and interband politics as they struggle to maintain their Carrier identity and to regain control over their lives. I argue that their formal education provided the skills necessary for women's political participation, while traditional Carrier values, in contradiction to Catholic precepts, encouraged their emergence in the public and political realm.

A variety of research methods was used to gather data on the residential school. Official records of the government and the Oblates of Mary Immaculate were searched. From the Fall of 1979 to May 1980, twelve former students and five former teachers, members of the Sisters of the Child Jesus, were interviewed. (The findings of this study were reported in 1981.) These lengthy informal interviews, held in respondents' homes, as well as conversational exchanges in casual gatherings, were the most valuable sources of information on school experiences. A second period of field work, 1983-1985, provided further insights into the paradoxical consequences of residential schooling. Concentrating on women's political involvement, I gained new data and understanding of the impact of schooling on adult experiences, in particular on community leadership.

The data presented in the following discussion contain verbatim quotes from interviews held during both periods of field work. Discussion of women's responses to colonization and their specific political and economic strategies is also drawn from this field work.

Theoretical Framework

This analysis of gender and education is based on a theoretical framework that focuses on three distinct political forces that shape women's strategies of survival and social mobility: (1) the philosophy and practices of colonized education experienced by the Carrier, with specific concern for gender ideology, (2) the historical transformation of family organization and female productive and reproductive roles, and (3) the sexual politics of the home community. As students, girls were subjected to patriarchal authority that paid scant heed to their specific needs and aspirations. As young adults, they were excluded from the formal political structures imposed by church and state upon their communities. Therefore, in order to understand the contradictory experiences and outcomes of indigenous women's education, we need to look at the gendered nature of power relations at each stage of female experience as women confront the constraints and options afforded in the process of colonization.

Colonial education is typically viewed as a cultural invasion:

> ... the invaders penetrate the cultural context of another group, in disrespect of the latter's potentialities; they impose their own view of the world upon those they invade and inhibit the creativity of the invaded by curbing their expression. (Freire, 1970, p. 150)

Colonial curricula ignore, contradict and deny the students' culture: their language is forbidden and their daily life is structured according to the foreign moral precepts of the colonizers. Official control remains in the hands of the church and state elite. The philosophy and practices of the educators are couched in paternalistic terms: the invaders assume a moral and intellectual superiority that carries with it the mandate to advance indigenous society by improving the morality of future generations.

Colonial education is, of course, but one facet of imposed change. It is designed to support and augment economic and social transformation enforced on the indigenous community as a whole. Universally, colonial educators have struggled to eradicate indigenous family and kinship structures in order that marital and parental relationships will conform to European gender roles (Altbach & Kelly, 1978). In Canada, this process has been aided by the state. Federal legislation known as the Indian Act intrudes into all family relations by granting the Minister of Indian Affairs (through his agents) the right to determine inheritance of personal property, post-marital residence, and access to land and housing.

Colonial education is also designed to support foreign notions of social order and leadership. Not only is education rigidly hierarchical and grounded in the assumption that social progress is to be achieved by inculcating notions of obedience, duty and obligation, it is premised on a European Christian assumption of male superiority. The church and state introduced new models of leadership to indigenous peoples. In Canada and elsewhere, missionaries of the Catholic church sought to impose a theocratic order that would augment the priests' powers. To this end they established local political hierarchies that explicitly excluded women and that were empowered to uphold Catholic notions of patriarchy (Fiske, 1981, pp. 90-92). The state followed a parallel route; under the Indian Act, women were excluded entirely from political participation; they could neither hold office nor elect office holders.

Colonial processes are, of course, shaped by dialectical relations. Harsh interventions are resisted as the colonized perfect strategies of rejection and subversion. Schooling is no exception; students develop effective strategies to retain their cultural identity and to rebel against severe authority (Haig-Brown, 1988; King, 1963). Indigenous communities manifest diverse responses. Even while parents and community leaders recognize the potential benefits of academic and vocational instruction, they protest against unwarranted cultural loss and the wholesale social disruption caused by the residential mission schools. Enforced use of English and the concomitant loss of aboriginal language, for example, provoke anger and resentment as the elderly become unable to communicate with the returning students. That the young lack practical skills (for instance, those of fishing, trapping) necessary to traditional economies creates further inter-generational tension and gives rise to disillusionment and resistance (Fiske, 1981; Haig-Brown, 1988; Miller, 1987).

The diversity of community responses is in part shaped by the gender division of labor and the indigenous gender ideology. Women and men may be served differently by the removal of young children to residential schools. Women find themselves caught between their desire to gain new skills for themselves and for their children, and sacrificing their children to a foreign control that is often cruel (Fiske, 1981; Haig-Brown, 1988; Miller, 1987). Yet the absence of children may release women from reproductive tasks, freeing them for productive labor. At the same time, industrial and agricultural schools, which depend heavily upon student labor, require an adolescent student body — girls and boys who normally would be engaged in productive and reproductive labor at home or in the labor force. Strict sexual segregation in the schools also means that students return home with different skills that may (differentially) affect their reintegration into the community. Furthermore, changes in economic opportunities, and state intervention alter the community's needs for and perceptions of formal schooling.

Philosophy and Practices of Colonial Education

Until very recently, Canadian Indian residential schools were viewed by state and church as a key mechanism for colonization and acculturation of aboriginal peoples. The federal government saw them as essential to altering the aboriginal economic order and to assimilating aboriginal peoples into the dominant society; the missionaries saw them as necessary to transforming the aboriginal moral order and to creating a segregated Christian society. Residential schools were set up when reserves were established for the aboriginal populations (Patterson, 1972, p. 70). From 1830 through to the turn of the century, the federal government steadily increased its support for residential schools, hoping that gradually the aboriginal population would be either absorbed into the labor force or resident in self-sufficient agricultural reserves (Miller, 1987, p. 3).

Residential schools were a joint enterprise of state and church. The Canadian government negotiated with missionary societies regarding the location and administration of the schools. The state limited its involvement to providing funds and land, while the missionaries provided teaching staff, hired industrial assistants and managed the school's farms, which were expected to become self-sufficient. Wherever possible residential schools were isolated from aboriginal communities. In the expectation that once familiar with Euro-Canadian values and vocational skills students would abandon their own culture, parental visits were discouraged. During their annual ten months of residency, the students had virtually no contact with the world beyond the school's border; they spoke English, ate Euro-Canadian foods, and played Euro-Canadian games and team sports (Gresko, 1986; Haig-Brown, 1988; Miller, 1987).

In British Columbia the Catholic educational strategy relied exclusively on residential schools, preferably ones isolated from both aboriginal and Euro-Canadian communities. The Catholic missionaries considered residential schools essential instruments to block the transmission of aboriginal culture and to prepare students for life in a segregated community dependent upon subsistence agriculture (Knight, 1978, p. 253).

Lejac Residential School, which opened in 1922 and closed in 1972, was one link in a chain of mission schools operated throughout British Columbia by the Oblates of Mary Immaculate, a French Catholic mission order that predicated its mode of missionization upon a reactionary, patriarchal pastoral idealism. In their view, the route to "advanced civilization" lay in the establishment of self-sufficient, patriarchal nuclear families (Fiske, 1981, p. 92). Hence, extended families and corporate kinship organizations were to be eradicated. The Oblates considered the matrilineal kinship system of the Carrier (which entailed membership in one's mother's clan and succession to positions of rank held by her or her siblings) to be a degraded state, the outcome of "looseness of morals and absence of social restraint" (Morice, 1902, p. 23) that would have to be abandoned before its adherents could "become thorough Christians" (Morice, 1902, p. 23). The priests also objected to women holding traditional positions of power. Among the Carrier, women as well as men acquired noble titles and were eligible to inherit a chieftainship provided they had adequate wealth to validate their claims. Ideally, the converted would dwell in autonomous, theocratic villages governed by an ecclesiastically controlled political hierarchy. The residential school, it was thought, would assure the perpetuation of the Catholic community and provide an educated male elite to lead it.

The patriarchal philosophy of the Oblates' agenda was reflected in their school organization and educational practices. School principalships and vice-principalships were reserved for Oblate priests. Orders of nuns were secured for classroom teaching, health care and daily domestic management. By example as well as by their teaching, the religious sisters reinforced the patriarchal values of Euro-Canadian society. The Sisters of the Infant Jesus who served at Lejac, for example, had no formal teacher training. Rather, they had received an education that stressed religion and domestic sciences at the expense of academic knowledge. In all aspects of their work and social relations they were subordinate to the male administration.

Like other missionary bodies, Protestant and Catholic, the Oblates stressed the importance of religious and moral education at the expense of classroom studies. The religious and moral instruction were shaped by negative assumptions about the psychology and character of aboriginal girls. While moral education was deemed essential for all students, the Oblate priests held it to be particularly necessary for girls, as the following statement indicates:

> I also consider a school for the Indian girls a far greater benefit here than a school for the boys. Both would be required. . . . But the girls' is undoubtedly the most required. In vain would we teach the boys so long as the girls are ignorant and wicked. (McGuckin, O.M.I., 1866, UBCL, Oblate Records, AWI, R4664)

Since the girls, more than the boys, had the onus of sexual morality placed on them, they faced a greater number of rules and more stringent demands upon their behavior. Notions of correct modesty dictated the girls' dress and behavior. They wore unbecoming uniforms, were denied personal adornment, and were subjected to standard hair styles. Sexual segregation was enforced rigidly. All social activities, routine chores and, where possible, lessons, were undertaken separately. The classroom was divided into a "girls' side" and a "boys' side"; it was considered a serious offense merely to glance across the room. Communication between girls and boys was forbidden; even sisters and brothers were prohibited from speaking to one another.

The Oblates imposed a severe routine intended to inculcate habits of obedience, cleanliness and punctuality. Daily activities were strictly regulated; routine bell ringing marked the change in activities. Infractions of established rules and alleged disrespect met with disciplinary measures ranging from a loss of privileges to corporal punishment. Like the daily routine, the students' lessons were repetitive and highly structured. At Lejac, as at all of the Oblates' schools (Haig-Brown, 1988, pp. 54ff), the students rarely spent more than two hours in the classroom. The curriculum was limited to the basic and "concrete" study of primary arithmetic and reading as a result of prevailing notions of Native mentality:

> In academic subjects the Indian child advances most satisfactorily in subjects that might be described as "imitative," as for example, reading, writing and very primary arithmetic. (Dunlop, 1946, p. 17)

Aboriginal culture was ignored at best, denigrated at worst. All instruction was in English and use of the aboriginal language brought swift and harsh punishment.

State and church were united in their goal for female education: to train future farm wives. Thus the girls spent at least half of each day performing domestic chores, which in the official records is categorized as "domestic sciences." Upon arising each day the girls performed routine cleaning tasks. Each afternoon all the girls retired to the sewing room. Here, following the appropriate prayers, the young girls mended socks, sewed on buttons, and so forth, while the older girls at their sewing machines set forth to make all the required school uniforms. Each year the items numbered in the hundreds. For example, in the school year 1927-1928, the girls completed "293 dresses, 191 aprons, 296 drawers, 301 chemises, 600 pairs [of] socks . . ." (Lejac Quarterly Report, 31 March 1928, PAC, School Files, RG 10, Vol. 6443, file 881-1, part 1). Similar inventories of the girls' production are intermittently recorded throughout 1924 to 1946 (Lejac Quarterly Report, 1924-1946, PAC, School Files, RG 10, Vol. 6443, file 881).

Although the government's practice was to provide girls with only a domestic education and literacy to grade 8, it supported the Oblates' frequent requests to retain girls long after their formal studies were completed. The church, ever cognizant of its self-assumed moral obligations to protect girls from so called "vices" of frontier and indigenous societies, frequently requested that they remain at school until a marriage was arranged for them. Hence, it was not uncommon for girls to stay Lejac until eighteen or twenty years of age. The presence of young women was an important advantage for Lejac; they became a full-time unpaid source of labor, assisting the sisters in the nursery and infirmary and taking charge of the kitchen.

Although the government and Oblates agreed on a common educational practice, they frequently differed on what was appropriate for the girls' future. The government favored their assimiliation into the work force, the church their permanent residence, as wives, on a reserve. Both were content that they had fulfilled their moral and social obligations to the female students. Neither questioned the limits of the education offered; rather, they appeared to share the view of one principal who, in 1938, stated,

> As far as the girls are concerned there is not much more that can be done. They already are taught all the branches of domestic science. . . . (PAC School Files, RG 10, Vol. 6443, file 881)

The girls, however, did question the limited course of studies and regretted the poor quality of instruction. They enjoyed learning, and chafed at the imposed routines and mundane labor. In her memoirs, one former student recalls,

> I found that I wanted to learn. I like to read; I even liked arithmetic and spelling. Sometimes I found myself wishing that we did more studying. (Moran, 1988, p. 43)

Girls found that their aspirations for future work and careers could not be fulfilled with their limited education, a situation later described by one as "criminal negligence . . . it was criminal what we weren't allowed to do" (cited in Fiske, 1981, p. 44).

When the federal government agreed to provide financial support for Lejac, it anticipated that with time the school would become self-sufficient. State enthusiasm for Indian education, however, had diminished by 1922, and the federal government became more and more hesitant to fund Indian education. Consequently, not only were the pupil subsidies meager, remaining at national rates set some twenty years earlier ($125 per pupil per annum), but the Oblate principal was denied funds for hired labor and routine maintenance (Lejac School Diaries, UBCL Oblate Records, AW1 R4664; Lejac School Registers, PAC School Files, RG 10, Vol. 6443, file 881). In the face of insufficient endowments, the girls' domestic work was critical to the survival of the school. As the farm was extended so was the range of the girls' chores. In regimented work parties the girls alternated in the kitchen, laundry and bakery. Eventually the girls assumed responsibility for making cheese and butter and preserving fruits and vegetables.

Despite the barriers facing girls, they did spend more time in class than the boys did. Because of the demands of farm labor, boys attended classes irregularly, while the majority of girls received regular, albeit minimal, instruction. Not only were girls in class more frequently than boys, it appears that they developed discrete strategies of resistance and accommodation that in turn affected the course of their school experiences. While the boys chose to be openly defiant of routines, the girls chose to be more subtle in their relationships with the sisters. They soon learned "you could get away with murder if you were a teacher's pet." Girls formed friendships with the more compassionate sisters and chose to be "good" in order to earn favors or to avoid punishment for breaching minor rules. Other girls chose to be obedient because it was easier to withdraw and "turn off" the nuns and priests. Some, shy and awkward, were submissive because, in their words, they "didn't want to stand out," or "didn't want to be noticed." These sentiments contrast sharply with those of the men who recall that, "We wanted them to know we were still 'wild'."

The contrast between compliant female behavior, with its more subtle forms of resistance, and the outright challenges of the boys, had some positive ramifications for the girls. In an effort to maintain amicable relations with the girls, the sisters generally treated their pranks with determined good humor rather than punishing them and rewarded their good behavior with small privileges. It comes as no surprise, therefore, that on average the girls were more successful in school than were the boys. More girls than boys completed the eighth grade. Between 1943 and 1948, when boys were released as farm laborers, no boys advanced beyond the sixth grade, while 16 girls were able to do so. Two years later the government permitted the Oblates to offer secondary classes and again it was the girls who enrolled.

There is some irony here, for the school's practices were not intended to favor the girls' classroom instruction. Neither were the Oblates primarily concerned with maintaining a large female enrollment. Rather, given their reliance on student labor, they were often desperate to find and to keep boys capable of strenuous farm labor. The reasons that the school failed to do so lie as fully in the changing Carrier socio-economic order and community responses to the school as in the school itself.

Reasons For Attendance

The Carrier had first requested an industrial school more than a quarter of a century before Lejac had opened. With Euro-Canadian settlement in the Nechako Plateau, the Carrier had diversified their economic strategies. Their aboriginal seasonal round of fishing (primarily salmon), hunting and trapping large and small game, and foraging vegetation first had been adapted to the requirements of trapping and fishing for trade and had been altered again with increased opportunities for wage or contract labor. From the turn of the century, the Carrier had enjoyed relative prosperity consequent upon wage and contract labor associated with railroad and agricultural expansion. Nonetheless, they recognized that with continuing depletion of natural resources, which threatened their trapping and subsistence production, and with increasing Euro-Canadian settlement, they would need the benefits of formal schooling.

Despite the Carriers' stated desire for educational facilities and their conviction that literacy would lead to social equality, responses to the school varied and affected girls and boys differently. Some families who occupied prominent positions within the villages, in particular positions endorsed by the Oblates, strongly supported the school (UBCL, Oblate Records). Changes in family organization and the diversification of productive tasks affected school enrollment. The shift of winter activities from extended family settlements to individually owned trap lines encouraged parents to enroll their children. Without the burden of young children, women were free to undertake a variety of productive tasks. They spent longer and more profitable periods on the trap line or at the lake shore where they fished. With men routinely working away from the community, women assumed sole responsibility for livestock or other farm work. Women also sought opportunities to earn cash. They joined the men in freighting goods, providing railroad ties for the newly constructed railroad, and clearing land for the white settlers.

Family dislocation also influenced school enrollment. Several Carrier communities were devastated by the 1918 Spanish influenza. In consequence, infants were handed over to the school to be cared for by the sisters and older girls. Older children who were not needed for their labor were sent by widowed parents or other relatives who were unable to provide well for them. Girls in particular were sent to school, often to remain there year round until they were adolescents.

Of course, not all parents wished to send their children away; emotional ties and dependence upon children's contribution to the family economy made many reluctant. Some parents complied only when urged or coerced by the Oblate priests; others refused entirely, hiding their children when the priests came for them, a source of frustration that led one priest to complain to his superiors:

the month of September was spent in collecting children from the camps . . . the parents doing nothing towards their education unless coaxed and threatened. (Allard, 1922, UBCL, Records of the Oblate Father, AW1, R4664)

Carrier parents were more reluctant to part with sons than daughters, apparently feeling that their sons' economic contributions were vital to the family subsistence (Allard, O.M.I., UBCL, Oblate Records, AW1, R4664). Mothers often refused to part with their very young sons. Local families assisted their sons' escapes and hid others from the priest. Families departed early for the trap line to avoid enrollment. Thus, on average, boys entered school at the age of ten and remained for no longer than three or four years (Principal's Report, 1944, PAC, School Files, RG 10, Vol. 6443, file 881).

The government exacerbated this situation by discharging boys before the school leaving age of fifteen. Either at the request of their guardians, who required the boys' labor, or in order to evade state financial responsibility for impoverished parents, the government chose to send the boys home. The government agents had learned that "Indian boys do not take well to trapping after they are sixteen or older" (Howe, 1944, PAC, School Files, RG 10, Vol. 6443, file 881). In addition, when their labor was in demand, as for example during World War II, boys were dismissed to become farm laborers (ibid.).

The school did not face the same difficulties in recruiting and retaining female students. Significantly, not only did more girls than boys attend, they also remained longer. Fewer girls were discharged to take on family economic responsibilities, and those who did leave often returned (Lejac School Registers, PAC, School Files, RG 10, Vol. 6443, file 881). Available figures show that between the years 1923 and 1936 female enrollment exceeded male enrollment (Department of Indian Affairs, Annual Reports 1923-1936). Furthermore, more girls than boys achieved an academic standing past sixth grade (Lejac School Registers, PAC, School Files, RG 10, Vol. 6443, file 881).

The Life Course of Former Pupils

Eventually, the girls and young women left Lejac to return home, most to enter marriages arranged by the priest or his appointed representative, the Church Chief. Despite the severe limitations of their schooling, many found themselves better prepared for adult life than their male peers whose years of hard work had failed to provide them with the vocational skills they had hoped would make them marketable in the labor force. While they had received no industrial training, the girls had learned a range of practical skills such as canning and pickling garden produce, knitting, and so on. These skills they easily assimilated into the domestic economy, since the Carrier now relied considerably on subsistence agriculture.[2] Small-scale mixed farming was incorporated into the annual subsistence cycle as women found it useful to tend gardens and raise poultry. Garden produce provided women with goods to barter or sell to their Carrier and Euro-Canadian neighbors. During the hard times of the Great Depression, for example, Carrier women traded food items to white women, receiving in return used clothing to be remade for their children.

Ironically, mission schooling can be credited with preparing Carrier women for social roles once abhorred by the Oblate missionaries. The Oblates placed some former students, mostly orphans, in the regional Catholic hospital. (Those who had remained at Lejac beyond eighth grade were particularly well-prepared for this role because they had assisted in the school infirmary.) The priests vehemently objected to women entering the labor force. With expanding settlement and economic development, however, women soon found their domestic skills marketable. Overriding the priests' objections, women took jobs as domestic workers in private homes, public hospitals, restaurants and hotels. Furthermore, having gained experience and self-confidence, many women left the hospitals to join the women working elsewhere (Fiske, 1981, p. 45).

By 1960 many women found themselves supporting large families, as the influx of Euro-Canadian men displaced Carrier men from the labor force while settlement and industrial expansion undermined fur trapping (Fiske, 1989, p. 92). The advent of community self-administration in the 1970s opened new doors for literate women. Former students of Lejac became office workers and band managers, frequently upgrading their credentials in adult education courses and in para-professional training.

Despite the overwhelming loneliness, hardship and boredom of their student years, former female students acknowledge these benefits. As one former student, who left Lejac at the beginning of the Great Depression, recollects,

> I learned useful things, sewing, crocheting, knitting, stuff like that. . . . I learned to look after myself and to be a good mother. I [can] my own salmon and . . . my vegetables too. I learned to do very delicate work with my hands. . . . Then I learned basketry to show my mother I could do it. I revived my traditional skills.

Another remembers,

> The girls learned useful things. We did work for the Red Cross. It came in handy when we were mothers. I have ten children. At least I learned to read, write, cook and bake. . . . Without Lejac I would have been nowhere.

Mary John, in telling her life history, poignantly describes the benefits she experienced.

> Even then, I knew that there were also good things about school. I could now speak English, and I was making what the teachers called excellent progress in reading, writing, and arithmetic. I had also learned other, more practical things: sewing, cooking, and other domestic skills which the nuns and missionaries hoped would turn girls like me into good farmers' wives. Sister Superior gave me singing lessons each day, and while the lessons were going on, I was as happy as I could be away from my village. (Moran, 1988, p. 48)

Economic advantages were not the only benefits women came to appreciate. Just as other mission schools were influential in forming the coming generations of Indian leadership (Gresko, 1986; Knight, 1978, pp. 252ff; Miller, 1987), so was Lejac instrumental in preparing Carrier women for community leadership. Proficiency in new domestic skills and use of new technology meant that women could diversify and increase their subsistence production. The most capable women were able to organize extended family productive units that, having collective claims to critical resources, provided the context for control over essential goods and shared labor (Fiske, 1989, chapter 6). Control over domestic resources not only afforded women considerable domestic authority and personal autonomy, it provided the material base for generating influence in larger kin networks, which are the primary political units of reserve communities (ibid.: chapters 6 and 8). As women drew on other skills essential to community well-being — for example, treatments learned while serving in the Lejac infirmary — they gained prestige and respect and widened their personal social networks within the community.

Although the Indian Act denied women direct participation in their band's affairs before 1951, women utilized their schooling to influence community decision making. In the 1940s, for example, former Lejac students organized local protests against the harsh conditions at Lejac. Carrier women refused to enroll their children and wrote letters to Ottawa demanding changes. During the same period, these same former students organized women's voluntary associations, which were initiated to provide assistance to young mothers and families experiencing personal crises. Soon, however, these leaders were able to draw upon association members to support their petitions to Ottawa for improved community facilities, to organize income-generating activities such as handicraft sales, and to assist their leaders in attending a range of conferences and meeting with other women's voluntary associations in Western Canada (Fiske, 1989, pp. 291-292). Here also, they drew on their student experiences, maintaining contact with former friends and classmates as they united in their social and political activities.

In the 1950s and 1960s, state intervention into their daily lives increased, and social and economic conditions deteriorated. Industrialization and steady, rapid increases in the white male population displaced Carrier men from the labor market. Incomes from trapping dove sharply. Simultaneously, the state assumed greater control over resource management, all too frequently to the Carriers' disadvantage (Fiske, 1989, pp. 97ff). Women broadened their community responsibilities. It was they, rather than men, who had the literacy essential to effective political action. Once again they lobbied and petitioned the government, this time struggling for improved housing, health services and social assistance.

When the federal government finally removed its ban against women's participation in community electoral politics in 1951, former students were well prepared. Not surprisingly, they were the first women to stand for and win elected office. Over time several have become prominent community leaders and remain active in interprovincial voluntary associations and regional tribal councils. When asked what Lejac did for her, one Carrier woman replied,

> I went on past Lejac, past school. . . . What did Lejac do for me? I became a chief and a professional person.

Paradoxes of Missionization

The irony of residential schooling for women can only be appreciated in the context of Catholic missionary activity and changes in Carrier society, which in themselves created paradoxical constraints and opportunities for women. Long before Lejac Residential School opened, the Carrier social organization had been influenced by Catholic notions of authority and patriarchy. As mentioned previously, the Oblates had sought to eliminate the Carrier matrilineal clan system, which had previously bound Carrier villages together in ties of marriage and trade, and to exclude women from positions of influence. The theocratic model of authority that they imposed upon the Carrier operated from the late nineteenth century through to the 1930s. It comprised a local hierarchy of chiefs, sub-chiefs, captains, watchmen, soldiers and councillors whose members the priests drew from established positions of clan and village leadership. The watchmen were the "eyes" of the council, the soldiers its policemen. The former reported misdemeanors to the soldiers, the latter brought the misdemeanants before the chiefs for discipline. Chiefs and sub-chiefs performed as lay magistrates, while the captains administered public whippings ordered by the chiefs. Although the matrilineal clan system did not disappear during this period, it lost significance. Because the potlatch (ceremonial property distributions) had been outlawed, succession to clan titles and noble positions could not be validated publicly by wealth distributions. Consequently, there was no public forum in which women could claim either traditional or Euro-Canadian positions of leadership.

Christian proselytizing eroded women's sources of autonomy and authority. As clan-based trade and exchange disintegrated, women lost opportunities for independently trading amongst themselves. Exclusion from public offices meant that women could not negotiate directly with Euro-Canadians regarding matters immediate to their domestic reponsibilities — for example, use of resource territories, access to medical care and reform of the education system. Women were even hampered in their efforts to indirectly influence community affairs. For not only did priests explicitly forbid women a public voice in church or village affairs, they ridiculed and berated men who took guidance from women (Fiske, 1981, pp. 17, 100).

The missionaries directed a great deal of energy toward the establishment of patriarchal nuclear family. Men were reminded that "in a family it is the father who is the master . . ." (Morice, 1930, p. 59). Priests demanded father-to-son inheritance of property and supported the government's outlawing of the potlatch on the grounds that sons were denied their rightful inheritance and entire communities were rendered destitute. Social stability was to be achieved through the eradication of matriliny, of so-called illicit sexual unions, and of marital dissolution. Watchmen and soldiers were expected to concentrate their attentions on informing against women who allegedly violated their marriage vows or entered into unsanctioned relationships with Euro-Canadians. Chiefs responded with harsh punishments, usually public floggings.

"Civilization" carried with it the domestication of women. The Oblates placed great emphasis on women remaining at home, busy with domestic tasks typical of the farm wife — which, in fact, corresponded to many of their aboriginal duties — sewing, cooking, food processing and child care. At the same time the priests attempted to restrict women's participation in such tasks as packing, trapping, guiding and land clearing, which took them away from the community. Priests also encouraged women to adopt European clothing and hair styles (Morice, 1930, p. 59).

The priests made further attempts to radically alter the behavior as well as the social importance of women. They attacked the practice of menstrual seclusion and where possible intervened to restrict or stop it. They denounced traditional healers as "witch doctors" and labelled elderly female practitioners "ancient hags." Where possible, however, the priests introduced midwife societies, with the expectation that, like the watchmen, midwives would report unsanctioned behavior of pregnant women to the church hierarchy or the priest (Cronin, 1960, p. 159). In conformity with Euro-Canadian gender roles, women's positions within the church organization were confined to informal auxiliary roles.

Carrier women resisted the missionaries' forceful efforts to eradicate traditional practices and to transform the organization of the domestic economy from extended family productive units to autonomous, male-headed nuclear family productive units. They continued to form co-operative productive units comprising female kin, over which senior women exercised authority. Female kin, furthermore, shared the burden of child care, enabling mothers to travel to their fishing sites or to migrate to agricultural jobs at considerable distance from their homes. Ironically, the priests' emphasis on maternal responsibilities served to enhance rather than diminish women's domestic and community leadership. Because men were frequently working away from home, women had ample opportunity to exercise authority beyond their own domestic units. As suggested above, women soon recognized that in order to provide for their families and to prevent infant mortality, political action was necessary. Improved material conditions — for example, a safe water supply, electric power or adequate housing — could only be obtained with aid from the federal government. Whether organized as a midwife society, church auxiliary, or a state-sponsored community service group, voluntary associations became critical to their political activism. Rather than remaining a subordinate church group, as the Oblates had envisioned, in at least two Carrier communities women's auxiliaries provided a forum for articulating grievances, making demands and influencing political action (Fiske, 1981, p. 100).

Women justify these actions on two grounds. First, some claim that aboriginal social organization was either matriarchal or egalitarian (Fiske, 1989, p. 128). Second, echoing Catholic ideals of motherhood, women argue that in order to discharge their parental obligations they must pursue explicit political strategies; failure to do so is failure to be responsible mothers and grandmothers (ibid., p. 292). In short, the interlocking processes of missionization and colonization created paradoxical conditions that unintentionally offered women opportunities to subvert the aims of the priests. Having learned English and having become literate, competent women emerged from Lejac with the knowledge essential for political action. Notwithstanding its patriarchal practice and its harsh routine, Lejac enabled some women to achieve positions of community leadership. As one former student stated,

My sister-in-law runs the reserve. She can do that with her education.

Conclusion

The implicit goals of colonial education are to persuade or compel a subordinate population to adapt to the dominant society and in so doing to acquiesce to the political and economic policies of the colonizers. The practices of colonial education are harsh, unremittingly sexist and unilaterally imposed without consultation with the parents or the community leaders. As is well-known, the consequences of colonial education have been unquestionably traumatic for many, perhaps the vast majority, of residential students. Nonetheless, Indian residential schools not only failed to assimilate aboriginal peoples into Euro-Canadian society, they unintentionally provided the foundation upon which aboriginal leaders successfully built structures of resistance. In the final analysis, the missionaries' forceful interventions into Carrier society did not facilitate the anticipated social changes. Carrier women did not accept Euro-Canadian models of patriarchal authority, nor did they accommodate themselves to the state's assimilatory policies. Women resisted efforts to undermine their social position and to restrict their personal autonomy. Women (and men) selectively utilized novel skills and knowledge beneficial to themselves; in so doing, they effectively subverted the missionaries' intentions by broadening their economic strategies and by developing sophisticated political responses, which to a large measure were spearheaded by a schooled female leadership.

Notes

[1]This paper was originally prepared for the National Symposium on Aboriginal Women of Canada: Past, Present and Future, Lethbridge, Alberta, 19-21 October 1989. I appreciate the editorial assistance of Patricia Chuchryk in revising the paper for publication. It will also appear in *Women of the First Nations of Canada,* a collection of papers presented at the National Symposium.

[2]According to Knight (1978, p. 71), Indian farming was already in a decline before Lejac School opened. Large-scale commercial farming and ranching in central British Columbia was constrained by the harsh climate and a lack of transportation and markets. Subsistence farming was far more significant than cash crops which failed to offer a secure source of earnings.

References

Altbach, P.G., & Kelly, Gail P. (Eds.). (1978). *Education and colonialism.* New York: Longman.

Balikci, A. (1963). *Vunta Kutchin Social change: A study of the people of Old Crow.* Yukon Territory: Department of Indian Affairs/Ottawa: Northern Co-ordination and Research Centre.

Cronin, K. (1960). *The cross in the wilderness.* Vancouver, BC: Mitchell Press.

Dunlop, H., O.M.I. (1946). The Indian residential school. *Oblate Missions II* (8), 16-17.

Fisher, R. (1977). *Contact and conflict: Indian-European relations in British Columbia, 1877-1890.* Vancouver: University of British Columbia Press.

Fiske, J.A. (1981). *And then we prayed again: Carrier women, colonialism, and mission schools.* Unpublished master's thesis, University of British Columbia.

Fiske, J.A. (1989). *Gender and politics in a Carrier Indian community.* Unpublished doctoral dissertation, University of British Columbia.

Freire, P. (1970). *Pedagogy of the oppressed (Myra Bergman Ramos, Trans.). New York: Herder and Herder.*

Gresko, J. (1986). Creating little dominions within the Dominion: Early Catholic Indian schools in Saskatchewan and British Columbia. In Jean Barman, Yvonne Hébert, & Don McCaskill (Eds.), *Indian education in Canada: Vol. I. The legacy* (pp. 88-109). Vancouver: University of British Columbia Press.

Haig-Brown, C. (1988). *Resistance and renewal: Surviving the Indian residential school.* Vancouver, BC: The Tillacum Library.

Iverson, K. (1978). Civilization and assimilation in the colonized schooling of Native Americans. In Philip G. Altbach & Gail Kelly (Eds.), *Education and colonialism* (pp. 149-180). New York: Longman.

King, A.R. (1967). *The school at Mopass: A problem of identity.* New York: Holt Rinehart and Winston.

Knight, R. (1978). *Indians at work: An informal history of Native Indian labour in British Columbia, 1858-1930.* Vancouver: New Star Books.

Miller, J.R. (1987). The irony of residential schooling. *Canadian Journal of Native Education, 14*(2), 3-13.

Moran, B. (1988). *Stoney Creek Woman: Sai'k'uz Ts'eke/The story of Mary John.* Vancouver, BC: The Tillacum Library.

Morice, Rev. Father A.G. O.M.I. (1902). *A first collection of minor essays, Mostly anthropological.* Quesnel, BC: Stuart Lake Mission.

Morice, Rev. Father A.G., O.M.I. (1930). *Fifty years in western Canada: The abridged memories of Father A.G. Morice, O.M.I.* Toronto: Ryerson Press.

Oblate Fathers, Archives of the Oblate Fathers, St. Paul's Province. Microfilm: Provincial Archives of British Columbia.

Oblate Fathers, Records of the Oblate Missions of British Columbia from Oblate Historical Archives St. Peter's Province Holy Rosary Scholasticate, Microfilm. Ottawa: University of British Columbia Library, AWI R4664.

Patterson, E.P. (1972). *The Canadian Indian: A history since 1500.* Toronto: Collier MacMillan.

Public Archives of Canada [PAC]. (1938). *Industrial school files annual report.* Records Relating to Indian Affairs RG 10. Vol. 6443, File 881-1, part 1, September 30th.

6

Adolescent Females and Computers: Real and Perceived Barriers

Betty Collis

Many Canadian educators believe that schools have a responsibility to prepare students for the very near future in which technology, work, and learning will be inextricably intertwined (Canadian Advisory Council on the Status of Women, 1982). Computers in particular have become commonplace in schools throughout Canada and the United States (Becker, 1986; British Columbia Ministry of Education, 1985), and there is a general expectation that some sort of competency with computers is a valuable and even necessary component of the contemporary school experience (Romaniuk, 1986). However, ever since microcomputer use first began to become popular in schools during the early 1980s, more males than females have been involved with their study and use (Phi Delta Kappa, 1983) and furthermore, there are both quantitative and qualitative differences in male and female students' access to computer opportunities (Schubert, 1986). This paper documents these differences and then presents a conceptual model that describes some of the barriers, both external and self-generated, that underlie the situation. The paper concludes with a discussion of intervention strategies whose aims are to reduce the incidence and influence of barriers that currently impede adolescent females' involvement with computers and technology.

Gender Differences in Access to Computers

School Participation

Computer use in schools is strongly established throughout Canada, with virtually all secondary schools and the majority of elementary schools having installed computers by 1985 (B.C. Ministry of Education, 1985). Extensive school-computer initiatives have been made in Ontario (Smith, 1986), Manitoba (Gonzalez, 1986), and Alberta (Romaniuk, 1986). As of March 1987, Alberta had the fifth lowest student-computer ratio of any province in Canada or state in the U.S. and the second greatest number of computers in schools, exceeded only by California (Yocam, 1987). However, despite the number of computers in schools, there is consistent evidence that females make less use of the technology than do males. This is particularly so with regard to participation in computer science courses at the secondary level (Becker, 1987; Lockheed, 1985; Smith, 1985). National assessments in the United States compared male and female enrolment in secondary school computer programming courses in 1978 and 1981-82. These assessments found approximately twice as many males as females enrolled in these courses in 1978, a difference that remained constant during the 4-year time period through 1982 (Anderson, Welch, & Harris, 1984). Although "computer programming" has come to be replaced by "computer science" as a senior secondary elective course, the same disproportionate enrollments of males and females continue to be documented (Anderson, Klassen, Krohn, & Smith-Cunnien, 1982; Lipkin & McCormick, 1985; Newsnotes, 1985a). If completion of secondary school computer science courses increases the likelihood of continued work with computers after secondary school, whether in university, other postsecondary training, or the workplace, then the long-range implications of male-dominated computer science courses in secondary school may be substantial.

These gender differences in participation are also seen at the junior secondary level, although the ability to make choices about participation is limited in these grades (Hess & Miura, 1985; Revelle, Honey, Amsel, Schauble, & Levine, 1984). Male to female ratios in these studies typically range from 5:1 to 2:1. Finally, in elementary grades, several studies also report significant gender differences in "computer class participation" (Fetler, 1985; Sanders, 1984). Teachers at all grade levels identify boys, rather than girls, as the students most actively involved with school computer use (Becker, 1987). For example, when teachers in a national U.S. survey were asked to indicate the sex of the three students most involved with computers in their schools, 74 percent of the elementary teachers and 78 percent of the secondary teachers cited a male as the first student named and overall indicated males twice as often as females.

Extracurricular Usage

Gender differences in extracurricular computer use are also well established (Lockheed, 1985). McKelvey (1984) notes in a study done in several Ontario schools that ten times as many males as females used computers during extracurricular time. Becker (1987) notes that boys outnumber girls 3 to 1 where computers are used either before or after school, and, at the "typical middle school" in a 1985 national survey of 2 331 U.S. schools, only 15 percent of the extracurricular users of computers are females. Males consistently outnumber females in enrollment at computer camps and at computer-related courses outside of school and, as costs and age increase, the proportion of females decreases (Miura & Hess, 1983). Although video game arcades have declined in popularity, they were and continue to be strongly identified with male users (Kiesler, Sproull, & Eccles, 1983). Finally, home use of computers is reported to be more likely for adolescent males than for adolescent females (Collis, 1984/86; Revelle et al., 1984).

Attitudes

Gender differences in adolescents' attitudes toward computers have been reported in a number of studies, with adolescent males consistently more positive than adolescent females (Collis, 1984/86; Lockheed, 1985;

Temple, 1986; Wilder, Mackie, & Cooper, 1985). Collis interviewed 156 Grade 8 and Grade 12 students to develop an item pool of statements relating to attitudes toward computers and computer users. The instrument developed from this item pool was subsequently administered to nearly 3 000 Grade 8 and Grade 12 students, the majority of the populations for those grades in two British Columbia school districts. Results from this study and subsequent replications of the study include the following:

1. Sex differences in attitudes toward computers are strongly established by Grade 8.

2. Males are consistently more positive about using computers than are females, and more likely to express interest in and pleasure in using a computer.

3. Males and females agree that males are most likely to be the computer users in their households, and that "mother" is the least likely person in their households to have any interest in using a computer.

4. Females are more likely than males to associate social and academic stereotypes with computer users. (Collis, 1985c)

Why Be Concerned About These Differences in Attitude and Participation?

It is not important or feasible that all adolescents have positive attitudes toward technology or participate in computer science courses in secondary school. If females were underrepresented in computer classes and in informal experiences with computers because of disinterest based on thoughtful decision-making processes on their parts, the situation might not be of serious concern to educators, especially now that early predictions of school computer literacy experiences being critical to future job prospects have been qualified (Levin & Rumberger, 1986). However, a number of research studies indicate that inequities and barriers to access, not thoughtful, well-informed decisions are involved. Females stay away from computers because their options become prematurely limited, either by themselves or by others.

They believe that working with these machines is appropriate for bright males, but not for them, that they indeed are "not cut out for computers," and that efforts they might make would be repaid with both social embarrassment and personal frustration. . . . Females expect they won't do well, won't enjoy the [computer] contact, and have no need for it (Collis, 1985b, pp. 180-81).

As personal expectations frequently become self-fulfilling, it is critical that educators respond to any influences that may relate to the stunting of academic achievement and self-esteem (Sadker, 1975). What are the influences that serve to erect or reinforce barriers between many adolescent females and constructive computer experiences in schools?

A Conceptual Model to Predict Adolescent Females' Computer Access

Models to Predict Participation

A number of models have been developed to predict females' participation and achievement in various school subjects (Armstrong & Price, 1982; Fennema, 1980; Marsh, Smith, & Barnes, 1985). All include perceptions of self-efficacy and personal relevance as well as perceived expectations of significant others as predictors. Some researchers have attempted to build a prediction model of influences on females' utilization of school computer resources (Dasho & Beckum, 1983; Lockheed, Thorpe, Brooks-Gunn, Casserly, & McAloon, 1985; Sanders, 1984; Schubert, 1986).

Dasho and Beckum (1983) identify five "problem areas" that influence secondary school students' computer access: (1) attitude-related, including motivational and self-concept variables; (2) software-related; (3) hardware access and "human interface" problems; (4) academic, including interest in and success in certain computer-related courses; and (5) social, including perceptions of peers and of home environments. Schubert (1986) lists (1) school policy, (2) software selection, (3) student encouragement, and (4) the role of family and peers as critical components. Lockheed and her colleagues (1985) have developed a complicated causal model which includes the interactions between task characteristics; cultural milieu; teacher, student, and family characteristics; and various domains of expectations (p. 24).

Based on analyses such as these, we propose a model with three dimensions as an efficient predictor of adolescents' access to constructive experiences with computers. The model has potential predictive and explanatory value and can also serve as a framework for intervention strategies. A study involving researchers from British Columbia, Alberta, and Quebec is being conducted (1986-87) to test the model with data from adolescents in rural, isolated, and urban areas in various geographic regions of Canada. As of March 1987, over 3 000 Grade 11 students from eight urban areas in Canada have been involved in the study. The three dimensions of the predictive model may be described as: (1) school policies and practices, (2) social expectations, and (3) personal factors. The dimensions, while distinct, are not independent.

1. School-Related Policies and Practices

(a) Policies relating to academic pre- and corequisites.

The majority of utilization of secondary school computer resources occurs within the context of computer science or computer studies courses (Becker, 1983, 1986). These course frequently require mathematics pre-requisites, have a mathematical orientation, and are taught by instructors who were originally mathematics teachers at the school (Lockheed & Frakt, 1984; Sanders, 1984). Little opportunity exists to use school computers outside of this mathematically oriented computer science framework, although business education students may have their own lab (Becker, 1983). More recent U.S. data show only 13 percent of secondary school computer use occurs outside computer science courses or business education courses (Becker, 1987). Data from a British Columbia survey show the same pattern of limited opportunities for computer use in secondary schools (Flodin, 1984), with students' choices typically limited to computer science (with senior mathematics pre- or corequisites) or word processing in business education courses.

Becker's surveys also document a revealing statistic. As secondary schools acquire more computer equipment, the new resources are typically not used to expand access to more students but instead to provide more extensive access to those already involved in computer science courses. In terms of inequities and barriers, this represents a systematic exclusivity that focuses computer opportunities on capable mathematics students. This in turn serves to disfranchise the majority of students for whom mathematics is neither a strong subject nor an interest, and this group includes proportionately more females than males (Fennema, 1980). Thus, the typical secondary school practice of allowing computer science teachers and courses to dominate use of school computers and to insist on mathematics prerequisites for access to these courses is a real and effective barrier to computer use for many females.

(b) Practices relating to a limited view of computer use.

Computer science and studies courses involve a narrow view of computer applications relative to the many valuable uses that can be made of computers in the secondary school setting. Computers can be used in English classes to support composition and as tools for functional writing done in a social context (Daiute, 1985). They can be used in science classes as data-capturing and display tools and as vehicles for the presentation of various types of simulations of scientific processes (Gredler, 1986; Lamk 1984-85). They can be also used in social studies as tools for the accessing and organizing of information and the display of information in graphic form (Parker, 1986) and in art and music courses for the support of new types of creative expression (Lamb, 1982). These and many other applications are available now for the secondary school. They do not require any substantial infusion of new equipment or reorganization of instructional timetables. Their incorporation has the potential of providing interesting and relevant computer experiences for a much larger group of students than those who are now interested in computer science courses (Sanders, 1985). In particular, word processing in an academic context rather than in the vocational context of business education courses has special potential for female students, in that females are frequently more self-confident about themselves as writers and communicators in English courses than they are of themselves as participants in mathematics, science, and computer courses (Collis & Ollila, 1986a; Lockheed & Frakt, 1984). However, the typical secondary

English, science, social studies, or mathematics teacher makes no use at all of school computer resources (Becker, 1986; Lehman, 1985; Newsnotes, 1985b). Thus, by school practice, probably based on a lack of awareness of the breadth of instructional uses of computers possible in all subject areas, the majority of adolescent females are never given any opportunity to use school computers in instructional settings where they could develop their awareness of the computer as a relevant tool, especially for language-related tasks. Through this omission, adolescent females as well as males are deprived of access to many valuable aspects of constructive computer usage.

(c) School policies with regard to the location of computers.

The most typical pattern for hardware organization in secondary schools is to cluster the majority of the school machines in a single computer laboratory (Becker, 1983, 1986). This may inadvertently result in the creation of more barriers for female students. The secondary school computer lab has become associated with males (Collis, 1985a; Lockheed & Frakt, 1984). Computer labs frequently become locker-room-type environments that are unattractive to most females (and to many male students as well) (Lockheed & Frakt, 1984; Smith, 1985). In addition, computer labs often become the responsibility of the computer science teacher, whose students absorb as much access time as they are allowed (Becker, 1986). Together, the computer teachers and students may be perceived as an elite group around whom others are not comfortable (Matson, 1985). Schools could mitigate many of the problems associated with computer laboratories by rotating access to the lab and responsibility for the lab among teachers in different disciplines or by limiting the lab access of computer science students to certain time blocks. However, these strategies rarely occur. School policy, or lack of policy, with regard to location of and access to hardware perpetuates a major barrier to equitable and relevant computer usage for females.

(d) School practices with regard to the organization of learning.

A final area in which school practices fail to relate to the interests and preferences of many females students involves the types of learning environments usually organized for computer use and computer-related assignments. Computer-related assignments frequently involve programming or program design done independently by each student as individual keyboarding practice in business education word-processing courses. However, there is evidence that many female students prefer cooperative learning situations to individual or competitive situations (Johnson, Johnson, & Stann, 1986; Peterson & Fennema, 1985). Johnson, Johnson, and Stanne assigned Grade 8 social studies students to three groups, all of which made use of a computer simulation within the context of a two-week unit on map reading and navigation. One group was told to work cooperatively, with their final grades based on an average of all group members' marks. Another group was told they would be graded on a competitive, norm-referenced basis within their group. The third group was told their grades would reflect only their individual work and would be based on criterion-referenced standards rather than through any sort of comparison with their classmates. Males in the competitive condition expressed a more positive attitude toward computers after the treatments were concluded than did any of the other male or female groups. However, females in the cooperative condition accomplished more work and achieved higher scores than did females in the competitive and individualistic conditions, and students in the cooperative condition (male and female) completed more work and correctly answered more items than did students in the other two groups. In addition, students in the cooperative condition nominated more female classmates as desired future work partners than did students working competitively or individually. Students in the individualistic condition ended the experience "liking computers" less than any other students. These results suggest that cooperative learning experiences involving computers have both social and achievement-oriented benefits for adolescents and may "equalize status and respect" for female group members (Johnson, Johnson, & Stann, 1986, p. 390). Thus, the typical secondary school practice of expecting students to work individually at computer terminals does not exploit a learning environment that is attractive to and productive for many female students.

2. Social Expectations

(a) Computers and masculine associations.

It is well established that gender-typed labeling of school subjects is related to students' achievement and participation in those subjects (Dwyer, 1973). Furthermore, expectancy of success in a task is also related to an individual's perception of its gender-appropriateness for him- or herself (Stein, Phly, & Mueller, 1971). Because of this, it is particularly significant that the computer domain is strongly identified as being a masculine one. Collis and Ollila (1986b) found that 3- to 6-year-old children already associate computers with boys rather than with girls. Wilder, Macker, and Cooper (1985) and Swoope and Johnson (1985) also found that young children perceive computers as more appropriate for boys than for girls and that this impression increases with age.

The computer-male association is reinforced by the marketplace. Sanders (1985) examined large-circulation computer magazines and found males to dominate the articles and illustrations. Ware and Stuck (1984) did a similar analysis with similar results. Men appeared twice as often as women and were overrepresented as managers and experts, whereas women were overrepresented as clerical workers or observers. It is not surprising that magazines display this type of gender difference with regard to computer use in the workplace. Men are more likely than women to be involved in computer use at a managerial or expert level, while females who use computers at work are more likely to be using them under someone's direction and for clerical tasks (Bodger, 1985; Stanton, 1983). In the home, males are the predominant computer users (Collis, 1984/86; Sanders, 1985) and the Director of Educational Marketing for Apple Computers was quoted in 1985 as saying, "The buyers of Apple computers are 98% male. We do not feel that women represent any great untapped audience" (Sanders, 1985, p. 23).

Secondary students have absorbed this message of computers being in a male domain (Collis, 1985a; Hawkins, 1985). Collis found female students to be significantly more likely than males to endorse a stereotype of a computer user as being a bright male who likes mathematics but is not particularly attractive socially. Lockheed and Frakt (1984) are among many others who document a male association attached to computer use for secondary school students. This gender typing is likely to erect or maintain a barrier that will inhibit the development of computer-related competences in many adolescent females.

3. Personal Factors

(a) Lower self-confidence.

It has long been documented that females express lower levels of self-confidence than do their male peers. Cross noted in 1968 that women are less likely than men to believe they have the ability to do university work even though they earn better secondary school grades. A survey of graduate students in science, engineering, and medicine at Standard University ("High Test Scores," 1984) showed that even the women in this group were "less self-confident and assertive than their male counterparts." March, Smith, and Barnes (1985) found females to have significantly lower self-concepts in mathematics than did their male peers, even though the females had significantly higher achievement levels in mathematics than the males.

With this inclination to express lower levels of self-confidence, it is not surprising that females have been found to be significantly less self-confident than their male classmates with respect to computer use (Collis, 1985c). Heightened anxiety level can create another barrier to adolescent females' constructive involvement with computers.

(b) "We can, but I can't."

There is an interesting extension that can be made to the examination of females' self-confidence with regard to computer use. The only computer-attitude items on Collis' survey (1984/86) to which females responded in a more positive manner than did males were those which described the ability of "women in general" to be competent computer users. Females in both Grade 8 and Grade 12 strongly agreed with all statements about females in the abstract being as computer-competent as men (while males were inclined to disagree). However, as soon as the females were asked to assess their own competencies and self-confidence with regard to computers, they shifted in their attitudes. The typical adolescent female respondent felt that women in general are capable, but that she as an individual is not likely to be a competent computer user. This "We can, but I can't" paradox may represent the collision of two different sets of cultural messages and may have psychosocial implications for contemporary adolescent females that range well beyond computer work (Collis, 1985c).

A similar finding has recently appeared in a Labour Canada survey of the career aspirations of Canadian school children (Ellis & Sayer, 1986). Ellis and Sayer found a definite trend among the Grade 1 to 8 students they surveyed. The students saw the development of a greater participation rate of women in traditionally male careers developing (interestingly, there was no similar trend for men toward traditional "women's work"). However, when girls were asked to indicate their own career aspirations, they tended to choose "women's jobs" rather than predominantly masculine professions.

> It was as though girls did not apply to themselves their general belief in the equality of the sexes. Many of them seemed to be saying, "Yes, women can become doctors, but I expect to be a nurse." (p. 55)

This "We can, but I can't" paradox has the potential to be a formidable barrier to equitable computer access for adolescent females, no less powerful because it is self-imposed.

(c) Perceived irrelevance of computer work.

Computer activities in schools may have little appeal to females because the females do not see any personal relevance for computers in their own lives, present or future (Lockheed & Frakt, 1984). One major reason for this may be that adolescent females still are less career-motivated than males (Tobin & Fox, 1980) and form career goals at a later age than males (Cooper & Robinson, 1985), and as a result, they may be less concerned about the importance of developing a strong base for further professional or vocational growth. Ellis and Sayer note that girls, at least in their Canadian sample, still "picture their adulthood as consisting of being mothers with small children" (1986, p. 56) and further assume they will have husbands to support them.

> Even Grade 8 girls of 14 years of age did not consider the possibility of their having to be in remunerative employment to support themselves or their children. There do not seem to be any unmarried mothers, deserted wives, widows, or divorcees among the imaginary women Canadian schoolgirls expect to become. (Ellis & Sayer, 1986, p. 56)

This "Cinderella" perspective (Dowling, 1981) has the potential to translate itself into a major barrier, a barrier of disinterest that can thwart motivated effort with computers in schools for adolescent females — "If it's for boys, anyway, and isn't very interesting, and I'm never going to need it, why bother?" Until girls realize that they will in all probability have to be breadwinners, not just "cakewinners," it is likely that more males than females will continue to involve themselves in computer opportunities in secondary school.

Recommendations

Intervention Strategies

As of 1986, there are at least seven large-scale intervention programs focusing on the reduction of barriers to females' utilization of school computers (Schuber, 1986). All of these programs are based in the U.S. Most involve materials for parents and teachers as well as descriptions of computer activities that are felt to be attractive to both boys and girls. However, similar intervention programs for females in mathematics and science have long been in existence (Ekstrom, 1979) but have apparently not made large-scale impacts on female interest and participation in these subjects. It is difficult to expect isolated intervention programs to have any sustained impact on the formidable assortment of barriers between secondary school females and equitable, constructive use of school technology. However, some recommendations do seem important.

1. Expand computer use in secondary schools beyond the computer science/computer studies courses so that *every* student has repeated opportunities to use computers as appropriate tools within the context of his or her ongoing school activities. Emphasize language and communication applications in order to capitalize on the positive attitudes females have about themselves and language (Collis & Ollila, 1986a). Build this orientation into teacher-training programs and teacher inservice so that teachers see the computer as a tool within a curriculum context rather than as an object of study in itself (Salomon, 1987).

2. Monitor the computer laboratory environments in schools so that all students have equitable access to the resources even if this means that some computer science students will have less access than they currently do. "Let the herd instinct work for you" (Sanders, 1985) by structuring cooperative computer activities for pairs or groups of students.

3. Counsel adolescent females to have more realistic expectations of the importance that work is likely to have for them in their adult lives. Articulate and discuss the "We can, but I can't" paradox and the "Cinderella" expectation and help the students identify the impact of these psychological constructs on their current and future academic decisions.

This last point is especially important. We as educators must share some of the responsibility for the barriers of perceived inadequacy that thwart female students. We have let male mathematics teachers become the computer educators in our secondary schools. We have allowed the content of school computer experiences to be weighted with mathematics and have minimized or ignored the central importance of language and communication in professional computer use in the workplace. We have allowed a few male students to dominate the school computers. More fundamentally, we have allowed females to grow up feeling they are inadequate. We have not reacted when we see them limit their options by erecting barriers marked "appropriate behavior — for a girl" and "not appropriate — for a girl." We have not communicated to them the importance of work, with or without a technological component, to their future financial and psychological health, nor have we communicated the extent to which the level of this health will relate to their ability to feel self-confident and productive in a technologically dominated society.

Removing some of the barriers to appropriate technological interaction will be a major challenge for both educators and students. Not removing them may lead to results too serious to ignore.

References

Anderson, R.E., D.L. Klassen, K.R. Krohn, & P. Smith-Connien. (1982). *Assessing computer literacy* (Publication 503). St. Paul, MN: MECC.

Anderson, R.E., W.W. Welch, & L.J. Harris. (1984). "Inequities in opportunities for computer literacy." *The Computing Teacher,* 11, 8:10-12.

Armstrong, J.M., & R.A. Price. (1982). "Correlates and predictors of women's mathematics participation." *Journal for Research in Mathematics Associations,* 13:99-107.

Becker, H.J. (1983). *School uses of computers. Reports from a national survey* (Issue 2). Baltimore, MD: The Johns Hopkins University, Center for Social Organization of Schools.

Becker, H.J. (1986). *Instructional uses of school computers.* (Issue No. 1.) Baltimore, MD:The Johns Hopkins University, Center for Social Organization of Schools.

Becker, H.J. (1987, February). "Using computers for instruction." *Byte,* pp. 149-62.

Bodger, C. (1985, January). "Sixth annual salary survey: Who does what and for how much." *Working Women,* pp. 65-72.

British Columbia Ministry of Education. (1985). *Computers in Canadian education.* (Research Report) Victoria, BC.: Author.

Canadian Advisory Council on the Status of Women. (1982). *Microtechnology and employment: issues of concern to women.* Ottawa: Author.

Collis, B.A. (1985a). "Psychosocial implications of sex differences in attitudes toward computers." *International Journal of Women's Studies,* 8, 3:207-13.

Collis, B.A. (1985b). "Reflections on inequities in computer education: Do the rich get richer?" *Education & Computing,* 1:179-86.

Collis, B.A. (1985c). "Sex differences in secondary school students' attitudes toward computers." *The Computing Teacher,* 12, 7:33-36.

Collis, B.A. (1986). "The development of an instrument to measure attitudes of secondary school males and females toward computers." Doctoral dissertation, University of Victora (1984). *Dissertation Abstracts International,* 46, 8:2274-A.

Collis, B.A., & L. Ollila. (1986a). "An examination of sex differences in secondary school student's attitudes toward writing and toward computers." *The Alberta Journal of Educational Research,* 32, 4:297-306.

Collis, B.A., & L. Ollila. (1986b). June. "Gender stereotypes about reading, writing, and computer use in preschool, kindergarten, and Grade 1 boys and girls." Paper presented at the Annual Meeting of the Canadian Society for Studies in Education, Winnipeg, Manitoba.

Cooper, S.E., & D.A.G. Robinson. (1985). "Students in highly technical careers: Sex differences in interpersonal characteristics and vocational identity." *Journal of College Student Personnel,* 26:215-19.

Cross, P. (1968). "College women: A research description." *Journal of the National Association of Women Deans and Counselors,* 32, 1:12-21.

Daiute, C. (1985). *Writing and computers.* Reading, MA: Addison-Wesley Publishing Co.

Dasho, S.J., & L.C. Beckum. (1983, April). "Microcomputers and educational equity: The promise and the peril." Paper presented at the Annual Meeting of the American Educational Research Association, Montreal.

Dowling, C. (1981). *The cinderella complex: Women's hidden fear of independence.* New York: Simon & Schuster, Inc.

Dwyer, C.A. (1973). "Influence of students' sex role standards on reading and arithmetic achievement." *Journal of Educational Psychology,* 66:811-16.

Ekstrom, R.B. (1979). "Intervention strategies to reduce sex-role stereotyping in education." In O. Hartnett, G. Boder, & M. Fuller, eds., *Sex-role Stereotyping.* London: Tavistock Publishing.

Ellis, D., & L. Sayer. (1986). *When I group up: career expectations and aspirations of Canadian school children.* Ottawa, ON: Minister of Labour, Government of Canada.

Fennema, E. (1980). "Sex-related differences in mathematics achievement: Where and why?" In L.H. Fox, L. Brody, & D. Tobin, eds., *Women and the Mathematical Mystique.* Baltimore, MD: The John Hopkins University Press, pp. 76-93.

Fetler, M. (1985). "Computer literacy in California schools." *Sex Roles,* 13, 3/4: 181-92.

Flodin, N. (1984). *British Columbia public schools microcomputer inservice survey.* Victoria, BC: British Columbia Teachers' Federation.

Gonzalez, E. (1986, May). "Manitoba strategy to stimulate the implementation of educational technologies." Paper presented at the Fifth Canadian Symposium on Instructional Technology, Ottawa.

Gredler, M.B. (1986). "A taxonomy of computer simulations." *Educational Technology,* 26, 4:7-12.

Hawkins, J. (1985). "Computers and girls: Rethinking the issues." *Sex Roles,* 13, 3/4:163-80.

Hess, E.S., & I. Miura. (1985). "Gender differences in enrollment in computer camps and classes. The extracurricular acquisition of computer training." *Sex Roles*, 13, 3/4:193-203.

"High test Scores don't bring confidence, automatic success." (1984, November). *The Stanford Observer*, p. 3.

Johnson, R.T., D.W. Johnson, & M.B. Stanne. (1986). "Comparison of computer-assisted cooperative, competitive, and individualistic learning." *American Educational Research Journal*, 23, 3:382-92.

Kiesler, S., L. Sproull, & J. Eccles. (1983, March). "Second-class citizens?" *Psychology Today*, pp. 19-26.

Lam, T. (1984-85). "Probing microcomputer-based laboratories." *Hands On!*, 8, 1:1, 4-5.

Lamb, M. (1982). "An interactive graphical modeling game for teaching musical concepts." *Journal of Computer-Based Instruction*, 9, 2:59-63.

Lehman, J.R. (1985). "Survey of microcomputer use in the science classroom." *School Science and Mathematics*, 85, 7:578-83.

Levin, H.M., & R.W. Rumberger. (1986). *Education and training needs for using computers in small businesses.* (Report 86-SEP1-7). Stanford, CA: Stanford University, Stanford Education Policy Institute.

Lipkin, J., & L.M. McCormick. (1985). "Sex bias at the computer terminal: How schools program girls." *The Monitor*, 24:14-17.

Lockheed, M.E. (1985). "Women, girls, and computers: A first look at the evidence." *Sex Roles*, 13, 3/4:115-22.

Lockheed, M., & S. Frakt. (1984). "Sex equity: Increasing girls' use of computers." *The Computing Teacher*, 11, 8:16-18.

Lockheed, M.E., M. Thorpe, J. Brooks-Gunn, P. Casserly, & A. McAloon. (1985). *Sex and ethnic differences in middle school mathematics, science, and computer science: What do we know?* Princeton, NJ: Educational Testing Service.

Marsh, H.W., I.D. Smith, & J. Barnes. (1985). "Multidimensional self-concepts: Relations with sex and academic achievement." *Journal of Educational Psychology*, 77, 5:581-96.

Matson, M. (1985). "Networks? Maybe. Computer rooms? No." *Micro-scope*, 16: 8-10.

McKelvey, G. (1984, January 25). Cited in: *Education Daily*, 17, 17:6.

Miura, I., & R.D., Hess. (1983). "Sex differences in computer access, interest, and usage." Paper presented at the Annual Meeting of the American Psychological Association, Anaheim, CA.

Newsnotes. (1985a). "Problems of equity in high school programming courses." *Phi Delta Kappa*, 66, 7:515-16.

Newsnotes. (1985b). "School use of micros spreading out of math classes." *Phi Delta Kappa*, 67, 2:165-66.

Parker, J. (1986). "Tools for thought." *The Computing Teacher,* 14, 2:21-23.

Peterson, P.L., & E. Fennema. (1985). "Effective teaching, student engagement in classroom activities, and sex-related differences in learning mathematics." *American Educational Research Journal,* 22, 3:309-35.

Phi Delta Kappa. (1983). "Sex differences in computer training: Why do boys outnumber girls?" *Research Bulletin.* Bloomington, IN: Phi Delta Kappa Center on Evaluation, Development, and Research.

Revelle, G., M. Honey, E. Amsel, L. Schauble, & G. Levine. (1984 April). "Sex differences in the use of computers." Paper presented at the Annual Meeting of the American Educational Research Association, New Orleans, LA.

Romaniuk, G., ed. (1986). *Computers in schools: A strategic planning symposium.* Edmonton, Alberta: Alberta Education.

Sadker, M. (1975). "Sexism in schools." *Journal of Teacher Education,* 26, 4:317-22.

Salomon, G. (1987, February). "Computers in education: Add-ons or levers?" Paper presented to the meeting of the International Committee of the International Council for Computers in Education, Tel Aviv, Israel.

Sanders, J.S. (1984). "The computer: Male, female, or androgynous?" *The Computing Teacher,* 11, 8:31-34.

Sanders, J.S. (1985). "Making the computer neutral." *The Computing Teacher,* 12, 7:23-32.

Schubert, J.G. (1986). "Gender equity in computer learning." *Theory Into Practice,* 25, 4:267-75.

Smith, L.R. (1986, May). "The Ontario initiatives introducing microtechnology to schools." Paper presented at the Fifth Canadian Symposium on Instructional Technology, Ottawa.

Smith, R.A. (1985). "Women, education, and computers." *The Monitor,* 24, 5/6:10, 27.

Stanton, P. (1983). *Women in the labour market: 1983.* Victoria: British Columbia Ministry of Labour.

Stein, A.H., S.R. Pohly, & E. Mueller. (1971). "The influence of masculine, feminine, and neutral tasks on children's achievement behavior, expectancies of success, and attainment values." *Child Development,* 42:195-207.

Swoope, K., & C.S. Johnson. (1985, April). "Students' perceptions of interest in using computers: Boys, girls, or both?" Paper presented at the Annual Meeting of the American Educational Research Association, Chicago.

Temple, L.E. (1986). *Gender differences in attitudes toward computers.* Unpublished master's thesis, University of Winnipeg, Winnipeg, Manitoba.

Tobin, D., & L.H. Fox. (1980). "Career interests and career education: A key to change." In L.H. Fox, L. Brody, & D. Tobin, eds., women and the mathematical Mystique. Baltimore, MD: The Johns Hopkins University Press, pp. 179-92.

Ware, M.C., & M.F. Stuck. (1984). "Sex-role messages vis-à-vis microcomputer use: A look at the pictures." Paper presented at the Annual Meeting of the American Educational Research Association, New Orleans, LA.

Wilder, G., Cooper, J., & Mackie, D. (1985). "Gender and computers: Two surveys of computer related attitudes." *Sex Roles,* 13, 3/4:215-28.

Yocam, D. (1987, March). "Computers in education." Presentation to Computers, Connections, Curriculum, Colleagues, Fifth Annual Conference of the Alberta Teachers' Association Computer Council, Edmonton.

7

Opportunities and Obstacles for Women in Canadian Higher Education[1]

Lesley Andres Bellamy and Neil Guppy

Background

Over the past century, and particularly in the last three decades, the Canadian post-secondary education system has experienced spectacular expansion. In this latter period, a significant proportion of the growth has been due to the increased participation of women. For the post-secondary student in the 1990s, equal representation of women at institutions of higher education probably seems commonplace. It is easy to forget that women's participation in mainstream higher education is a relatively recent phenomenon.

While formal education at institutions of higher education in Canada can be traced to the beginnings of the nineteenth century, the presence of women at these institutions cannot. In 1802, the University of King's College in Windsor, Nova Scotia, was the first institution in the British Commonwealth, outside of the British Isles, to be granted a university charter. By 1860, 1 381 first and professional degrees, including law, medicine, engineering and music, had been granted by 11 degree-granting institutions. It was not until 1875, however, that Mount Allison University conferred upon Grace Annie Lockhart the first bachelor's degree granted to a woman by a university in the British Empire. Curiously, given women's enrollment patterns in recent years, the degree bestowed upon Lockhart was a Bachelor of Science. Seven years later, in 1883, the same university awarded the first Bachelor of Arts to a woman, Harriet Starr Stewart, and in 1884 Stewart received the first Master of Arts awarded a Commonwealth woman. Before 1890, 23 degrees from nine other institutions had been awarded to women. In 1890, however, 803 degrees were awarded to men at 19 universities (Harris, 1976).

In these early years, the admission of women to universities was a topic for heated debate. Once women gained admission to universities and the issue of exclusion was laid to rest, other equally contentious debates ensued on such topics as residential facilities for women, appropriate models of co-education, and whether education for women should consist of the same course content that was offered to men. Of considerable import was the Victorian ideal of womanhood wherein women were seen to be neither physically nor mentally fit to endure the rigors of advanced study. Those so brash as to pursue a post-secondary education were considered destined to endure lives void of love, marriage and children (see Gillett, 1981 and

Stewart, 1990 for in-depth histories of women at, respectively, McGill University and the University of British Columbia).

Throughout the twentieth century, women were required to argue the merits of their obtaining a post-secondary education. Stewart (1990) outlines some of these justifications:

> During the First World War, derogatory insinuations that the university had become a 'ladies college' forced women to claim that their higher education served patriotic purposes. In the twenties and thirties, women asserted the benefits of higher education for social usefulness and economic indepen-dence 'if marriage does not come'. By the forties and fifties, they suggested that educated women could better further the interests of their middle-class husbands, whether as full-time housewives or part-time career women. Before the sixties, the purposes of women's education continued to be defended within the limits of social expectations. (p. 125)

She suggests these justifications may be "more myth than real," and that women pursued post-secondary education for the same reasons as men — to "secure employment according to their own aptitudes and preferences," at least until the time of marriage (p. 125).

As this remark suggests, education has long been viewed as critical to the enhancement of one's life chances. Educational credentials provided, and continue to provide, a route to autonomy and thus power over one's life (see Prentice, 1989). As Table 1 demonstrates, level of educational attain-ment is a good predictor of employment opportunities and earnings.

Table 1
Distribution of Individuals by Average Income, by Education and Sex
Unemployment Rate, by Education and Sex
Canada, 1988

	Average Income			Unemployment Rate		
	Total	Male	Female	Total	Male	Female
	$	$	$	%	%	%
0-8 years	14 867	19 239	9 970	10.6	10.1	11.7
Some high school and no post-secondary	18 708	24 087	13 128	9.1	8.7	9.7
Some post-secondary	19 013	23 452	14 297	7.4	6.9	8.0
Post-secondary diploma/certificate	23 765	30 272	17 920	5.5	5.1	5.8
University degree	35 237	42 035	26 301	4.0	3.4	4.8

Sources: Statistics Canada (1989b, 1990a).

Also, Table 1 clearly demonstrates that for women, the economic benefits from education are not as great as for men. An individual woman may be able to increase her income level in relation to other women by furthering her education, but spending more time in school does little to reduce the male-female wage gap. On average, a woman with one university degree earns barely more than a man with a high school education. Education is nonetheless a key route to upward mobility in a society that is increasingly characterized by escalating divorce rates, lone-parent families consisting of a female parent, and increasing numbers of women living in poverty (Gunderson & Muszynski, 1990; Statistics Canada, 1990b). Women may earn less than men, but income increases sharply for women as they attain more schooling.

Our purpose in this chapter is to review the opportunities and obstacles faced by women enrolled in Canadian higher education. We pay particular attention to issues of change, documenting the significant trends over the last century. We also, however, stress the degree to which women still face barriers to full participation in all areas of colleges and universities.

We begin by outlining the participation rates of women and men, showing specific trends in enrollments and degree completion. We note where and when these rates have changed, examining in particular what this has meant for the composition of the student body on college and university campuses. This entails an examination of gender differences in fields of study and a consideration of gender differences among post-secondary faculty. We conclude with a brief review of explanations and issues that emphasize the current context of women's post-secondary experiences.

Women's Participation in Higher Education

Post-Secondary Enrollment Patterns

Historically, the average number of years of schooling has been approximately equal for women and men. Considerable differences, however, are apparent in the level of education attained by each group. Compulsory attendance, legislated by most provinces since the turn of the century, ensured that school attendance at least to the minimum leaving age was an obligation as well as a right for both girls and boys (Phillips, 1957). Beyond this point, however, girls and boys have tended to follow different educational trajectories. Historically, girls were more likely to attend and complete secondary school, but less likely to continue to university. For example, in British Columbia in 1929-30, girls accounted for 48% of elementary enrollments, but almost 54% of secondary enrollments. Yet, in that same year women represented only 23.5% of all university enrollments in Canada (Statistics Canada, 1971, 1978b). Women were more likely to attain a non-university education. For men, the pattern of high school leaving and post-secondary participation was somewhat different. As Table 2 demonstrates, while men had higher secondary school dropout rates, they were also more likely to attend and complete a university education.

Table 2
Educational Attainment of the Population, 15 Years and Older,
by Sex, Selected Years

Level of Education		1971	1976	1981	1985	1988
0 to 8 years	M	32.1	26.0	22.4	19.7	17.5
	F	30.5	25.0	21.5	18.9	17.2
9 to 13 years	M	50.1	45.7	49.4	48.6	47.4
	F	54.2	50.2	53.1	51.6	49.3
Some post-secondary	M	17.8*	10.1	8.6	9.3	9.5
	F	15.3*	8.4	7.6	8.9	9.4
P.S. certificate/diploma	M		8.9	9.0	10.6	11.7
	F		11.4	11.2	12.3	14.1
University degree	M		9.3	10.5	11.8	13.6
	F		5.0	6.6	8.3	10.0

*Includes college or university and attendance or degree completion.
Sources: Statistics Canada (1971 through 1988; 1990a).

In recent years, differences between the sexes in high school attendance, completion and transition to post-secondary education have been reduced. Statistics Canada (1990a) reveals that while in 1950-51 only 50% of sixteen-year-olds remained in school, by 1988-89, 93% of this age group was still in school, with little difference between the sexes. Similarly, as transition rates from high school to post-secondary education have increased, sex differences have declined. Overall, the transition of high school graduates directly to the post-secondary system, as portrayed in Figure 1, has increased from 44.5% in 1978-79 to 53.2% in 1985-86 (Standing Senate Committee on National Finance, 1987). In 1978, fewer female high school graduates (22.1%) went directly to university than did male (28%). In that same year, approximately equal numbers of women and men (19.7 and 19.6%, respectively) went directly to college. By 1985, the transition of females (29.2%) directly from high school to university equalled that of males (29.5%). Transition directly to community colleges was 24% for females and 23.7% for males.

Post-Secondary Enrollments

In the 1901 Census year, women represented 12% of the 6410 full-time undergraduate and professional enrollments and 30% of the 100 full-time graduate enrollments in Canadian universities. In 1925, 20% of all enrollments were women, and by 1931, the number of women enrolled full-time in universities had grown by almost 41% to 7 494, or 23.5% of total full-time university enrollment. As Figure 2 reveals, enrollments of both men and women increased slowly but steadily over the next ten years, with the proportion of women remaining constant at around 23%. In 1945-46, although the absolute number of women attending universities had reached

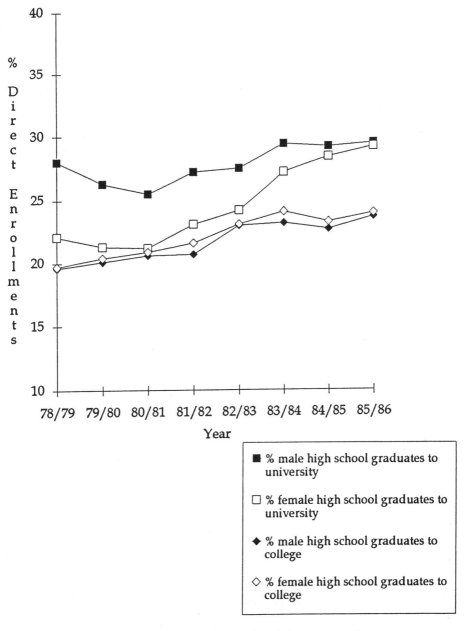

Source: Standing Senate Committee on National Finance (1987).

Figure 1
Post-Secondary Enrollment Directly from High School as a Percentage
of High School Graduates, 1978-1985

12 870 — up by 59% from the 1940-41 figure of 8 107 — this increase was obscured by burgeoning male enrollments (an increase of 77%) due to returning Second World War veterans whose education was paid for by the government. The proportion of full-time university students who were women in 1945-46 actually dropped to less than 21%, then plateaued at this level until 1960-61. By 1960, the full-time male university student body had soared to over 80 000, compared to 27 000 full-time female participants.

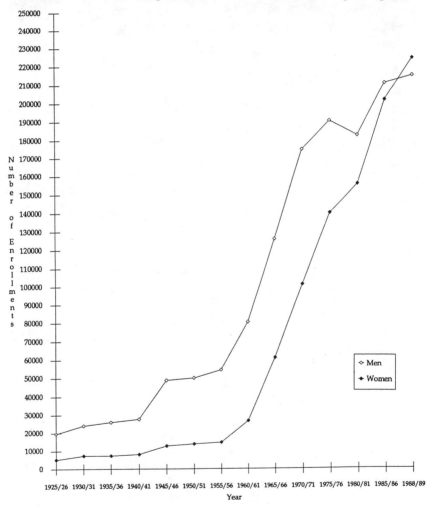

Figure 2
Canadian University Full-time Undergraduate Enrollments by Sex,
1925-1988

Sources: Statistics Canada (1978b, 1990a).

In contrast, as Figure 2 so dramatically illustrates, the most important period of full-time enrollment increase for women began in the 1960s. By 1970 over 100 000 women were enrolled in universities, representing an increase from 1960 of 74 000 or almost 300%. From 1960 to 1970, the proportion of enrollments by women grew from less than 25% to almost 37%. This increase continued steadily through to today, avoiding the modest decline exhibited in male enrollments in the 1970s. By 1985, participation by women in universities had approached 49% of all full-time enrollments, and by 1988 women's enrollment had actually surpassed men's. One way of illustrating the trend in enrollment patterns is to note that in the last 35 years, the number of male students has increased by 294%, while female enrollments have risen by an astounding 1420%.

Full-time enrollment only partially describes the extent to which women now participate at universities. Part-time enrollment by women has also increased dramatically. In 1988-89, over 170 000 or 64% of the total part-time enrollments were women. This represents an increase of 16% since 1984-85, compared with an increase of less than 1% in the part-time enrollment of men during the same period of time.

A second avenue for women to pursue studies beyond high school arose with the establishment and subsequent expansion of the Canadian community college system. Women have historically dominated in post-secondary non-university educational institutions principally because training for traditional female occupations such as nursing and teaching were, before the early 1970s, offered outside the university context in teachers' colleges and hospitals. For example, in 1959 over 68% of full-time enrollments in non-university post-secondary institutions were women. Even after universities began to offer degrees in nursing and education, women's participation in the growing community college system flourished. While equal enrollment opportunities for women were not explicitly cited as one of the goals of community colleges, offerings of university-equivalent courses (as well as vocational, technical, career, academic upgrading, and continuing education courses), lower tuition fees, flexible admission requirements, and programmes located within commuting distance, all facilitated women's enrollment. As early as 1969, 41% of the total enrollments at Lethbridge Community College (established in 1958 as the first community college in Canada) were women (Dominion Bureau of Statistics, 1970).

Of 317 729 full-time community college students in 1988-89, almost 54%, or 171 017 were women. Interestingly, full-time participation by men has declined by 6.8% since 1984-85, whereas that of women has increased by over 4% in the same time period. Of 185 253 part-time community college students in 1988-89, almost 60%, or 110 326 were women. Part-time participation by women has increased by over 24% since 1984-85, compared to an increase of just over 11% for men during the same period.

Distance education provides a third route to the Canadian post-secondary system. According to Coulter (1989), while equal proportions of males and females now participate in traditional undergraduate education, distance education is disproportionately appealing to women. For example, at Athabasca University, female enrollment has increased from 63% in 1985 to 66% in 1988-89 (Ross & Powell, 1990).

Over the last 30 years, tremendous change has occurred in the demographics of post-secondary educational participation in Canada. Women now clearly represent the majority of all post-secondary enrollments (both full-time and part-time) at universities, community colleges and distance education institutions. Access, however, is only one frame from which to analyse women's experiences in higher education. Examination of degree completion rates and levels of achievement provide other insights.

Undergraduate Degree Attainment

If gaining entrance to institutions of post-secondary education presented a major hurdle to women in the nineteenth century, demonstration of competence and receipt of recognition proved to be others. In an address entitled "The Female Sex" printed in 1852 in the Nova Scotia monthly *The Provincial,* W.T. Wishart asserted that women's minds should be enhanced by intellectual pursuits. However, he believed that: "the severe searching mind that gives eminence to the lawyer is foreign to their usual constitution. . . . [and women's abilities were] not calculated for those impetuous and concentrated efforts that are deemed requisite for the career of the politician and orator" (cited in Phillips, 1957, p. 378).

Events at various universities illustrate how prevailing attitudes and practices militated against participation and degree completion by women. For example, the practice of prohibiting women from attending classes at the University of Toronto was challenged in 1880 and 1882 when three girls won scholarships, two of which were "not in the congenial field of modern languages, but in the stern discipline of mathematics" (Phillips, 1957, p. 383). Although the myth of female intellectual inferiority was demolished by these women's accomplishments, admission to full student status required nothing less than a motion in the provincial legislature to admit women to the university (which, incidentally, was opposed by the President and the university council). In 1885, when such legislation came into effect, eleven women students began classes at the University of Toronto (ibid., p. 384).

At other institutions, recognition for advanced study did not necessarily coincide with academic effort. Although Mount Allison University, the first degree-granting institution to open a Female Academy, began admitting women in 1848, the first bachelor degree was not awarded until 1875. Prior to 1875, female graduates were granted "Tokens of Merit" and "Mistress of Liberal Arts" diplomas — certificates of recognition that held no substantive value (Harris, 1976, p. 11).

In 1925, 50 years after Grace Lockhart had attained the first degree granted to a woman, almost 26% of the graduating cohort across Canada was composed of women (1 276 of 4 922 undergraduate degrees were awarded to women in 1925). Over the next 15 years, degree attainment by women fluctuated between 27% and 29%, and peaked at 31% in 1945 (especially high considering that in 1945, women represented less than 21% of total university enrollment). But in the years immediately following the war, the numbers of women graduates actually declined. Fuelled by the return of war veterans and the educational opportunities provided these men, the graduating class numbered 17 185 in 1950, but the percentage of woman graduates declined relative to 1945, falling below 22% (equivalent to the pre-1925 figure). At least part, if not all, of this decline can be accounted for by relegation of women back to family obligations, leaving higher education and the world of paid work for men. Stewart (1990) comments that for married students at the University of British Columbia who were living in family residences during this period, the student was rarely the female partner. In the UBC annual *Totem,* one commentator was quoted as saying "in most, but not all cases, it is the male member of the household who makes the daily pilgrimage to Point Grey. The wives stay home and vie with neighbours in inventing new and different ways to make a four-room army hut liveable" (cited in Stewart, 1990, p. 87).

In 1950, the proportion of woman university graduates was lower than at any other time since 1920. Not only did the percentage of woman graduates decline, but between 1950 and 1955 the absolute number of women graduates dropped by 629 to 3 146. From 1955 onwards, as Figure 3 shows, the number of degrees awarded to women steadily escalated. By 1965 the percentage of woman graduates had returned to the levels of 1945, and by 1975, over 49% of university degrees were awarded to women. In the interval spanning 1970-71 to 1988-89, the number of degrees awarded to women rose by almost 120%, while for men the increase was not quite 16% (see Figure 3). Since 1981-82 more women than men have acquired bachelor and first professional degrees, and by 1988-89, 12 000 more undergraduate and professional degrees were awarded to women than men.

As increasing numbers of undergraduate degrees were awarded to both men and women, and as the demand in recent years for advanced credentials soared, overall enrollments in postgraduate programmes increased. At the graduate level, the majority of degrees are still conferred on men, although at both the masters and doctoral level dramatic increases for women are evident. As Figure 4 reveals, since 1970-71 the number of masters degrees granted by universities has grown by 69.3%, and the number acquired by women has escalated by 245.3%, representing 44.9% of all masters degrees awarded in 1988-89.

Figure 3
Undergraduate Degree Attainment by Sex,
1920-1988

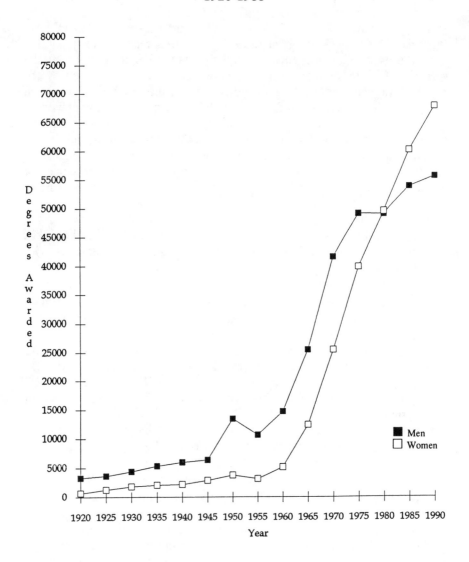

Source: Statistics Canada (1978b, 1990a).

At the doctoral level the overall increase in numbers of degrees awarded has been 48.6%, but the increase for women has been 388.7% (compared to a 12.2% increase for men). Yet only 30.6% of all doctorates in 1988-89 were awarded to women. Men still dominate in graduate schools; however, steady progress in graduate degree attainment by women continues and women's participation in the educational hierarchy continues to increase.

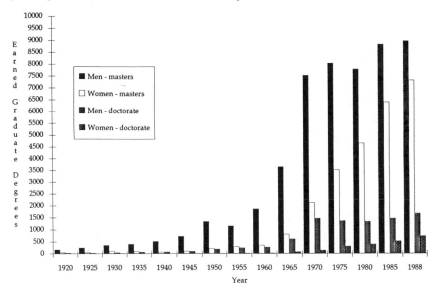

Figure 4
Masters and Doctorate Degrees by Sex, 1920-1988

Source Statistics Canada (1978, 1990a).

Success and Excellence

Stephen Leacock, in an essay entitled "Oxford As I See It," openly doubted the ability of women to compete with men at advanced study. He exclaimed:

> On all that goes with physical and mathematical science, women, on the average, are far below the standard of men. There are, of course, exceptions. But they prove nothing. It is no use to quote to me the case of some brilliant girl who stood first in physics at Cornell. There is an elephant in the zoo that can count to ten, yet I refuse to reckon myself his inferior. (cited in Gillett, 1981, p. 15)

This humorist's viewpoint was probably an accurate reflection of the general sentiment in the early 1900s. The evidence, however, in terms of degree completion and academic achievement, contradicted this view. In 1925-26, women constituted 21.2% of all university undergraduates; yet in that same year they received 26% of all undergraduate degrees granted by Canadian universities. This imbalance between enrollment and degree completion is not some historical anomaly, as Leacock implies. Women made up 54% of the total enrollment in 1984, yet they received almost 56% of degrees granted. In other words, women have historically received a greater percentage of undergraduate degrees than their proportion of enrollments would seem to warrant.

This observation is buttressed by findings of recent studies. Dennison, Forrester and Jones (1982) found that female undergraduate students at British Columbia universities were more likely than their male counterparts to attain degrees. Similarly, in a follow-up study of students who first enrolled at the the University of Guelph in the late 1970s, Kupferschmidt and Vanderkamp (1987) report that the success rates of female students is "striking." They found that by the mid-1980s, 57.1% of women had graduated, compared with 50.3% of men. Even after controlling for high school grades (since women entering university generally have superior records of high school achievement), women were still more likely than men to graduate from university.

Women are also more likely to complete university courses through distance education. For example, at Athabasca University, an analysis of completion rates of 1987-88 registrants showed that, irrespective of the area of study, a greater proportion of females passed the courses in which they were registered. Most notable was the 79.7% completion rate for women in senior level science courses, compared to a 62.3% completion rate for men (Ross & Powell, 1990).

In terms of academic achievement, women demonstrate equal if not superior performance levels. According to Axelrod and Reid (1989), during the early years at Dalhousie University women were able to successfully compete with men. They state:

> Despite the "male" orientation of the curriculum [in the years spanning 1881 to 1921], women held their own in the classroom, capturing an impressive share of the honours in proportion to their minority percentage of the student population. Half of the Avery Prize winners — the graduating students with the highest grades in the general degree programs — were women. (p. 27)

More recently, in an analysis of university course grades of women and men, Decore (1984) found that achievement of women attending the University of Alberta, in a variety of courses from inorganic chemistry to sociology, was slightly higher than that of men. Furthermore, this difference was maintained throughout the 1970s, although this gap would appear to be closing. Similarly, in a longitudinal study of academic achievement of education students at the University of Calgary, Violato (1990) found that females in both elementary and secondary education consistently, over a ten-year period from 1973 to 1984, outperformed males in earned mean grades.

Several competing interpretations may be used to account for women's apparent superiority in obtaining degrees. These include higher expectations of women who enter institutions of higher education, the types of programmes in which women enrol, and/or discriminatory admission practices allowing entrance to only the very best female students (as suggested by testimony provided to the 1970 Royal Commission on the Status of Women in Canada). Alternatively, there is some evidence to suggest that women come disproportionately from upper-class backgrounds, arriving at university already enriched by cultural capital, abetted by educational capital, and supported by social and economic capital; thus, they may be less likely to drop out of university than men. This latter explanation implies a differential class composition for women relative to men at university, an issue to which we now turn.

Social Origins of Women in Higher Education

In 1900, the typical university student was male, white and upper-class. Students from upper-status backgrounds have always been overrepresented at university. Axelrod and Reid (1989) note that from 1920 to 1950, nearly half of the student population at Memorial University of Newfoundland came from middle- and upper-class backgrounds, while only 10% of Newfoundland society was composed of these groups. Fathers of women attending Dalhousie University from 1880 to 1900 were most likely to be businessmen or clergy. At Queen's University in the early 1900s, 16% of students came from working-class backgrounds. Yet the women of Queen's were far more likely to come from wealthier backgrounds.

Little convincing evidence exists to suggest that this inequality by social class has diminished much over time (Guppy, 1984). The 1985 *Report of the Royal Commission on the Economic Union and Development Prospects of Canada* reported that the likelihood of university attendance by children whose parents hold bachelors degrees is three times greater than by children of parents without degrees, and that participation in post-secondary education of young people from high-income families has always been greater than for young people from low-income families.

Also less apparent are the disparities in characteristics among those who *do* participate in the various institutions of post-secondary education. Although reductions in socioeconomic disparities among participants in post-secondary education are evident, this reduction was largely attributed to the expansion of the non-university sector of higher education. A recent joint study by Statistics Canada and the Department of the Secretary of State (1987) shows that (1) undergraduate levels of education continue to be dominated by children of parents who fall in upper-middle- and upper-class categories, (2) the rate of overrepresentation is not rapidly decreasing, and (3) parents of students at community colleges — institutions with an over-representation of women — tend to have lower levels of education (cited in Fortin, 1987). Guppy and Pendakur (1989), using data from a national survey of post-secondary students, found that the reduction of one ascriptive characteristic — gender — which in the past has been related to post-secondary participation, resulted in the exacerbation of another form of ascription — family origin.

As Table 3 indicates, in 1983-84, while women from families having all levels of education were more likely to attend university than in 1973-74, only those women from the most educated families were more likely *than men* to attend university. Also, men from the most educated families were the least likely to attend community colleges.

Table 3
Attendance of Students in Higher Education
by Institution, Family Education*, and Year

	Women Family Education			Men Family Education		
	Lo Ed	Med Ed	Hi Ed	Lo Ed	Med Ed	Hi Ed
1974-75						
University	56.1	60.8	72.8	63.6	67.1	76.6
College	43.9	39.2	27.2	36.4	32.9	23.4
1983-84						
University	61.2	64.4	76.7	63.8	65.2	72.8
College	38.8	35.6	23.3	36.2	34.8	27.2

*Family Education is defined by average length of parents' education: Lo Ed - less than 11 years; Med Ed - 11 to 13 years; Hi Ed - more than 13 years.
Source: Guppy & Pendakur (1989).

Violato and Travis (1990) report similar findings. They found that, in a national survey of students enrolled in Canadian faculties of education, the socioeconomic backgrounds of these students were slightly higher than those of Canadians in general. However, the women in the sample came from more privileged backgrounds than did the men. Of women education students, 64% came from families whose fathers held professional/managerial or entreprenerial positions, compared to 52% of the male students. Twenty-two percent of men originated from families whose fathers were unskilled laborers, compared to 11.9% of women. Also, more women than men had fathers who had attended university.

Women now constitute the majority of students in, and graduates from, colleges and undergraduate university programs. While women are still underrepresented in graduate education, steady gains continue to be made at both the masters and doctoral levels. It appears, however, that social class inequalities in post-secondary participation which have historically existed for women, persist.

Opportunities and Divisions in Higher Education

Any portrayal of women in higher education would be woefully inadequate if it told only about access and growth. Since higher education is composed of various parts, it is also essential to ask about the opportunities women have in each of these (separate) parts. Greater access to colleges and universities does not guarantee equal opportunities within these institutions. More women entering post-secondary schools is not evidence that women have attained equal representation in all spheres of college and university activity. There is also, then, an important story about gender divisions within higher education.

Recall that Grace Annie Lockhart obtained her university degree in 1875. She could not, however, have done so in any field she might have wanted. She could not, for example, have graduated from medicine, because only men were permitted to study for a degree in this professional field. As Lockhart's example attests, women had access to certain higher education disciplines over a century ago. But women have been excluded from or discouraged from entering many fields. In this section we discuss the current extent of this exclusion and segregation.

Although opportunities for girls to enter the elementary school system existed in the 1800s, a variety of devices were used to differentiate their status from that of boys. Not only were girls discouraged from taking courses like classics (which were required for later entrance to professional fields), but the physical set-up of the school and the organization of the curriculum treated girls and boys differently.

> Common school architecture and pedagogy as well as Education Office advice throughout the period [late 1800s] insisted on separate entrances, separate playgrounds, separate seating and even separate recitations for boys and girls. . . . (Prentice, 1977, p. 112)

Separate entrances and play areas for girls and boys have largely vanished (although private schools for each sex persist), but the courses students take still vary substantially by gender. This can be seen quite starkly, for example, in the high school courses pursued by young women and men. Table 4 shows the percentage of women and men enrolled in physics, advanced mathematics, and computer science courses in various provinces during the 1980s.

In every case a majority, and often a large majority, of the students in these courses were male. This is clear evidence that gender streams continue in the education system, that women and men tend to congregate in different "gender-tracks" or in separate fields of study.

Fields of Study

Hidden from view in the earlier graphs and tables showing women's increasing participation in higher education, are the patterns of that participation. The content of courses and degree programmes followed by women and men are very different. This produces a "gendered division of education."

Table 4
Percentage of Women and Men in Selected High School
Courses (Various Provinces, Various Years)

Course	Women (%)	Men (%)
Physics		
Ontario, 1982	29	70
Alberta, 1983	24	76
Manitoba, 1986	37	63
B.C., 1987	21	79
Mathematics (Advanced)		
Alberta, 1983	28	72
Manitoba, 1986	36	64
B.C., 1986	44	56
Computer Science		
Manitoba, 1986	29	71
B.C., 1987	23	77

Source: Status of Women Canada and Manitoba Women's Directorate (1989).

Table 5 documents the fields of study from which women and men graduated in 1970-71 as compared to 1988-89. The bottom row of the table ("Total") shows that in 1970-71 women attained 38% of all degrees, and that by 1988-89 this had risen to 58% (this parallels Figure 1). This comparison repeats the story of women's increasing participation.

The most remarkable feature of Table 5 is the significant concentration in 1988-89 of women in some fields and of men in others. Women continue to attain the vast majority of degrees in social work, household science and nursing but are conspicuously absent from the graduation rolls in such fields as engineering and applied science. These comparisons point to a story of divisions and restricted opportunities.

In certain fields, however, women have made remarkable gains, especially in commerce, veterinary medicine and engineering. These are the only fields in which women's degree attainment increased at least ten-fold between 1970-71 and 1988-89. Indeed, there have been important gains in all fields represented in the lower portion of Table 5 where women's participation had been low (and in some cases, despite major gains, remains low — notably engineering). That is, in all areas where women previously were underrepresented there has been movement toward greater gender balance. The underrepresentation of the earlier period persists (except for veterinary medicine and pharmacy), but the pattern of change is toward a more equal representation of women and men in these selected fields.

What makes this finding so striking is that the same cannot be said for areas where historically women have been overrepresented. In the upper portion of Table 5, in fields where women's participation was greater than men's in 1970-71, the gender balance has moved away from greater equality. That is, in those areas where women have long predominated, the over-representation of women has intensified. Weis (1985), using data from the United States, found similar patterns of representation by women in various university programs.

Table 5
Degree Attainment by Sex, Field of Study, and Year
(Bachelor and First Professional University Degrees)

	1970-71			1987-88		
	Total Degrees	Degrees to Women		Total Degrees	Degrees to Wom+ ..	
Field of Study	N	N	%	N	N	%
Household Science	629	625	99.4	1 078	1 021	94.7
Nursing	1 258	1 221	97.0	2 406	2 313	96.1
Health Occupations	280	221	78.9	1 514	1 105	73.0
Social Work	319	175	54.9	1 749	1 403	80.2
Applied Arts	1 165	639	54.8	3 559	2 324	65.3
Education	15 406	8 129	52.8	16 196	11 339	70.0
Arts	19 393	7 802	40.2	33 841	19 867	58.7
Pharmacy	441	169	38.3	725	461	63.6
Biological Sciences	1 837	517	28.1	5 133	2 546	49.6
Physical Sciences	3 870	751	19.4	7 229	2 019	27.9
Medicine	1 432	211	14.7	2 274	951	41.8
Agriculture	502	61	12.2	741	341	46.0
Law	1 958	183	9.3	3 334	1 505	45.1
Veterinary Medicine	132	11	8.3	258	153	59.3
Commerce	3 444	215	6.2	12 567	5 592	44.5
Dentistry	369	16	4.3	504	151	30.0
Engineering	4 426	51	1.2	7 113	782	11.0
Non-Classified	10 090	4 453	44.1	3 554	1 860	52.3
Total	66 951	25 450	38.0	103 775	55 733	56.1
IQV[1]		.749			.849	

[1]IQV — Index of Qualitative Variation: this statistic measures the extent to which degree attainment is concentrated in certain fields; a higher figure indicates greater dispersion or less concentration [non-classified degrees have been excluded in the calculation].
Sources: Statistics Canada (1984, 1990a).

The trend for women to acquire more degrees in traditionally male-dominated fields of study acts to break down historic patterns of gender-tracking. However, the expansion of women's degree attainment in fields such as social work and education has acted in exactly the opposite direction by further entrenching gender imbalances. Since the former trend is stronger, there has been a positive shift toward greater gender balance across all fields, a change that is almost exclusively due to women entering fields of study where men have historically predominated.

An alternative way to examine the changing gender balance is to focus on those fields that have experienced rapid expansion over the time period in question (no fields have contracted). The largest growth has been in commerce, where the number of degrees granted has almost quadrupled. In 1987-88, women attained a significant number of those degrees, at 44.5% up significantly from only 6.2% in 1970-71. In general women have attained more degrees in those fields of study that have expanded. This is a very important finding since it demonstrates that women's growing participation in higher education has not resulted from simply increasing their degree completion in traditional areas of study by women.

Growing degree completion in non-traditional areas also illustrates that women have made significant inroads in areas of higher education that typically lead to higher paying, career-line employment prospects. Women's participation in professional education programmes has risen dramatically, signalling an important shift in the labor market jobs these women pursue upon graduation. However, as we saw earlier, women still remain under-represented in graduate study (master's and doctoral levels) and here the gendered division of education has not altered much. For example, in the late 1980s about 50% of doctoral degrees in education were awarded to women while the number of female doctorates in engineering was only 3%. Overall, the gender imbalance of 1970-71 was reduced slightly by 1987-88. In all areas traditionally dominated by men, women have significantly increased the proportion of degrees they attain. However, in areas where women have always obtained the vast majority of degrees, there has been either no shift or a shift away from greater gender balance (i.e., men continue not to enter these fields).

These general findings about fields of study are based on university data and it is important to see whether a similar pattern is found also in community colleges. Table 6 provides the relevant information for colleges, although unfortunately Statistics Canada does not have field of study data (broken down by sex) for colleges prior to 1975-76.

The gendered division of education is found at community colleges as well. Men are much more likely than women to be in fields of transportation, engineering and natural resources, whereas women are overrepresented in such fields as health and medicine, and education. Once again the overall trend is toward a greater gender balance but notice that here too some traditionally female fields of study (i.e., education and business) are becoming increasingly female-dominated.

Tables 5 and 6 use fairly crude divisions among fields of study. For example, university arts programmes are divided into many different fields, and the divisions between economics, psychology, and so forth have been ignored in our tables. But there are different gender distributions within each of these sub-fields, with, for example, men outnumbering women 2:1 in economics but women outnumbering men 3:1 in pychology. Had even finer divisions within arts, or engineering, or other fields of study been available to us for each time period, the results would show even greater division and concentration. Our use of coarse categories makes the Tables less complex and easier to interpret, but understates the degree to which there is a gendered division of higher education.

Table 6
Diploma Attainment by Sex, Field of Study, and Year
(College Diplomas)

	1975-76			1987-88		
	Total Diplomas	Diplomas to Women		Total Diplomas	Diplomas to Women	
Field of Study	N	N	%	N	N	%
Medicine	11 742	10 847	92.4	11 249	9 466	84.1
Education	5 096	4 148	74.1	2 316	2 117	91.4
Business	8 684	5 182	59.7	15 671	10 432	66.6
Arts	3 106	1 338	43.1	4 678	2 684	57.4
Natural Resources	2 018	382	18.9	2 654	795	30.0
Engineering	2 119	179	8.5	12 647	2 066	16.3
Transportation	253	5	2.0	197	21	10.7
Technologies	2 553	226	8.9	n.a.	n.a.	n.a.
Other/Misc.	393	123	31.3	7 525	5 139	68.3
No Report	561	222	39.6	92f	37	40.2
Total	38 334	23 082	60.2	57 029	32 757	57.4
IQV[1]		.737			.836	

Note: Field of study as designated by Statistics Canada. Technology field not designated by Statistics Canada in 1987-88.
[1]IQV — see explanation in Table 5; higher figure, less concentration.
Source: Statistics Canada (1989a), p. 184.

Explanations for these patterns are diverse and there is little consensus in the research literature as to exactly what factors account for this patterning of participation and course selection (see Collis in chapter 6). As our Table 4 shows, the gender imbalance begins prior to post-secondary education and so the explanations must begin there as well.

The Post-Secondary Labor Force

It is not just female *students* who are concentrated in certain fields of study. Female faculty members in college and university are also likely to be overrepresented in selected fields and underrepresented in others.

One way to illustrate the imbalance between women and men on the teaching staffs of Canadian colleges and universities is to examine the sex composition of higher education faculties. In 1990 there were over 61,000 full-time instructors in higher education (36 000 at universities and 25 000 at colleges). Of these, only about one quarter are women.

Figure 5 shows the changing sex balance of university instructors between 1961 and 1991. In 1961, just over 1 in 10 university faculty members were women. Thirty years later this ratio has changed to just under 2 in 10. While Figure 3 showed that the number of degrees awarded to women almost tripled between 1970-71 and 1989-90, Figure 5 shows much, much slower change in the growth of women on university teaching staffs.

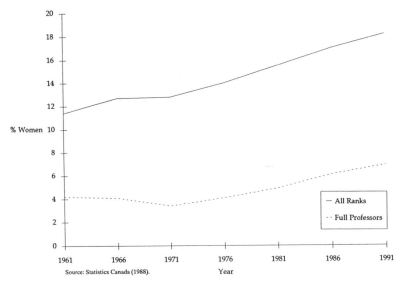

Figure 5
Women on University Faculty (as percentage of total faculty), 1961-1986

One of the most discouraging features of the nominal change in the percentage of women on university teaching staffs, is that in other professional fields the pace of change in altering the sex balance has been quicker.

In male-dominated professions, of which university teaching is one, Marshall (1987) has shown that women's participation between 1971 and 1986 has grown from 11.0% to 22.9%. That is, the proportion of women has doubled over 15 years in all male-dominated professions. In universities, however, the change has been from 12.8% (1971) to 17.0% (1986) — a growth rate of less than half that in other male-dominated professions.

Not only has the entry of women into the male-dominated university teaching profession been slow, women's prospects for promotion have also been poor. New members of the university teaching staff normally begin as instructors, lecturers, or assistant professors. They may, as their careers develop, advance through a series of ranks to associate, and then full professor. Figure 5 shows the percentage of women who occupy the top rank, full professor. Not only is the percentage low, but it has a rather flat trajectory, meaning that the proportion of full professors that are women has changed only slowly over the last three decades.

The position of women in the university teaching hierarchy can be seen more clearly in Table 7. First, although women now make up the majority of people attending universities, fewer than 1 in 5 of the teaching staff is female (see the bottom right-hand corner of the Table).

Table 7
Number of Full-time University Teachers by Rank, Sex, and Year

Year	Rank									
	Full Professor		Associate Professor		Assistant Professor		Lecturer		Total	
	F	M	F	M	F	M	F	M	F	M
1970-71	166	4 677	522	5 948	1 241	7 736	888	2 181	3 140	21 472
	3%	97%	8%	92%	14%	86%	29%	71%	13%	87%
1975-76	302	013	1 017	9 130	1 694	7 390	707	1 552	4 317	26 467
	4%	96%	10%	90%	19%	81%	31%	69%	14%	86%
1980-81	476	9 328	1 600	10 950	1 773	5 594	668	1 029	5 169	28 130
	5%	95%	13%	87%	24%	75%	39%	61%	16%	84%
1986-87	803	11 809	2 096	10 673	2 093	5 045	623	761	6 212	29 241
	6%	94%	16%	84%	29%	71%	45%	55%	18%	82%

Note: An ambiguous "other" category has been dropped from the original table.
Source: Statistics Canada (1988) p. 185.

Second, among those women who are on the teaching staff, the great majority find themselves in the lower ranks of the profession. To illustrate the latter, in 1986-87 one out of every three university faculty members was a male full professor compared to one in forty-four faculty members who was a female full professor. Comparing percentages (in any column) back to 1970-71 reveals some change, but the overall pattern is stable.

As in the general labor force, women are more often found in the less secure, less prestigious positions. At colleges and universities this means that women tend to spend more time teaching than do men, often on part-time or limited-term contracts. Not only do they on average teach more hours, but they also teach more students and do more student advising (see, for example, Finkelstein, 1984; Rosenblum & Rosenblum, 1990). The consequence is that women have less time to devote to research and scholarly writing — the very activities essential for promotion in higher education.

In addition to being concentrated in the lowest and least secure echelons of the university profession, women also receive significantly lower wages than do their male colleagues (see Table 8). In 1986-87 the difference in the median salaries of women and men was $9 156. Need it be said, the difference favoured men! This monetary advantage for men existed at every level of the profession, such that even among those few women whose accomplishments had secured them full professorships, they still earned over $3 000 less, on average, than their male counterparts.

Table 8
Median Salaries of Full-time University Teachers
by Rank and Sex, 1986-87

	Sex		
Rank	Female	Male	Difference
Full Professor	$60 123	$63 178	- $3 055
Associate Professor	$48 405	$50 839	- $2 434
Assistant Professor	$36 851	$38 475	- $1 624
Rank below Assistant	$32 960	$34 304	- $1 344
Other	$34 976	$42 432	- $7 456
Total	$46 115	$55 271	- $ 9 156

Note: Only faculty with Ph.Ds are included.
Source: Statistics Canada (1988), p. 186.

There are certain explanations for the persistence of this wage gap. Women faculty members tend to be younger than men and hence they often have not been in specific ranks as long as their male peers. This could, of course, account for some salary difference. However, after examining detailed salary data for 1985-86, Guppy (1989, p. 753) concluded that nearly 30% of the wage difference for women and men was due to discrimination. Even after adjusting salary data to take into account differences between women and men in rank, age, size of university, and so forth, women were found to earn, on average, $2 600 less than men.

As well as receiving less pay and being concentrated in the lower ranks of the profession, women faculty also tend to be overrepresented in certain disciplines. Women compose a sizeable proportion of the faculty in fields such as nursing, education and French. There are, however, very few female faculty, and almost no female full professors, in such fields as engineering, physiology, mathematics and anatomy. In senior administrative positions, women are rarely found, except of course as deans or directors of women's studies or gender relations programmes.

The consequence of all this is that the majority of students on both college and university campuses (i.e., women), are instructed by men of senior rank, especially in traditionally male-dominated fields of study from which growing numbers of women graduate (e.g., commerce, law, medicine). As well, the differentiation in the fields of teaching interacts with the differences by sex in fields of study, such that, for example, female English instructors serve as role models for undergraduate female students who then aspire to become experts in the specialties of their mentors, thereby perpetuating the initial gender divisions.

Explanations and Discussion

All of the preceding evidence points to major changes in women's participation in higher education. The changes have not been superficial, they have been profound. Indeed, there has probably been no other major social institution where women's lives have, collectively, been altered so dramatically in the past few decades. Certainly more change is necessary but the student population on Canadian campuses in the 1990s is radically different in its sex composition relative to the 1960s. What accounts for this dramatic change?

We approach answers to this question in two ways. First, we examine whether or not traditional explanations for the expansion of higher education adequately capture the dramatic changes by sex we have documented. Second, since these older theories are generally inadequate, we offer alternative explications for the changing sex composition in programmes of study in college and university.

Demographic Changes

In Canada in 1959 more children were born than in any previous or subsequent year. Indeed, 1959 represents the peak of the baby boom which lasted through the 1950s and early 1960s. As this population bulge made its way through the educational system, there had to be expansion. Growing student numbers required more teachers, more schools, and so forth. This baby-boom cohort fuelled much of the expansion of education in the past few decades (see Clark, Devereaux, & Zsigmond, 1979).

Children born in 1959 entered colleges and universities in the late 1970s and graduated in the early 1980s. In fact, over the 1980s the numbers of post-secondary-aged students declined (that is, the size of the 18- to 24-year-old cohort shrank as the 1980s progressed), since the baby boomers were passing into their late twenties and early thirties by 1990.

For men, a demographic explanation focusing on the size of the age cohort does a reasonably adequate job of predicting the number of men enrolled in, and graduating from, higher education. That is, over the last few decades a relatively stable proportion of men in the 18- to 24-year-old age cohort have participated in traditional post-secondary education. For women, the demographic account is virtually useless. As documented in Figure 2 and 3, women's participation in post-secondary education has surged from 1960 onward. Women participate full-time and part-time in universities, community colleges and institutions of distance education. This increase has been well beyond anything predictable by changes in the numbers of women between the ages of 18 and 24. In short, a traditional demographic explanation fits the patterns for men but is nonsensical in terms of explaining women's participation in higher education.

One demographic change often cited in the American literature as a reason for women's increased educational attainment is the timing of major life events, especially marriage and motherhood (see Bianchi & Spain, 1986; McLaughlin et al., 1988). In both Canada and the United States, the age at first marriage has been increasing since the Second World War (in 1988, the median age at first marriage for Canadian women was 24.6 and for men, 26.5). Also, the age at which parents have their first child has been increasing. Particularly for women, early marriage and motherhood (or just one of the two) tend to be incompatible with educational attainment.

The causal direction of this link is unclear, however. Are women postponing these major life events to obtain an education, or are women obtaining an education because these major life events have been postponed? Like the chicken and the egg, it is not clear which comes first. What is clear, though, is that the correlation between educational attainment and these life-course events is far stronger for women than for men (in other words, men often marry without it affecting their education plans).

Equality of Opportunity

The 1970 report of the Royal Commission on the Status of Women in Canada argued that "education opens the door to almost every life goal. Wherever women are denied equal access to education they cannot be said to have equality" (p. 161). Indeed, in the pursuit of a fair and just society, education is something that should be open to all, restricted to none. Since schooling does play the most important role in determining a person's occupational destiny and income, access to education is fundamentally important (see Creese, Guppy, & Meissner, 1991).

The rapid growth of higher education following the 1950s can be partly explained by an emphasis on equality of opportunity. Certainly evidence from the legislative debates of politicians demonstrates that equality of educational opportunity had a great deal of political currency, especially in the 1960s and 1970s. Offering more and better schooling was seen as an important way to provide opportunities for the best and brightest of Canada's young people.

Increasing accessibility to post-secondary education was part of this process, and as we have seen, access for women improved dramatically. But we have also seen that obstacles existed. Opportunities appear to have been much more constrained in certain fields of study and women still remain underrepresented in graduate schools. As we move from first-year college and university through to initial graduation, up through graduate school and on to college or university faculty, we find the proportion of men rises with each step. This suggests that equality of opportunity has opened up certain avenues for women, but that important omissions remain, where access for women is still less available.

Especially important in explaining women's growing presence in higher education has been the influence of the women's movement in empowering women to take advantage of opportunities that were available. This influence has been crucial not just in encouraging women to take more control of their own lives, but also in forcing post-secondary institutions to restructure in order to provide programmes and opportunities relevant to women.

Human Capital Explanations

Economists are prone to treat decisions to continue in school as an investment. Using a rational choice model, people are thought to make economic calculations concerning the relative costs (e.g., tuition fees, foregone wages) and benefits (e.g., future earnings) of higher education. People will "purchase" a university education if they can expect an appreciable "return" on their "investment."

If these accounts were to have any validity in explaining trends in both enrollment and graduation rates over the last few decades, they would need to be sensitive to the very different experiences of women and men. Such sensitivity has not existed. Traditional human capital accounts (e.g., Foot & Pervin, 1983; Vanderkamp, 1984) have failed to explain the distinct patterns apparent when comparing women with men.

Indeed, given that women earn less than men in the labor market, even when they work full-time and full-year, it is difficult to imagine how women could use human capital calculations to determine that college or university education was economically beneficial — under this logic a sex change operation might seem more rational! Certainly women's growing labor-force participation suggests that more women may have an eye to skill acquisition (witness the rising female enrollments in Commerce), but a human capital cost accounting model, blind to differences in women's and men's experiences, offers little in the way of explanation.

Wannell (1990) has recently shed important light on the economic consequences for the relative economic returns of women and men who graduate from university. A representative national sample of 1982 university graduates was contacted in 1987. Women who were employed full-time had average earnings of $31 000, or 82% of the average earnings of men, at $38 000. Given the identical educational backgrounds, and their similarity in age and labor-force experience, the earnings gap is hard to explain under the guise of human capital accounting.

The Changing Context in Higher Education

Unfortunately, it was not just growth in women's participation that was occurring in universities and colleges in the last few decades. Coincident with this expansion has been fiscal retrenchment. Just as women began to enter post-secondary institutions in growing numbers, the monetary support for colleges and universities began to soften (see, for instance, Decore & Pannu, 1986). Also, there is evidence that the value of post-secondary degrees has waned over this same period. Goyder (1980) shows that the economic value of degrees and diplomas has begun to erode, not to the point where they have no economic value, but certainly to the point where their "purchasing power" is weaker.

There has also been a more noxious undercurrent. With growing clamour throughout the 1980s, questions about the "standards" of higher education have been posed (see, for example, Bercuson, Bothwell, & Granatstein, 1984). Contention that excellence has been eroded or that quality has been lacking in higher education have been voiced at precisely the same time that women's participation has increased. And, of course, there have been frequent attacks on feminist teaching and women's studies programmes as "ideological" or as unscholarly (see, for example, Byfield, 1991).

These latter challenges, documenting yet again many people's tendency to see women's work as less valuable than men's (Eichler, 1983), demonstrate that the struggles of women in higher education continue. There are not just issues of enrollments and degrees, fields of study, and ranks among faculty, but also conflicts over ideology, bias and censorship.

Conclusions

In the past few decades, Canadian women have seized opportunities to participate at all levels of higher education. Women have outnumbered men at community colleges for many years. Among undergraduates, women now receive more university degrees than men. In several Canadian universities, women constitute the majority in the graduating classes in faculties of law and medicine.

Obstacles remain. The gender-divided nature of higher education persists. Certain fields of study (for instance, engineering) continue to attract relatively few women, and at graduate levels of education men continue to receive the bulk of degrees. Female instructors continue to predominate at the lower ranks of the college and university faculty, where they still receive significantly less pay than their male counterparts.

The evidence we have provided runs counter to widely accepted theoretical accounts of educational expansion. The sad fact is that adherence to these theories demonstrates that the patterns of women's presence in postsecondary education continues to be largely ignored. Even when gender differences are fundamental to the social issues at hand (here, the expansion of post-secondary education), the explanations devised to account for the changes ignore women.

In this paper we have used statistics to document the relative absence or presence of women in higher education; that is, we have analysed changes over time in access, enrollments, degree completion, levels of achievement, participation within university and college faculties, and representation within faculty ranks. We have only alluded to some other aspects central to understanding women's post-secondary participation — for example, the struggle by women, both in the past and in the present, for inclusion, and the *quality* of women's experiences in post-secondary institutions. Equal enrollments and degree completion rates do not necessarily mean parity of experiences for women and men at institutions of higher education. The extent to which a "chilly climate for women" (Hall & Sandler, 1982) exists, and persists, warrants further comment.

Note

[1]This is a substantially revised version of a paper appearing in the first edition of *Women and Education.* Doug Balson and Susan Vellutini co-authored the initial paper, and we are grateful to them for many of the ideas in that paper that we have retained.

References

Axelrod, P., & Reid, J.G. (Eds.). (1989). *Youth, university, and Canadian society.* Kingston: McGill-Queen's University Press.

Bercuson, D.J., Bothwell, R., & Granatstein, J.L. (1984). *The great brain robbery . . . Canada's universities on the road to ruin.* Toronto: McClelland & Stewart.

Bianchi, S.M., & Spain, D. (1986). *American women in transition.* New York: Russell Sage.

Byfield, V. (1991, January 7). Fembos in academe. *Alberta Report.*

Clark, W., Devereaux, M.S., & Zsigmond, A. (1979). *The class of 2001: The school age population — trends and implications — 1961 to 2001*. Ottawa: Statistics Canada.

Coulter, R. (1989). Women in distance education: Towards a feminist perspective. In R. Sweet (Ed.), *Post-secondary education in Canada: Policies, practices, and priorities* (pp. 11-22). Athabasca, Alberta: Athabasca University/Ottawa: Canadian Society for the Study of Education.

Creese, G., Guppy, N., & Meissner, M. (1991). *Ups and downs on the ladder of success: Social mobility in Canada, 1986*. Ottawa: Statistics Canada.

Decore. A.M. (1984). Vive la différence: A comparison of male-female academic performance. *Canadian Journal of Higher Education, 14*(3), 35-58.

Decore, A.M., & Pannu, R.S. (1986). Educational financing in Canada 1970-71 to 1984-85: Who calls the tune, who pays the piper? *Canadian Journal of Higher Education, 16*(2), 27-49.

Dennison, J., Forrester, G.C., & Jones, G. (1982). Degree completion at British Columbia's universities. *Journal of Higher Education, 12*(2), 43-57.

Dominion Bureau of Statistics. (1970). *Canadian community colleges and related institutions*. Ottawa: Minister of Industry, Trade, and Commerce. Catalogue no. 81-222.

Eichler, M. (1983). *Families in Canada today: Recent changes and their policy consequences*. Agincourt, ON: Gage.

Finkelstein, M. (1984). The status of academic women: An assessment of five competing explanations. *Review of Higher Education, 7*(3), 223-246.

Foot, D., & Pervin, B. (1983). The determinants of post-secondary enrolment rates in Ontario. *Canadian Journal of Higher Education, 13*(3), 1-24.

Fortin, M. (1987). *Accessibility to and participation in the post-secondary education system in Canada*. Saskatoon: National Forum on Post-Secondary Education.

Gillett, M. (1981). *We walked very warily: A history of women at McGill*. Montreal: Eden Press Women's Publications.

Goyder, J. (1980). Trends in the socioeconomic attainment of the university educated: A status attainment model interpretation. *Canadian Journal of Higher Education, 10*(2), 21-38.

Gunderson, M., & Muszynski, L. (1990). *Women and labour market poverty*. Ottawa: Canadian Advisory Council on the Status of Women.

Guppy, N. (1984). Access to higher education in Canada. *Canadian Journal of Higher Education, 14*(3), 79-93.

Guppy, N. (1989). Pay equity in Canadian universities, 1972-73 and 1985-86. *Canadian Review of Sociology and Anthropology, 26*(5), 743-758.

Guppy, N., & Pendakur, K. (1989). The effects of gender and parental education on participation within post-secondary education in the 1970's and 1980's. *Canadian Journal of Higher Education, 19*(1), 49-62.

Hall, R.M., & Sandler, B.R. (1982). *The classroom climate: A chilly one for women? Project on the Status and Education of Women.* Washington, DC: Association of American Colleges.

Harris, R. (1976). *A history of higher education in Canada 1663-1960.* Toronto: University of Toronto Press.

Kupferschmidt, M., & Vanderkamp, J. (1987). *Success and drop-out patterns of B.A. students.* Unpublished manuscript, University of Guelph.

Marshall, K. (1987). *Who are the professional women?* Ottawa: Statistics Canada, Catalogue no. 99-951.

McLaughlin, S., Melber, J.B., Zimmerle, D., Winges, L., & Johnson, T. (1988). *The changing lives of American women.* Chapel Hill: University of North Carolina Press.

Phillips, C.E. (1957). *The development of education in Canada.* Toronto: W.J. Gage and Co. Ltd.

Prentice, A. (1977). *The school promoters.* Toronto: McClelland and Stewart.

Prentice, A. (1989). Scholarly passion: Two persons who caught it. *Historical Studies in Education, 1*(1), 7-27.

Rosenblum, G., & Rosenblum, B.R. (1990). Segmented labour markets in institutions of higher learning. *Sociology of Education, 63*(3), 151-164.

Ross, L.R., & Powell, R. (1990). Relationships between gender and success in distance education courses: A preliminary investigation. *Research in Distance Education, 2*(2), 10-11.

Royal Commission on the Economic Union and Development Prospects of Canada. (1985). *Report of the Royal Commission on the Economic Union and Development Prospects of Canada.* Ottawa: Information Canada.

Royal Commission on the Status of Women in Canada. (1970). *Report of the Royal Commission on the Status of Women in Canada.* Ottawa: Information Canada.

Standing Senate Committee on National Finance. (1987). *Federal policy on post-secondary education.* Ottawa: Minister of Supply and Services.

Statistics Canada. (1971). *A century of education in British Columbia: Statistical perspectives.* Ottawa: Minister of Industry, Trade, and Commerce.

Statistics Canada. (1971 through 1988). *The labour force* (issues for: 1971, 1976, 1981, 1985, 1988). Ottawa: Minister of Supply and Services. (Catalogue No. 71-001)

Statistics Canada. (1978a). *Enrolment in community colleges.* Ottawa: Minister of Supply and Services. (Catalogue No. 81-222).

Statistics Canada. (1978b). *Historical compendium of educational statistics: From confederation to 1975.* Ottawa: Minister of Industry, Trade and Commerce. (Catalogue No. 81-568)

Statistics Canada. (1984). *Educational statistics for the seventies.* Ottawa: Minister of Supply and Services. (Catalogue No. 81-569)

Statistics Canada. (1988). *Teachers in universities, 1986-87.* Ottawa: Minister of Supply & Services. (Catalogue No. 81-241)

Statistics Canada. (1989a). *Enrolment in community colleges.* Ottawa: Minister of Supply and Services. (Catalogue No. 81-222)

Statistics Canada. (1989b). *Income distributions by size in Canada, 1988.* Ottawa: Minister of Supply and Services. (Catalogue No. 13-207)

Statistics Canada. (1990a). *Education in Canada: A statistical review for 1988-89.* Ottawa: Minister of Supply and Services. (Catalogue No. 81-229)

Statistics Canada. (1990b). *Women in Canada: A statistical report.* Ottawa: Minister of Supply and Services. (Catalogue No. 89-503E)

Status of Women Canada and Manitoba Women's Directorate. (1989). *Participation of girls and women in math, science, and technology. Report submitted to the Joint Meeting of Federal/Provincial/Territorial Ministries responsible for Education.* Toronto.

Stewart, L. (1990). *"It's up to you": Women at UBC in the early years.* Vancouver: University of British Columbia Press.

Vanderkamp, J. (1984). University enrolment in Canada 1951-1981 and beyond. *Canadian Journal of Higher Education, 14*(2), 49-62.

Violato, C. (1990). A longitudinal comparative study of the academic achievement of education and other undergraduate students, *Canadian Journal of Education, 15,* 264-276.

Violato, C. & Travis, L. (1990). A national survey of education students: Some data on background, habits, and reasons for entering education. *Canadian Journal of Education, 15,* 277-292.

Wannell, T. (1990). Male-female earnings gap among recent university graduates. *Perspectives on Labour and Income, 2*(2), 19-31.

Weis, L. (1985). Progress but no parity: Women in higher education. *Academe, 71*(36), 29-33.

8

Gender Relations in the Classroom:
A Fresh Look at Coeducation[1]

Linda Eyre

School policies and initiatives dealing with gender inequality have burgeoned in recent years. Typically, schools focus on correcting gender bias in student-teacher interaction, eliminating sex stereotyping in school texts and resources, and balancing the ratio of female and male students in specific school subjects. These gains have not come about without concerted efforts by feminist teachers and parents (Weiner & Arnot, 1987). However, these solutions can still allow traditional gender relations of domination and subordination to flourish. Mary O'Brien (1990), for example, says solutions that deal with equality of opportunity while avoiding equality of condition are "fundamentally patriarchal in theory and in practice" (p. 12).

The research reported in this chapter attempts to illuminate the inadequacies of one solution to gender inequality in schools: balancing enrolments of female and male students in specific school subjects and producing coeducational classrooms. I use evidence from a study of gender relations in grade 8 home economics classrooms to show how coeducation does not fulfill its promise as a solution to gender inequality in schools. I show how gender as a social relation of power operates in coeducational classrooms. In particular, I show how the actual practices of students and teachers constrain gender equity in coeducational home economics classrooms and I raise questions about appropriate pedagogic responses.

Home economics is a particularly interesting area of study because it has a distinct history with regard to coeducation. In the early 20th century, home economics and technical studies were excluded from the coeducational movement. Whereas other school subjects, for utilitarian reasons only, became coeducational (Lasser, 1987), home economics and technical studies remained strictly sex differentiated. This move reflected the ideology of gender, delegating women and men to their "natural," separate, private and public spheres (Prentice, 1988). In the early 1970s, however, in direct response to Sex Discrimination Acts and feminist concerns about women's equality and the role of schooling in the sexual division of labor, home economics was promoted as a coeducational subject. Now many schools require all junior high school students take a coeducational home economics and technical studies program, organized on a rotational basis, for at least one school year. Little attention, however, has been paid to how goals of gender equity through coeducation are realized in coeducational home economics classrooms.

Coeducation implies an equal education for girls and boys. Some feminist theorists, however, argue that girls and boys do not receive an equal education in coeducational settings. The argument, briefly, is that coeducation means giving girls and boys an education designed for males. As Adrienne Rich (1985) writes:

> If there is any misleading concept, it is that of 'coeducation': that because women and men are sitting in the same classrooms, hearing the same lectures, reading the same books, performing the same laboratory experiments, they are receiving an equal education. They are not, first because the content of education itself validates men even as it invalidates women. Its very message is that men have been the shapers and thinkers of the world, and that this is only natural. The bias of higher education, including the so-called sciences, is white, and male, racist and sexist: and this bias is expressed in subtle and blatant ways. (p. 24)

Educational researchers have provided data to support the belief that girls and boys receive unequal treatment in coeducational classrooms. Many studies have shown that boys and men dominate interaction and shape curriculum in coeducational settings (Kramarae & Treichler, 1990; Sadker & Sadker, 1986).

Jane Roland Martin (1981), an educational philosopher, has been influential in calling attention to masculine bias in school knowledge. Martin says that schools are permeated with masculine values of competition, power and control, and prepare students only for the public world. She says schooling should be informed with feminine virtues of care, concern, connectedness and nurturance, and should also prepare students for the private world of home and family. In describing her conception of the educated person, Martin (1981) writes:

> We need a conception of [the educated person] which does not fall into the trap of assigning males and females to the different processes of society, yet does not make the mistake of ignoring one kind of process altogether. We all participate in both kinds of processes and both are important to all of us. Whether we adopt one or many ideals, a conception of the educated person that is tied only to one kind of process will be incomplete. (p. 107)

Martin argues that both masculine and feminine dimensions must become an integral part of the education of all students and across all subjects in the curriculum. She believes it advantageous to girls and boys to understand both perspectives.

Martin (1981) also challenges the notion, implicit in "coeducation," that girls and boys should be treated "the same," arguing that gender equality is more likely to be achieved if teachers are sensitive to differences between girls and boys, differences based on their past, gendered experiences. She says teachers should provide different treatments to reflect the interests of the disadvantaged group:

> When sex or gender are thought to make no difference, women's lives, experiences, activities are overlooked and an ideal is formulated in terms of

men and the roles for which they have traditionally been considered suited. . . . Sex or gender has to be taken into account if the ideal of the educated person is not to be biased. (p. 109)

Whereas Martin is somewhat vague about what a gender-sensitive strategy would look like in a coeducational classroom, Mary Belenky, Blythe McVicar Clincy, Nancy Rule Goldberger and Jill Mattuck Tarule (1986) relate gender sensitivity specifically to theory about how women learn. They argue that schooling should be sensitive to women's ways of knowing: ways of knowing grounded in life experience rather than abstractions. A pedagogy more conducive to women's ways of knowing is proposed: "banking" and "doubting" models of education would be replaced with more collaborative, cooperative and caring learning environments.

Women's past experiences and ways of knowing, however, are determined by many dimensions of their lives. In particular, writings of black women, Native women, refugee women and lesbian feminists have shown how their experiences as women are tied to oppressions stemming from capitalism, racism, colonialism and heterosexism. Teresa De Lauretis (1990) writes:

> But what this string of seemingly coequal terms, conveying the notion of layers of oppression along parallel axes of "difference," does not grasp is their constant intersection and mutual implication or how each one may affect the others — for example, how gender affects racial oppression in its subjective effects . . . the layers are not parallel but imbricated into one another; the systems of oppression are interlocking and mutually determining. (p. 133)

Solutions to gender inequality in schooling, therefore, should recognize that woman students experience oppression in different ways. Gender inequality should be looked at in conjunction with other forms of oppression that exist in schools (Amos & Parmar, 1981; Pelleschi, 1988; Trenchard & Warren, 1987).

The study of gender inequality in coeducational settings reveals the issue of power to be even more complex than the question of diversity. Sandra Kessler, Dean Ashendon, Bob Connell and Gary Dowsett (1985), and Robert Connell (1987), for example, argue that most solutions to gender inequality in schools focus too simplistically on predetermined categories of "male" and "female." They argue that attention should be paid to variation within categories and to how particular kinds of femininity and masculinity are constructed as cultural ideals and how other kinds are suppressed. Kessler et al and Connell refer to the dominant patterns as "hegemonic heterosexual masculinity" and "emphasized femininity." Connell (1987) writes:

> Hegemonic masculinity is always constructed in relation to various subordinated masculinities as well as in relation to women. The interplay between different forms of masculinity is an important part of how a patriarchal social order works.

> At the level of mass social relations . . . forms of femininity are defined clearly. . . . It is the global subordination of women to men that provides an essential basis for differentiation. [Emphasized femininity] is defined around compliance with this subordination and is oriented to accommodating the interests and desires of men. (p. 183)

Connell says individuals do not simply resist or reproduce oppressive structures, but are constantly constituting their own culture. He also argues that as well as embodying oppressive structures, practice can turn against and oppose structures:

> The crucial point is that practice . . . is always responding to a situation. Practice is the transformation of that situation in a particular direction. To describe structure is to specify what it is in the situation that constrains the play of practice. Since the consequence of practice is a transformed situation which is the object of new practice, structure specifies the way practice (over time) constrains practice. . . . Practice can be turned against what constrains it; so structure can be deliberately the object of practice. But practice cannot escape structure . . . it is always obliged to reckon with the constraints that are the precipitate of history. (p. 95)

Solutions to gender inequality in schools, therefore, should explore how individuals build as well as respond to oppressive social structures.

Valerie Walkerdine (1981, 1989) and Rosie Walden and Valerie Walkerdine (1986) show how girls and boys and the teacher negotiate power in the classroom; how they at once seize and relinquish power. Walkerdine (1981) argues that individuals do not represent fixed positions of power. She says power is "produced as a constantly shifting relation" (p. 23). According to Walkerdine, power is not determined by the fact that individuals are boys, girls or teachers; power is constantly negotiated between them. However, Walkerdine describes the power held by girls as having a "double edge," reinforcing traditional notions of femininity and tying them to domesticity and economic dependence:

> the contradictions, the struggles for power, the shifting relations of power, all testify the necessity for an understanding of subjectivities not a unique subjectivity. These contradictions also point to the necessity to rethink our strategies for action within education. . . . It no longer seems enough to believe that we are in a process of simply oppressing children. Neither can we be comforted by the thought that 'progressive education' will free children to explore their own experience, without understanding precisely how that experience is understood and how that produces the children as subjects. (p. 24)

For several reasons I have found the work of Connell (1987), Kessler et al. (1985), and Walkerdine (1981) useful in analyzing gender relations in the study reported in this chapter, and for raising questions about appropriate pedagogic responses. Because power was negotiated among and between girls and boys in the study, it was not appropriate to speak of differences between girls and boys. Rather, as Walkerdine (1981) says, there were "a multiplicity of subjectivities" (p. 23). In addition, because there was division within gender categories, what became of interest was how particular kinds of femininity and particular kinds of masculinity were supported and others suppressed. The "particular kinds" of femininity and masculinity fitted with Kessler and her colleagues' and Connell's notion of "emphasized femininity" and "hegemonic masculinity." Their work also provided a way of analyzing the posturing of heterosexuality and homophobia evident in this study.

The Study

The setting of this study was a mandatory, grade 8, coeducational, home economics/technical studies program in an inner-city, multi-ethnic, secondary school in British Columbia. The study is based on participant observation and interviews with a classroom group of 24 grade 8 students (10 girls and 14 boys), and six teachers, during a school year. Students represented a variety of ethnic and cultural groups. The majority of students were of Chinese and Vietnamese origins, with the remainder having various backgrounds, including First Nations, Indo-Canadian and English-Canadian.[2]

This chapter deals only with the home economics section of the program. This section consisted of three separate courses: Food and Nutrition, Clothing and Textiles, and Family Management. Students moved through the program on a rotational basis, spending approximately 18 hours in each area. Each home economics course was taught by a different teacher. All of the teachers were "white" and from so-called majority backgrounds, and they all were women.

I stayed with one group of students throughout the school year, attending almost every home economics period with them. I sat with the students and participated in activities as best I could with notebook in hand. I took detailed notes about what I observed, and transcribed these daily. I interviewed students and teachers during lunch hours, free periods, or after school. I audio-taped the interviews and transcribed them later.

Throughout, I attempted to break the hierarchy of researcher-researched (Stanley & Wise, 1983), with varying degrees of success (Eyre, 1989). I tried to make interviews more like conversations (Oakley, 1981), while pushing for students' and teachers' understandings of coeducational home economics, domestic labor, and gender relations. I also sought students' and teachers' responses to what I had observed in the classroom. Following Shulamit Reinharz (1983), I kept a diary of my own thoughts and feelings as a researcher in order to provide information about my subjective experience in the research enterprise.

In addition, I avoided imposing my authority by taking all transcripts of my classroom observations back to the respective teachers for their analysis. I asked the teachers for their responses to my descriptions of life in their classrooms. Teachers' reflections on their own practices opened possibilities for pedagogical change.

Although I gave careful attention to accuracy of findings, the information presented here does not claim to represent reality. At best, ethnographic accounts are only partial truths and are necessarily incomplete (Clifford, 1986). I do not claim to speak about all coeducational home economics classrooms, nor do I claim that the evidence presented here consitutes a complete picture of the classrooms studied. Observations and interviews are mediated through conventions of research, and through the researcher's own lens (Atkinson, 1990), as is the writing of this chapter. The information is presented as a beginning point of entry into understanding gender relations and classroom life. Readers must take it from here and mediate it through their own experiences.

In examining practice my intention is not to universalize teachers' experiences, nor girls' or boys' experiences. Nor do I intend to position girls and boys against each other, or to blame teachers. My intention is to show how, despite plans for gender equity through coeducation, social relations of the wider society enter into daily lives in classrooms and how, through actual practices, gender inequality is maintained.

This chapter focuses on two themes: issues of knowledge and competence, and issues of segregation and domination.[3] Although I discuss the themes separately, they are interconnected and act together to constrain gender equity in the classroom.

Issues of Knowledge and Competence

It is important to look at teachers' constructions of the curriculum and how this intersects with the different experiences and preferred ways of knowing that students bring with them to the classroom. A gender-equitable curriculum allows for a variety of subjectivities. It is also pertinent to examine how knowledge and practice contribute to the sexual division of labor, and it is essential to understand how teachers' and students' practices contribute to traditional power relations and ultimately to social inequality.

In this study gender equity was constrained because girls and boys had different experiences and interests but received the same instruction, instruction tailored to the teachers' perceptions of boys' needs. Teachers assumed boys preferred a technical approach to curriculum and that boys had little experience in domestic work. This was not immediately apparent in the way teachers described the program to me. Teachers said:

> "It is intended to give the students an introduction to the basic areas of home economics. Content is secondary. I think what we are doing is introducing them to a space, to a teacher, to a subject area. Hopefully turn them on in some areas so when they have an option in grade 9 they will know where they want to go."

> "You don't want to stereotype these roles. It gives them the chance to make some kind of decision for their electives next year . . . and it's something they have to do all of their lives."

"I want the students to be able to criticize traditions in terms of what they do to women, what they say about women, the position they put women in."

The teachers' conceptualization of the program differed, however, from descriptions they presented to students and from their actual practice. Whereas all teachers told me that the program was designed to give students broader experiences and prepare them for non-stereotyped roles and relationships, both Foods and Clothing teachers described their courses differently to students. Rather than talking about the domestic division of labor and the the importance of life-long sharing of work in the home, they talked to students about specific technical skills students needed to know in order to make specific products or to meet a certain standard. Teachers said:

"I don't intend to make you sewers. . . . You may never sew again. . . . I'd like to introduce you to a new machine. You learn to master the sewing machine. You control it — it doesn't control you. So you can all succeed. . . . You are going to make a kite and a pincushion. . . . We learn about the machine. Learn to master and control it and learn to make simple projects."

"I'm trying to introduce you to what foods and nutrition is all about, and the importance of it. It just isn't cooking and eating . . . I want you to learn about why food is important for the body. . . . I'm also going to teach you some basic techniques. . . . How to make a sauce without it going lumpy. . . . You will learn how to work safely in the kitchen. . . . I teach you the Canadian way of tablesetting. . . . It's not the only way or the correct way but if you are going to be working in food institutions then you will be expected to know the Canadian way."

Although Foods and Clothing teachers conceptualized the program as promoting women's equality through breaking down the sexual division of labor, their practice followed a traditional pedagogy, placing emphasis on manipulative skills and techniques and on meeting standards defined by the teacher. Though the ability to perform domestic tasks would no doubt contribute to sharing work in the home, one does not necessarily lead to the other. Interviews with students showed that girls and boys still held traditional views regarding domestic labor. Learning domestic skills did not necessarily change students' minds about who should be doing domestic work.

Content in the Family Management section, however, was specifically focused on issues of gender. For example, the Family Management teacher said:

"I am asking you to think about the roles of women and men and to question them. . . . I want you to be able to observe television critically and be critical of how that image is portrayed."

By emphasizing gender roles, however, the teacher limited the discussion of gender inequality. Gender inequality was viewed as a matter of individual practices and personal behaviors rather than social relations of power.

Although teachers said that girls and boys should be treated "the same," they also said they adapted their programs to make boys feel comfortable:

"I just treat them the same. I figure they've all got the same intelligence. I think I make allowances for the boys if they do blunder but I do for the girls too. . . . But I do just cover the basics because the boys would get a little lost."

"I want to get boys more comfortable with the things women have traditionally done . . . so that women can get out and have careers and so forth . . . to help boys later on in their relationships with women."

One particular teacher said she was trying to achieve a delicate balance between treating students the same and yet differently, and she recognized the inherent contradictions. She said:

"As human beings we should treat each other equally to a certain extent as far as respect and the basic kinds of things we expect from one human being to another. But you have to treat them differently. I have difficulty talking about it. When you are speaking to a whole class of kids you speak to them as asexuals. You don't even think about it, but when you are dealing with them, one to one you have to. I certainly don't treat them the same. . . . You have to make a distinction because they need to feel comfortable. . . . I say 'This is a machine. It has a clutch. . . .' All these similarities to things that are masculine helps. I think I joke with the boys more than I do with the girls. . . . They need to feel secure in what is traditionally a girls' area."

One of the difficulties for teachers was providing for different levels of experience. All of the girls and a couple of the boys were familiar with the language of foods and sewing, and were already socially oriented to work in the home.

Rita:[4] "My dad cooks and cleans and goes to work and everything. I like sort of help out, sort of like a mom does. Like I clean up and I cook and I look after my brother and sister cause they're little."

Tina: "I already knew some of the stuff we made here. I could do it in a couple of hours by myself . . . like with my aunt I usually do everything in half an hour. . . . I make muffins and macaroni and cheese, I already knew that years ago. I always make fried rice at home."

Jill: "Well, at home the cloth is not cut. Like it's not already cut for me. [At home] we have to measure and all that to make our own clothing."

A boy also commented on girls' proficiencies:

Jaspal: "Most girls already know how to cook and how to sew. You can watch them and learn something. Even on the first sewing day they knew what to do already, like for ironing. . . . The food they made looked good. It looked better than ours."

A few boys also possessed some basic skills, particularly in sewing. They told me they had learned sewing skills from their mothers in the home sewing industry, and cooking skills from women at home. Boys said:

Trung: "I already learned how to use the sewing machine. My mother taught me. I learned by watching my mother. I don't make stuff. I just mend stuff, rips and stuff. I just mend it."

Thanh: "Cooking was the easiest cause you have experience with it. You might do a little yourself or you might see your mom do it. I just cook for myself . . . eggs or something."

For most boys, however, domestic work was a new experience.

David: "It's not difficult really. It's just knowing what to use I guess. I don't know some of those things that we use. Like she says to use these things and I forget. Just one little thing like a wooden spoon, and then she gets mad at me when I ask her what to use."

Jaspal: "I know how to iron pretty good now, better than before. . . . Before it was hard to sew. Now it's easy, just putting the thing in. Like I didn't know which way to sew at all, it was confusing. . . . I can thread the needle now and I can do those stitches on the outside and those on the inside."

These examples show also that being oriented to domestic work required using a specific language and boys were not as proficient in its use as were girls.[5]

There were similarities and differences between and among girls and boys in their responses to the program. In the Foods and the Clothing sections, boys were more outwardly enthusiastic than girls. Boys said they loved what they were doing, they raced to finish first, jostled for the teachers' attention, and talked often about who, among the boys, was going to get the highest mark. Girls' enthusiasm was different. Whereas some girls said they were bored in the classroom, they also talked to me and to each other about their interests in making clothes and preparing meals.

For example, at the beginning of Clothing and Textiles students had to practice using the sewing machine by sewing on paper. Though one girl said she enjoyed what she was doing:

Tina: [Sewing on paper] "That was fun!"

Jill: [Disgusted tone] "It's fun?"

Tina: "I've never done that before, that's all."

Most girls were not similarly enthused:

Tanya: "We were making clothes" [in previous school].

Jennifer: "Yeah. What do we do? — sew paper."

Maria: "Are you bored, Tanya?"

Tanya: "Yeah . . . I'm finished. It's so boring."

Maria: "So am I."

Many boys, however, were excited about the technology of sewing:

Jay: "I love it! [sewing on paper] It's fun."

Rick: "Isn't it weird when you put it [stitch regulator] on different lengths."

Stuart: "Wow. A computer in a sewing machine."

Rick: "I know. Computerized patterns."

And in finishing first:

Stuart: "Are you at the last part yet, Danny?"

Danny: "Yes."

Stuart: "Which one?"

Danny: "Second one. Third small one. I haven't made a mistake yet."

Bao: "I bet."

Danny: "I haven't."

Stuart: "Winner! I'm done. Are these the only sheets we do?"

Rick: "I'm finished."

Teacher: "Good, Rick. What are you going to do now?"

Anthony: "Damn it. Rick got finished before me. Shit face."

Although Danny talked about wanting to make other projects — "When you get to grade 12 you can come in here and do what you want. . . . [Looking at senior work] What's this? It's nice. . . . I wanted to do that bag, man. I wanted to make that bag instead of this kite" — it was mostly girls who wanted to produce objects that they perceived as being more useful and more interesting than what they were doing in the classroom:

Rita: [Looking at a poster] "I want to make a poodle skirt like that."

Maria: [Looking at senior projects] "Look, they're all making shirts."

Lily: "They always make kites [in grade 8], but I want to make the grade 9 bag. . . . I think I don't want to make the kite. It's very useless. You're not going out and play with it. It's just — just decoration. It's no good."

In interviews I tried to find out if students would have liked to have had an opportunity to talk about food and clothing in relation to their own lives. Whereas most boys said they did not want to talk about their own experiences, some girls were keen on a less technical approach. For example, Poonam, said:

"I would tell them about the religion that we talk and what kind of clothes we wear. Mostly it's shiny material like when we go to parties. Like my mom, she wears a sari, right? It's just a long piece of material that has different designs. It's almost like a skirt but it goes all around the waist part and over your shoulder — there's this long thing that comes over it."

Poonam's comments were particularly meaningful because this was the most I heard her say all year. She was usually very quiet, but on this topic she spoke confidently and enthusiastically.

The different responses suggest that girls were more sophisticated in their interests than boys. For most boys sewing was enjoyable because it involved knowing how things work and because boys made it into a competitive activity. Girls and some boys, however, were more interested in clothing itself than in the activities offered in the program.[6] The responses also suggest that while emphasizing manipulative skills, the curriculum supported a particular kind of masculinity, one interested in technology and control.

The Family Management section of the program involved different knowledge and competencies. While the teacher still controlled what counted as knowledge, students were expected to share their personal experiences in the classroom. Although only a few girls and boys actually participated in this way, none of the girls said they objected to this approach, whereas many of the boys did object. Some boys said that the activities were "too private"; others just did not complete the activities as requested by the teacher; and others fooled about in class, or tuned out. Danny's comments were typical of most boys:

"Most of us [boys] didn't really like Family Management. I sort of didn't like it. Sort of boring 'cause most of the time you had to get your chair [into a circle] and you'd get bored just sitting around. Get bored after a while."

A few boys were more explicit about their difficulties in the course:

Trung: "It was hard trying to express myself. I find it easier talking about other people than myself. [Why?] I don't usually tell other people about my feelings. I keep it to myself."

Ptan: "Sometimes you feel so nervous because you say stuff that is really intimate, really deep inside yourself. Today what I said was really personal — about someone judging me because of my height. I felt sad."

Some girls, however, wanted more from the course:

Rita: "It's kinda boring. I like assignments, but she doesn't give us that many. Like we started one. We had to write about me. I liked that one. I like writing stories and stuff like that, but she doesn't give us many."

Lily: "We mostly talked about western culture. I think it would be nice — it would be interesting — to know about other cultures, how you can make other cultures better. Because when you only stick to your own you think it's not that good and you don't know how lucky you are."

These comments suggest that in determining classroom activities, the Family Management teacher inadvertently overlooked the interests of most girls and some boys. Also, while focusing her course on verbal descriptions of personal experience, the teacher inadvertently overlooked the difficulties many boys had with this approach, but at the same time didn't take the notion of experience far enough for some girls. Thus, while treating students "the same," teachers inadvertently neglected to recognize the diversity of girls' and boys' interests and ways of knowing; and the teachers' technical approach did not allow such diversity to be revealed in the classroom.

Whereas this work points to the importance of being sensitive to gender differences, as Martin (1981) and Belenky et al. (1986) suggest, it also alerts one to the dangers of categorizing girls and boys and of making assumptions about their previous gendered experiences. It was clear that students' gendered experiences intersected with other dimensions of their lives.

Issues of Segregation and Domination

Another issue of coeducation concerns male dominance in classrooms. Though the prefix "co" suggests mutuality and complementarity (Stimpson, 1987), as stated previously many studies have shown that male students dominate classroom interaction. In some ways this study was no exception. In other ways, however, there were important differences. Participant observation and interviews with students revealed the internal dynamics of the classroom. There were a variety of subjectivities and there were divisions within gender categories.

In all sections, girls and boys segregated themselves into same-sex groups. Girls and boys gave similar reasons for this segregation. They said they were "more comfortable," "more confident," and "less embarrassed" with people of the same sex, and most of all, they wanted to be with their friends. A friend was someone they could talk to and relate to, and was also of the same sex.

> Anne: "Girls like to be near each other so we can talk to each other. Girls don't talk to boys 'cause they don't understand. Girls don't like to talk to guys. . . . We talk about clothes, shopping, girls talk, stuff like that."

> Jaspal: "Boys talk to each other more. They share things with each other. . . . Like what we talk about is what we do together. We don't know what girls talk about so we don't talk to them."

Some girls gave other reasons for their desire to be segregated from boys. Jill and Tina had already internalized messages of girls' promiscuity:

> Jill: "Like if you sit with the guys the girls would say 'You're boy-crazy' and all those things."

> Tina: "We don't want boys to think we like them. . . . Don't want to give them ideas."

Melanie spoke of the power boys held in the classroom:

> "We just go in the room and we know we shouldn't sit there cause the boys sit there."

And Lily spoke of how Anthony made her feel:

"There's nothing wrong except that — well, he takes a knife, you know, and he pokes the bench. He scares me sometimes. And then sometimes he's always in a bad mood or something, but he's really quite nice. It's just well — it's crazy. He cares about how other people look at him, right? He wants to be tough."

Maria talked about what boys did to girls:

"They're brats in grade 8 mostly. They're immature, mostly . . . I'm not saying that about all the boys, just most of them. . . . They spit on you and like stupid things; one guy broke into my friend's locker and started writing all over it. The teacher caught him but he did nothing. He just goes apologize to that girl. That's all."

And Poonam spoke of what boys said to girls:

"Sometimes the boys make fun of you and the girls don't like it. . . . Sometimes they make fun of the clothes you're wearing, or if they get their hair permed, they call them names or something."

Most girls, however, did not speak about what boys actually said to them. I observed that boys called girls "cows," "bitches," "witches," "whores" and "lesies," and they said they were "evil" and they "smelled." Boys' talk was frequently homophobic and misogynist, and linked to their sexuality. For example:

[Maria walked past the boys to get stuffing for her kite.]

Bao: "How come she transfer out of Art class?"

Stuart: "Who cares!"

Danny: "Who?"

Stuart: "Maria. What a gay — no, what a lesbian name, eh? I don't know why the girls like the gay guys on the block. They suck."

Danny: "That's why they like them, 'cause they're gay."

[Maria returned to her table without saying anything.]

Teacher: "Orange vegetables have lots of vitamin A."

Jay: [Pretending to be serious] "Is it hard?"

Teacher: "The carrot is crisp. Would someone like to have it?"

Danny: "Jennifer will have it. She likes long things."

[Laughter.]

Girls did not raise boys' talk as an issue. When I drew girls' attention to such talk, girls substantiated my observations, but their reaction was usually one of denial:

Rita: "What do you mean? Like what?"

LE: "Like 'cow.'"

Rita: "Oh, 'cow' is a normal one, yeah. That's what guys call girls when they get mad at them. . . . It doesn't bother me 'cause I don't really care, you know. I know they don't know any better so I don't say anything back. I don't care. Even if they do say something to me I don't listen, or if I'm really mad I'll call them a name back."

LE: "Do they call you anything else?"

Rita: "'Slut,' 'tramp,' 'ig,' 'whore,' 'bitch'; stuff like that. I just tell them to shut up."

This reaction of Rita's, echoed by other girls, suggests that girls took boys' language for granted. It was an accepted part of their everyday experience.

Though teachers showed concern about the amount of noise boys were making, they did not usually address the content of boys' talk. Teachers said:

"Boys, I don't mind you socializing. You have to remember we can all hear what you are talking about. You talk too much."

"Keep it gentleman-like. There's too much chatter. . . . Just remember this isn't the locker room."

"Be quiet. We don't need details here."

"I don't like the conversation here."

"Some of you are quite rude."

By suggesting that such talk should be kept private, or reserved for the locker room, and by not being explicit about the content, teachers may inadvertently have condoned the content of boys' talk.

Although girls and boys segregated themselves most of the time, and teachers did not insist on other arrangements, there were a few instances in the Family Management section when students were expected to work together in small, mixed-sex groups. On these occasions girls and boys each blamed the other, either for not working or for not listening to their points of view.

Jill: "We were supposed to write things down and participate in the answers and stuff. The boys didn't participate at all, they wouldn't give any answers. They would just sort of sit there."

David: "I didn't want to work with Rita. Then the teacher started getting really mad. She said she would send me to the office, so I said I would work with her. But the girls kept saying, 'Oh we did all the work,' and stuff. I didn't do lots but I did my fair share. Rita was the recorder, so that didn't help much."

David's comments also illustrate how the teacher, while attempting to provide an interactive pedagogy, reprimanded students who did not participate, thereby resorting to the security of a more traditional pedagogic model.

Girls and boys also came together during teachers' demonstrations or large-group discussions. On these occasions a small group of boys dominated student-teacher interaction. They answered most of the teachers' questions, they asked questions, and they corrected and ridiculed teachers. The following scene is typical of what happened during the teacher's demonstrations in the Food and Nutrition section of the program:

Teacher: "What did I do with the margarine for the biscuit mixture?"

Jay: [Shouting] "Cut it in!"

Rick: "Chop it!"

Teacher: "What did I use to mix it?"

Tanya: "A spoon."

Jay: [Shouting] "A fork!"

Rick: [Shouting] "A fork!"

Teacher: "A fork is okay. How do I add the liquid?"

Jay: [Shouting] "Pour little by little."

Teacher: "Right."

Jay: "Don't you have to turn on the stove stuff?"

Rick: [Laughing and mimicking Jay] "Turn on the stove stuff!"

[Laughter from boys' side.]

Teacher: "As it forms [a dough], what do you do?"

Jay: [Loudly] "Mix it together! You use your fingers. You forgot the flour!"

Teacher: "I haven't got there yet. Have any of you made biscuits at home?"

Jay: "I made it. I fed it to the birds and the birds died!"

[Loud laughter from boys.]

[The teacher made the dough and rolled it out to make a pizza]

Rick: "Isn't that small?"

Teacher: "It's plenty big enough. If it sticks what do you do with the dough?"

An: "Put flour on it."

Bao: "Isn't that thin?"

Rick: "Man, that's thin!"

[Loud laughter from boys]

[The teacher pricked the bottom of the pizza dough. She explained the reason for this with reference to a hot air balloon. Jay and Vinh started to make farting noises, Danny and Bao joined in. Loud laughter from the boys.]

Teacher: "You can add lots of ingredients to pizza. I know someone who even likes banana."

Vinh: [Pointing to Jay's neck] "Hey, look at this."

Trung: [Quietly] "A hickey."

Jay: [Laughing] "Jenny gave me this. Jenny gave me a banana split."

[Boys laughed quietly.]

Danny: [Thinking boys were laughing about banana on pizza] "Banana's good with it, you know."

[Boys laughed loudly.]

This example, among many, illustrates how a few boys typically dominated student-teacher interaction. Girls and most boys were silenced. Whereas girls rarely laughed at the boys' talk, laughter from the quieter boys had the effect of supporting the dominant boys' behavior. Boys displayed their heterosexuality, showing how sexuality was interwoven with power. In addition, the example shows how the teacher tried unsuccessfully to relate to students' experiences because of the power of the dominant boys.

Most quiet girls and boys rarely spoke out. Rita, Jennifer and Ptan, however, occasionally tried to break their own silence. In Family Management, for example, they tried to interject their own experiences into the curriculum. Those who spoke out, however, were corrected, interrupted, made fun of, or drowned out by the dominant boys.

Teacher: "Does anyone know what joint custody means?"

Rick: [Loudly] "They cut her in half."

Rita: "They have joint custody of me. They both have to agree about me. They both have a say in it."

Stuart: "They both have to give you money."

[Laughter]

Jennifer: "My aunt is East Indian and she lives with her aunt and her brothers. They are all from India and they have nowhere to go."

Rick: [Shouting] "A hundred aunts living in a house."

[Loud laughter from boys' side.]

Ptan: "Somebody said about me, 'You know, that shrimp is the shortest guy in the whole school.'"

[Silence]

[Bao laughed loudly.]

[Jennifer and Rita said something to Bao in Ptan's defence. Inaudible noise level high.]

Teacher: "Yes that's a really hurtful thing. Why do we value taller people? In the long run does it make a difference how tall someone is?"

Rick: "Yeah. You can't reach the cookie jar."

[Laughter.]

There were also occasions when girls' contributions were overlooked by teachers. For example:

Teacher: "Can you give an example of a television show where women are invisible and unnecessary?"

Rick: "I've never seen an invisible woman!"

[Laughter.]

Jennifer: "'Night Street.'"

Teacher: "Rick, you seem to be choosing to absent yourself from the discussion. I would like you to move further away from Jay."

This example also illustrates how difficult it was for the teacher to hold a serious conversation with the group.

Many of these examples show how teachers' techniques of asking questions to the group, thereby allowing anyone to respond, enabled the same group of boys to dominate question-and-answer sessions. Also, because the same boys fooled about, made fun of, and corrected the teacher, they received more criticism, and because they answered more questions they received more praise, than girls and quieter boys. In addition, by giving power to the dominant boys, teachers indirectly reinforced a particular kind of femininity for themselves and in turn sustained a particular kind of masculinity among boys.

Although girls and quieter boys did not comment on their own silencing, Ptan said:

"If I was a girl I would get angry, because sometimes the boys they kind of criticize what the girls say, so I think if I was a girl I would get angry inside."

Whereas most of the dominant boys were unable to explain their behavior, Rick said:

"I talked a lot, but off call, when I wasn't supposed to. I guess I did a fair amount of that. . . . It could have been a bit of protection, but I doubt that, um I'm not too sure . . . I don't know, it just kind of pops out — out of nowhere. . . . Just making fun of what we were talking about . . . I guess because we found it boring, or I'm not too sure. . . . Because we had already reviewed all this, I guess. She was practically reviewing half the stuff that I did in the grade 7, in the Family Life program. . . . Grade 7 was a preview to what we did."

Quiet students explained their silence by blaming themselves or the teacher. Quiet boys said they just didn't want to speak out in class or get into trouble; girls said they wanted to absorb the information, or they were bored, or too shy. Teachers' frustration with asking questions and receiving no response from girls was clearly evident. Occasionally teachers drew attention to girls' silence:

> Teacher: "The boys are doing all of the answering here."
>
> Jay: "They [girls] don't know anything."
>
> Teacher: "I think they know, they're just more quiet."

> Teacher: "I would like to hear from someone who hasn't said anything yet. What about you, Melanie?"

Although this approach sometimes initiated a response from girls, it made a problem of girls' quietness rather than of boys' dominance and inability to listen. As well, by encouraging girls to speak out, teachers assumed girls had equal opportunity to speak without being interrupted or made fun of by others. This approach also ignored boys who were quiet and who received little attention.

Quiet girls, however, were not always passive in the classroom. Girls frequently responded to boys' comments by telling them to "shut up" or calling boys "stupid" or by ignoring them. Also, on the rare occasions when girls and boys worked near each other in the classroom, girls often chastised boys for not performing domestic tasks correctly. The following scene shows how girls seized power in the classroom:

> [David and Hung worked in an adjacent unit to Lily, Poonam and Tina. Although each group worked separately, they shared a table for their meal. During the meal:]
>
> Tina: [Looking over to the boys' pile of dishes] "You shouldn't wait until the last minute to do dishes."
>
> Lily: [Pointing to the girls' dinner plates] "We only have to clean up these."
>
> [Hung got up from the table and began to wash the dishes. He put the draining rack on the counter without a tray underneath. Water flowed over the boys' books left on the counter.]
>
> David: [Shouting] "Hey, Hung, use the thing under there, so you don't get water all over the counter. Use the what do you call it, the blue thing. It's underneath!"
>
> [David got up from the table to help Hung with the dishes. The girls smiled as they watched the boys doing dishes. David was using a dishcloth to dry dishes.]
>
> Lily: "You don't dry dishes with that!"
>
> David: [Angrily] "Well, the other thing's totally soaked."
>
> Poonam: "Well, get another one."
>
> David: [Angrily] "I'm almost done. I'm not stopping now."
>
> [The girls quickly cleaned up their unit. Lily began to help David with the dishes.]
>
> David: [Firmly] "We don't need your help. It's okay."

[Lily stayed. She wiped the boys' counter and put their dishes in the cupboard. David tipped the water out of the bowl left by Hung and he quickly wiped the counter.]

David: "Miss, we're ready!"

[Lily quickly dried the boys' sink and polished the taps ready for inspection.]

In sewing:

[Vinh was revving the sewing machine.]

Rita: "You nerd. You're gonna break the machine."

[Vinh laughed but stopped what he was doing.]

[Ptan was ironing.]

Tina: "Push it! You're waving it around."

While girls' confidence with domestic tasks gave them an advantage over boys, their busyness and attention to cleanliness tied them to particular notions of femininity. Girls' correcting of boys in the domestic setting, and cleaning up after them, while giving power to girls, may have reinforced the notion that women are better suited to domestic work than men.

Some girls took their domestic tasks very seriously, but others participated as if they were playing a game. Nevertheless, these girls still complied with the image of domesticity:

Jill: "Now I have to dry the sink." [Dried sink and polished the taps.]

Tanya: "I'm housekeeper. I've got to sweep the floor. [Sarcastically] It's so bad!"

Tanya: [Sweeping meticulously around the unit] "There's totally nothing to clean on the floor. I always sweep at home but not with a brush like this broom."

Girls also corrected and policed each other in the domestic setting. The following scene is typical of girls' conversations:

Tanya: "Okay, let's clean up."

Jill: "You can dry; I want to wash. Wash the tray first so you can stack everything on it."

[Tanya washed the tray and put it on the counter.]

Jill: "Did you wash the bottom of it as well?"

Tanya: [Glaring at Jill] "Who's doing the washing here?"

Jill: "I just want to check."

Tanya: "How come you used so many dishes?"

Jill: "I always do. Hey look at my apron — no spots!"

Tanya: [Looking at her apron] "No spots. We're clean chefs!" [Laughed]

The teacher gathered students around to look at each others' muffins.

Jennifer: "Are they supposed to be round or pointed on the top?"

Teacher: "Round."

Jennifer: [Shouting across the unit] "Tanya, if they're peaked it means you have mixed them too much!"

Jill: [Shouting back, angrily] "We didn't mix them too much!"

What is particularly interesting about girls' power was that it was not held by any girl for long. There was a constant back and forth between girls as they corrected each other. Similarly, particularly when sewing, girls constantly helped each other. There was a sharing of power among them. Girls' practice supported Walden and Walkerdine's (1986) description of girls in elementary school mathematics classrooms: "Girls are not subordinated in any once and for all way but . . . move from powerful to powerless positions from one moment to the next" (p. 125). At the same time, again similar to Walkerdine's findings, girls' power tied them to domesticity and economic dependency.

Although all girls all of the time did not illustrate a particular kind of femininity, these examples show how a pattern was established where girls were domestic, silent, and subservient to boys. Although all boys all of the time did not present the same kind of masculinity, a pattern was established where a group of boys held power and control over girls and their woman teachers, and over boys who did not support their particular practices.

Although girls were silent in the classroom, in interviews girls spoke confidently and assertively. It was as if, as Connell (1987) says, "What most women support is not necessarily what they are" (p. 186). Similarly, with boys, while only a small group of boys actually held power in the group, their practice was supported by other boys. The effect was to subordinate the girls and to reinforce the boys' power.

Teachers' Reflections on their Practice

Taking the observations back to the teachers for their analysis was an important part of this study. Teachers' comments provided understanding of the difficulties teachers face and the conditions under which teachers work.

Teachers were immediately aware of paying more attention to boys. Teachers said:

"When I read your observations I was thinking, 'Have I crossed over the field so far that I almost teach to the boys?' 'Have I developed a style that is more exciting for them than for the girls?' I really want them to like it."

"In one way it would be nice to have a boys' class and a girls' class, because then you could adapt it at a higher level for the girls. . . . I'm teaching to the lower level, when I think of it."

"I have thought a lot about whether I would like to have separate classes because it may be too early for some of these boys . . . to talk about their relationships with women. . . . But maybe we need to have separate classes not so much for the boys but for the girls. So we can talk about those things without the boys there to put them down, laugh, or chatter or whatever."

The single-sex solution is not a panacea, however, because teachers would still have to attend to diversity of experience within sex groups. Some boys, particularly in sewing, demonstrated as much proficiency as girls. Power relations in classrooms would still need attention; quiet boys, like girls, were humiliated and controlled by dominant boys.

Teachers also recognized that their practices facilitated segregation and domination in the classroom. Teachers described their predicaments as follows.

"I certainly try not to give boys more attention than the girls. I think sometimes I do. Maybe it's trying to compensate — to make sure they are with me more than the girls. But they also seem to demand more attention than the girls . . . the girls work quietly whereas the boys are always wanting help. They're louder than the girls so they get more attention. . . . I was aware that I was doing it . . . but obviously you interact with the kids that need you or that come to you."

"I focused on the rowdy boys . . . I wasn't so aware of the quieter boys . . . and I didn't interact too much with the girls. . . . Because they wouldn't say anything. Even if I ask them right out they won't say anything. . . . The boys call out the answers and I don't stop them. . . . I like the class to be really sort of casual and it's very hard for me to know how to make it casual and comfortable and still structure the questioning techniques."

Teachers were surprised at the content of boys' talk. They explained their lack of response in relation to the demands of teaching. Teachers said:

"I don't pick up on any of what they are saying . . . you don't have time or bother to listen. . . . I am too busy with other things."

"I don't know how to stop them from doing all those putdowns. I've only got 18 hours with them. How am I going to stop them from putting other people down right away?"

One teacher described her approach as follows:

"Well, if I hear something really nasty I would certainly take them aside or something. I tend to humour that kind of situation and make light of it. . . . Not to make a big deal of it because that isn't good sometimes. . . . I kind of do diversionary tactics like bring the conversation back to something we are doing here. I don't usually do a direct response. If I hear anything I don't usually respond directly with a value judgement on it. Not that I hear much."

Teachers explained the gender relations of the classroom as biologically and psychologically based:

"Boys always have to show off — they are always performing, competing and performing. . . . They are more involved with sex. But isn't that to be expected with that age boy?"

"Maybe boys are having a hard time dealing with their puberty . . . the girls seem to be more accepting of themselves."

"I guess they [girls and quiet boys] have to learn to fend for themselves. I guess that is all part of the growing-up process — speaking up for yourself."

Walkerdine (1981) explains a similar response by teachers in her study as fitting with "scientific pedadogy":

> Its purpose is to produce better control through self control and that ironically is what helps to produce the space in the practice for the children to be powerful . . . thus the very discourse helps to produce the children as powerful. . . . Similarly, the discourse of the naturalness of male sexuality to be expressed not repressed produces and facilitates in the teacher, collusion in her own oppression. Since, if she reads actions as normal and natural, and suppression of those actions as harmful, she is forced into a no-choice situation. She cannot but allow them to continue, and she must render as harmless their power over her. (p. 18)

Unlike Walkerdine's teachers, teachers in this study also explained gender relations of the classroom in terms of ethnicity:

"Maybe I'm talking in opposition to girls' Chinese tradition, and that may make life very difficult for them. . . . I think I am talking about things that are very foreign to them. . . . Because boys are Chinese, I think they probably don't want to do it because it may be in conflict with the messages they may be getting at home."

"When they are still young children they don't work well together . . . when students are more advanced sexually then I don't think you have that. . . . A lot of those Chinese girls haven't gone through puberty yet. . . . They must mature later."

These arguments showed that the teachers were trying to be sensitive to what they perceived to be characteristics of Chinese students, which they generalized to all Asian students. The origin of these perceptions requires further study. It is clear, however, that teachers' arguments indirectly supported traditional gender relations by explaining students' practices in psychological and physiological discourse, and through culture, rather than in terms of men's dominance over women.

Discussion

Participant observation and interviews with students and teachers provide a deeper understanding of gender relations than is evident in earlier approaches to classroom interaction research. Whereas previous studies focused on teachers' questioning techniques, this study shows how traditional gender relations are supported not only through curriculum content and classroom pedagogy, but also through the actual practices of students and teachers themselves.

This study supports concern about gender bias in curriculum content and classroom pedagogy. It was clear that treating students "the same" meant catering to the perceived interests and experiences of boys. Following Connell (1987), however, I suggest that the curriculum supported a particular *kind* of masculinity, one interested in authority, technology, and control.

Voices of students showed the necessity of a more gender-sensitive approach, but one sensitive to what Teresa De Lauretis (1990) describes as "axis of difference" (p. 133). Students brought to the classroom different experiences in domestic work. This not only illustrated traditional practices regarding how domestic work is organized, but also the importance of teaching to different competencies and of providing for different ways of knowing.

It is also clear that misogyny and homophobia in classrooms is a serious problem. Classroom observations day after day showed that a group of boys not only dominated student-teacher interaction, but they also corrected, interrupted and ridiculed girls and quieter boys and woman teachers. Whereas the silence or the laughter of most girls and quieter boys had the effect of giving power to the dominant boys, those who tried to break this control were subject to further abuse. Girls had good reasons for segregating themselves from boys. For teachers to insist on non-segregated seating arrangements would have shown a lack of sensitivity to girls' experiences.

Although boys in the classroom clearly had more power, I concur with Walkerdine (1981) that it was more complicated than this. First, not all boys held power. A hierarchy existed among boys: a few dominant boys intimidated and controlled other boys. Second, girls exerted power in the domestic setting, where they policed each other and where they ridiculed or corrected boys. Such reversal of power, however, reinforced the notion of girls' domesticity and tied them to traditional notions of femininity.

It is possible that in order to maintain a particular kind of masculinity, boys may not only have wanted to distance themselves from the domestic nature of the course and from girls in the class, but also from their teachers, because they were women. Hegemonic masculinity required that they take power away from women — who happened in this case to be their teachers. It is also possible that boys' responsiveness provided intrinsic rewards for teachers. Boys' enthusiasm, therefore, may have caused the teachers in this study to overlook issues of power in their classrooms.

Although "emphasized femininity" and "hegemonic masculinity," as described by Kessler et al. (1985) and Connell (1987), do not describe all of the girls and boys in this study, many supported these images, and those who did not conform were subordinated. Inequities result because a particular kind of femininity and a particular kind of masculinity are buttressed through schooling, while other kinds are suppressed. It is clear that this perspective needs to be added to understandings of gender inequality in schooling.

The information presented here shows the importance of Connell's argument about practice. Classroom observations and interviews challenged the view that girls and boys merely reproduce or produce traditional gender categories. Variation within categories, particularly among boys, was clearly evident, as was the part that students and teachers played in building social structures. Similar to Connell's structures of labor, power and cathexis, participants in this study built and responded to academic structures, sexual division of labor, segregation and domination, and sexuality and social relations.

It is also tempting to speculate about how different dimensions of oppression intersect in the classroom. Rita and Jennifer were both "white," from so-called "majority" backgrounds. They were also the most dominant of all the girls. Although other dimensions such as class may have played a part and other "white" girls along with girls from so-called "minority" backgrounds were silenced, Rita's and Jennifer's "whiteness" was to me the most striking feature in their dominance. Similarly, Anthony, the only First Nations student in the classroom, exhibited the most anger and aggression, showing possibly how a particular kind of masculinity intertwines with the experiences of belonging to a particular so-called "minority" group. Unlike dominant boys, however, Anthony's drawings and his comments to himself revealed that his anger was directed more at society generally than it was towards the girls in the classroom. Further analysis is needed before more than token words can be said on this issue, though I recognize that my own "whiteness" and dominance may have prevented me from being sensitive to the complexity of segregation and domination in the classroom.

Teachers' reflections on their practice draws attention to the importance of understanding teachers' work. This means understanding the intersection between what teachers do every day in their classrooms and the conditions of their work. Over the school year each teacher in this program met almost 150 grade 8 students, in addition to those they dealt with in other areas of their teaching load. Working with groups of approximately 24 students in one-hour time slots, teachers hardly had time to get to know students' names, let alone to develop sensitivity to these students' particular gendered experiences.

The organization of the program must also be understood in relation to the gender politics of schools. As Martin (1981) points out, school systems place little value on knowledge for the private sphere. Home economics is relegated little space in the overall school timetable. Inclusion of both girls and boys in home economics did not result in more time being given to this area: what it meant was less time, but more students. As a result, teachers' workloads increased and curriculum content and pedagogy became standardized.

What are we to do about the gendering that goes on in schools? What can be done about traditional gender relations and gender regimes in classrooms? Is it possible to bring about change when working within a system that itself embodies ideologies of a particular kind of male supremacy? If, as Connell (1987) says, practice can be turned back on itself, what would this look like in the classroom?

This work points to the need for feminist pedagogy. Linda Briskin (1990), for example, provides some hope. She calls for a pedagogy that empowers students through knowledge about oppressive societal structures and calls into question the gender relations of classrooms. She calls this an "anti-sexist" pedagogy toward gender equity:

> An anti-sexist strategy makes gender an issue in all classrooms in order to validate the experience of students, to bring it into consciousness, and to challenge it. It makes gender an official rather than an unofficial factor in classroom process and curriculum; by extension, an anti-sexist strategy takes up race, class, and sexual orientation, which interrelate in complex patterns with gender. . . . Anti-sexism shifts the focus from the realm of morality (I am not sexist) to the realm of political practice (What can I do about sexism?). (p. 14)

Thus gender equity involves more than questions of access, sex stereotyping, and gender bias in student-teacher interaction. As Rich (1985) says, it means taking women students seriously. It means understanding the inequities that result when traditional power relations enter into our daily lives in classrooms. It means examining the taken-for-granted experiences we have as women and men, girls and boys. It means recognizing the diversity of human experience, revaluing women's knowledge and women's work, and changing traditional ways of relating. It means placing gender relations on the agenda in the classroom.

Notes

[1]This paper is part of a larger study entitled "The Social Construction of Gender in the Practical Arts." The study explores gender relations in home economics and technical studies classrooms. The research was supported by a grant (#452-90-2555) from the Social Sciences and Humanities Research Council of Canada. I would like to thank Jane Gaskell and Arlene McLaren for their helpful comments on earlier drafts of this paper.

[2]I would like to thank Josette McGregor, Robin Van Heck and Tim Stanley for their help in describing the ethnic and cultural diversity of the classroom.

[3]Other themes were issues of utility and domestic labor and issues of sexuality and social relations. Though not developed fully in this paper, these themes interconnect with those described here.

[4]These are not the students' real names. I chose pseudonyms to match the original name of the student. Where the student's real name indicated the student's ethnic background, I replace it with a similar pseudonym. Where the real name did not match the student's ethnic background, niether does the pseudonym.

[5]Language and competence also became important in technical studies. Boys, to varying degrees, already possessed many of the manipulative skills needed in technical studies and they worked hard at posturing the required language. The skills required in technical studies, however, were not a part of most girls' experiences, nor were girls interested in posturing the language of this subject area.

[6]Students' conversations while they worked also revealed their divergent interests. Although the intensity of interest varied among girls and among boys, girls talked about fashion, makeup and romance; boys talked about sport, electronics and parts of women's bodies.

References

Amos, V., & Parmar, P. (1981). Resistances and responses: The experiences of black girls in Britain. In A. McRobbie & T. McCabe (Eds.), *Feminism for girls: An adventure story* (pp. 129-148). London: Routledge & Kegan Paul.

Atkinson, P. (1990). *The ethnographic imagination: Textual constructions of reality*. New York: Routledge.

Belenky, M.F., Clinchy, B.M., Goldberger, N.R., & Tarule, J.M. (1986). *Women's ways of knowing: The development of self, voice and mind*. New York: Basic Books.

Briskin, L. (1990). *Feminist pedagogy: Teaching and learning liberation* (Feminist Perspectives No. 19). Ottawa: Canadian Research Institute for the Advancement of Women.

Clifford, J. (1986). Introduction: Partial truths. In J. Clifford & G.E. Marcus (Eds.), *Writing culture: The poetics and politics of ethnography* (pp. 1-26). Berkeley: University of California Press.

Connell, R.W. (1987). *Gender and power*. Sydney: Allen and Unwin.

De Lauretis, T. (1990). Eccentric subjects: Feminist theory and historical consciousness. *Feminist Studies, 16*(1), 115-151.

Eyre, L. (1989, May). *Feminist ethnography: Reflections from the field*. Paper presented at the Canadian Association for Research in Home Economics, the Learned Societies Conference, University of Victoria, B.C.

Kessler, S., Ashenden, D.J., Connell, R.W., & Dowsett, G.W. (1985). Gender relations in secondary schooling. *Sociology of Education, 58*(1), 34-48.

Kramarae, C., & Treichler, P.A. (1990). Power relationships in the classroom. In S.L. Gabriel & I. Smithson (Eds.), *Gender in the classroom: Power and pedagogy* (pp. 41-59). Urbana: University of Illinois Press.

Lasser, C. (Ed.). (1987). *Educating men and women together: Coeducation in a changing world*. Urbana: University of Illinois Press.

Martin, J.R. (1981). The ideal of the educated person. *Educational Theory, 31*(2), 97-109.

O'Brien, M. (1990). Political ideology and patriarchal education. In F. Forman, M. O'Brien, J. Haddad, D. Hallman, & P. Masters (Eds.), *Feminism and education:*

A Canadian perspective (pp. 3-26). Toronto: Ontario Institute for Studies in Education.

Oakley, A. (1981). Interviewing women: A contradiction in terms. In H. Roberts (Ed.), *Doing feminist research* (pp. 30-61). Boston: Routledge & Kegan Paul.

Pelleschi, A. (1988). Pastoral care and girls of Asian parentage. In R. Dale, R. Ferguson, & A. Robinson (Eds.), *Frameworks for teaching: Readings for intending secondary teachers.* Toronto: Hodder & Stoughton.

Prentice, A. (1988). *Canadian women: A history.* Toronto: Harcourt Brace Jovanovich.

Reinharz, S. (1983). Experiential analysis: A contribution to feminist research. In G. Bowles & R.D. Klein (Eds.), *Theories of women's studies* (pp. 162-191). London: Routledge & Kegan Paul.

Rich, A. (1985). Taking women students seriously. In M. Culley & C. Portuges (Eds.), *Gendered subjects: The dynamics of feminist teaching* (pp. 21-28). Boston: Routledge & Kegan Paul.

Sadker, M., & Sadker, D. (1986). Sexism in the classroom: From grade school to graduate school. *Phi Delta Kappan, 67*(7), 512-520.

Stanley, L., & Wise, S. (1983). *Breaking out: Feminist consciousness and feminist research.* London: Routledge & Kegan Paul.

Stimpson, C.R. (1987). New consciousness, old institutions, and the need for reconciliation. In C. Lasser (Ed.), *Educating men and women together: Coeducation in a changing world* (pp. 155-164). Urbana: University of Illinois Press.

Trenchard, L., & Warren, H. (1987). Talking about school: The experiences of young lesbians and gay men. In G. Weiner & M. Arnot (Eds.), *Gender under scrutiny: New inquiries in education* (pp. 222- 231). London: Open University.

Walden, R., & Walkerdine, V. (1986). Characteristics, views, and relationships in the classroom. In L. Burton (Ed.), *Girls into math can go.* London: Holt Rinehart & Winston.

Walkerdine, V. (1989). *Counting girls out.* London: Virago.

Walkerdine, V. (1981). Sex, power, and pedadogy. *Screen Education, 38,* 14-23.

Weiner, G., & Arnot, M. (1987). Teachers and gender politics. In M. Arnot & G. Weiner (Eds.), *Gender and the politics of schooling* (pp. 354-370). London: Open University.

Part Three:

The Nature of Curriculum: Whose Knowledge?

In this section we come to the heart of the feminist critique of education. Feminists argue that our very conception of education, of what counts as important knowledge and good pedagogy, has a male bias. It has been designed by men for men, it treats women as "other," and it ignores women's experience.

What is taught in school classrooms? How do we determine whether it is correct and important? Who decides what belongs in school and what should be learned elsewhere? How do schools decide who learns what parts of the curriculum? Why has the curriculum changed over time and how should it change in the future? The study of curriculum involves fundamental questions about what is worth knowing, who decides and how we should teach. By and large, schools teach how to conjugate irregular verbs in French, but not in Chinese; they teach about Beowolf but not about Harlequin romances; they teach gymnastics but not break dancing. What is taught in school is a selection from among the vast number of often contradictory things that different people "know" at any particular time. Some people have more power than others to include "their" knowledge in the curriculum. Moreover, curriculum involves the organization of knowledge in particular ways for teaching purposes.

What is taught reflects conscious and unconscious decisions by a variety of people acting in particular social and economic contexts. Influential work in the so-called "new" sociology of education (Bernstein, 1977; Young, 1977) and in social history (Cuban, 1984; Kliebard, 1986; Tomkins, 1986) has renewed academic interest in the social and historical processes involved in creating a curriculum. Feminist scholarship has a variety of contributions to make to this debate about what counts as important knowledge in schools and how it is shaped by social processes.

We often fail to notice the selection and organization of knowledge that is involved in arriving at a curriculum, taking for granted that multiplication will be taught in grade 4, that the politics of confederation is central to Canadian history, and that discipline boundaries will separate the teaching of history from the teaching of literature. But struggles over curriculum do erupt, and when they do, the decisions involved in arriving at the curriculum become visible and debatable. When AIDS curriculum is criticized because it impinges on the role of the family, or a school board bans *The Merchant of Venice* because it stirs up anti-Semitism, the politics of curriculum hits the headlines. Feminism has called into question some of our taken for granted assumptions about curriculum, put them on the political agenda and struggled to bring about change.

The feminist critique of curriculum in the late 1960s was not a new phenomenon. As historian Veronica Strong-Boag (1986) points out,

> Women have been part of a broad ranging assault on the assumptions, substances and methods of educators and educational institutions. . . . First

and second wave feminists have had much to say specifically about the education of girls and women, and the failure to reflect female reality in the structures of teaching or scholarship. To a large degree they have believed that to control education is to control the future and the outrage of their foes would seem to suggest that they believe it as well!

One of the first attempts organized women's groups in Canada made to change the curriculum was to try to get home economics taught in public schools. At the turn of the century, when labor and industry were arguing for the inclusion of industrial and technical subjects, many women's groups were arguing for the inclusion of home economics. As the Local Council of Women told the Royal Commission on Industrial Training and Technical Education in 1913, "The Local Council of Women would like to see service in the home lifted to the same plane as the profession of nursing. The Council does not believe the home should continue to be the only place for which special training is not regarded as necessary." They wanted women's work to be publicly recognized as worthy of study; they wanted its scientific knowledge base acknowledged. They saw that putting something in the curriculum was a way of publically acknowledging its value (Danylewcyz et al., 1985; Stamp, 1977). They accepted as natural the division between men's and women's spheres, and they wanted recognition for women's. There were a few dissenting ("equal rights") feminists who challenged the notion of separate spheres for men and women, arguing that the inclusion of home economics would channel women away from industrial and technical studies and confirm their position in the domestic sphere (Powers, 1984). But when home economics was eventually introduced, it was seen as a victory for women. Today, on the other hand, the class and ethnic biases in what was taught in home economics are clear, and the status of the subject as a "ghetto" for women is criticized. As curriculum changes, the feminist critique of it also changes and develops.

The debate about home economics illustrates some of the different strands of thought that contribute to a feminist debate around curriculum. There are those who would have women move into the existing curriculum in a more equal fashion — taking more science and more industrial arts, while boys would be encouraged to enroll in home economics. There are those who would add to the curriculum the concerns of women, from home economics to women's studies, on the assumption that these concerns are different from men's, in both the short and the long run. There are those who would diversify the notion of women's concerns, to include women in poverty, and women from the Third World. There are those who would replace the existing curriculum with one that more fairly represents the concerns of both men and women. To continue the home economics example, this would mean replacing both home economics and industrial arts with a course that provides a new amalgam of both under the rubric of something like life skills (a solution discussed by Linda Eyre in chapter 8).

The feminist critique has no single voice. Some feminists want to add women's concerns to an existing curriculum; others want to reshape the entire curriculum. Some believe there is a distinctive women's way of discovering and knowing the world; others want to focus on the differences among women. Some focus on the content of what is taught; others focus on how it is taught, arguing that the medium is the message. Some women are frustrated and angry at the recalcitrance of those who refuse to respond to women's concerns about curriculum; others are excited and optimistic about the potential for renewing and revitalizing education which the discovery of women's voices brings. In all cases, feminists critically examine what counts as education and want it changed.

Equal Representation in the Curriculum

The argument that women should be more equally represented in different subject areas was taken up in part two. As a critique of curriculum, it suggests eliminating sexism in classrooms so that women feel welcome in all areas of the school. This entails the development of bridging programs and remedial classes to allow women access to new areas. It means changing classroom interaction to eliminate discrimination against female students. Trying to make the curriculum more hospitable to women, more "girl friendly" as Whyte et al (1985) put it, often involves an extensive critique of curriculum, administration and pedagogy.

To make schools "girl friendly" involves, among other things, representing female experience in the curriculum. The most straightforward index of women's omission from the curriculum is a count of various indices — the number of female characters in elementary school readers, the number of female authors on the reading list, the number of women mentioned in a history text, the number of women in tenured university positions who are responsible for creating scholarship. The omission of, or as Tillie Olsen (1978) so eloquently phrases it, the silences of women, are clear.

But adding women means re-examining the rules that determine inclusion in the first place. If the people mentioned in history texts are those who have played an important role in governing the country, clearly women cannot be equally represented. The process of adding women involves changing conceptions of what students should learn in history and why they should study history in the first place. It means learning about the ways ordinary people lived their lives so children can understand the history of people like themselves. It means including more social history, more studies of how families were organized and how work was distributed in other historical periods. It means understanding the ways gender has shaped the organization of Canadian society.

The omission of women is not just a question of oversight. Our very conceptions of education, of what is worth knowing, and of the disciplines are challenged by the process of including women.

Revaluing the Female

In an oft-quoted address to a group of female college graduates in 1977, the poet Adrienne Rich said,

> What you can learn here (and I mean not only here but at any college or in any university) is how men have perceived and organized their experience, their history, their ideas about social relationships, good and evil, sickness and health, etc. When you read or hear about 'great issues', 'major texts', 'the mainstream of western thought', you are hearing about what men, above all white men, in their male subjectivity, have decided is important. (p. 232)

O'Brien (1981) has felicitously dubbed this curriculum the "malestream."

To add into the curriculum what women think important can mean a variety of changes. It can mean adding home economics, parenting education, or assertiveness training. But most often it means adding feminist perspectives, in what has come to be called "women's studies."

Women's studies curricula focus on what women want to know, on developing knowledge from, as Smith (1974) puts it, "the standpoint of women." Feminist curricula are distinctive. They begin with women, with their sense of what they are, with their own experience (Smith, 1977 p. 13).

Jane Roland Martin (1985) has articulated the underlying concern that informs the feminist project on women's studies. The curriculum has been designed to prepare men for the public and "productive" spheres of work and citizenship, she argues. It has ignored the private and "reproductive" spheres of family, love, intimacy, for these were the domains of women. Women and women's concerns did not belong in the public world of the school, or if they did, they belonged only as long as women were willing to adopt a masculine stance, and give up the feminine, at least while they were there. Martin argues that we must reintegrate the feminine and the masculine by incorporating reproductive concerns into the curriculum for all students. We can no longer expect women alone to learn the three C's of caring, concern and connection, and to do these things for everyone.

Many books point out how knowledge must change when women's experiences are addressed (Dubois et al., 1985; Finn & Miles, 1982; Harding, 1987; Keohane, Rosaldo, & Gelphi, 1982; Langland & Gove, 1981; Sherman & Beck, 1979; Spender, 1981). Examples could be taken from a variety of areas, but perhaps in re-examining our conceptions of science, feminist criticism makes the most radical break with male epistemology. Feminist thought joins recent work in the history and philosophy of science in calling attention to the way scientific knowledge has been shaped by its particular social and political context, and especially its practice by men. Keller (1982, 1983) has argued that women tend to do science, and talk about it in different ways from men. In her 1983 biography of Barbara McClintock, who won the Nobel prize for her work in corn genetics, Keller contrasts McClintock's "feeling for the organism," her "conversations" with nature, with male conceptions of science as domination and imposition. Keller argues that these ways of doing science have been denigrated by the scientific establishment, but that they must reexamined, revalued, and recognized as an intrinsic part of the scientific process.

Gilligan (1982) makes similar arguments in relation to moral reasoning. She argues that women do it differently, and that women's ways of working through moral problems have not been recognized in moral philosophy and moral education. Individualized arguments about justice, which underpin our legal system and our tests of moral reasoning, ignore the kind of contextualized reasoning and concern for community and commitment, Gilligan termed "the ethic of care." Women, she argues, are more likely to articulate this ethic.

In other disciplines there are many examples of how feminist scholarship challenges such basic assumptions as the relation of public and private (Elshtain, 1981), the ways to read a text (Silverman, 1985), and the nature of the economy (Cohen, 1982). In all cases, the argument is that if one starts from the standpoint of women, things appear in a different light. The questions one asks are different; the ways one goes about looking for answers are different.

It is not only the content of curriculum that concerns feminists. "We know that to bring women fully into the curriculum means nothing less than to reorganize all knowledge and that changing what we teach means changing how we teach" (Culley & Portuges, 1985). Feminists have charged that the organization of educational institutions and the ways knowledge is transmitted to students have a male bias and that this is because institutions have failed to incorporate the ways women prefer to organize and learn (Briskin, 1990).

The notion of a distinctive feminist pedagogy arises from the experience of consciousness raising in the women's movement in the late 1960's. Consciousness raising involved small, leaderless groups of women coming together to share their life experience and to use it to discover what was common among them and how women's oppression was organized. This mode of learning was enormously powerful and politically influential. The method has been compared to Freire's (1970) "conscientization," a mode of literacy training for peasants that combined political action and the active reconstruction of knowledge by learners.

Feminist pedagogy is based in a questioning of traditional authority relations between teacher and student, and a distrust of bureaucracy (Bowles & Klein, 1983; Gardner, Dean, & McKaig, 1989; Tancred-Sheriff, 1987). It eschews the separation of the public classroom from private experience, and does not recognize any clear distinction between emotion and reason. It is based in a feminist politics which demands the sharing of power and authority. It makes gender visible and in so doing lays the basis for exploring and validating the multiplicity of experiences students have, according to their class, race, ethnicity, sexual orientation and many other factors. Feminist pedagogy, then, is quite opposed to traditional academic structures.

This wide ranging critique makes the process of putting women into the curriculum a difficult, indeed revolutionary task. It is relatively straightforward to add to the history books the suffragettes and the Native women who organized the fur trade, to add to the literature curriculum a few novels written by women and to add to the arts syllabus some woman artists. It is quite another thing to change the way we approach historical, literary and artistic study. While it may be possible to formulate plans to stop discrimination against female students and encourage interaction between teachers and female students, it is difficult to do away with bureaucracy, hierarchy, political neutrality and competition in educational institutions.

A New Synthesis: Integrating Women's Studies

The desire of feminists to transform curriculum and pedagogy has led to a debate about whether scholarship should be a separate discipline or should be integrated into the mainstream disciplines (Bowles & Klein, 1983; Boxer, 1982; Strong-Boag, 1983). Those who want to keep women's studies as a separate course, department or field argue that feminist scholarship must first develop alongside, then enter into and transform the mainstream disciplines. Others argue that women's studies becomes a ghetto that allows most students to continue in "men's studies."

Most feminists, however, would agree that whatever the best means, the ultimate goal is not to continue with two versions of knowledge, the male version and the female version, but to develop a new synthesis that is richer for paying attention to both male and female perspectives. To return to Keller's (1982) views on science, she concludes that, rather than rejecting science, the feminist critique can enrich our understanding of how science is accomplished, and can "bring a whole new range of sensitivities, leading to an equally new consciousness of the potentialities lying latent in the scientific process." It adds an understanding of the reflexive subject to traditional notions of objectivity. Similarly, Gilligan (1982) argues that understanding both the ethic of justice and the ethic of care will lead to "a more generative view of human life."

One of the most influential Canadian documents to address the way feminism must transform all knowledge, *On the Treatment of the Sexes in Research,* was published in 1985 by the Social Sciences and Humanities Research Council. Its authors, Eichler and Lapointe, point out that scholarship that does not take adequate account of women is simply bad scholarship. The pamphlet gives specific examples of how male bias operates and what can be done about it. Eichler and Lapointe discuss how research has transformed statistical differences into essential differences (as in psychological scales of masculinity and femininity), how it has overgeneralized concepts that apply to males ("universal" suffrage was granted before women got the vote) and how it has failed to consider the way assumptions about gender affect data gathering ("Do you think women doctors are as good as men doctors?" does not allow the response that women are better doctors).

Such sensitivity to the standpoint of women however, has too often meant taking the standpoint of white and privileged women. The feminist movement often cites its origins as the publication of Betty Friedan's *The Feminine Mystique,* a book that, as bell hooks (1984) points out, actually referred to the plight of "a select group of college-educated, middle and upper class, married white women — housewives bored with leisure, with the home, with children, with buying products, who wanted more out of life." To define these women's experience as "women's" experience is to commit the sin of overgeneralizing the experience of the powerful to others. It is exactly this sin that the feminist movement has been most concerned with, for men have done it to women. Feminist scholarship has its value in pointing to difference, in validating difference, in criticizing the ways one side of a difference gets privileged through inequitable social relations. It respects the voices "on the margins." It is for this reason that postmodern theory has been attractive to feminists, even while its masculine origins, its often apolitical stance, its treating of the world as merely text, its abstruse discourse and its bid for hegemony in the academic world have also made it suspect for many feminists.

To point to the ways gender organizes our lives, it is necessary to see how it works in a wide variety of times and places. Women's experience of mothering, women's experience of paid labor, women's experience of school, women's experience of books, of the law, of housing, of anything is hugely different depending on which women we are talking to or about. To universalize "women's experience" is tremendously risky and politically suspect because of what it eclipses. The point is not to define one experience which is female. The point rather is to see that gender relations have been relations of power, and that they need to be examined in whatever forms they take, and to be challenged and reformulated. The point is not to privilege the examination of gender over the examination of race, class, handicap, ethnicity, nationality and all the other factors that shape our lives. The point is to see that these things do not necessarily work the same way for men and women, and to look for gender relations as they coexist with and influence and interact with other relations of domination and exclusion.

The articles in this section represent a variety of feminist approaches to curriculum. Because of its important influence on feminist scholarship in Canada, Dorothy Smith's essay on ideological structures introduces the section. Smith argues that women have been excluded from the production of the forms of thought which describe and explain experience. It is men's perspectives and interests which are represented in the dominant ideology and in curriculum, despite the fact that women as the majority of teachers in the lower grades are responsible for transmitting this ideology to children. Her analysis of the roots of this dominance, and of its maintenance have had a major impact on the way feminists understand the curriculum.

Magda Lewis and Roger Simon take up the same issues at the level of a graduate seminar in education. They start with their experience of the classroom, they examine its gendered dynamics, and they explore the fundamental issues of what a curriculum should look like if it is to grapple with educational issues seriously, and just as seriously engage men and women equally in the discussion. The value of theoretical discourse for women is debated clearly in their discussion of this class.

Seema Kalia looks at the feminist project from the point of view of a non-white university student. She points out the ways white middle-class women have dominated the discourse and tried to define "women's experience" in a way that excludes most women. She knows feminist instructors and students can be racist. She adopts the feminist project, but points to the many ways in which it must be reworked to account for the experience of women of color.

To include discussion of sexuality, reproduction and birth control in the official curriculum instead of leaving it to the private discussion of students is to offend many people's notion of the proper role of schooling, as Jane Roland Martin has pointed out. Many battles have been waged over whether such discussion should be included in the school at all. Helen Lenskyj takes the debate a further step by looking at what is actually taught. She points out the heterosexual assumptions of sex education, and its normative definitions of sexuality. She provides some discussion of the Ontario Ministry of Education's policy, and offers a vision of sex education that validates difference and helps all students understand their experiences.

Finally, Roberta Lamb explores the subject of music education for feminists. As she notes, the implications of feminist theory for the visual and performing arts has not been taken up much by educators. The sound patterns of music are based in theory, but whose theory? Feminism requires daring and "terrible vulnerability," rethinking and being "insubordinate." The form of Lamb's writing and the dialogue she creates among feminist voices takes us into the style of postmodern feminism. Knowledge comes from dialogue; dialogue is situated in each participant's experience and theory; the result of the dialogue is to move towards new understandings of music, of curriculum, and of education.

References

Bernstein, B. (1977). *Class, codes and control: Vol. 3. Toward a theory of educational transmission* (2nd ed.). London: Routledge and Kegan Paul.

Bowles, G., & Klein, R.D. (Eds.). (1983). *Theories of women's studies.* London: Routledge and Kegan Paul.

Boxer, M. (1982). For and about women: The theory and practice of women's studies in the United States. In N. Keohane, M. Rosaldo, & B. Gelphi (Eds.), *Feminist theory: A critique of ideology.* Chicago: University of Chicago Press.

Briskin L. (1990). *Feminist pedagogy: Teaching and learning liberation.* Ottawa: Canadian Research Institute for the Advancement of Women.

Cohen, M. (1982). The problem of studying economic man. In G. Finn & A. Miles (Eds.), *Feminism in Canada.* Montreal: Black Rose Books.

Cuban, Larry. (1984). *How teachers taught: Constancy and change in American classrooms, 1890-1980.* Stanford: Longman Publishers.

Culley, M., & Portuges, C. (Eds.). (1985). *Gendered subjects: The dynamics of feminist teaching.* London: Routledge and Kegan Paul.

Danylewcyz, M., Fahmy-Eid, N., & Thiverge, N. (1985). L'enseignement ménager et les "Home Economics" au Québec et en Ontario au début du 20e siècle: une analyse comparée. In J.D. Wilson (Ed.), *An imperfect past: Education and society in Canadian history.* Vancouver: University of British Columbia, Centre for the Study of Curriculum and Instruction.

Dubois, E.C., Kelly, G.P., Kennedy, E.L., Koremeyer, C.W., & Robinson, L.S. (1985). *Feminist scholarship: Kindling the groves of academe.* Urbana: University of Illinois Press.

Eichler, M., & Lapointe, J. (1985). *On the treatment of the sexes in research.* Ottawa: Social Sciences and Humanities Research Council.

Elshtain, J.B. (1981). *Public man, private woman: Women in social and political thought.* Princeton, NJ: Princeton University Press.

Finn, G., & Miles, A. (1982). *Feminism in Canada.* Montreal: Black Rose Books.

Freire, P. (1970). *The pedagogy of the oppressed.* New York: Continuum.

Gilligan, C. (1982). *In a different voice.* Cambridge: Harvard University Press.

Gardner S., Dean, C., & McKaig, D. (1989). Responding to differences in the classroom: The politics of knowledge, class and sexuality. *Sociology of Education, 62*(1), 64-74.

Harding, S. (Ed.). (1987). *Feminism and methodology.* Bloomington: Indiana University Press.

hooks, bell. (1984). *Feminist theory: From margin to centre.* Massachussetts: south end press.

Keller, E.F. (1982). Feminism in science. In N. Keohane, M. Rosaldo, & B. Gelphi (Eds.), *Feminist theory: A critique of ideology.* Chicago: University of Chicago Press.

Keller, E.F. (1983). *The feeling for the organism: The life and work of Barbara McClintock.* San Francisco: W.H. Freeman.

Keohane, N., Rosaldo, M., Gelphi B. (Eds.). (1982). *Feminist theory: A critique of ideology.* Chicago: University of Chicago Press.

Kliebard, H. (1986). *The struggle for the American curriculum, 1893-1958.* Boston: Routledge and Kegan Paul.

Langland, E., & Gove, W. (Eds.). (1981). *A feminist perspective in the academy: The difference it makes.* Chicago: University of Chicago Press.

Martin, J.R. (1985). *Reclaiming a conversation.* New Haven: Yale University Press.

O'Brien, M. (1981). *The politics of reproduction.* Boston: Routledge and Kegan Paul.

Olsen, T. (1978). *Silences.* New York: Delacorte Press.

Powers, J.B. (1984, April). Feminist politics, pressure groups and personalities: Trade training versus home economics in Smith-Hughes. Paper presented at the American Educational Research Association meeting, New Orleans.

Rich, A. (1977). Claiming an education. In her *On Lies, secrets and silence.* New York: W.W. Norton.

Roberts, H. (Ed.). (1981). *Doing feminist research.* London: Routledge and Kegan Paul.

Royal Commission on Industrial Training and Technical Education. (1913). *Report.* Ottawa: Author.

Sherman, J.A., & Beck, E.T. (Eds.). (1979). *The prism of sex.* Madison: University of Wisconsin Press.

Silverman, K. (1985). *Subject of semiotics.* New York: Oxford University Press.

Smith, D.E. (1974). Women's perspective as a radical critique of sociology. *Sociological Inquiry, 44*(1), 7-13.

Smith, D.E. (1977). *Feminism and Marxism: A place to begin, a way to go.* Vancouver: New Star Books.

Spender, D. (Ed.). (1981). *Men's studies modified: The impact of feminism on the academic disciplines.* Oxford: Pergamon Press.

Stamp, R.M. (1977). Teaching girls their God given place in life. *Atlantis 2*(2), 18-34.

Strong-Boag, V. (1983). Mapping women's studies in Canada: Some signposts. *Journal of Educational Thought, 17*(2), 94-111.

Strong-Boag, V. (1986). *Commentary on women and the curriculum.* Paper presented at the Women and Education Conference, University of British Columbia, Vancouver, B.C.

Tancred-Sheriff, P. (1987). *A century of women in higher education: Canadian data and Australian comments.* Lecture at Macquarie University.

Tomkins, G.S. (1986). *A common countenance: stability and change in the Canadian curriculum.* Scarbrough, ON: Prentice-Hall.

Young, M.F.D. (Ed.). (1977). *Knowledge and control: New directions for the sociology of education.* London: Collier McMillan.

Whitty, G. (1985). *Sociology and school knowledge: Curriculum theory, research and politics.* London: Methuen.

Whyte, J., Deem, R., Kent, L., & Cruikshank, M. (Eds.). (1985). *Girl friendly schooling.* London: Methuen.

9

An Analysis of Ideological Structures
and How Women are Excluded:
Considerations for Academic Women[1]

Dorothy E. Smith

To a large extent, men appropriate the positions that govern, administer, and manage our society. Men hold the positions from which the work of organizing the society is initiated and controlled. A distinctive feature of this social form is that the work of organizing is largely done symbolically. Things get done, or rather their doing originates and is coordinated, in words, in mathematical and other symbolic forms, on paper. It is an ideologically structured mode of action. Images, vocabularies, concepts, knowledge of and methods of knowing the world are integral to the practice of power. The work of creating the concepts and categories, and of developing the knowledge and skills which transform the actualities of the empirical into forms in which they may be governed, the work of producing the social forms of consciousness in art and literature, in news, in TV shows, plays, soap operas, etc. — this work is done by institutions which are themselves an integral part of the ruling structure. Universities, schools, broadcasting and publishing corporations, and the like are the ideological institutions of the society. They produce, distribute, and socialize in the ideological forms upon which this social organization depends.

The mode of organizing society ideologically had its origin some four or five hundred years ago in Western Europe. It is an integral aspect of the development of a capitalist mode of production. Women have been at work in its making as much as men, though their work has been of a different kind and location. But women have been largely excluded from the work of producing the forms of thought and the images and symbols in which thought is expressed and ordered. There is a circle effect. Men attend to and treat as significant only what men say. The circle of men whose writing and talk was significant to each other extends backwards in time as far as our records reach. What men were doing was relevant to men, was written by men about men for men. Men listened and listen only to what one man says to another. A tradition is formed in this discourse of the past within the present. The themes, problematics, assumptions, metaphors, and images are formed as the circle of those present draws upon the work of the past. From this circle women have been to a large extent excluded. They have been admitted to it only by special licence and as individuals, not as representatives of their sex. They can share in it only by receiving its terms and relevances and these are the terms and relevances of a discourse among men.

Throughout this period in which ideologies become of increasing importance first as a mode of thinking, legitimating, and sanctioning a social order, and then as integral in the organization of society, women have been deprived of the means to participate in creating forms of thought relevant or adequate to express their own experience or to define and raise social consciousness about their situation and concerns. They have never controlled the material or social means to the making of a tradition among themselves or to acting as equals in the ongoing discourse of intellectuals. They have had no economic status independent of men. They have not had until very recently access to the educational skills necessary to develop, sustain, and participate in it. The scope of their action has indeed over time been *progressively narrowed* to the domestic.

Women have of course had access to and used the limited and largely domestic zone of women's magazines, television programs, women's novels, poetry, soap operas, etc. But this *is* a limited zone. It follows the contours of their restricted role in the society. The universe of ideas, images, and themes — the symbolic modes which are the general currency of thought — have been either produced by men or controlled by them. Insofar as women's work has been entered into it, it has been on terms decided by men and because it has been approved my men. This applies of course even to the writers of the women's movement.

In this paper I shall be concerned with some aspects of how the socially organized production and transmission of ideas and images deprive women of access to the means to reflect on, formulate, and express their experience and their situation. It is aimed at defining the distinctive role for women's studies which follows from the analysis. Much of what I shall say is not new as information. In fact what I want to do is to make observable some of the socially organized aspects of what we already know. It is a problem of tying things into a single framework which shows how they belong together. I want therefore to make use of the familiar in drawing up an account as a context within which the character and objectives of women's studies in sociology and in other academic fields might be conceived.

The Concept of Ideology

The conceptual framework used in the analysis makes the concept of ideology its key. In developing this analytic framework, I have returned to the formulation made by Marx and Engels in *The German Ideology* bypassing some of the very different traditions of use which are built into the contemporary practice. The meaning of the word ideology has been reduced to the notion of political beliefs.

There are two aspects of Marx and Engels' formulation of the concept, only the second of which will be used here. First, they use ideology as a key term in a methodological critique of ways of thinking of social concepts and categories (the forms of thought) as if they were autonomous powers or agents in society, independent of those who think them and of the actual practical situations in which that thought arises and to which it is relevant.

Second, they are concerned with ideology as a means through which the class that rules a society orders and sanctions the social relations which support its hegemony. The concept of ideology here focuses on social forms of consciousness (the ways in which people think and talk with one another) which originate outside the actual working relations of people going about their everyday business and are imposed upon them.

Marx and Engels held that how people think about their social relations and the social order and the ways in which they define themselves and their environment in relation to the social order arise out of their actual working relations and the discourse which accompanies and expresses them. The production of ideas, of conceptions, of consciousness, is at first directly interwoven with the material activity and the material intercourse of men, the language of real life. Conceiving, thinking, the mental intercourse of men appear at this stage as the direct efflux of their material behavior. The same applies to mental production as expressed in the language of politics, laws, morality, religion, metaphysics, etc. of a people (Marx & Engels, 1970:47). Originally then and perhaps in some sense "naturally" (though this term must always be used with caution) the forms of thought arise directly out of and express people's working relations, their actual situation, their experience. With the emergence of a class society, however, "mental production" becomes the privilege of a ruling class. Note here that Marx and Engels do not use the term ruling class as it has come to be used since then. It does not with them refer to a political elite. It refers rather to that class which dominates a society by virtue of its control of the means of production (1970:64). Among those means are the means of mental production.

In following their use of the concept of ideology we attend to the production of ideas by a specialized set of persons located in a ruling class. The ideas, images, etc., are produced for others to use, to analyze, to understand, and to interpret their social relations, what is happening, the world that they experience and act in. These systems of ideas are a pervasive and fundamental mode in which the organizing and control of this form of society is done. It is important to recognize that these social forms of thought originate in a practice of ruling — or management, or administration, or other forms of social control. They are located in and originate from definite positions of dominance in the society. They are not merely that neutral floating thing, the "culture."

The contrast implicit in their formulation is on the one hand between the social forms of thought — ideas, images — which are directly expressive of a world directly known and which arise where it needs to be thought and to be said and, on the other, the social forms of thought which come to us from outside, which do not arise out of experience and the need to communicate with others in working contexts. Characteristic of the latter is a way of proceeding which begins from a knowledge of the ideas and images and how to use them, and examines, interprets, assembles and formulates the world of direct experience as instances of them. We come thus to know it in terms in which it is ruled.

The forms of thought are learned. We receive them in what we read, whether books, magazines, comic-books, newspapers, or whatever; we receive them both conceptually and as images (a powerful and new ideological form in this type of society) on television and in movies; we hear them on the radio and second-hand in the ways in which the ordinary talk depends upon these media resources. The scope and intensiveness of the production of the social forms of thought is greater in this type of society than in any previously known.

The ideas and images are a pervasive and fundamental mode which serves to organize, order, and control the social relations, the working practices, the ideals and objectives, of individual members of the society. They are the forms given to people to understand what is happening to them, what other people are doing, particularly those not directly part of their lives. These are the means we are given to examine our experience, our needs and anxieties, and to find out how they can be made objective and realized (made real) as a basis for action. Ideology in our form of society provides an authorization of social reality. Perhaps more than that which can become recognized as real in the socially constructed reality is what is already interpretable in the ideological forms of thought. The practice of the ideological analysis of experience is circular, not proceeding by hypothesis, inference, and evidence, but by a process called "typification" (Schutz, 1966) which analyzes and assembles what is given in experience to find in it the type which it intends. The concept of ideology as I am developing its use here identifies a *practice* or *method* in the use of ideas and images which is ideological rather than a determinate object or type of object. I want to be able to recognize the ideological aspects of, or methods of using, the work of poets and artists and religious thinkers as well as the work of sociologists, political scientists, economists, etc. I do not, however, want to reduce the poem to its ideological use. I am not trying to suggest that everything that is produced by an intelligentsia can be reduced to this. I am holding rather that many types of literary as well as religious works have an ideological dimension and lend themselves to ideological uses. Works of many kinds may serve to order, legitimate, and organize social relations and the socially relevant aspects of experience. It is this function which is identified as ideology here. Insofar as these works are produced by that section of a ruling class known as the intelligentsia; in so far as they present as generally valid and authoritative the view and sense of the world from the specific position of its ruling class; insofar as they sanction and formulate determinate forms of social relations and serve to organize the local, particular, and directly known into the social forms of thought and discourse in which it is or can be ruled — they are ideological.

The model of manipulation from behind the scenes, the model of ideology as ideas designed to deceive and fool the innocent and ignorant put forward consciously and with malign intent by a ruling elite, is quite inadequate to analyze the phenomena we are concerned with. We are describing a class phenomenon. This means that we are locating a determinate set of positions in relation to a structure of power which constitutes a common perspective, set of relevances, conditions of experience, interests and objectives. People who occupy these positions arrogate certain powers. They have these powers because of their positions. Because of their positions they view the world in particular ways; they experience common conditions with others similarly placed. Things make sense to them in terms of projects and relevances which are not only similar but often directly related to one another. This class of positions controls the means of "mental production" as Marx and Engels describe it. Hence what is produced takes for granted the conditions of their experience, their interests and relevances. The forms of thought which are produced in this way assume the background conditions and knowledges which these positions are embedded in. They assume the moral and political values of the discourses of which they are part. They assume the dilemmas and contradictions and anxieties they give rise to. *And above all they take for granted the silences of those who do not hold these positions, who are outside.*

And as we know, those who occupy and appropriate those positions are men. Marx's and Engels' account of ideology identifies it with the ruling class. It is now clear that the class basis of ideology is articulated yet further to a sex basis. For it is men who produce for women, as well as for other members of the society, the means to think and image. In the various social apparatuses concerned with the production and distribution of ideas and images, or with the training of people to participate in and respond to these forms of thought, it is men who occupy the positions of authority, men who predominate in the production of ideas and social knowledge, and men who control what enters the discourse by occupying the positions which do the work of gatekeeping and the positions from which people and their "mental products" are evaluated.

Women's Exclusion Actively Enforced

The exclusion of women from these positions is not a function of their biology. Of course there have existed bases of exclusion in the social determinants of their role, but in this sphere there is a history of active repression. Women who have claimed the right to speak authoritatively as women have been repressed. I have made up from various sources a short list of instances.

Though we cannot assign a definite date to the emergence of ideological formations, the translation of the Bible into the vernacular languages of Europe is a good place to begin. At this point a written source which sanctified direct interpretations of moral and cosmological order became assessible to anyone who could read. The authority of the scriptures thus became anyone's authority and women were among those who could grasp it. Our first example then is from this period.

Sylvia Thrupp in *The Merchant Class of Mediaeval London* tells us of Joan Boughton and her daughter Lady Yonge: "The only evidence of heretical leanings in the city's merchant class concerns women. Sir John Yonge's mother-in-law, Joan Boughton, was burnt as a heretic in 1495, at the age of eighty, defying all doctors in London to shake her faith in the tenets of Wycliffe, and a few years later Lady Yonge followed her to the stake. Pecock had complained of women 'which maken hem self so wise bi the Bible.' who would insist on disputing with the clergy and would admit not practice to be virtuous, 'save what thei kunnen fynde expresseli in the Bible' (Thrupp, 1962:252).

Sheila Rowbotham gives an account of the trial and banishment of Anne Hutchison from Massachusetts in the seventeenth century: "'You have stepped out of your place,' the Calvinist church fathers in the Massachusetts Bay colony told Anne Hutchison in the mid-seventeenth century. 'You have rather been a husband than a wife, and a preacher than a hearer, and a magistrate than a subject, and so you have thought to carry all things in Church and Commonwealth as you would and have not been humbled for it'" (Rowbotham, 1973:17). Notice here a theme which we shall find again. It is not what she said that she is condemned for. It is rather that as a woman she claimed to speak as one who had authority. "They worked hard at humbling her. She had gathered round her a group of followers, mostly women. They met together and Anne Hutchison preached on texts, criticized some of the ministers, and became respected for her knowledge of scripture and of healing herbs. . . . She upset Calvinist dogma, political differentiation, and masculine superiority. She was accordingly tried by both civil and religious authority. Pregnant and ill, at one stage while she was being questioned she almost collapsed, but they wouldn't let her sit down. . . . Finally she faltered and confessed to heresy. But they were still not satisfied. "'Her repentance is not in her countenance.' She was banished by the colony" (Rowbotham, 1973:17).

Many women were active in the French revolution. They were organized in active revolutionary clubs. In the fall of 1793 after Marat's assassination, the Convention decided to prohibit women's clubs and societies. Two of the leading women, Olype de Gouges (on November 3, 1793) and Manon Roland (on November 8, 1793) were guillotined. Here is the official interpretation of what women were to learn from their deaths: "In a short time the Revolutionary Tribunal has given women a good lesson which will no doubt not be lost on them. . . . Olype de Gouges wished to be a statesman, and it seems that the law has punished that conspiratoress for having forgotten the virtues appropriate to her sex. The woman Roland was a mother, but wished to rise above herself; the desire to be a savant led her to forget her sex, and that forgetfulness, always dangerous, finished by causing her to perish on the scaffold" (des Jacques, 1972:139).

Mrs. Packard was imprisoned in the State of Illinois Insane Asylum for three years from 1860 to 1863 under a law which permitted a man to commit his wife or child to an asylum on his word alone and without other evidence of insanity. Mrs. Packard was married to a Calvinist minister. She came to hold religious and political views very different from those of her husband. Her attorney describes the difference as follows: "Her views of religion are more in accordance with the liberal views of the age in which we live (than those of her husband). She scouts the Calvinistic doctrine of man's total depravity, and that God has foreordained some to be saved and others to be damned. She stands fully on the platform of man's free agency and account-ability to God for his actions. . . . She believes slavery to be a national sin, and the church and the pulpit a proper place to combat this sin. These, in brief, are the points in her religious creed which were combated by Mr. Packard, and were denominated by him as 'emanations from the devil,' or 'the vagaries of a crazed brain'" (Szasz, 1973:57-58). It was not, however, the content of her beliefs alone which led to the decision that she was insane. Her husband had called in three physicians who as expert witnesses testified in the court procedures to her insanity. Her claim to speak as authority in religious and moral matters was judged insane: "QUESTION: What else did she say or do there, that showed marks of insanity? ANSWER: She claimed to be better than her husband — that she was right — and that he was wrong — and that all she did was good, and all he did was bad. . . ." (Szasz, 1973:66). Her case became a *cause célèbre*. After her release from the asylum in which she had been held, Mrs. Packard was active in getting the law changed in Illinois.

In Paris during the student uprising of 1968 a feminist group on the Left had prepared leaflets: "As we walked around we handed out leaflets, particularly to women. A crowd of about a hundred people followed us around; most of them were hostile. We had been prepared for significant opposition from men, even afraid of it; but even so were not prepared for such depth and breadth of outrage. Here were 'movement' men shouting insults at us: 'Lesbians,' 'Strip,' 'What you need is a good fuck'. . . ." (quoted by Mitchell, 1972:86).

In 1969 a major demonstration in Washington was organized on the occasion of Nixon's inauguration. A women's group had arranged to burn their voter's registration cards to demonstrate how little getting the vote had done to change women's oppression. As the rally went on, the group began to sense that they were not going to be given a chance to speak. "Dave Dellinger introduces the rally with a stirring denunciation of the war and racism. 'What about women, you schmuchk,' I shout. 'And, uh, a special message from Women's Liberation,' he adds. Our moment comes, M., from the Washington group, stands up to speak. This isn't the protest against the movement men, which is the second on the agenda, just fairly innocuous radical rhetoric — except that it's a good looking woman talking about women. The men go crazy. 'Take it off!' 'Take her off the stage and fuck her!'" (Ellen Willis, quoted by Mitchell, 1972:85).

This is the rough stuff. It points to a boundary which we are not aware of until we read such instances. They show us that more is involved than can be met simply by a work of reasoning and persuasion. There is a social structuring of authority which is prior to and a condition of the development among women of the means to express themselves and to make their condition actionable. Women are defined as persons who have no right to speak as authorities in religious or political settings. Deprived of this right, how can what they might have to say become a basis for knowledge, symbol, moral sanction, complaints, claims, or action? In most of the instances I have cited, it is the claim to authority which is the crucial impiety.

Male Control of the Educational System

The exclusion of women from participating actively in making and creating the forms under which social relations are thought and spoken of has seldom to be so violently repressive. The ordinary socially organized process of socialization, education, work, and communication perform a more routine, generalized, and effective repression. The educational system is an important aspect of this practice. It trains people in the skills they need in order to participate, at various levels, in the ideological forms of social control (they must be able to read); it trains them in the images and the forms of what the ideology sanctions as real; it trains them in the appropriate relations and in how to identify authoritative ideological sources (what kinds of books, newspapers, etc., to credit, what to discredit, who are the authoritative writers or speakers and who are not). It is part of the system which distributes ideas and ensures the dissemination of new ideological forms as these are produced by the intelligentsia. It is also active itself in producing ideology, both in forms of knowledge in the social sciences, psychology, and education, and in the forms of critical ideas and theories in philosophy and literature.

Prior to the late nineteenth century, women were almost completely denied access to any form of higher education beyond the skills of reading and writing. One of the first major feminist works, Mary Wollstonecraft's *Vindication of the Rights of Women,* places their right to education at the centre of her argument. She is responding specifically to Rousseau's prescriptions for educating women which aim to train them for dependency, for permanent childishness, and for permanent incapacity for the autonomous exercise of mind (Wollstonecraft, 1967). During the latter part of the nineteenth century in both Europe and North America opportunities for women in higher education were a major focus of women's struggle. Though women's participation in the educational process at all levels has increased in this century, this participation remains within marked boundaries. Among the most important of these boundaries, I would argue, is that which reserves to men control of the policy-making and decision-making apparatus in the educational system.

In this section I am going to present some of the by now familiar figures which describe how women are located in the educational system as teachers and administrators. I shall not be concerned with viewing these under the aspect of social justice. I am not concerned here with equality of opportunity. I want rather to draw attention to the significance of the inequalities we find for how women are located in the processes of setting standards, producing social knowledge, acting as "gate-keepers" over what is admitted into the systems of distribution, innovating in thought or knowledge or values and in other ways participating as authorities in the ideological work done in the educational process.

In 1970-1, according to the Canadian Department of Labour statistics, women were 62.6 percent of teachers in public schools at all levels.[2] In 1969-70 at the elementary school level where the major focus is the teaching of basic skills, they formed 75.0 percent of teachers (this figure is for eight provinces only; Quebec and Ontario data were not available.[3] At the secondary school level young people receive not only a training in academic and vocational skills, they are also given substantive training in the ideological forms which regulate the social relations of the society (in sports as much as in history or English literature). At this level men predominated, and only 34.0 percent of teachers were women (eight provinces only).

At each next point upward in the hierarchy of control over the educational process, the proportion of women declines. In 1969-70 only 23.6 percent of principals were women (eight provinces only), though there is considerable variation by province.[4] The figures showing the proportion of women school superintendents or the location of women in Departments of Education are not readily available, but there is no reason to believe that we would see a different over-all picture.[5] Figures on the educational staffs of community colleges show distributions in the same direction. In 1970-7 women were only 18.6 percent.[6] At the university level the same pattern is apparent. Gladys Hitchman has brought together the data from studies of six Canadian universities (Alberta, Queen's, McGill, McMaster, UBC, Waterloo). An average of the percentages of women at all ranks in these six is 12.54 percent. Overall, the figures from schools, community college, and universities indicate an inverse relation between level in the educational "hierarchy" and the proportion of women.

Within the university the same pattern is repeated. The data brought together by Gladys Hitchman (1974) appear in Table 1. The inverse relation between status level and proportion of women is obvious at every level and in all six universities. Women are most heavily concentrated in the positions of lecturer and instructor which are not part of the promotional system leading to professorial rank (the so-called "ladder" positions), and are usually held on only a one-year contract. There is an appreciable drop even to the next level of junior positions, the assistant professors — the first step on the promotion ladder. Women form a very small proportion of full professors.

Table 1
Percentage of Women in Academic Status Categories
for Six Canadian Universities*

	Alberta	Queen's	McGill	McMaster	UBC	Waterloo
	(1971)	(1972)	(1970-71)	(1969)	(1972)	(1972)
Lecturers/ instructor	68.1	25.0	46.3	26.6	41.9	11.9
Assistant professor	20.0	13.0	19.2	11.9	18.7	9.5
Associate professors	9.1	3.5	12.3	7.2	9.3	3.6
Full professors	4.8	0.5	5.5	3.1	3.4	1.5
Chairpersons	n.d.	0.0	n.d.	n.d.	n.d.	0.0
Total Faculty	16.1	7.7	16.8	11.0	18.1	5.3

*Based on Hitchman, 1974.
n.d. = no data.

It is important to keep in mind that we are looking at rather powerful structures of professional control. It is through this structure of ranks and the procedures by which people are advanced from one to another that the professions maintain control over the nature and quality of work that is done and the kinds of people who are admitted to its ranks and to influential positions within it. Two points are of special importance; first the concentration of women in the relatively temporary non-ladder positions. This means that they are largely restricted to teaching, that their work is subject to continual review, and that reappointment is conditional upon conformity. The second point to note is the marked break in the proportion of women between tenured and non-tenured positions. I have made averages from Hitchman's tables in order to bring this out (see Table 2). However, please note that this is a rather rough procedure and the results can be treated as estimates only.

There are considerable variations between universities, largely produced by the differences in proportions of women at the lecturer and instructor level. However, here we are concerned not with accounting for the variations of the over-all pattern but with looking at what it tells us about the structures of professional control in the university. The figures show very clearly a marked jump between proportions of women in tenured and non-tenured positions, ranging from a difference of 8.15 percentage points at Waterloo to 37.55 at Alberta. (The lower break at Waterloo is a function of the lower proportions of women employed at any rank.)

These figures show us that at these six Canadian universities women are markedly underrepresented in positions of full membership of university and profession. These are positions in which their continued employment is no longer subject to the continual scrutiny of their senior colleagues. They are also those from which decisions are made about the continued employment of those as yet without tenure. If we look at these figures as if they represented votes, we find women woefully underrepresented: only two votes in every hundred at Queen's, and at best only about nine in every hundred at McGill.

Table 2
Percentage of Women in Non-tenured and Tenured Positions
for Six Canadian Universities*

	Alberta (1971)	Queen's (1972)	McGill)1970-71)	McMaster (1969)	UBC (1972)	Waterloo (1972)
Non-tenured	44.50	19.00	32.71	19.25	30.30	10.7
Tenured	6.95	2.00	8.90	5.15	6.35	3.55
Differences	37.55	17.00	23.85	14.10	23.95	8.15

*Estimate based on Hitchman, 1974.

The tenured faculty, to a large extent, control those admitted to its ranks and what shall be recognized as properly scholarly work.[7] This minimal "voting power" of women helps us to understand why women in more senior positions in the university do not ordinarily represent women's perspectives. They are those who have been passed through this very rigorous filter. They are those whose work and style of work and conduct have met the approval of judges who are largely men. And, in any case, *they are very few.*

There is, I have suggested, more than one type of ideological function in contemporary society. There is that which is concerned with the general moral and expressive modes and with the political and philosophical interpretations which are generalized in the society. There is also that which is directly built into the modes of organizing the various corporate, bureaucratic and professional enterprises which govern the society. There are, we might say, two forms of ideology: the ideologies of expression, evaluation, and theory, and the ideologies of organized action. Women's relation to these two modes are different. Their access to the means of expression and the means of representation of their interests and perspectives in the ideological forms which govern the society are very differently structured. Some figures from a study done by the Women's Action Group (1972) at the University of British Columbia gives us a clearer picture of the effect I am now trying to describe. The faculties of arts (which at the University of British Columbia includes the social sciences) and education represent the ideologies of expression and theory; the fields of commerce and law represent ideologies of organized action. these have of course very different relations to the power structures of the society — the latter being directly implicated in the formations and media in which power is exercised, while the former exercises primarily a control of regulatory function. Table 3 shows how women are located in these fields. It shows quite clearly that from those ideological fields which are directly involved in preparing people for positions in the managerial and governing structure, namely commerce and law, women are completely excluded. They are excluded thereby from occupying the positions in which innovative thinking in those professions is most likely to be done. Therefore they do not participate, at least from positions of authority from which their thinking may enter directly into the training and preparation of professionals, in forming the conceptual framework and relevances in which professionals in these fields are trained.

Table 3
Percentage of Women by Rank with
Ideological Function, UBC, 1972

	Arts	Education	Commerce	Law
Lecturer	44.8	44.4	0	0
Instructor	57.0	38.0	0	0
Assistant Professor	21.2	33.3	0	0
Associate Professor	10.8	17.0	0	0
Full Professor	2.7	15.0	0	0

Source: Report on the Status of Women and the University of British Columbia, Table VIII.

The differences between arts and education are also suggestive. Faculties of education are concerned with training and distribution of knowledge, skills, and the forms of thought. Though innovative work is done in educational theory and practice, it is innovative as a means of transmitting a substance which originates elsewhere. At least in some of the arts fields, critical standards and procedures are being developed and concepts and knowledges originate. The direction of the difference between education and arts indicates the same effect. In the "ladder" positions from assistant professors up, there are lower percentages of women at each rank in arts than in education. The loci of ideological production are largely controlled by men.

In this section I have suggested that we can see two major aspects with respect to how women are located in the educational system. One is that the closer positions come to policy-making or innovation in ideological forms, the smaller the proportion of women. The second is that the closer the ideological forms are to the conceptual and symbolic forms in which power is exercised, the less likely women are to be found in the relevant professional educational structures.

Authority

The control by men of the ideological forms which regulate social relations in this form of society is structured socially by an authority they hold as individuals by virtue of their membership in a class. Authority is a form of power which is a distinctive capacity to get things done in words. What is said or written merely means what the words mean until and unless it is given force by the authority attributed to its "author." When we speak of authority we are speaking of what makes what one person says count. Men are invested with authority as individuals not because they have as individuals special competencies or expertise but because as men they appear as representative of the power and authority of the institutionalized structures which govern the society. Their authority as *individuals* in actual situations of action is generated by a social organization. They do not appear as themselves alone. They are those whose words count, both for each other and for those who are not members of this class. (Note, I am not using the term "class" here in a Marxist sense. It bears its ordinary dictionary meaning only.)

We have by now and in various forms a good deal of evidence of the ways in which this social effect works. It is one which Mary Ellman has described as a distinction between women and men in intellectual matters, "which is simple, sensuous and insignificant: the male body lends credence to assertions, while the female takes it away" (Ellman, 1968:148). A study done by Philip Goldberg which was concerned with finding out whether women were prejudiced against women demonstrates this effect very clearly (Goldberg, 1969). Here is Jo Freeman's description: "He gave college girls sets of booklets containing six identical professional articles in traditional male, female and neutral fields. the articles were identical, but the names of the authors were not. For example, an article in one set would bear the name John T. McKay and in another set the same article would be authored by Joan T. McKay. Each booklet contained three articles by 'women' and three by 'men.' Questions at the end of each article asked the students to rate the articles on value, persuasiveness and profundity and the authors on writing style and competence. The male authors fared better in every field, even such 'feminine' areas as Art History and Dietetics" (Freeman, 1971). There seems to be something like a plus factor which adds force and persuasiveness to what men say and a minus factor which depreciates and weakens what is said by women.

A study reported by Jessie Bernard describes this effect in the context of teaching. A woman and a man were chosen by their department as being roughly equal in their ability to communicate. Each gave two identical lectures, which were in fact chapters from books by established sociologists.

The study was concerned with finding out whether students learned more from one sex than the other. As determined by examination results, there was no difference. However, other differences did emerge and it is these that are relevant here. "The young woman had less impact than the young man. Many more of her listeners have neutral or impersonal résumés of the talk when tested. The young man evoked much more reaction" (Bernard, 1964:256). There was a difference in "credibility": "Fewer of the young man's listeners than of the young woman's hid behind the 'he said' dodge. They accepted what he said as fact. The implication is that material presented by a man is more likely to be accepted at face value than material presented by a woman: it seems to have more authority; it is more important" (Bernard, 1964:257). This effect must generally diminish the authority of women teachers (at all levels) vis-à-vis students. I refer the reader to a moving retrospective account by one of Suzanne Langer's students which expresses this (Pochoda, 1972). Once brought into focus it is, I believe, an effect which academic women can recognize at once as an ordinary working condition.

It is not of course confined to academia. The way in which the sex of the speaker modifies the authority of the message has been observed in other ideological fields. Lucy Komisar reports that in advertising women "receive instructions about how to do their housework from men: Arthur Godfrey, who probably never put his hands into soapsuds, tells women across the country why they ought to add still another step to their washing routine with Axion Pre-Soak. Joseph Daley, president of Grey Advertising, says the *men are used because the male voice is the voice of authority* (Komisar, 1972, my emphasis). Chesler's study of preferences among psychotherapists and their patients shows that the majority of women patients prefer male therapists and that the majority of male psychotherapists prefer women patients. The reasons the women give for preferring male psychotherapists are that they generally feel more comfortable with them and that they have more respect for and confidence in a man's competence and authority. Chesler reports that both men and women in her sample said that they trusted and respected men as people and as authorities more than they did women (Chesler, 1972).

A study done by Fidell on sex discrimination in university hiring practices in psychology shows the intersection of this effect with the educational system of controls described in the preceding section. She used an approach very similar to Goldberg's, constructing two sets of fictional descriptions of academic background and qualifications (including the Ph.D.) Identical descriptions in one set had a woman's name attached and in the other a man's. The sets of descriptions were sent to chairpersons of all college an universities in the United States offering graduate degrees in psychology. They were asked to estimate the chance of the individuals described getting an offer of a position and at what level, etc. Her findings supported the hypothesis of discrimination on the basis of sex: "The distributions of level of appointment were higher for men than for women.

Further, men received more 'on line' (academic positions leading to tenure) responses than women. Only men were offered full professorships" (Fidell, 1970). It seems as though the class attribution of authority which increases the value of men's work constitutes something rather like a special title to the positions of control and influence and hence to full active membership in the intelligentsia.

This effect is socially constructed. It is not a biological attribute. This becomes more observable when we attend to the social class dimensions of authority. It is not, as Ellman (1968) suggests, merely the male *body*, but rather the male body literally *clothed* in the trappings of his class which "lends credence to assertions." The working man, the native Indian, the black man are also depreciated. It is a social effect which preserves the status and control of male members of the ruling classes over the ideological forms and at the same time renders that control effective as authority.

These patterns are integral to the *social organization* of the ideological formations of this type of society. More than one study has shown that well-educated and middle-class people have what may be described as greater deference[8] to the opinions and perspectives of interviewers who represent the "university" than do people with relatively little education (Komarovsky, 1967; Schatzman & Strauss, 1966) Pheterson's findings in a study using procedures similar to Goldberg's, but limiting the topics of articles to matters within the women's domain, found that middle-aged "uneducated" women did not respond as Goldberg's college student respondents had (Goldberg, 1969). Hochschild describes her findings thus: "Pheterson (1969) explored prejudice against women among middle-aged, uneducated women. This time the professional articles were on child discipline, special education, and marriage. The women judged female work to be equal to and even a bit better than male work" (1973). Some women at least appear not to be fully integrated into the social organization of ideological formation. In some areas of discourse at least men are not constituted as authority. The class structure mediated by educational middle-class women are fully part of it. Their subordination is the second term which constitutes the grammar of authority. Their silence is integrated into and generated by its organization (Gornick, 1972; Smith, 1974).

Circles

The metaphor of a "circle" of speakers and hearers relevant to one another is helpful in conceptualizing this as an aspect of the social organization of ideology. It seems likely that the process of developing ideological forms is controlled by restricting participation in such "circles" to properly authorized participants. Only the perspectives and thinking of these get *entered* into the discourse as its themes and topics. Jessie Bernard describes this in the academic context as "the stag effect" (Bernard, 1964:157) and refers to an informal experiment in which professional subjects were asked to name the top 10 in their field. Leading women members of the profession were unlikely to be mentioned. "When this was pointed out to the subjects, they tended to look sheepish and say they never thought of her. She was not in the same image of their profession as were the men. . . . It is not that the work of distinguished academic women scholars was not taken seriously; it was only that in most disciplines the image of the professional did not include them" (Bernard, 1964:176).

It seems that women as a social category lack proper title to membership in the circle of those who count for one another in the making of ideological forms. To identify a woman novelist as a woman novelist is to place her in a special class outside that of novelists in general. The minus factor attached to what they say, write, or image described in the previous section, is another way of seeing how what they say, write or image is not "automatically" part of the discourse. I suggest that if we observe how these things get done in our professions, in literary reviews, and in ordinary situations of meeting among professionals, we would see that what women say and do has a conditional status only. It awaits recognition by a fully qualified male participant. It awaits sanction. It must be picked up (and sometimes taken over) by a man if it is to become part of the discourse.

The previous discussion has been concerned largely with the authority of the written or printed word. But these are patterns which are clearly observable in face to face interaction also. We can and have observed them ourselves. There are by now a number of studies which serve to fill out our description of how male control over the topics and themes of discourse is maintained in actual situations of interaction. For example, Stodtbeck and Marm in their study of jury deliberations report that men talked considerably more than women. The differences, however, were more than quantitative. They also describe what seems to be a general pattern of interaction between women and men. Men's talk was more directed towards the group task while women reacted with agreement, passive acceptance, and understanding (Strodtbeck and Marm, 1956). The pattern I have observed also involves women becoming virtually an audience, facilitating with support or comments, but not becoming among those who carry the talk and whose remarks are directed towards one another.

Characteristically, women talking with men use styles of talk which throw the control to others, as for example, by interspersing their talk with interjections which reassign the responsibility for its meaning to others, as by saying "you know" or failing to name objects or things or to complete sentences. Expectations for men's and women's speech differ and must have an effect on how people are seen with respect to how and how much to talk. Cudill describes a supervisor of nurses as "an assertive person," "willing to express her opinion in unequivocal terms." Yet his data show that in meetings she spoke less on the average than the hospital administrative and psychiatric personnel, including a resident described as "passive and withdrawn" (Caudill, 1958:249).

Candy West has made a study of differences between single sex and mixed sex conversations which focuses upon the differential rights to speak of men and women (1974). She observed a variety of different "devices" used by men apparently with women's consent which serve to maintain male control of the topics of conversation. For example, men tended to complete women's sentences, to give minimal responses to topics initiated and carried by women, and to interrupt without being sanctioned. She gives one example from a transcribed conversation which went as follows: "After thirty lines of talk, during which the female lays out a problem she's having and the male responds minimally on every occasion of his turn arising, a twenty-five second pause ensues. Then he commences to discuss a paper *he's* working on — without semantically having ever acknowledged her subject" (West, 1974:37). Her study describes "a pattern of male control of conversation, principally through the use of interruptions and the withdrawal of active participation in topic development" (West, 1974:19-20).

In professional conversations we can also identify a collection of devices which may be used to restrict women's control of what West calls "topic development." Among them are devices which are used to recognize or enter what women have said into the discourse under male sanction. For example, a suggestion or point contributed by a woman may be ignored as its point of origin. When it is re-introduced at a later point by a man, it is then "recognized" and becomes part of the topic. Or if it is recognized at the time, it is re-attributed by the responder to another male (in the minutes of the meeting, it will appear as having been said by someone else). Or the next speaker after the woman may use a device such as, "What Dorothy really means . . ." Or the woman's turn is followed by a pause following which the topic is picked up at the previous speaker's turn as if she had not spoken. We can, I am sure, add to the list of these devices and also cite many exceptions to these patterns. They arise, however, out of very general assumptions about the socially organized relations of men and women in relation to control of the ideological forms of the society. Their specifics may vary, but the over-all patterns of control over topics and themes recur. The social organization of men-women relations in such contexts can be understood as generating the appropriate practices, devices, and perceptions as these are situationally relevant and appropriate. The grammar of these relations is understood by both sexes. It is not simply imposed by men upon women. Women participate in the ways in which they are silenced.

Women as Subject

I have focused here on the various ways in which women have been and are excluded from full participation in creating the forms of thought which constitute the social consciousness of a society. By this point in the women's movement I believe we must be familiar with the effect of this. Modes of thinking and imaging our experience are produced for us by others who do not share our experience or position in the world. They are produced by those who hold the superordinate positions in the society and whose consciousness extends into the world as a reflection on the structures of power within which they act upon and know it. De Beauvoir in *The Second Sex* (1961) has made an important distinction between men as subjects and women as other. It is as if the world is thought from the position of a consciousness which has its centre in a ruling class of men — what Kate Millett has described as "the patriarchy" (Millett, 1971). From this centre women appear as objects. In relation to men of these classes women's consciousness does not appear as an autonomous origin of knowledge, an authoritative perspective on the world from a different position in and experience of it. Women do not appear to men as men do to one another, as persons who might share in the common construction of a social reality. It is the social organizational substructure of this relation which we have been assembling in the preceding sections. We have begun to look at this relation as it is actually practised and enforced. If women have failed to find a position from which we might reflect back upon men as subjects, it is these institutionalized structures and practices excluding us from functioning as subject which *enforce* our failure.

It is important to recognize that the deprivation of authority and the ways in which women have been trained to practice the complement of male control of "topic development" (West, 1974:20) have the effect of making it difficult for women to treat one another as relevant figures. We have difficulty in asserting authority for ourselves. We have difficulty in grasping authority for women's voices and for what women have to say. We are thus deprived of the essential basis for developing among ourselves the discourse out of which symbolic structures, concepts, images, and knowledges might develop which would be adequate to our experience and to devising forms of organization and action relevant to our situations and interest. In participating in the world of ideas as objects rather than as subjects we have come to take for granted that our thinking is to be authorized by an external source of authority. Thus, as Bostock says: "one of the consequences of living in a world intellectually dominated by men . . . is that women try to have opinions which will satisfy the approved standards of the world; and in the last analysis, these are standards imposed on them by men, which, in practice, means that our opinions are kept fairly rigorously separated from our own lived experience. If a woman today wants to have opinions which are truly her own, she has to check them against her experience, and often not against her personal experience alone, *but against a collective one* (Bostock, 1972, my emphasis). Bostock is laying down an essential condition to the development by women for women of social forms of consciousness. But it has not been easy for women to take what women have to say as authoritative, nor is it easy for women to find their own voices convincing. It is hard for us to listen to ourselves. The voice of our own experience is equally defective.

Lack of authority then is lack of authority for ourselves and for other women. We have become familiar in the women's movement with the importance of women learning to relate to one another. We need also to learn how to treat what other women say as a source and basis for our own work and thinking.

The institutionalized practices of excluding women from the ideological work of society is the reason we have a history constructed largely from the perspective of men, and largely about men. This is why we have so few women poets and why the records of those who survived the hazards of attempting poetry are so imperfect (Bernikow, 1974). This is why we know so little of women visionaries, thinkers, and political organizers (Rowbotham, 1973). This is why we have an anthropology which tells us about other societies from the perspective of men and hence has so distorted the cross-cultural record that it may now be impossible to learn what we might have known about how women lived in other forms of society. This is why we have a sociology which is written from the perspective of positions in a male-dominated ruling class and is set up in terms of the relevances of the institutional power structures which constitute those positions (Bernard, 1973). This is why in English literature there is a corner called women in literature or women novelists or the like, but an over-all critical approach to literature which assumed that it is written by men and perhaps even largely for men.

The ideological practices of our society provide us with forms of thought and knowledge which constrain us to treat ourselves as objects. We have learned to practice, as Rowbotham points out, a nihilistic relation to our own subjectivity and experience (Rowbotham, 1974:29-37). We have learned to live inside a discourse which is not ours and which expresses and describes a landscape in which we are alienated and which preserves that alienation as integral to its practice. In a short story, Doris Lessing describes a girl growing up in Africa whose consciousness has been wholly formed within traditional British literary culture. Her landscape, her cosmology, her moral relations, her botany, are those of the English novels and fairy tales. Her own landscape, its forms of life, her immediate everyday world do not fully penetrate and occupy her consciousness. They are not *named* (Lessing, 1966). This is the ideological rupture which Marx and Engels have given us the means to understand. Lessing's story is a paradigm of the situation of women in our society.

It is important, I think, to remember that we are not alone in this. Sheila Rowbotham has drawn a parallel between the experience of women in this relation and that of working class men (alas, she does not refer to working class women, but we are all learning all the time). She writes:

> There is a long inchoate period during which the struggle between the language of experience and the language of theory becomes a kind of agony. In the making of the working class in Britain the conflict of silence with "their" language, the problem of paralysis and connection has been contin-uous. Every man who has worked up through the labour movement ex-pressed this in some form. The embarrassment about dialect, the divorce

between home talking and educated language, the otherness of "culture" —
their culture is intense and painful. The struggle is happening now every
time a worker on strike has to justify his position in the alien structures of
the television studio before the interrogatory camera of the dominant class,
or every time a working-class child encounters a middle-class teacher
(Rowbotham, 1974:32).

In insisting that women appear as subjects in the formation of a social
consciousness, we represent ourselves. We cannot break, though we can be
aware of, the other enforced silences. And we can assert that there is not one
way of seeing the world, not one way from which it may be known. There
is not one universal subject from whose perspective knowledge can be
simply transformed into an objective and universal account. We can recognize and explore the implications of this recognition. We can also confront
the institutional practices which in an everyday and routine way constitute
women as other in the ideological relation. These are the same or similar
practices by which others are excluded and by which the appearance of a
single subject is created out of the silences of many.

Conclusions

The implications of this analysis for women academics are far-reaching.
Matters are not improved simply by including women in the professional
and academic positions of influence. The professional discourse has by now
a momentum of its own. The structures which have been developed have
become the criteria and standards of proper professional performance. Being
a professional involves knowing how to do it this way and doing it this way
is how we recognize ourselves as professionals. The perspective of men is
not apparent as such, for it has become institutionalized as the "field" or the
"discipline." Similar considerations apply to the left-wing intelligentsia
whether the perspectives of men are institutionalized as the issues and topics
of radical discourse in relation to which people locate themselves and are
located politically.

We cannot be content with working as academics in the box created by
the male monopoly of artistic, ideological, and other symbolic resources so
that what we do in relation to women and arising out of our interests and
experience as women is defined as "women's business" and confined in the
same way as women's magazines, women's novels, women's programs, etc.
This essentially restricts our topics to those of the relevance of women's
roles. I now distrust that orientation in sociology (undoubtedly with its
parallels in other disciplines) which makes the topic of "sex roles" a central
aspect of women's studies courses. Further, if I teach a sociology *of* women
I am perpetuating the status of women as objects in relation to the ideological
constructions written from the position of men. We must, it seems to me,
begin an examination and critique of how women are constituted as other in
the ideological formations which establish the hegemony of male consciousness.

In developing forms of thought and knowledge *for* women, academic women must offer a major critique of the existing disciplines and theoretical frames. We are confronted virtually with the problem of reinventing the world of knowledge, of thought, of symbols and images, not of course by repudiating everything that has been done but by subjecting it to exacting scrutiny and criticism from the position of women as subject (or knower). This means, for example, claiming the right to examine literature from the perspective of women. That is to do much more than to establish the right of women to honor and examine the work of women poets and novelists or to study the role of women in fiction or drama. In sociology it means, I think, constructing a sociology *for* women rather than *of* women. By this I mean a sociology which will analyze and account for women's position in society and is capable of examining social structure from the perspective of women as subjects. Research is needed which begins with questions that could not have been posed before. I have learned from colleagues with whom I share an interdisciplinary course in women's studies what it means to examine anthropology and psychology from this point of view. I have begun to have a sense of the extraordinary depth and extent of what remains to be discovered by women working from the perspective and experience of women. I believe it goes much farther than I could have thought before participating in this course and approaching it from this (shared) perspective.

There are other implications. Some of them are difficult to come to terms with given the social organization of ideological formation and the productive organization of which it is part, but we should begin to find out how to think them anyway. Insisting on constituting women as subject (rather than that abstract mythical "woman") raises questions about the relation of women members of the intelligentsia and their work to the existence and experience of other women. Exploration of what it means to be *responsible* to women in the society as *subjects*; what it means to develop forms of thought and knowledge capable of expressing their experience, examining and being capable of making intelligible to them how the world as they know and suffer it is determined, providing them with the knowledge, information, and means to think and act in relation to it; these are tasks proposed by the contradiction implicit in our situation as academic women (as it has been analyzed here). We cannot just turn our backs on it by opting for membership in an elite whose ideological forms claim a spurious universality. A critique of the social organization of the academic enterprise is indicated which would examine how it is rendered academic, that is, how the forms of knowledge, relevances, conceptual frameworks, etc., are bounded by an institutionalized discourse which is an integral part of the institutions doing the work of ruling in this type of society.

Notes

[1]Reprinted from *The Canadian Review of Sociology and Anthropology*, 12, 4, Part 1, 1975.

[2]*Women in the Labour Force: Facts and Figures* (1973 edition). Table 78, p. 201.

[3]*Women in the Labour Force: Facts and Figures* (1971 edition). Table 37, p. 91. The percentages are my computation. The 1973 edition of *Women in the Labour Force* did not give this information, so I used the 1971 edition.

[4]*Women in the Labour Force: Facts and Figures* (1971), Table 35, p. 87.

[5]Linda Shuto of the British Columbia Teachers' Federation in an address to the Department of Education workshop on "Sexism in Schools" (North Vancouver, 12-13 June 1975) reported that there were no women superintendents in British Columbia and no women senior officials in the Department of Education.

[6]*Women in the Labour Force: Facts and Figures* (1973), Table 71, p. 187. This percentage is my computation. For both high school and community college we need to take into account the effect of a second factor on these percentages. In both, vocational and technical courses are a significant part of the curriculum. However, even the 10 subjects most representative of women show only 39 percent women (my computation from Table 76, p. 197).

[7]This is generally true at least in a negative sense. The administrative structures of the universities provide for various forms of control over the collegial decision-making process, but it is only in exceptional cases that renewal, tenure, or promotion awards are made against collegial recommendation.

[8]Differences between middle and working class respondents are described in terms of greater ability on the part of middle-class respondents to "take the role of the other" etc. My renaming is ironic but not I think unwarranted by the descriptions. See in particular Komarovsky's discussion of the differences between her interviews with wives of "blue-collar" workers and earlier studies of college-educated women (Komarovsky, 1967:14-22). She notices the respondents' relative "unconcern with the interviewer's attitude" (p. 15).

References

de Beauvoir, S. (1961). *The second sex.* New York: Bantam Books.

Bernard, J. (1964). *Academic women.* New York: New American Library.

_____ (1973). "My four revolutions: an autobiographical history of the ASA." *American Journal of Sociology*, 78, (4).

Bernikow, L. (1974). *The world split open: Four centuries of women poets in England and America, 1552-1950.* New York: Vintage Books.

Bostock, A. (1972). Talk on BBC Third Program published in *The Listener* (August).

Caudill, W. (1958). *The psychiatric hospital as a small society.* Cambridge, Mass.: Harvard University Press.

Chesler, P. (1972). "Patient and patriarch: women in the psychotherapeutic relationship." In V. Gornick & B. Moran, (Eds.) *Women in sexist ssciety: Studies in power and powerlessness pp. 362-92.* New York: Signet Books,

Ellman, M. (1968). *Thinking about women.* New York: Harcourt Brace Jovanovich.

Fidell, L.S. (1970). "Empirical verification of sex discrimination in hiring practices in psychology." *American Psychologist,* 25, (12), :1094-7.

Freeman, J. (1971). "The social construction of the second sex." In M. Garskof, (Ed.) *Roles women play: Readings toward women's liberation (pp. 123-41).* Belmont, California: Brooks/Cole Publishing.

Goldberg, P. (1969). "Are women prejudiced against women?" *Transaction* (April); 28-30.

Gornick, V. (1972). "Women as outsider." In V. Gornick & B. Moran, (Eds.) *Women in sexist society: Studies in power and powerlessness (pp. 126-44).* New York: Signet Books.

Hitchman, G.S. (1974). "A report on the reports: the status of women in Canadian sociology." *Bulletin of the Canadian Sociology Anthropology Association,* (October): pp.11-13.

Hochschild, A.R. (1973). "A review of sex role research." *American Journal of Sociology,* 78, (40).

des Jacques, S. (1972). "Women in the French Revolution: The thirteenth brumaire of Olympe de Gouges, with notes on French Amazon battalions." In A. For freedom, (Ed.) *Women out of history: A herstory (pp. 131-40).* Culver City, Calif.: Peace Press.

Komarovsky, M. (1967). *Blue-collar marriage.* New York: Vintage Books.

Komisar, L. (1972). "The image of woman in advertising." In V. Gornick & B. Moran, (Eds). *Women in sexist society: Studies in power and powerlessness (pp. 304-17). New York: Signet Books.*

Labour, Department of, Government of Canada: Women's Bureau (1971). *Women in the labour force: Facts and figures.*

_____ (1973). *Women in the labour force: Facts and figures.*

Lessing, D. (1966). "The old chief MshLanga." In *The black madonna (pp. 83-106).* St. Albans, Herts: Panther Books.

Marx, K. & Engels, F. (1970). *The German ideology.* Part One. New York: International Publishers.

Millett, K. (1971). *Sexual politics.* New York: Avon Books.

Mitchell, J. (1971). *Women's estate.* Harmondsworth, Middlesex: Penguin Books.

Pochoda, E.T. (1972). "Heroines." In L.R. Edwards, M. Heath, and L. Baskin, (Eds.) *Woman: an issue (pp. 177-86).* Boston: Little, Brown.

Rowbotham, S. (1973). *Women, resistance and revolution.* Harmondsworth, Middlesex: Penguin Books.

_____ (1974). *Women's consciousness, man's world.* Harmondsworth, Middlesex: Penguin Books.

Schatzman, L., & Strauss, A. (1966). "Social class and modes of communication." In A.G. Smith, (Ed.) *Communication and culture.* New York: Holt, Rinehart and Winston.

Schutz, A. (1966). *Collected papers.* 116-32. The Hague: Martinus Nijhoff.

Smith, D.E. (1974). "Women's perspective as a radical critique of sociology." *Sociological Inquiry,* 44, 1.

Strodtbeck, F.L., & Marm. R.D. (1956). "Sex role differentiation in jury deliberations." *Sociometry,* 19 (March), 9-10.

Szasz, T.S. (Ed.) (1973). *The age of madness: The history of involuntary hospitalization presented in selected texts.* Garden City, New York: Doubleday Anchor Books.

Thrupp, S.L. (1962). *The merchant class of mediaeval London 1300-1500.* Ann Arbor, Michigan: Ann Arbor Paperbacks, University of Michigan Press.

West, C. (1973). "Sexism and conversation: Everything you always wanted to know about Sachs (But were afraid to ask)." M.A. Thesis, Dept. of Sociology, University of California, Santa Barbara, California.

Wollstonecraft, M. (1967). *A vindication of the rights of women.* New York: W.W. Norton.

Women's Action Group of the University of British Columbia. *A Report on the status of women at the University of British Columbia* (January).

10

A Discourse Not Intended for Her:
Learning and Teaching Within Patriarchy[1]

Magda Lewis and Roger I. Simon

Listen to the voices of the women and the voices of the men; observe the space men allow themselves, physically and verbally, the male assumption that people will listen, even when the majority of the group is female. Look at the faces of the silent, and of those who speak. Listen to a woman groping for language in which to express what is on her mind, sensing that the terms of academic discourse are not her language, trying to cut down her thought to the dimension of a discourse not intended for her. (Rich, pp. 243-244).

In the spring of 1985 the two of us participated in a graduate seminar, one as faculty/teacher, the other as student; one of us is a man, the other a woman. Our common interest in this seminar was in exploring questions concerning the relation between text and discourse seen in the light of a consideration of the relation between language and power.[2] Although our interests were common, our experience of the class was very different. This paper tells of this difference as it emerged and as it continues to be understood by us. We struggled over finding a common voice in this shared — yet different — experience. But the results of our search for a single voice were never satisfactory, as one or the other of us was unintentionally but inevitably silenced. As our dialogue continued, it became clear to us that the difficulty we were having in our attempt to speak with single voice had not so much to do with us as individuals but rather more powerfully with our different relations to those social, political and economic practices that make possible the privilege of men over women: patriarchy.

In her now classic article, Hartmann (1984) defines patriarchy as a social system characterized by "the systematic dominance of men over women" (p. 194). It emerges as a "set of social relations between men, which have a material base, and which, though hierarchical, establish or create interdependence and solidarity among men that enable them to dominate women. Though patriarchy is hierarchical, and men of different classes, races, or ethnic groups have different places in the patriarchy, they also are united in their shared relationship of dominance over their women; they are dependent on each other to maintain that domination" (p. 197). Hartmann goes on to say that "*patriarchy is not simply hierarchical organization* but hierarchy in which *particular* people fill particular places. It is in studying patriarchy that we learn why it is women who are dominated and how" (p. 199).

Patriarchy so defined has the potential to obliterate the will, desire and capacity of particular individuals, be they women or men, to form personal and collective relationships that are not based on an acceptance of male prerogative. We do not minimize the importance of such struggles. None-

prerogative. We do not minimize the importance of such struggles. None-theless, what we sometimes think of as private lives are not separable from the social forms within which they are constituted. Patriarchy is a social form that continues to play on and through our subjectivities, affecting conceptu-ally organized knowledge as well as elements that move us, without being consciously expressed. It continues to provide us with different vantage points, and positions us differently within relations of power. For this reason we have decided to keep our voices separate, not in order to provide a dialogue but to juxtapose our differences as the ground on which we could formulate a reconstructed practice that would counter patriarchy.

We realize that women constitute only one of many disadvantaged social groups that include people of color, people of racial and ethnic minorities, people in countries dominated politically and economically by imperialist powers, and people who must work in exploitative relations of wage labor or commodity exchange, all of whom suffer disempowerment and silencing. Within this paper we do not discuss race and class dynamics, not because we think such concerns less important than gender or that gender relations can be understood outside the context of other social relations, but because the specific event we speak about in this essay occurred among a homoge-neous group of people with respect to race and class. Our discussion of patriarchy, however, is clearly linked to other forms of domination and we would argue that counter-patriarchic practices have a strong relevance to other struggles against unjust social relations.

Magda Lewis

The overwhelming experience of women in a society dominated by men is that of being silenced.[3] This has not only been shown over and over again by a growing number of feminist writers but can be graphically documented in the daily lives of all women. The search for examples does not have to be long or intensive. A woman I sat next to on a recent trip summed it up exquisitely. After the conductor, the steward and the railroad's public relations representative overlooked her in their various dealings with the passengers, she turned to me and said, "Sometimes I think I must be invisible. People don't see me. They don't hear me. Sometimes I wonder if I am really here." This was a woman, a grandmother, a secretary, who had never read Spender's (1982) *Invisible Women.* I passed on that reference along with a couple of others and she promised to read at least one of them. But she admitted feeling reluctant to buy books with titles like *Sex, Gender and Society* (Oakley, 1972) or *Women's Oppression Today* (Barrett, 1980). *Invisible Women,* she thought, sounded sufficiently like the title of a science fiction novel that she could smuggle it into the house without arousing her husband's suspicion. She implied that if her husband were aware of its subject, the book would surely be banned from the house and her reading even more closely monitored.

Is this an extreme example? I don't think so. It is simply a particular manifestation of a general social condition that is played out among men and women on a daily basis in a variety of forms and places.[4] The example is instructive, however, in that it uncovers the power relations within which men's lives and interests circumscribe those of women. I equivocate deliberately on the word "interest" for I do indeed intend both meanings of the word — what interests men as well as what is in their interest.

As we parted company, my seatmate said, "You younger women have it made. You know what you want and you are so outspoken, people listen to you. Women my age never had a chance." Had there been time I could have explained; I could have told her what I am about to say here, that she and I inhabit the same world, that we are both engaged in the collective struggle to claim our voice, to be heard, to become visible.

Roger Simon

The department we are in consists largely of male faculty members. While this department is not the most extreme example of the male character of academic institutions, it is important to make this point simply to highlight the fact that woman graduate students are familiar with the negotiations and accommodations that are required of them in order to survive in the world of male academia.[5] Shaped by the political/theoretical discourse of socialist feminism and critical pedagogy, my daily experiences in this context have fed my interest in the project of feminist pedagogy.[6] What has made me most uneasy is the growing realization of my complicity in the practice of gender domination, which is constructed on the one hand through the relationship between language use and nonverbal practices, and on the other, through the moral regulation of people that results from the limitation of what are considered appropriate forms of thought, expression and behavior.

In the spring of 1985 I developed and taught a new graduate course entitled "Discourse, Text, and Subjectivity." This course was designed to explore questions concerning the relation between language and power. I intended that the participating students would develop with me a way of framing questions that explore the relation between language and the enhancement of human possibility; for example, how language enters into such questions as who we are and what we are able to be and do. It is an issue that begins to crystallize when we ask how language can be not only a vehicle for learning but, in Foucault's terms, a form of "government" as well.[7] Foucault allows this word the broad meaning it had in the sixteenth century. "Government" referred then not only to political structures or the management of states, but, in addition, to the way in which the conduct of individuals or groups might be directed: the government of children, of souls, of communities, of families, of the sick. To govern, in this sense, is to structure the possible field of human action. To think in these terms is to ask how language is linked to the freedom of women and men, a question which points to a concern with discourse as the concrete process of morally regulated expression and the central component of the production of subjectivity.

Magda Lewis

While all of us — students and teacher, women and men — came to this new course for a variety of personal and professional reasons, we also came with an intact social repertoire. We came carrying the baggage of our governed selves. For the women this meant that we already knew that what we said and how we said it was not quite as important to our male colleagues as the fact that we spoke at all. In a set of social relations where women's ideal discursive state within patriarchy has been defined as silence, a woman speaking is itself a political act (Spender, 1980). Under these conditions the very act or intention of speaking becomes an intrusion and a potential basis for a violent reaction on the part of those who have decreed our silence. Ultimately for individuals who transgress the limits of patriarchy, the forces of regulation are without a doubt swift, sure, and relentless.

As we began to take up the first of the assigned readings, the interesting and significant work by Dorfman, *The Empire's Old Clothes* (1983), the social dynamics in the class were aggravating but not unusual: the men monopolized not only the speaking time but the theoretical and social agenda as well. They sparred, dueled and charged at each other like gladiators in a Roman arena. Yet their camaraderie intensified with each encounter. Throughout this exchange, the women were relegated to the position of spectators. When a woman speaks, it means that a man cannot speak, and when a man cannot speak it means that the social relations among the men are disrupted. Women, therefore, have no place on this playing field. Independently, we felt our exclusion more and more intensely the more we struggled to find room for our voices and to locate ourselves in the discourse.

Roger Simon

For several weeks I held discussions after class with a few students on how to break the discursive monopoly. I felt I had to do something to alter the situation, and so I became more and more of a "gatekeeper," trying to make room in the discussion for people who were not speaking. At one point we thought that introducing literature on men's dominance of conversation in mixed gender groups might help, but I resisted this as I thought it too much of a "diversion" from my planned agenda. I held to the steady but not very successful path of "space-making": asking for comments from those women who had not yet spoken, repositioning myself at the table so that I could see most of the women and perhaps through eye contact and body language encourage their entry into the conversation, noticing when a woman did try to speak, and cutting off those men who had been speaking most often.

Of course, these tactics did nothing to alter the deeply sedimented forms of inequality at work in the class. These tactics simply shifted the focus from a masculine discursive monopoly to women's silence. What I missed here was the fact that the women knew (despite my efforts) that it was not a safe place to speak. Women know that being allowed to speak can be a form of tyranny.[8] I was and still am unsure of why I backed away from confronting this fact — and my complicity in the situation. Knowing, however, that one cannot donate freedom, I deliberately imposed one limit on myself. I knew that as a male teacher I could not, from my position of authority (a position established by my being a man and a professor) overtly name and make topical the oppressive relations in the class. Perhaps this was partly the reason for my reluctance to introduce special readings in the course as a vehicle for raising the issue of the gender relations of the class. Retrospectively, what was needed was not a pedagogy that itself structured not "women as the question" but rather a practice wherein women could "enunciate the question" (Felman, 1981).

Magda Lewis

The feeling of being in a space that is not one's own is familiar to women in a society marked fundamentally by patriarchy.[9] It is not that there were not ideological differences among the men in how they took up the agenda of the class or in how they envisioned its pedagogical implications. In many instances, there was more in common both pedagogically and ideologically between groups of men and women than between people of the same gender. But since the overriding issue in this class was not the politics of curriculum but rather the politics of gender, ideological differences among the men were obliterated by the desire to structure gender solidarity.

Because patriarchy organizes the political and economic forms within which we must survive, regardless of our gender, class, or racial and ethnic identification, all men can benefit in some way from belonging to the dominant group. At the most mundane level, this means that, for men, the boundaries of social relations are so extended that a whole range of social behaviors that is seen to be acceptable for them is deemed to be inappropriate for women, irrespective of their social class or ethnic and racial origin.

In the context of our course this meant that the men were allowed to speak at length — and did. Their speaking was seldom if ever interrupted. When a woman and a man began speaking at the same time, the woman always deferred to the man. Women's speaking was often reinterpreted by the men through phrases such as "what she *really* means. . . ." More than just a few times the actual talk of women was attributed in a later discussion by a man to a man. Women's ideas — sometimes reworded, sometimes not — were appropriated by men and then passed off as their own. Whenever a woman was able to cut through the oppressive discourse, the final attempt at silencing took the form of aggressive yelling. It became clear to us that the reversal of this dynamic would have been totally unacceptable to those who held the power of legitimation.

Gender solidarity is not rooted first and foremost in some vague notions about sociality but rather in the politics and economics of patriarchy. This is not to say, however, that "homosociality" is not an important strategic position from which to maintain and reinforce male dominance, or that such homosociality does not have extremely effective and deeply felt results.[10] Rather, men's political and economic advantage continues to be confirmed, supported and legitimized through a social discourse that arises from their particular relations to one another.

Women have found legitimation only to the extent that we have been able or willing to appropriate the male agenda, a particularly self-violating form of escape from domination which in the end turns out to be no escape at all. The price we pay for this appropriation is the disclaiming of our collective experience of oppression, an act that forfeits our voice and gives overt support to the dominant social, political and economic forms. We, as women, have appropriated to a large extent the terms of our own subjection. This is not a case of false consciousness. Rather, we have accepted the powerlessness of these terms to define a discourse within which we can speak partly because we are powerless to do otherwise. While many feminists are clear about the need for women to legitimate each other and thereby begin to break away from the patriarchic stranglehold, it is also clear that intellectual assault is just one of many forms of violation that act in concert to disempower women. Given the complexity of the relationships between physical, emotional, psychological and intellectual abuse, it is clearly not easy for women to subvert this assault.

Roger Simon

From the beginning I had planned to use Radway's *Reading the Romance* (1984) as a key text in the course. At the time I had no idea how pivotal a text it would be. In this book Radway examines extensively both the production and consumption of mass-marketed popular romance novels. Radway's work is unique in that she not only develops an ideological critique of the novels she examines, but she also analyzes empirically and theoretically the reading of these books as part of the discursive practices of a particular group of women. She not only identifies the way they use and read romance novels, but also gives us an understanding of how packaged forms of romance are integrated into daily lives that are historically and structurally constituted within patriarchic social practices of courtship, sexuality and marriage. Radway questions how, why, by whom and with what purposes and meanings such books are read. In examining the readings produced by the women she studies, Radway reveals contradictory constructions of resistance and regulation. Hence, she shows how we can investigate the reading of a text as a form of social practice that can be examined for the work it does in organizing subjectivity. What provoked me to rethink my pedagogy was not our examination of women reading romance but the experience of the women students' reading Radway's text under the determinant conditions of our graduate seminar.

Magda Lewis

Despite conversations and discussions that took place between small groups of women as the course proceeded, by the time we came to Radway's book the women in the class had been all but muted. Either because we had been oppressed into silence or because we had made a conscious decision to refrain from the discussion as a form of resistance to being silenced — how ironic that the result in both cases should be the same — we had become prisoners or exiles within a wall of silence. In part the reason the text of the book enraged us was the context within which we read it and our realization that what was going on with the women in Radway's study was precisely what was going on with us in the classroom. Her study demanded a response. As the male-defined resistance to the formulation of our response intensified, it became clearer to us (the women) that what we were engaged in in this class was a struggle not just for ourselves but for all women — including those women who are reading the romance.

Had we not been required to read Radway's study in this context we might never have been pushed to the outer limits of our marginality. While we could doubt ourselves, our capabilities, our understanding and even our experiences within the context of most male-defined academic discourse, in this instance the disjunction between content and process became obvious. We knew we had not only an experiential base from which to take up Radway's agenda, but a lived theoretical framework from which to understand it as well.

Women are politically disempowered, economically disadvantaged and socially delegitimated, not as individuals (although it is as individuals that the effects are felt most often and most brutally) but as a group. We occupy particular positions in our homes, in our employment and in the street that lead to experiences different from those of groups who are more advantageously positioned. The material basis of women's and men's lives, therefore, plays a major role not only in how they are positioned but also in how their particular social perspective arises. What is often forgotten by both women and men but is important to remember is that this process is man-made — although not without a struggle — and therefore neither natural nor neutral.

We needed to understand that what we were experiencing was indeed a collective experience, and we needed to know what this collective experience was about. Our reading of Radway's *Reading the Romance* was the catalyst that enabled us to understand the divisive and individualizing process embedded in the taken-for-granted prerogative of male discourse.[11] As a collective we could more easily challenge the oppressive boundaries and limited interpretations imposed through such discourse.

It is important to understand that the disjunction between male and female discourse does not arise out of the distinction between objective knowledge on the one hand and subjective knowledge on the other. Rather it is reflective of the disparity in the relations of power between men and women. This implies that women's experience and discursive forms are defined by men as illegitimate *within the terms of men's experience and men's discursive forms.* The assertion that women's knowledge is based on personal experience while men's knowledge is based on objective grounds obliterates, first and foremost, the relationship between education, personal experience and politics. The only education that can have meaning is education that is personal and therefore political. The ingenuousness of an educational process that attempts to obliterate the personal and political is profoundly silencing.

Roger Simon

With the introduction of *Reading the Romance* into the course more was at stake than just the struggle for "air-time." I did not realize at the time that Radway's book, as a text dealing with how particular women named their own experience within patriarchy, would have the capacity to crystallize a perception of past events in the class in a way that made the present visible as a "revolutionary moment" (Buck-Morss, 1981).

What was about to happen has subsequently become a significant episode in my attempt to clarify the basis of a counter-patriarchic pedagogy. Being clear about the concrete conditions that prefigure this episode seems to require an elaboration of what it means to be "muted." Being muted is not just a matter of being unable to claim a space and time within which to enter a conversation. Being muted also occurs when one cannot discover forms of speech within conversation to express meanings and to find validation from others.

As we began the discussion of *Reading the Romance,* the majority of male students in the class and I defined the issues raised within the text in an abstract and distanced language. In my authoritative position as instructor I validated and legitimated this "preferred" theoretical discourse insofar as I encouraged it and — more important — participated in it. Through this very particular and academic form of homosociality, we simultaneously excluded and silenced the women sitting among us. This is not at all to say that the women in the class were incapable of full participation in our theoretical mode of conversation. Rather it is to acknowledge that women experiencing patriarchy not only in our class but also at home, at work and in the streets would have something different to say about Radway's text from that which is abstractly constructed by men.

Within the frame of patriarchy, the men in the class could not speak any other way about the substance of this text. While our own lives do not preclude our considering female oppression, for us it can only be the experience and situation of an Other. We can discuss this experience and situation, we can analyze it, and it can become a provocation for our moral anger. But if we alone take up women's experience of patriarchy, it will be within a discourse that is distanced and abstract. The double problem in this case was that my own objective for the course included the development of a "theoretical fluency," which meant, in part, legitimating and *encouraging* the meaningful use of what for many of the students were new terminology and concepts. I had wanted to use *Reading the Romance* as an example of how we could understand the relation between language, power and subjectivity. It was to this end that I was encouraging a discussion of Radway in abstract terms, appropriating her text to my agenda of introducing students to a new theoretical position. But at this moment the women did not wish to engage in these abstractions. Thus the lived relations of patriarchic power which specified who controlled how we would study mediated our "difference" into inequality. Worse, with the women silenced, we were doing what I said earlier should never be done, enunciating women's problems.

Magda Lewis

Silence can turn into rage when we realize that who "speaks" and whose authority governs that speaking cannot be disassociated from those relations of power that mark the structures within which individuals live their daily lives. How we knew that the occasion we chose to cast aside our silence was the right one demands an articulation of "soft" data about body language and a profound sensibility to non-verbal discourse that at times becomes the only means of communication between and among members of oppressed groups. As women in the class, we knew we had to confront our silencing concretely.

It is important to signal that what happened to the women in this class was not just consciousness-raising — as important as that is — but, more important, it was a moment of politicization. This always implies collective action and, to the extent that it challenges the status quo, such action is always revolutionary and difficult. Suddenly and forcefully the revolutionary moment became concrete. While we were waiting for the elevator during one of our breaks, a moment of solidarity was precipitated by what may have seemed an offhand comment made to me by one of the other women: "I can't go back into that room."

I responded with an invitation to talk. The usual practice during breaks had been for the men and women students to sit together — a time of informal discussion during which the same dominant discourse prevailed. The two of us took our coffee and tea and moved to a private space. Other women noticed and joined us. Some went to get the rest of the women until all but one of us were gathered. The possibility of this action was facilitated by the deliberate practice of the instructor to absent himself during our breaks. Our gathering was not unnoticed by the male students, whose body language and joking demands to know "what's going on" punctuated our construction as the Other. Only one of the men asked if he could join us, in a show of solidarity. While his gesture was appreciated, his presence, however unobtrusive, would have been silencing. We said no. Our meeting was seen to be and was an overtly political act. As we talked, the anger came in floods.

Without jeopardizing personal confidences, I want to relate some of the discussion that took place during our break.

"I don't understand what they [the men] are talking about. I feel like I'm not as well educated as them. I haven't done too much reading in this area. They know so much more than I. I just feel that if I said anything they'd say, what is she doing in this class, she doesn't know anything, so I keep my mouth shut."

"I haven't got the right language so I always feel like such a dummy. I don't really want to talk because if I do they [the men] will realize how stupid I am."

"I feel very angry and uncomfortable in that room. They have no right to talk about us like that. I feel so embarrassed. It's like men passing around pornographic pictures. I don't think it's appropriate."

"I've talked a few times, but nothing I say seems to make a difference. What I say never gets taken up. It's like I hadn't said anything. So I've given up. Why bother?"

"They talk about those women [in Radway's study] as if they were me. I don't sit at home reading junk like that. I've worked all over the world and have done many interesting things. In this class it's like none of that counts. You're a woman so you must sit at home reading cheap romance novels. That life isn't my life, and I resent being compared to them. But then I get angry at myself for saying that. Why do I want to distance myself from those women? We are no different, they and I."

"I always have the feeling you get when people are talking about you as if you don't exist but in fact you're sitting right there. It's the way people talk about children or mental incompetents."

"You know, they are just like little boys, always demanding attention and monopolizing all the time. I just sit back and think, let them have their say. Sometimes I think it's quite funny."

It was now not as individuals but as a group that we uncovered the perspective from which the men in the class discussed Radway's work, drawing as they did on their own version of what women were supposed to be like. Thus we were able to discern the subtleties of how they twisted the analysis until the subjects of Radway's study fit the image that was required to sustain the notion of male superiority. We came to understand the oppressive relation within which women become the subjects of male discourse. It became clear that the only difference between us and the women in Radway's study was that as graduate students we lived out and contested the patriarchic social relations under different circumstances. The oppression was no less felt, and the struggle was no less difficult. We were the women in Radway's study.

The women in Radway's study were us. In a moment of collective insight we understood that we are our history, and our history is laid within patriarchy. To deny that we are a collective body is to deny not only our history but the possibilities for healing and recovery. Realizing our identity with the women in Radway's study was the first step in releasing us from the bonds of patriarchy.

When we connected with, talked to, and listened to each other we became a viable political force in this context. We reappropriated our voice, found support in each other and were able (for a short time and certainly not completely) to lift the oppression. Our act of refusing silence produced a moment of speaking. After our extended break we returned to the class, each of us prepared to make a statement. What we could never have accomplished individually became possible for us as a group. We disrupted the male agenda and appropriated our space.

But this is not altogether a happy story. On the one hand it was clear that, as the term continued, a true sense of equality and understanding was achieved on occasion between some of the women and some of the men. On the other hand this was not a miraculous transformation of patriarchy. The men became conscious of their own speaking and began to monitor themselves and each other. Moreover, being "given" time and space had its oppressive moments in that the power of control over such time and space had not changed. Nonetheless, the power dynamics were made explicit.

I suspect all women, like those of us in this class, have lived this struggle, have felt anguish in response to the strength-sapping power of the oppressor pushing us to the edge and demanding us to conform, and felt terror and rage welling up from the depths of our being when sometimes in hopelessness we think that conforming would be so much easier. Most of the time the strength is there to keep up the struggle. But when it seeps away, it is these golden touchstones, the reference points signifying a collective struggle, that enable us to say we are not alone.

Roger Simon

It is ironic to realize in retrospect that we were producing concretely a "textbook" example of how the privileged use of language can be an act of domination and an occasion for resistance, while I strove to show the class that same point through reading Radway's book. This course met for two-and-one-half hours a week for thirteen weeks. Within this constraint I had an agenda which I thought gave form and justification to naming our collective weekly meetings as a credit course in a graduate department of education. My agenda is most simply described as the systematic discussion of an assigned set of readings (supplemented by lectures and assignments) examining various aspects of the relation between language and power. I have long felt that an important purpose of graduate teaching is to empower students through the development of the practical competence that is inherent in theorizing. Theorizing has meant to me exploring ways of comprehending and thinking about situations. What I had to offer was the possibility of a discourse which might clarify and critique existing educational practices and create new possibilities.

How this agenda is to be accomplished so that it might work to empower all our students remains a central teaching problem. Barthes (1982) has emphasized that "what is oppressive in our teaching is not, finally, the knowledge or the culture it conveys, but the discursive forms through which we propose them. Since our teaching has as its object taken in the inevitability of power, *method* can really bear only on the means of loosening, baffling, or, at the very least, lightening this power." Corrigan (1984) agrees with this point and emphasizes that "we face a plenitude of naming claims which erase, by mentalizing, our very bodies. Language embodies power never more strongly as where it renders bodies powerless. We have been colonized (and subsequently have become the colonizer) through the enforced modalities of a required, encouraged, rewarded discursivity" (p. 8). We must beware of discursive forms which colonize and silence bodies — all bodies.[12] Forms of discourse that do not allow an answer to the question, "Where is *my body* in that text?" silence us.

I am trying to understand how particular discursive forms — those social, political and economic relations extended over space and time in concrete practices — subjugate the experiences of some people. This happens when a particular text is taken to be *the* text and therefore the locus of silence and terror. Discourse becomes the assertion of certainty when it naturalizes a specific regime of truth manifested in patriarchy as the Law of the Father, God, Nature, or any other form of rule.

We must ask ourselves: Does our teaching, our use of particular sets of practices and forms of discussion, subjugate? It is clear to me that mine sometimes does. As an example, read the words of one of my doctoral students. I had suggested that she read some of Foucault's work in light of the problems she had in analyzing her thesis data. After reading the text she wrote me a short note:

> To sort out the content from how Foucault projects it is impossible for me. He is disembodied, disassociated, beyond knowledge, beyond human frailty, a single phallus waving in the breeze, frightened of the breeze and certainly wretchedly ambivalent about the need for communication imposed by writing. To read Foucault means entering that space, becoming part of it (because of the inseparability of content/context of utterance) which is very destructive for me, despite the possibilities Foucault holds out for what I am trying to study.

Now I do not read Foucault that way. I cannot dismiss the type of discourse associated with Foucault. It always seems so rich to me and teaches me so much about the very issues we have been writing about here. Within the political/ethical project out of which I teach, I identify it as a discourse that can make an important difference in how we understand our world and our lives so as to make possible practices of justice, caring and solidarity. This is a crucial paradox for any male teacher within patriarchy. What can we offer that will not become a form of malefic generosity?

Towards Counter-Patriarchic Practice

Aided by our juxtaposed reflections, what can we say together about teaching and learning within patriarchy that encourages a collective educative practice bound by a politics of solidarity rather than opposition? We pose this question in particular reference to mixed-gender education. This is not to deny the importance of recent feminist reconsiderations of the value of all-female learning situations,[13] but rather to pose the possibility of a counter-patriarchic pedagogy in the mixed gender institutions within which we work and study.

We begin by suggesting several qualities required by a counter-patriarchic form of teaching and learning, qualities for which both students and teachers must take responsibility. The first is the embodied quality of discourse: the fact that oppression is enacted not by theoretical concepts but by real people in concrete situations. Put most simply, this means that theories don't oppress, people do. In that people are differentially placed socially, politically and economically, there can be no text that one can claim as displaying a rational, neutral, androgynous form. To the extent that academic discourse appears objective and distanced (and is understood and privileged in this way) it becomes a vehicle for domination. It devalues alternative perspectives, understanding and articulation of experience. It denies the lived reality of difference as the ground on which to pose questions of theory and practice. It favors one set of values over others as they are generated by the multiplicity of human experiences.

It is the experience of the reality of lived difference that critical pedagogic practice must claim as the agenda for discussion. This means that both students and teacher must find space within which the experience of their daily lives can be articulated in its multiplicity. In practice this always implies a struggle — a struggle over assigned meaning, a struggle over discourse as the expression of both form and content, a struggle over interpretation of experience, and a struggle over "self."[14] But it is this very struggle that forms the basis of a pedagogy that liberates knowledge and practice. It is a struggle that makes possible new knowledge that expands beyond individual experience and hence redefines our identities and the real possibilities we see in the daily conditions of our lives. The struggle is itself a condition basic to the realization of a process of pedagogy: it is a struggle that can never be won — or pedagogy stops. It is the struggle through which new knowledge, identities and possibilities are introduced that may lead to the alteration simultaneously of circumstances and selves.

We emphasize that our position does not require teachers either to suppress or abandon what and how they know — essential aspects of what they bring to teaching. Indeed, the struggle over meaning-making is lessened without such resources. However, teachers and students must find forms within which a single discourse does not become the locus of certainty and certification. In particular, teachers must ask how they can help create a space for the mutual engagement of lived difference that is not framed in oppositional terms requiring the silencing of a multiplicity of voices by a single dominant discourse.

It is clear from the separate accounts of the episode we have written about that such a meeting must rest on a politics of solidarity which requires the contestation of patriarchic relations. What does this mean? If social relations are to change, it is not enough for women to be explicit about their experience of oppression. It is necessary for those men who believe that liberating politics and practices can truly humanize our world to question the privileged status of their own practices. Men have to resist using male prerogative to shape social relations and set the historical agenda. Women's struggles are not just against the silence imposed from within and without: they are also against the silence created by our failure to make explicit men's experience of the practice of domination. We need to understand the meaning of this powerful form of male silence. An emancipatory pedagogy requires that explicitness be taken up as a political position by men as well as women. This questioning of one's privileged practices is not a call for declarations of guilt but rather for the unequivocal acknowledgement that one's embodiment as "man" accrues privileges and prerogatives that are not equally available to all and which therefore must be refused. It requires that we understand that emancipation is not just freedom from power over us but also freedom from our power over others. Hence, men need to be located differently not just in relation to women but in relation to themselves.

Irigaray (1985) has suggested that "the first question to ask is . . . how can women analyze their own exploitation, inscribe their own demands, within an order prescribed by the masculine? Is a women's politics possible within that order?" (p. 81). This is neither the first nor the only question to ask. As our colleague Ann-Louise Brookes has suggested, we must simultaneously ask the following: "In an order prescribed by the masculine, how might men analyze the methods of exploitation which they use to inscribe and make legitimate their claims about human freedom? How might men move from a voice of authority to a voice of questioning in their attempt to freely speak about exploitation?"

In the context of our seminar, what could men have done differently that would have rejected the assumption of male privilege? First of all, it would have been necessary for them not to see the women's developing political protest as individual moments of hysteria, for which the cure was the calming hand of the Father. Second, it would have been necessary for them to take equal responsibility for naming patriarchy as an immorally oppressive social form that denies freedom and human possibility. There is no easy answer to how this could have been done. If men are to participate in the emancipatory project, they can neither assume the burden of providing women's freedom and legitimacy nor enjoy the luxury of remaining silent in the face of oppression. To declare solidarity with women under either of these conditions can be rightly challenged as insincere. Learning how to listen, how to hear, how to see, and how to watch is a precondition to becoming fully aware. But this is insufficient. The men needed to risk more than a comfortable indignation that declares solidarity with women without requiring action on their conviction. Men need to embody forms that do not express and construct masculinity as defined within patriarchy. One cannot simply donate freedom from a position that does not challenge privilege. As is that case for any oppressor group, for men to ally themselves with the oppressed, they must understand the power of their privilege and the privilege of their power, and self-consciously divest themselves of both. It is important to note that emancipatory practices are only truly emancipatory when they challenge our own privilege, whether we accrue such privilege by the color of our skin, our class position, our age, or our gender.

In the context of our seminar, what was required was a position from which a man could say, "While I have had complicity with and benefit from what is happening here, it has become offensive and is no longer acceptable to me." The pre-condition is that men accept that no single voice can speak for our multiple experiences; that no simple understanding of how things are and how they ought to be can derive from a limited perspective; and that ultimately, in the push and pull of social and political relations, they might have to yield.

We are arguing here for a pedagogical project that allows a polyphony of voices, a form which legitimates the expression of difference differently. To struggle for a practice supportive of the equality and possibility we need to speak on our own terms, ones framed by *our desire for solidarity and freedom.* But such desire cannot be taken for granted. We must ask and ask again, who needs to listen?

Notes

[1]This article first appeared in the *Harvard Educational Review, 56*(4), November 1986, 457-472.

[2]"Discourse" refers to particular ways of organizing meaning-making practices. Discourse as a mode of governance delimits the range of possible practices under its authority and organizes the articulation of these practices within time and space although differently and often unequally for different people. Such governance delimits fields of relevance and definitions of legitimate perspectives and fixes norms for concept elaboration and the expression of experience. "Text" refers to a particular concrete manifestation of practices organized within a particular discourse. In everyday life, meaning-making does not exist in isolation, but forms complexes that are organized contingently through time and space. Examples of text include written passages, oral communication, nonverbal communication accomplished through body movement and expression, and visual forms of represen-

tation such as paintings, photographs and sculpture. For further elaboration of these concepts, see Terdiman (1985).

[3]For discussions of various forms of such silencing, see Rich (1979), Smith (1978), and Spender (1980, 1981).

[4]Radway (1984) documents the extent to which men are not tolerant of women's reading, particularly if it can be construed as a challenge to the balance of power in a marriage.

[5]For a detailed first-person analysis of such negotiations, see Finn (1982).

[6]No single perspective defines the notion of feminist pedagogy. For a variety of discussions see, for example, Bunch and Pollack (1983), McVicker, Belenky, Goldberger and Tarule (1985), and Thompson (1983).

[7]Corrigan (1984) points out that the English translation of the concept to which Foucault (1982) refers is better expressed as *governance* not government. For explicit discussion of how governance works within patriarchic social forms, see Fox-Genovese (1982).

[8]My thanks to Ann-Louise Brookes for pointing this out to me.

[9]For an excellent discussion of this issue see Imray and Middleton (1983).

[10]The concept of homosociality is introduced and discussed in Morgan (1981).

[11]Individualizing refers to a process of constructing the "self" so that a person views herself or himself as the unique proprietor of one's thoughts, capacities and feelings. It is a construction basic to the historically constituted political formation which has arisen in Canada and the United States since 1850. For an extensive discussion, see MacPherson (1962).

[12]There is an extensive body of literature about the issue of language colonizing bodies in the context of discussions of racism and colonialism. See, for example, Fanon (1967).

[13]See, for example, the discussion of feminist proposals for sex-segregated schools and classes in Shaw (1980) and Howe (1984).

[14]We take the notion of "self" to be nonunitary and multiple. A struggle over self refers to the situation where one is confronted with multiple, often contradictory, discursive possibilities for naming and claiming one's identities.

References

Barrett, M. (1980). *Women's oppression today*. London: Verso Editions.

Barthes, R. (1982). Inaugural lecture, Collège de France. In S. Sontag (Ed.), *A Barthes reader* (pp. 457-478). New York: Hill & Wang.

Buck-Morss, S. (1981, July-August). Walter Benjamin — Revolutionary writer. *New Left Review, 128,* 50-75.

Bunch, C., & Pollack, S. (Eds.). (1983). *Learning our way: Essays in feminist education.* Trumansburg, NY: Crossing Press.

Corrigan, P. (1984). *The body of intellectuals/the intellectual's body.* Unpublished manuscript.

Dorfman, A. (1983). *The empire's old clothes: What the Lone Ranger, Babar, and other innocent heroes do to our minds.* New York: Pantheon Books.

Fanon, F. (1967). *Black skins, white masks.* New York: Grove Press.

Felman, S. (1981). Re-reading femininity. In *Feminist readings: French texts/American contexts* (pp. 19-44). (From *Yale French Studies, 62*).

Finn, G. (1982). On the oppression of women in philosophy, or whatever happened to objectivity? In A. Miles and G. Finn, *(Eds.),Feminism in Canada: From pressure to politics* (pp. 145-173). Montreal: Black Rose Books.

Foucault, M. (1982). The subject and power. *Critical Inquiry, 8,* 777-789.

Fox-Genovese, E. (1982, May-June). Placing women's history in history. *New Left Review, 133,* 5-29.

Hartmann, H. (1984). The unhappy marriage of Marxism and feminism: Towards a more progressive union. In R. Dale, G. Esland, R. Ferguson, & M. McDonald (Eds.), *Education and the state: Politics, patriarchy, and practice* (Vol. 2, pp. 191-210). Sussex: Falmer Press.

Howe, F. (1984). *Myths of co-education.* Bloomington: Indiana University Press.

Imray, L., & Middleton, A. (1983). Public and private: Marking the boundaries. In E. Gamarnikow, D. Morgan, J. Purvis, & D. Taylorson (Eds.), *The public and the private* (pp. 12-27). London: Heinemann.

Irigaray, L. (1985). *This sex which is not one.* Ithaca: Cornell University Press.

MacPherson, C.B. (1962). *The political theory of possessive individualism.* Oxford: Clarendon Press.

McVicker, C., Belenky, M., Goldberger, N., & Tarule, J. (1985). Connected education for women. *Journal of Education, 167,* 28-45.

Morgan, D. (1981). Man, masculinity, and the process of sociological inquiry. In H. Roberts (Ed.), *Doing feminist research* (pp. 83-113). London: Routledge & Kegan Paul.

Oakley, A. (1972). *Sex, gender, and society.* London: Temple Smith.

Radway, J. (1984). *Reading the romance: Women, patriarchy, and popular literature.* Chapel Hill: University of North Carolina Press.

Rich, A. (1979). *On lies, secrets, and silence: Selected prose, 1966-1978.* New York: Norton.

Shaw, J. (1980). Education and the individual: Schooling for girls, or mixed schooling — A mixed blessing? In R. Deem (Ed.), *Schooling for women's work* (pp. 66-75). London: Routledge & Kegan Paul.

Smith, D. (1978). A peculiar eclipsing: Women's exclusion from man's culture. *Women's Studies International Quarterly, 1,* 281-295.

Spender, D. (1980). *Man made language.* London: Routledge & Kegan Paul.

Spender, D. (Ed.). (1981). *Men's studies modified: The impact of feminism on the academic disciplines.* Toronto: Pergamon Press.

Spender, D. (1982). *Invisible women: The schooling scandal.* London: Writers & Readers Publishers.

Terdiman, R. (1985). *Discourse/counter-discourse: The theory and practice of symbolic resistance in 19th century France.* Ithaca: Cornell University Press.

Thompson, J. (1983). *Learning liberation: Women's response to men's education.* London: Croom Helm.

We acknowledge Ann-Louise Brooks and Phillip Corrigan for their insightful comments during the completion of this article and thank them for their courageous participation in emancipatory pedagogy.

11

Addressing Race in the Feminist Classroom

Seema Kalia

Throughout my undergraduate studies in sociology and anthropology, it seemed that when class discussion turned to explore race analysis, there was little interest, yet a great deal of discomfort. Are those of us with an interest in addressing racism in an academic forum left to assume that others do not care enough to prepare for, or to pursue such controversial discussions? Is it something that white, socially conscious students feel should be left to persons of color to discuss in a segregated environment, that they may then return to the larger classroom with a prepared race theory? Does this inadvertent apathy surface only in my presence? These questions, among others, are almost exclusive to the student of color in the Canadian feminist classroom.

As a woman of color, I would like to see a working race scholarship developed to incorporate a feminist/socialist analysis in all my studies. I would like others to increase their understanding of existing knowledge with respect to race dynamics. I would like my experiences as a woman of color included or recognized in the social sciences, particularly in feminist scholarship. More than anything, I would like to have a mature, respectful, sensitive way to confront racism and race bias when I see it in my academic environment, and in my personal relations within academia.

Race inclusion in a meaningful way is an admirable endeavor. As much so as male-stream scholarship, predominant feminist Western scholarship has marginalized the experience of women of color, or has reduced it to convenient assumptions and superficial examination. To encounter feminist scholarship through the more predominant literature (as most of us initially do), is to be left with the impression, if any at all, that the gender oppression of women of color is somehow drastically worse than the gender oppression experienced by our more "civilized" white counterparts. I often have to correct faulty assumptions with respect to arranged marriages and other East Indian customs for my colleagues in sociology and anthropology. Ethnocentrism prevails when dominant Western culture judges what it perceives to be archaic or barbaric social customs. I continually have to clarify the concept of and purpose behind arranged marriages to my white colleagues, yet I am always caught at a precarious point of validating a sexist custom or upholding racist assumptions. Arranged marriages are not ideal family forms from a feminist perspective, but there are many arguments as to why they are preferable to Western concepts of courtship for women's status.

Although I acknowledge the need to radically alter feminist perceptions of East Indian culture, I do not believe it appropriate simply to disregard feminist analysis of marriage and the family when faced with different cultural contexts. This brings up an important point: sometimes when we attempt to revise feminist analysis for application to other cultures, the language permits us only complete rejection of mainstream feminist "revelations." Part of colored women's struggle for inclusion will involve reformulating mainstream and feminist language to communicate our experiences with greater meaning and precision.

The first step toward increasing awareness of and sensitivity to issues of race bias is articulating carefully, with meaning and precision, the real struggles of all groups fighting a dominant and silencing white culture. Race struggle in the United States can no longer assume a meaning of just White versus Black, or in Canada of White versus Native. Our language needs to expand to accommodate the multitude of experiences that await adequate inclusion, and we all need to manipulate language in order to speak previously silenced truths. Friedan's "problem with no name" had a name for women of color. We called it racism, race struggle, discrimination, ignorance, race bias, ethnocentrism and denial. Essentially, people fighting racism are left with a handful of terms to express an entire history of race dynamics. The message starts sounding tired and vague when one lacks adequate vocabulary, and one cannot rely on the existing race scholarship as a basis for validation and academic credibility.

Many students of color in the social sciences tire of sounding like one-issue politicians in the classroom, where they are often the only "visible minority." That is, if they are brave enough, or even concerned with race analysis to begin with. Too often I had the experience of being the only student to bring up issues of race bias in discussion or study. I got tired of feminist instructors going on the defensive or intellectually grandstanding when I questioned the approximately 5% of class time allotted to all women of color and women of poverty in the women's studies classroom. I got tired of being told that the bias or preoccupation with the issues of white petit bourgeois women in feminist studies existed only in my imagination, or that this bias was somehow necessary for the full understanding of feminist theory. Towards the end of my degree, I became silent. I chose my battles carefully, knowing that in some classes it was better to "lay low," to avoid a strong political identity, never to make the instructor feel defensive, in order to get the marks I needed to continue in academia. If instructors wonder why their students of color are not taking the kind of initiative in race discussion that they themselves are afraid to take, it may be valuable to consider who has silenced them already. One instructor expressed to me her concern in teaching at a law school, that by incorporating a race dynamic into legal scholarship, she made uncomfortable the few very conspicuous students of color. This is sensitive, but not accurate. Silencing the issues is not protecting us. What is ideal is to advise students in the course outline that race dynamics (like class or gender) will be examined in the course. This sort of inclusion is so rare it will not go unnoticed, and I doubt that the astute student will not prepare for the discussion, whether through preparation of materials or choosing to remain absent for those lectures. Students of color that I know have to be constantly prepared to harden themselves to a clumsily handled race-related remark. Insensitivity cannot and will not break us. If it could, we would not have made it as far as your classroom.

Words of warning about dealing with such a precarious area such as race analysis: there are no guidelines, and there is no real structure in terms of "politically acceptable" and "politically incorrect" language or behaviour except for the obvious racial slurs. Accept outright that you will use at least one term that offends someone, that opposition to any approach is guaranteed. Be prepared to have any fact, statistic or theory disputed, and to have no visible means of evaluating "credibility" that will help you screen your information. In short, imagine the struggles you would have incorporating a feminist analysis without a documented history or an existing scholarship and you will be somewhat prepared to undertake the elusive task of discussing race theory.

It is troubling that the term "Women Of Color" is used to summarize such a multitude of women's experiences and perspectives. I resent that it can be used as a convenient way for the ruling class to lump my experiences as an East Indian immigrant with those of an 8th-generation Black Canadian. Women of color can claim very few experiences with other racial and ethnic groups, except those arising from being non-white in a white-supremacist culture. This is the commonality which is meaningful to those who label us. This labelling is, unfortunately, necessary for our own empowerment and union.

The fact that I am made more uncomfortable when a white woman attacks my ideas in class (whether or not they pertain to race) than when another woman of color does is something of which I am not proud. I have grown to recognize my response and to work on it, the way I have grown to realize that I will always be in the minority in my viewpoints on class and race in the university classroom — especially since the higher I advance, the more of a minority I become.

I secretly enjoy the fact that my opinion in small discussion groups is often the "last word" on issues of race or class, if I am the only woman of color in the room. I also exploit opportunities to utilize my experiences as a "visible minority" in women's studies courses as a "fresh, new perspective." I resent not always having those opportunities, or having to assume a white, middle-class experience that is not my own. I'm tired of being asked to (continue to) identify with models that are not reflective of my experience. I am offended that we read Betty Friedan's *The Feminine Mystique* in a third-year women's studies class. Lack of race consciousness, in any "major work," even when keeping in mind "the context in which it was written," is intolerable in any discipline, but particularly in women's studies, which claims that it examines the fight for freedom from oppression for all women.

I am annoyed when treated as some sort of authority on Third World women's issues because of my appearance. Immigration at an early age is not conducive to a social experience reflective of the country of origin. My social experience is that of a woman of East Indian origin adjusting to perceived Canadian values and social structures. Only recently has it become apparent to me that my lack of identification with my culture of origin could stem from the fact that characteristics shared amongst a group of immigrants have to be different from those of a group that did not immigrate (examples of such characteristics include attitudes towards Western ideology, political attitudes, social attitudes, level of income, and education).

Why is it my responsibility to make the harsh realities of racism within feminism more palatable to a socially conscious white liberal audience? Why do I feel guilty when white women become upset about a seminar that deals with race that they feel is "too harsh"? Why are blatantly race-biased feminist works, regarded as having redeeming scholarly merit despite this "minor flaw," used in women's studies courses when any other discipline would at least acknowledge this race bias as problematic? *Who* decided that Friedan's *The Feminine Mystique* was an important feminist work? From the perspective of a woman of color, it can be argued that it is works such as this one that defined the North American women's movement as a "white bourgeoisie movement" and incorporated exclusion in popular feminist thought. When one looks back and wonders how women of color have been and continue to be marginalized from mainstream feminism, it might be a good idea to examine the models that are still being held up as typical, and to examine their contribution to the invisibility of women of color. There seems to be an understanding that a work that is non-sexist is not necessarily anti-sexist. This is an important distinction when addressing race-consciousness. A book that is not explicitly anti-racist is not going to reduce the domination of mainstream feminism by white feminists.

How is it possible to attain a bachelor's degree in social science at a Canadian university in a medium-sized urban centre without even once encountering a woman (or man) of color as an instructor? In one case, a lone student of color called a professor's remark in a women's studies course racist. The instructor became defensive, insulted by the suggestion that she had made a racist statement, and backed up her statement with a type of "Well, I know a Japanese feminist who would say the same thing" claim. The defense that "they have internalized white supremacy, so let's use that to justify continued racism" does not work. After a few heated words were exchanged between the professor and the sole woman of color in the room, the woman of color left in tears. Soon after, the class took a break, and some of the remaining women left in protest. My question is, why didn't all the feminists in the course choose to leave?

Many reasons come to mind: confusion, insensitivity, academic opportunism, fear. I would suggest that anger kept the students from protesting. No one likes to be made to feel guilty. If many students didn't recognize the race bias in the professor's statement until it was raised by a woman of color, what does that say about their own race biases? Feminists, as a group that has recognized the institutionalized oppression of women, have come to recognize sexism as the norm in a patriarchal culture. We all deal with our own, socialized sexist assumptions when growing as feminists, and we forgive ourselves and each other when we "slip up" into old patriarchal models. Most of us would acknowledge the patriarchal bias from which we have all emerged, and would recognize that it is through not tolerating sexism, especially in its most subtle forms, that it can be successfully fought.

One of the students who chose not to leave the women's studies classroom defended the professor. As she was an otherwise "race-conscious" individual, I was shocked that this friend of mine had not even mentioned the incident to me. We had shared other non-feminist courses where we were united in our outrage over race, sex and class biases in the teaching. When I had asked her why she didn't feel that this professor should be called on her race bias, she said, "Calling someone a racist is a *very* serious accusation. I would hate to think we would apply a label like that lightly." She also directed her anger not at the professor for the comment, but at the student who "didn't give us any idea what she wanted." Why was it the responsibility of the lone woman of color in the room to bring race bias to the forefront, and why was she to blame when the topic was not handled well? Most North American women of color, like everyone else in North America, are raised in a white supremacist culture which generally ignores its race bias. "We" have no real opportunities to unite, nor to articulate our dismay at race bias. "We" don't know how to handle it any better than "you" do. It was not until I started to compare racism with sexism that I could convey the unfairness in this woman's assessment of the situation. If she was in a room full of men, all trying to ignore yet never completely ignoring her gender, and one made an equally "subtle" sexist remark, how would she feel? Most likely silenced. If the remark was "women are less rational then men," would it be acceptable, or would it be her responsibility to feminism, to call the man on this remark? What if the person who made the remark was a professor? What if it seemed that all of her "peers" defended the sexism with statements like: "Well, he was not trying to be maliciously sexist, so don't overreact," or "'Calling someone sexist is such a *serious* allegation, I don't think that it is appropriate," or "You didn't handle it very well; you just left, instead of explaining to us men your feelings in a way that is meaningful to us, and in a way with which we are completely comfortable"? Would it be fair to put the onus on her? No. It just often ends up this way.

If we could just come to recognize our racism in the same ways progressive academic minds have come to recognize sexism, we would all be much more comfortable in dealing with it. And comfort seems to be what this is all about. When I brought forth my anger at the race bias reflected in the course curriculum of a women's studies course, groans were heard and guilty eyes became downcast, and the instructor, sensing the other students' impatience, presented no alternatives. Coming in late to a course, I was faced with the unfortunate task of presenting critically the "contribution" of Betty Friedan's *The Feminine Mystique* to the feminist movement. Throughout my reading of this work (no part of which was inspirational to my feminist soul), I became more and more angry that this model for so many years and even today was presented as one of the few existing "historical examples" of women's oppression. Not to say that the experience of the white petit bourgeois housewife is not a valid expression of sex-role stereotyping gone to an extreme, but what about those of us who do not identify with this model? Not only women of color, but also white women of poverty, disabled women and lesbian women were excluded from Friedan's "problem with no name." The same thoughts kept recurring as had occurred when I first came to understand the North American feminist movement. How nice that being bored in the suburbs was all that these women had to worry about. How nice that they are (over)represented in the literature, that most of the emphasis in feminist scholarship is on that which is of concern to the white petit bourgeois feminist. When the issues of women of color and women of poverty (I use the two together, although they are not necessarily synonymous, because I feel that they are equally invisible to the predominant feminist academia) finally did surface in women's studies, it was tacked on at the end, as if an afterthought. Bell hooks' *Feminist Theory: From Margin to Center* was the first and only book I encountered out of about 30 required and recommended readings in women's studies, that dealt explicitly with feminist race analysis. In my experience, the courses that offer materials relating to women of color are hidden away in the "Third World Development" section in the anthropology department. Again, this material is not reflective of the reality of being non-white in a white-supremacist culture.

The writing of women of color often takes on the form of early women's writing. We write short works, because we are generally not supported by a class structure or academia that facilitates our scholarship (as it did that of, for instance, Betty Friedan and Simone de Beauvoir), articles that can be researched and written in addition to our daily work, as we are generally not academics exclusively, and which are published by obscure collective publishing houses with limited resources and limited means of distribution. Yes, the scholarship of women of color is difficult to find. Does that justify its very limited inclusion within women's studies curricula? Mari Matsuda puts the onus on mainstream feminist academia to seek out the work of marginalized groups in "Affirmative Action and Legal Knowledge: Planting Seeds in Plowed-Up Ground," in the *Harvard Women's Law Journal, Volume 11* (Spring 1988):

> Established scholars can start the process of eradicating apartheid in legal knowledge by making a deliberate effort to buy, order, read, cite, discuss and teach outsiders' scholarship . . . If none are available, a formal inquiry is appropriate. The scholar can put pressure on the book selling and publish-

ing industries to supply outsiders' scholarship. Quotas will help the particularly recalcitrant buyer. (p. 4)

Lesbian scholarship, as a minority and stigmatized voice in the feminist movement, has managed to find its rightful place in the consciences and classrooms of feminism. We have just started to become aware of our own heterosexist biases within the feminist movement. Despite its advances the lesbian movement has further to go in educating not only feminists but heterosexuals in the broader society.

The increased accessibility to lesbian perspectives in feminist scholarship is a great relief to all of us who couldn't identify with liberal models of feminism. The problem with almost all expressions of feminism, from liberal to radical, is the limited and unimportant voice of women of color within those political identities. When will the feminist academia, through its women's studies programs, make a true commitment to race-consciousness in the feminist classroom? Aside from political and procedural restructuring (perhaps a commitment to study a minimum number of women writers of color per course), how is race bias going to be addressed in the classroom? As I was advised by one (white) feminist professor, addressing me after a poorly handled class discussion on race bias, "If you want to educate others, do not 'intimidate' them." I took this to mean that accusations should be non-accusatory, that identifications of race bias should be as subtle as possible, and that I must be fully armed with every last word on the subject of race bias in academia if I ever hoped to discuss it with a feminist instructor with greater academic experience than myself.

The difficulty in writing as a woman of color about being a woman of color is knowing just what is exclusive to my experience as an individual, as a visible minority, or as a woman. Do others resent accusations of racism because they are painful, or is it because those accusations are truly unfounded on my part? Do they avoid discussing issues of race openly and honestly only in my presence, or all the time? Do they interact with me in a particular way because I am a woman of color? Because I am a woman? Because I am vocal? I am angered when I think that those who felt confronted by a vocal woman of color would not feel nearly so threatened by a vocal white woman, or a more passive woman of color. In a heated discussion about race I had with two white women and a white man, tempers flared and voices were raised so that each individual was speaking over the next. At one point one of the women pointed at me and said "As I was going to say before *you* cut me off. . . ." I wondered if my lack of manners was being singled out by this woman as somehow exclusively inappropriate for me. Was it because I was the only one with whom she disagreed, or was my rudeness somehow less excusable than that of the other woman and man who were arguing (from my subjective view, far more aggressively than I). I wonder if others are dismayed because I defy cultural stereotypes of female docility and enduring politeness. The "reasons" for the reactions of others will never be known. It is irrelevant, even if it could be proven, that all negative reactions I encounter are personal, not race-related — what is relevant is that I am in the particular position of having to consider the possibility that how others treat me personally may be motivated by race politics.

I am almost always aware now, in the classroom, of my ethnicity. I didn't used to be. As a child in a Canadian classroom I was completely oblivious to it. As I grow older, I see a need to recognize it, politicize it and identify myself with it, as the need for those around me to identify me with it increases. It is impossible to grow up in a patriarchal culture and not learn to think in sexist terms. Feminism is about destroying those terms through their recognition. Eradicating racism is about challenging it in all its forms. Not just the Neo-Nazis, or tasteless "ethnic jokes," but in the subtle forms as well. For women of color challenging racism means speaking out when we hear a stereotypical statement, when we feel excluded by what we are asked to accept as a reflection of our reality, and when we see the same old ruling-class models being presented as the norm. For women without color, it means accepting, and hence combatting, white supremacy in our culture, not curling up your back at the identification of race-bias in your words (Yes, women of color have racist thoughts too — remember, we were all raised with the same dominant ideology), and not being so unrealistically repulsed at the suggestion of race-bias that it blinds you to the reality. Our reality.

12

Beyond Plumbing and Prevention:
Feminist Approaches to Sex Education[1]

Helen Lenskyj

Introduction

School sex education programs have frequently been criticized for their "plumbing and prevention" focus, and for their failure to consider the emotional and moral dimensions of human sexuality. Feminists, too, are rightly critical of conservative sex education curricula that fail to challenge sexism, homophobia and male sexual violence in the private and public realms. The majority of programs developed in recent years focus on preventing pregnancy and sexually transmitted diseases, and the dangers rather than the joys of sexuality demand the most attention (Brick, 1985; Dorio, 1985; Mills, 1988).

Although there is clearly a need for adolescents to have accurate information about reproduction, contraception and safe sex practices, it is also necessary for sex educators to take questions of gender and sexual orientation into account. This means more than simply segregating classes by gender for purposes of comfort or propriety, and more than dealing with homosexuality only in relation to AIDS prevention.

A feminist approach to sex education requires that teachers promote among both male and female students the notion that human sexuality is not, or should not be defined exclusively in male heterosexual terms; that women are developing autonomous sexual identities; and that lesbians and gays are defining their sexuality in fulfilling and responsible ways. Such programs will of necessity challenge sexism, homophobia and male violence against women and children, and may ultimately bring about a celebration of the differences and diversity within human sexuality.

This article represents an attempt to integrate these various progressive agendas. First of all, we will examine existing sex education policies and programs in Canada and will review common right-wing arguments against more progressive approaches. Two major forces shaping adolescent girls' developing sexuality — male sexual violence and compulsory heterosexuality — will then be discussed, and recent initiatives in Ontario to introduce these issues into sex education programs will be evaluated. Focusing on the Toronto Board of Education's new policy regarding sexual orientation, and the Ontario Ministry of Education's AIDS Education Curriculum, we will explore the school's potential to promote acceptance and celebration of sexual difference.

Sex Education: The Current Situation

In a context where male heterosexual hegemony prevails, adolescents are unlikely to view sexism, homophobia and male sexual violence as essential components of a sex education curriculum. Recent research by Tricia Szirom among Australian youth aged 15-16 confirmed that, while girls thought boys should be exposed to the full range of sex education topics, including puberty, menstruation, contraception and pregnancy, most boys treated these issues as "girls' stuff" and showed little interest in understanding female physiology and sexual response, or in sharing the responsibility for pregnancy prevention. In fact, the majority of boys viewed sexuality issues exclusively in terms of their own sexual satisfaction during heterosexual intercourse; everything else was "the girl's problem." A small percentage of boys and girls indicated some interest in getting information about male homosexuality, but lesbians and lesbianism were rarely mentioned. It seems reasonable to assume that similar patterns exist in North America and the U.K., and Szirom's feminist methodology and interview questions would provide a very useful model for researchers in other countries (Szirom, 1988).

As well as looking at adolescents' needs and interests, we need to examine the views of parents and the community. As early as 1943, a Canadian Gallup poll showed that more than 75% of Canadian adults favoured sex education in the schools, although 1940s "family life education" gave primacy to the school's role in preparing young people for marriage and parenthood (Laycock, 1945). By 1984, the proportion favouring sex education in schools was 83%, and 90% of Canadians agreed that everyone should have the right to use birth control. Ninety-four percent believed that sex education should also take place in the home, although only one in five adults surveyed was given the "facts of life" as a child. Only 50% of schools in Canada offered any sex education, and only 25% had a separate course (Gallup Poll, 1984).

Although child welfare policies vary from province to province, educators are increasingly recognizing their responsibility to identify and report suspected incidents of physical or sexual abuse among students. In Ontario, teachers face a substantial fine for failing to report child abuse, and they are also required by law to report cases of sexual assault involving individuals under age 16. Although these legislative initiatives are commendable, they may discourage some teachers from raising these topics for classroom discussion. However, a 1986 survey showed that family violence and child abuse were listed as policy and program issues by six out of ten provincial ministries of education across Canada (Julien, 1987).

Confusion about the legality of talking about lesbian or gay sex to young people may also be a deterrent to open classroom discussion. Same-sex sexual activity is illegal between people under 18 in Canada; the age of consent for lesbian or gay sex is 21. Counselling about sexual orientation issues is permitted as long as abstract topics, and not actual sexual practices, are discussed, since this could be construed as encouraging illegal acts among minors. Young people may inadvertently make it difficult for the teacher or counsellor if they disclose that they are currently sexually active with same-sex partners. Clients at the Toronto Centre for Counselling Lesbians and Gays require parents' permission if they are between 18 and 21 years of age, and the centre does not provide counselling on sexual orientation issues for youth under 18.

Anti-discrimination statutes that include sexual orientation as prohibited grounds are included in four provincial/territorial human rights codes: those of Quebec, Manitoba, Ontario and the Yukon. In these provinces, lesbians and gays are protected from discrimination with respect to services, goods, facilities, housing, contracts or employment. Although such legislation offers some protection to lesbian/gay students and teachers, it does not necessarily prevent harassment, ostracism or violence.

Neither the Canadian Charter of Rights and Freedoms nor the Canadian Human Rights Act, which covers federal jurisdictions, specifically identifies sexual orientation as prohibited grounds. However, it is hoped that a test case to be put forward at some future date by the Women's Legal Education and Action Fund, an organization that funds Charter challenges, will set a precedent regarding discrimination on these grounds.

Understanding the Right-Wing Opposition

Most opponents of school sex education adhere to right-wing arguments upholding the rights and responsibilities of parents to pass on, or to withhold, "the facts of life," and claiming that such information promotes teenage sexual activity, promiscuity and pregnancy. The gender bias in this kind of opposition is clear. It is *girls'* knowledge about birth control that is viewed as the green light to unfettered adolescent sexual activity; boys who "sow their wild oats" are not a new phenomenon, and are only seen as a problem if they overstep class or race divisions. Moreover, the fear of "putting ideas into teenagers' heads" is probably unfounded. Some studies have shown that teenagers who have received sex education are less active sexually, more likely to form responsible relationships and more likely to use some form of birth control. Others have revealed that sex education does little to change adolescent patterns of sexual activity (Adame, 1985; Kirby, 1980). Programs aimed specifically at dispelling rape myths have been shown to make young men less susceptible to the harmful effects of violent pornography, because they know that the message that women enjoy violent sex is false (Donnerstein et al., 1987).

There are parents of various political persuasions who oppose school sex education on the grounds that the school program is overcrowded, that teachers do not receive adequate preparation for the task, particularly about the values aspect of sex education, or that they are too embarrassed about the subject matter to be effective (Noble, 1986).

When the teaching profession comprised mostly unmarried women, many parents scoffed at the idea that these teachers were capable of teaching about sexuality. Today, the number of unmarried female and male teachers, many of whom are lesbian or gay, has not passed unnoticed among parents, or for that matter, among students. It is a sad fact that many children will experience the death of a gay teacher or principal from AIDS before their schooling has ended. Yet it is rarely recognized that at least 10% of the student population also have a lesbian or gay orientation, and that these students have no role models within the school and receive little, if any, validation for their sexual identities in sex education classes.

Those who argue that sex education falls into the realm of morals and values, and is therefore a parental responsibility, appear to believe that parents are the only force shaping a child's value system. They are certainly correct in believing that sex education cannot be value-free, even if only the mechanics are taught. Physiology texts provide a good example when they deal with reproduction: sperm were traditionally described as active and aggressive, swimming upstream to penetrate the passive ovum. In contrast, the revisionist version portrays the ovum as actively enveloping the sperm. The male-dominant explanation fitted neatly with the traditional view of sex-appropriate behaviour during heterosexual intercourse, in which neither the woman nor her ovum was expected to take an active role.

Right-wing individuals are justifiably concerned that progressive sex education programs may cause their children to question traditional sex roles and men's control of female sexuality in both the public and private realms. Some of the opposition comes from right-wing women as well as men, a testimony to the power of male ideological control. One example is a Canadian group which calls itself R.E.A.L. Women (Realistic, Equal, Active for Life). This group is also opposed to no-fault divorce and universal, subsidized child care. On the issue of homosexuality, R.E.A.L. Women are predictably hostile: they oppose any human rights protection for homosexuals, whom they lump together with public nudists, drug addicts or members of motorcycle gangs. They claim that human rights protection for homosexuals constitutes validation of a "chosen lifestyle" which is "contrary to the beliefs and religious practices of the majority of Canadians" (R.E.A.L. Women, 1986; 12-13).

A sex education program that is sensitive to the issues of gender, sexual orientation and sexual violence is of course a potential challenge to "the traditional family" as it is envisioned by groups such as R.E.A.L. Women. Young women who are aware of other options will not necessarily choose traditional marriage and a life of economic, sexual and emotional dependency upon men, nor will they stay in abusive relationships; young men who have experienced caring, egalitarian relationships with women, and/or with men, may question men's right to control and oppress women.

Equally controversial is the inclusion of child sexual abuse as a sex education topic. Children who learn to identify "good touch" and "bad touch" will have the words and the validation they need to identify their experience of physical and sexual abuse. The threat to male power in the private realm and the implications for patriarchy at large are no doubt responsible for much of the opposition by so-called men's rights groups.

Power Issues in Sex Education

The problems resulting from unprotected heterosexual intercourse — pregnancy and sexually transmitted diseases — have a central place in most existing sex education programs, evidence of the generally reactive rather than proactive approach. Yet even in teaching the mechanics of contraception, a program that fails to recognize power relations between the sexes is unlikely to succeed. In many adolescent subcultures, as elsewhere in society, a double standard exists: it is the women who are expected to take sole responsibility for birth control, and yet if they take oral contraceptives or have an IUD, they are seen as "sluts" because it appears that they are expecting to have sex — and sex, so the argument goes, should be as spontaneous and "natural" as it is in the soap operas (Kostash, 1987).

A proactive approach to female sexuality issues would first of all adopt a woman-centred perspective, one that challenges the view that girls' and women's lifework is, in de Beauvoir's words, "to reflect men at twice their normal size." The primacy of the male sex drive in the eyes of both sexes is borne out in any casual observation of adolescent male/female interaction, as well as in formal investigations carried out by feminist researchers. As Kathleen Barry (1979) explains, "girls learn that the locus of sexual power is male"; they abandon primary relationships with girls and their subsequent male-identification robs them of their own sexual identity (p. 218). Young women who are equipped to claim personal and sexual power for themselves will be better able to deal with two of the dominant forces in school and society: male sexual violence and compulsory heterosexuality.

Challenging Male Sexual Violence

Male sexual violence is a fact of life in schools; female students and teachers are the major targets, and homosexual students are also victims. There is little documentation of the extent and nature of sexual violence that take place on school premises, although girlfriend assault and rape, which usually take place in other locales, are now receiving researchers' attention. A few recent examples from both rural and urban centres in Ontario, gathered from teachers and anti-rape activists as well as from the literature, will reveal the nature of the problem. There have been two sexual assaults in the girls' washroom of a Toronto high school. An attempted rape in a classroom at a Catholic elementary school involved a boy under twelve years of age. A teacher reported that young boys were observed mutilating dolls in the play centre in an elementary classroom. Elementary schoolchildren were observed playing a game which they called "gang rape." Violent sexual imagery is frequently appearing in the compositions that children are writing at school (Smith, n.d.).

Some progressive educators are incorporating the issue of sexual violence into the sex education curriculum. A play entitled *Thin Ice* (Rubess & Cooper, 1987), produced by Theatre Direct and first staged in Ontario schools in 1987, tackles the problem of coercive sexuality, or, more accurately, girlfriend rape. The difference between sharing and caring, persuasion and coercion in sexual relationships is the major theme of *Thin Ice*. The teenage angst is palpable, as both boys and girls struggle towards ways of relating sexually that feel comfortable for them. The challenge of developing caring heterosexual relationships occurs in a social context that overwhelmingly opts for violent, coercive sex. One of the female characters in *Thin Ice* reflects that the women on Dynasty (a soap opera) don't get bruises; presumably they just "give in." Yet this is the same girl who once took a self defence class; she knows how to use her keys to fend off an attacker in a dark alley, but this is hardly a useful technique to deter the young man who is using charm and persuasion, and just a hint of physical force (because he wouldn't "stoop" to hitting a girl) to get her to "give in" (Rubess & Cooper, 1987). Students have little difficulty identifying with the characters and scenarios in this production, which has received a very positive student response.

Challenging Compulsory Heterosexuality

The pressure to be (hetero)sexually active is a central theme in *Thin Ice*; there is only one passing reference to the (homophobic) suspicions that a young man, in particular, might arouse if he fails to conform. Similarly, even the most progressive sex education literature defines "sexually active" as "engaging in heterosexual genital intercourse." Except for literature that specifically addresses lesbian and gay issues, there is little critique of the heterosexist bias within the sex education field (Dorio, 1985; Ellis, 1985; Newton & Risch, 1981). Since pregnancy prevention is currently one of the major goals, it would seem useful for sex educators to promote alternatives to genital/genital contact among heterosexually active youth and to discuss the possibility that some students may prefer same-sex partners. It is interesting to note, therefore, that the Ontario Ministry of Education's 1987 AIDS Curriculum guidelines are quite explicit about these possibilities. The discussion guide notes that sexual activity which may transmit the AIDS virus involves the mouth, the penis, the vagina or the anus, and that there are "safe alternatives" to heterosexual intercourse such as "talking, masturbation, fantasizing and close physical contact without intercourse" (Ministry of Education, 1987, Part C, p. 38).

Somewhat unexpectedly, the Ministry discussion guide goes on to provide an explication of compulsory heterosexuality. "In spite of the fact that the majority of young people are heterosexual, they have no experience of heterosexuality. They have simply assumed that they are heterosexual because that is the societal norm. Heterosexuality can represent success and acceptance by one's peers whereas homosexuality is seen negatively" (Ministry of Education, 1987, Part C, p. 39). It also makes the point that it is acceptable for adolescents to say "no" to pressure to become (hetero)sexually active, but the gender-neutral language used throughout disguises the fact that the person in a heterosexual relationship who is responsible for that pressure, often accompanied by the threat of violence and rape, is the adolescent male.

Sex Education for Sexual Pleasure

For teenage sex education programs, the preoccupation with (heterosexual) genital intercourse is particularly inappropriate. If sexual pleasure were the goal, as teenagers usually say it is, then young women in particular would opt for alternative sexual practices, since there is ample evidence that women are less likely to have an orgasm through penile penetration than through stimulation directly involving the clitoris. Yet only a very small minority of teenagers express interest in sex education that provides information about sexual arousal or techniques to increase sexual pleasure. Apparently, it is the actual practice rather than the quality of heterosexual sex that provides status for adolescents, male and female, and sex education that does not take this into account is unlikely to be effective.

More importantly, we cannot assume that adolescent girls have sufficient power in their relationships with boys to insist on the kinds of sexual activities that bring them pleasure. In her study of adolescent girls in Canada, Myrna Kostash (1987) found that emotional security was as important as physical stimulation to girls' enjoyment of sex. In a societal context where coercive sex is the norm, and where the major consumers of pornography are adolescent males, the chances of girls' sexual fulfilment with adolescent male partners are slim. The Australian research cited above reinforces Kostash's findings. Jaded but ever hopeful, one sixteen-year-old girl in Szirom's study stated: "a lot of guys that maybe we haven't met have a lot of respect for girls. Maybe *they* have different ideas" (Szirom, 1988, p. 7). It seems that sexual fulfilment is a distant dream for adolescent girls, many of whom no doubt internalize the message that they are inferior, and not worthy of respect.

Lesbians and Gays in the School

While teachers and parents have reluctantly accepted the fact that a significant proportion of adolescents are heterosexually active, there is usually strong community reaction to the realization that lesbian and gay adolescents are also interested in dating and sexual relationships. Over the past ten years or so, the print media have reported a number of incidents in the United States where same-sex couples have attempted, with varying degrees of success, to attend high school proms together. Some have been openly lesbian or gay, others have not, but all were treated as "deviant" by students and teachers alike. When girls attended dances "alone" (i.e., with each other, rather than with male dates) students expressed the fear that they would take the other girls' (male) dates (Burkett, 1986; "A prom night to remember," 1987).

Conformity to sex roles is the cornerstone of heterosexuality, and provides a reassuring answer to adolescent confusion about personal and sexual identity, especially for males. Feminists have argued that in coeducational settings, girls serve as a negative reference group to establish male identity and to boost male self-esteem (Shaw, 1980). The same may be said of lesbians and gays in relation to the adolescent male's heterosexual identity. A boy might not know exactly who he is, but he does know who he isn't: he isn't a girl, and he isn't queer.

Conservative parents and administrators believe that lesbian and gay teachers provide inappropriate role models for young people, and/or that these teachers will indoctrinate, seduce or molest children. Although some provincial human rights codes protect lesbians and gays in the workplace, few teachers, aware of parental and community attitudes, are willing to put the codes to the test. Catholic teachers have few illusions about human rights legislation in the face of the church's stand on homosexuality. In a number of U.S. civil rights cases, lesbians and gays unsuccessfully protested their firing from jobs in church-affiliated organizations. Although Catholic schools are exempt from some aspects of provincial legislation covering education, some legal opinion holds that the provincial human rights codes, as well as the Canadian Charter of Rights and Freedoms, will provide protection for Catholic teachers who are lesbian or gay (Johnston, 1987).

As for lesbian and gay youth, the Ontario Human Rights Code now protects them from being expelled from school, but offers no protection on the job since employees under 18 are not covered. Again, the situation for Catholic youth has its own difficulties. In 1985, three Toronto girls who attended a Catholic high school were expelled for "inappropriate" behavior that involved putting their arms around each others' shoulders. In 1986, a Catholic high school principal in Malton, Ontario, banned the publication of an editorial supporting Bill 7 which was to appear in the school paper, on the grounds that it undermined Catholic doctrine (Pennant, 1987; Wheeler, 1985). (Bill 7 introduced sexual orientation into the Ontario Human Rights Code as a prohibited ground for discrimination in 1986.)

Harassment and discrimination often precede actual violence. In a recent survey of the National Gay Task Force (U.S.), approximately 20% of lesbians and 50% of gays reported that they had been harassed, threatened or physically abused (Sears, 1987). The incidence may be lower in Canada, but the threat of violence remains a reality, particularly in the school context. While teachers will often confront instances of racist or sexist name-calling, many are paralysed when they hear homophobic comments, either unwilling or unable to deal with them. Toronto students have reported that teachers observed verbal or physical harassment and did nothing to intervene on behalf of gay or lesbian students. A former student at Western Technical School reported that homosexuality was dismissed in the sex education class as "just lust" (Chow, 1986a, p. 3). Unfortunately, the male physical education teachers who are responsible for boys' sex education in most high schools are unlikely to present the most progressive views on homosexuality. After all, male team sport constitutes the classic training ground in machismo, and acceptance of different sexual orientations is not compatible with the rigid sex role conformity required in the male "jock" subculture.

There is a sad irony in the proposed strategies for confronting homophobia in the school suggested in sex education literature: proposals that teachers explain why homophobic jokes are not funny, support the victims of homophobic teasing, and encourage discussion of homophobia and its links with other kinds of discrimination such as racism and sexism (Gordon, 1983). Such responses stand in stark contrast to the behavior typically cultivated by teachers who hide their sexual orientation, and who may choose to ignore homophobic jokes in the classroom and staffroom, to withdraw from discussions of sexuality issues and to avoid showing solidarity with lesbians and gays, because to do so would be to risk disclosure and the loss of one's job.

It is the invisibility of lesbians and gays that complicates the analogy with racism and sexism. A white teacher who confronts students' racism will not be labelled black, and to be labelled a "women's libber" because of one's anti-sexist stand is almost commonplace; but any teacher, homosexual or heterosexual, who confronts homophobia will almost certainly be suspected of being homosexual. And in this situation it is obviously counterproductive to make a public assertion of one's heterosexuality. Hence there is a paralysis around the homophobia issue.

Lesbian and Gay Youth: Their Stories

In September 1988, Lesbian and Gay Youth Ottawa-Hull prepared *A Report on High Schools* for the Coalition for Lesbian and Gay Rights in Ontario. In the introduction, they state: "Thousands of lesbian and gay youth across Ontario are being silenced by a society that is hostile and homophobic. By raising our voices, we hope to lessen the oppression and provide hope for our lonely friends" (p. 1).

Pressure and hostility faced by young lesbians and gays is responsible for problem behavior that often comes to the attention of teachers and counsellors — drug and alcohol abuse, delinquency, heterosexual promiscuity and pregnancy, behavior that some see as an escape from a bleak future as social outcasts (Lesbian and Gay Youth Ottawa-Hull, 1988; Schneider, 1988). One third of the young people interviewed in the Ottawa-Hull survey admitted that they had dated members of the opposite sex in order to conceal their lesbian/gay identities. They all reported that they knew more about heterosexual than homosexual sex, and that media images of "effeminate" gay men and "macho" lesbians shaped their perceptions of what it meant to be lesbian or gay.

Parental hostility exacerbates the problem. Some young people are grounded, physically abused, kicked out of the home or threatened with psychiatric treatment for their "sickness." Because of the stigma attached to a lesbian or gay identity, many young people make last-ditch efforts to prove that they are heterosexual, and for girls, pregnancy is often one of the outcomes. It is not uncommon to hear of lesbians and gays in their thirties or forties who, as adolescents in a more conservative era, were persuaded that marriage would "straighten them out," and it is perhaps a sign of the conservative backlash that young people are still being directed into this disastrous path. It is unlikely that the average heterosexual teacher or counsellor would interpret this kind of indiscriminate heterosexual activity accurately without specific training about sexual orientation (Schneider, 1988; Sears, 1987).

The Toronto Board of Education: A Case Study

Toronto's Board of Education may well be one of the most progressive in Canada on sexual orientation issues. Its current work in curriculum development and inservice training was sparked by a tragic event in June 1985, when a gay teacher was murdered by four adolescent males who attended Toronto schools. In December 1985, the president of the Ontario Secondary School Teachers' Federation wrote to the Director of Education urging him to take steps to deal with intolerance and homophobia in the schools (Templin, 1985).

Early in 1986, Ward 6 trustee Olivia Chow, working with lesbian and gay students and groups, began to investigate sex education programs. She reported the virtual nonexistence of curriculum material on sexual orientation, noting that, since board policy required that the topic be discussed only by physical education teachers, human rights and tolerance aspects of the issue were ignored in the curriculum. Furthermore, approximately one professional development day every two years provided training for PE teachers, and only 40 out of about 200 PE teachers had attended the last session — in other words, 40 teachers were distributed among about 7,000 lesbian and gay students in Toronto schools. An occasional lesbian or gay speaker could be brought into the school with the principal's approval (Chow, 1986a, 1988).

Not only were curriculum materials silent on the issue of sexual orientation; they were deafening in their prescription of heterosexual activity. A survey of five family studies texts that were on Circular 14 (the list of books approved for use in Ontario schools) in the 1980s confirms this trend (Brinkley et al., 1978; Cowan, 1977; Goodspeed & Smith, 1977; Kieren,

1986; Schlesinger, 1979). In a section of *This is the Life,* that uses the question and answer format, two girls complain that their boyfriends never leave them alone to have a day to themselves. The response begins with the gratuitous aside that "lots of girls would like to have your problem." Another question comes from three boys who prefer to spend time together working on their cars rather than dating girls. The response: "give the girls a break" and start dating (Goodspeed & Smith, 1977, pp. 187-188).

One approved text, the most recently published of those surveyed, stands out as an exception to the trend: *Discovering Yourself,* by Diane Kieren (1986). In the section entitled "How relationships develop," Kieren begins with the following example: "Sue meets Rebecca on her soccer team and finds out they like the same music." The next example describes Darryl and Peter, who are on the same swim team. The author does not assume that a relationship has to be heterosexual, or for that matter, sexual at all, and her choice of soccer and swimming are refreshingly non-stereotypical (Kieren, 1986, pp. 62-63).

Ron Langevin, a Toronto psychologist who testified at the Toronto Board inquiry, pointed out that lesbian and gay students, as targets of homophobic discrimination in the schools and in the community, experienced stress-related mental and physical ill-health which the board had an ethical responsibility to alleviate. Explaining human sexual development, he stressed that sexual orientation is not changeable, but is fixed by adolescence (Langevin, n.d.). This psychiatric explanation was apparently more palatable than the notion of choice proposed by lesbians like Marilyn Frye and others (and, ironically, the same notion of choice that R.E.A.L. Women used to argue against sexual orientation in human rights codes). Parents, in particular, are less likely to oppose sexual orientation topics in sex education if they know that their child's sexual preference is already fixed, and that her/his exposure to information on this subject will not serve to tip the scales in the "wrong" direction.

The policy that was eventually approved by the Toronto Board in April 1986 focused on curriculum and professional development, and included the following recommendations: that "discrimination, harassment and violence will not be tolerated" in school environments; that steps will be taken, in collaboration with the Ministry of Education, to develop programs to "sensitize students to the basic human rights of *all* students and staff of the Board, including those who are homosexual"; and that inservice training programs be provided for *all* teachers (not just physical education teachers) (Chow, 1986b; School Programs Committee, 1986). A motion to include sexual orientation in Board policy as a prohibited ground for discrimination was defeated, although subsequently the Ontario Human Rights Code was amended to protect lesbians and gays.

With the new policy in Toronto schools, it is possible that lesbian and gay speakers will receive a warmer welcome than in the past. However, there are problems with the idea that the occasional guest speaker can serve as a role model for students. Sexual identity is the speaker's salient feature; students see a lesbian, not a journalist, or a mother, or an accountant. The Ottawa-Hull brief addresses this problem by proposing that speakers be invited with a "dual intention": a gay politician would discuss human rights issues, or a lesbian doctor would discuss lesbian health issues, so that students would see a multi-dimensional person. But the most effective role models are teachers themselves. Students need to see openly lesbian and gay teachers doing what teachers routinely do: teaching. And it is virtually impossible in the current climate for any openly homosexual teacher to do so safely and comfortably.

Given the barriers and risks to lesbian and gay teachers in dealing with homophobia, there is an urgent need to educate heterosexual teachers about appropriate ways of confronting homophobic name-calling, at least as a first step in the long process of developing a gay- and lesbian-positive climate in the schools. Teachers repeatedly state that many young children don't even know the meanings of the words they use as insults: gay, queer, lezzie, fag, homo. They are simply looking for an insulting name, and words like "gay" are seen as synonymous with "stupid." This is an appropriate time to educate young children about the potential damage caused by name-calling. Various strategies for experiential learning have been developed by sex educators and classroom teachers who report success even with young children (Gordon, 1983; Sears, 1987).

AIDS Education

Another potential opportunity for combatting homophobia comes with the AIDS education program that is now required in Ontario and elsewhere. In October 1987, the Ontario Ministry of Education released a document entitled *Education about AIDS: Materials for Use in the Mandatory Health Education Units*. We cannot assume, of course, that the implementation of the AIDS education program corresponds to the Ministry guidelines. However, an examination of curriculum materials does provide insights into educators' values and attitudes, as well as revealing what teachers may be telling children about AIDS and about homosexuality.

In an introductory discussion, the Ministry guidelines explain some of the broader implications of AIDS education: "Education around AIDS requires that attention be given to values and to the discussion of sex roles, equity, violence, the ethics of choice and tolerance of individual and group differences in behaviour and belief" (Ministry of Education, 1987, Part B, p. 6). It presents three major approaches: the information approach (facts and figures), the living skills approach (values) and the case study approach. The living skills section discusses some central AIDS-related issues, including: the right to privacy; discrimination in life- and health-insurance policies: stigmatization of homosexuals, prostitutes, etc.; attitudes of health care workers; the issue of infants and children with AIDS; and discrimination against people with AIDS in the areas of jobs, welfare, housing and drug therapy. These topics, although controversial, would undoubtedly stimulate classroom debate which a skilled facilitator could use to identify and change homophobic attitudes and behaviours. However, a survey of AIDS curriculum materials in use in three Ontario boards of education — Etobicoke (public), Simcoe County (public) and Simcoe County (Roman Catholic) — and the AIDS publications of the Institute for Catholic Education (Toronto) demonstrates that many educators are avoiding this kind of debate (Institute for Catholic Education, 1987).

The Ministry's case study materials were more popular than its living skills unit. Reproduced, in part, in all the school board publications, they present six AIDS-related examples: a boy born without an immune system; transmission through a blood transfusion; a baby born to an IV drug user; and a male IV drug user with AIDS; a situation illustrating peer pressure to have heterosexual sex; and a case of a homosexual man with AIDS. Since the most common form of AIDS transmission is unprotected sexual contact, and since most people with AIDS in North America are homosexual or bisexual men, the most significant case study is the last one, which states explicitly that the young man is homosexual and describes the reactions of his sister and his "roommate."

The discussion questions following the case studies raise issues of attitudes, emotions, the need for nurturing and support, safer sex practices and alternatives to sexual intercourse. Interestingly, one school board only included the first five case studies in its resource kit, and thus avoided the homosexual content, while the Catholic curriculum materials used modified versions of the first three cases. As well, Catholic teachers were advised that the Ministry curriculum materials were only to be used as teacher resource material. Clearly, these kinds of modifications have diluted what was a potentially progressive set of curriculum materials. We can only assume that, in the hands of predominantly heterosexual, and possibly homophobic, teachers, department heads and principals, the original intent will be further diluted and distorted.

Looking Forward

What would an anti-sexist and anti-heterosexist sex education program look like? It would validate the full range of human sexual preferences and practices: heterosexuality, bisexuality, homosexuality, celibacy, genital sex, non-genital sex, and so on. It would recognize differences between male and female experience of sex, and between lesbian, gay and heterosexual sex, but it would also consider the common ground between them. And it would not spend time on the "causes" of homosexuality, unless equal time was given to discussing the "causes" of heterosexuality.

Furthermore, the curriculum would take into account the social context in which males as a group have power and privilege, and females do not; therefore, it would be woman-centred, rather than gender-neutral. It would recognize that girls and women are affected in distinct and significant ways by such issues as contraception, pregnancy, abortion, homophobia and male sexual violence in all its forms. For the same reason, a feminist model of sex education would include courses organized by and for women, in addition to coeducational programming. Finally, it would attempt to develop woman-positive images of sexuality — a celebration of our bodies and our selves.

Note

[1]This article was originally published in *Gender and Education, 2*(2), 217-230. The research on which it is based was partly funded by a grant from the Lesbian and Gay Community Appeal of Toronto.

References

Adame, D. (1985). On the effects of sex education. *Health Education, 16,* 8-10.

Barry, K. (1979). *Female sexual slavery.* Englewood Cliffs, NJ: Prentice-Hall.

Brick, P. (1985). Sex education in the elementary school. *SIECUS Report 13*(2), 1-4.

Brinkley, J., et al. (1978). *Teen guide to homemaking.* Toronto: McGraw-Hill.

Burkett, K. (1986, August). Stepping out. *Ms Magazine,* p. 30.

Chow, O. (1986a, April 8). *Report to School Programs Committee re Policies and Programs Regarding Sexual Orientation.*

Chow, O. (1986b, April 8). *Notice of Motion to Toronto Board of Education School Programs Committee.*

Chow, O. (1988, November 29). Interview.

Cowan, B. (1977). *A family is. . . .* Toronto: Copp Clark.

Donnerstein, E., et al. (1987). *The question of pornography: Research findings and policy implications.* New York: The Free Press.

Dorio, J. (1985). Contraception, copulation domination, and the theoretical barrenness of sex education literature. *Educational Theory 35*(3), 238-254.

Ellis, M. (1985). Eliminating our heterosexist approach to sex education: A hope for the future. *Journal of Sex Education and Therapy 11*(1), 61-63.

Gallup P. (1984, May). *Canada Gallup Poll.*

Goodspeed, L. & Smith, E. (1977) *This is the life.* Toronto: Copp Clark.

Gordon, L. (1983). What do we say when we hear "faggot"? *Interracial Books for Children Bulletin 14*(3/4), 25-27.

Institute for Catholic Education. (1987). *AIDS education: Teachers' guidebook and resource materials, grades 7-10; and, Lessons and masters, grades 9 & 10.* Toronto: I.C.E.

Johnston, B. (1987, February). Separate schools not exempt from human rights. *G.O. Info,* p. 1.

Julien, L. (1987). *Women's issues in education in Canada.* Toronto: Council of Ministers of Education.

Kieren, D. (1986). *Discovering yourself.* Toronto: GLC Silver Burdett.

Kirby, D. (1980). The effects of school sex education programs: A review of the literature. *Journal of School Health, 50,* 559-563.

Kostash, M. (1987). *No kidding: Inside the world of teenage girls.* Toronto: McClelland & Stewart.

Langevin, R. (n.d.) *Report to the Toronto Board of Education.*

Laycock, S.R. (1945). New approaches to sex education. *The School, 34,* 310.

Lesbian and Gay Youth Ottawa-Hull. (1988). *Report on high schools: A study prepared for the Coalition for Lesbian and Gay Rights in Toronto.*

Mills, J. (1988). "Putting ideas into their heads": Advising the young. *Feminist Review, 28,* 163-174.

Ministry of Education, Ontario. (1987). *Education about AIDS: Materials for use in the mandatory health education units.*

Newton, D., & Risch, S. (1981). Homosexuality and education: A review of the issue. *The High School Journal, 64,* 191-201.

Noble, K. (1986). Sex education and the educational administrator. *CAHPER Journal, 53,* 9-12.

Pennant, R. (1987, January 17). Rights editorial banned. *Extra,* p. 3.

A prom night to remember. *Off our backs* (1987, July), p. 7.

R.E.A.L. Women of Canada. (1986, November 18). *Brief to the Members of Parliament.*

Rubess, B., & Cooper, B. (1987). *Thin Ice* (Dir. Maureen White). Toronto: Theatre Direct.

Schlesinger, B. (1979). *Families: Canada.* Toronto: McGraw-Hill.

Schneider, M. (1988). *Often invisible: Counselling gay and lesbian youth.* Toronto: Central Toronto Youth Services.

School Programs Committee [Toronto Board of Education]. (1986, April 23). *Amendment to Report No. 3 of School Programs Committee, Board Meeting.*

Sears, J. (1987). Peering in the well of loneliness: The responsibility of educators to gay and lesbian youth. In A. Malnar (Ed.), *Social issues and education: Challenge and responsibility.* Alexandria: Association for Supervision and Curriculum Development.

Shaw, J. (1980). Schooling for girls, or mixed schooling: A mixed blessing? In Rosemary Deem (Ed.), *Schooling for women's work.* London: Routledge & Kegan Paul.

Smith, A. (n.d) *A resource guide on sexual coercion for educators.* Toronto: Theatre Direct.

Squirrell, G. (1989a). Teachers and issues of sexual orientation. *Gender and Education, 1,* 17-34.

Squirrell, G. (1989b). In passing . . . teachers and sexual orientation. In S. Acker (Ed.), *Teachers, gender and careers.* Lewes: Falmer Press.

Szirom, P. (1988). *Teaching gender? Sex education and sexual stereotypes.* Sydney: Allen and Unwin.

Templin, M. (1985, December 17). *Letter from the President, Ontario Secondary School Teachers' Federation, to Dr. E.N. McKeown, Director, Toronto Board of Education.*

Wheeler, G . (1985, October 31). Separate schools of sex ed. *NOW Magazine,* p. 7.

13

Medusa's Aria:
Feminist Theories and Music Education

A Curriculum Theory Paper Designed as Readers' Theatre

Roberta Lamb

Prologue

This essay developed from my reading of three significant feminist texts within a few months of each other while I was searching for and exploring the possibilities of a feminist theory of music education. "Medusa's Aria" is designed to be heard rather than read silently. In a sense it is a drama with four separate characters, each speaking in her own voice. Consequently, the paper looks like a script to a play. As in a playscript, each character is identified by name and, in addition, each has a different type face to further delineate her voice. Nicole Brossard's speech is in this font; Catherine Clément's is in this font; and Madeleine Grumet's is in this font.

Cast of Characters:

Nicole Brossard

Catherine Clément

Madeleine Grumet

Narrator

The Play

Narrator:

I teach music education courses in a university school of music. I used to teach music in the public schools. And I am a feminist. For some time it has distressed me that music teaching is not informed by feminist or critical pedagogy. Whether one examines the research literature, attends professional conferences, or participates in practical workshops, the absence of feminist awareness is apparent (Lamb, 1987/1989). Indeed, the presence of unquestioned stereotypes is disheartening.

Consider, for example, this episode from a 1989 research conference in general music: Women and men were equally represented as participants and presenters. The women's research focused on early childhood through elementary levels. The men's research focused on junior high school through university. There were no exceptions. Consequently, when questions of gender were raised as potential research areas, the response was an uncomfortable, "but women have always been a part of music education, so what is there to research?" The next day, however, more than one woman cautiously mentioned to me some aspect of gender that warranted examination — the history of women in music education, the possibility that computer use in music composition might differ quantitatively and qualitatively by gender, the greater voice men have in running a professional organization the majority of whose members are women. These thoughts, presented in hushed tones, express an awkward tension between fear and interest in naming and in shaping the pattern of women's existence in music education.

Thus begins the difficult work of discovering how we women can make musical sense collectively. I seek as a voyageur, searching for voices of women — listening for statements of our creation, listening for questions about our knowledge, about how we define, create and share knowledge — within these musical arts, and specifically within music education. And, though I speak in the first person singular, though it has been necessary to look to other fields or disciplines to propose a structure within which a feminist critique of music and music education could grow, I do not speak in isolation. Other women are speaking in a similar manner in related arts, in related discourse.

Madeleine Grumet states,

Grumet:

"if I am a teacher";

Narrator:

Catherine Clément,

Clément:

"if I love opera";

Narrator:

Nicole Brossard,

Brossard:

"if I know ecstasy."[1]

Narrator:

In each case the author has transformed the conditional "if I" into a statement, a fragmentary statement, but a statement nevertheless. "If I" becomes the statement of women as artists envisioning. I will return to Brossard's, Clément's and Grumet's statements shortly.

Marilyn Frye (1989) has suggested the possibility of recognizing patterns as metaphor for that which is as yet unnamed as a means for developing feminist theory. Patterns were first a part of feminist practice in consciousness-raising groups where women would "hear each other into speech," thus building from isolation to commonalties as each woman voiced her experiences. According to Frye, when this concept is used to build feminist theory, pattern recognition opens rather than closes the questions, generates more rather than summarizing or limiting. She suggests we sketch the schema within which certain patterns function as sense-makers. Frye proposes articulating, judging and understanding the scope of patterns as metaphor as a way of making sense, but not a single sense. When sense-making becomes uniform it is not possible to perceive pattern. Ways of discovering patterns may be found in novel practices or in familiar strategies for creativity. Since a pattern is like a metaphor, it can make only so much intelligible; therefore, it becomes necessary to explore the limits and range of the pattern, to work the pattern until it dissolves.

I do not know whether or not from her philosophical viewpoint Frye had the arts in mind when she identified patterns as metaphors for sense-making or cited creative strategies as a means for uncovering patterns. But as I heard her speak I felt that here was a conceptual framework encompassing expressive envisioning wherein feminist theory could offer a new paradigm for the arts. After all, patterns organize the arts, both visual and performing. The creation of art itself is sense-making in non-verbal media; therefore, the intelligible in art is primarily non-verbal. Verbal description and analysis may appear to be precise, but are only metaphors for the patterns of art. So rather than working with metaphor to symbolize sense, working pattern in the arts is exploring sense-making itself, unmediated by metaphor. That is to say, in the arts, when a musician attempting to define a musical theory (in this case, a feminist theory of music education), explores patterns of sound to the points of dissolution, she is making sense; however, when she verbalizes this pattern, transforming sound-vision into word-patterns, those words become metaphors for theory. I think this circular problem is central to the difficulty in naming women's experience in music, and in framing a feminist critique of music education.

I see patterns connecting Madeleine Grumet's *Bitter Milk* (1988), a critique of women and teaching, Catherine Clément's *Opera; Or, The Undoing of Women* (1979/1988), a critique of women and opera, and Nicole Brossard's *The Aerial Letter* (1985/1988), a critique or analysis of women and writing — common thoughts and an unusual declaration, "if I." As I play with this particular pattern, I look to extend the range of that "if I" from the arts of teaching, opera and writing, through the metaphor of literary theory to music education. Perhaps it is like working a quilt. All these treasured scraps I carried with me from attic to attic, knowing that someday they would be made useful and artistic. Tracing shapes over graph paper, cutting and piecing until, finally, a thematic form appears which may be as visible to and understood by those who have not worked it as it is to me, the artisan who crafted it.

In looking for patterns, I read. I listen. I wonder. If I. I read biographies of women musicians. I read critiques of women composers. I listen to their music. I play their music. I talk to women who teach music, who write music, who perform music. I talk to women who study music. I read their work. But I find only a few connections to my own experience as a feminist voyageur exploring gendered boundaries in the political-cultural world of music education. I wander into Clément's operatic world, caught between text and music such that

Clément:

"I have seen these operas at work; if I am touched . . . they speak of women. . . ." (p. 8)

Narrator:

I wander into Brossard's literary world full of ironic metaphors where she

Brossard:

"make[s] text of their voyage." (p. 50)

Narrator:

I stumble across Grumet's emblem of

Grumet:

"aesthetic experience as a metaphor of education." (p. 80)

Narrator:

Now I find a connection that reminds me. . . .

I remember seventeen years ago, as a recent graduate, telling my favourite music history prof that I was going to research women composers. He told me curtly not to waste my time, which would be better spent studying the wives who inspired, supported the great composers. . . . Then, in 1985, while writing a dissertation chapter, I referred to one of the older volumes of the current generation of researched texts on women in music. I was sure it had been published several years before; I had used that book so much; I had referred so many people to it. And yet when I checked the date in my reference list, I was surprised to find that it was merely three years since its publication (Neuls-Bates, 1982). . . . Last year half a dozen first-year students asked for assistance with a project on women composers for their music history class. One of the young women wondered if they should abandon the project because she could find only six books on women in music in the music library (Ammer, 1980; Bowers & Tick, 1986; Cohen, 1981; LePage, 1980; Neuls-Bates, 1982; Zaimont & Famera, 1981), while her friend had located at least a dozen about Beethoven. I am grateful for those six books! I only wish my book budget had been greater and there had been dozens more to order! I am grateful for the extensive research on women in music, women and music that has been published during the past ten years.

Even so, as a feminist voyageur in music, seeking women's voices, I feel lost: Something is missing from this recent work. Some guiding questions have not been asked. After more than a decade of this most recent wave of research on women in/and music, some voices are unheard in this music I love. If I.

We (feminists studying music) identify a need for a feminist critique of music and music education that goes past the questions of "who were the women musicians/composers in our history?" and "how do we eliminate gender stereotyping in music classes?" This is not to belittle these kinds of questions, nor to suggest that they have been fully answered. Much work remains to be done in the identification of women's contributions to music and in the development of nonsexist curricula and teaching strategies in music education. Still, that sense of being lost perturbs me. If I.

I read. I listen. I wonder. I read more feminist literature and criticism. I read more educational theory informed by feminist perspectives. There, in the art of literature and the critical theory of education, I find the questions, questions that examine the entire structure of those disciplines, that wonder about and critique the reasons for the particular organization, the substance, the style, the practice, the process, the meaning. This happens in many, nearly all disciplines, yet we have not attempted this in music and music education. As Joseph Kerman (1985) puts it: "post-structuralism, deconstruction, and serious feminism have yet to make their debuts in music" (p. 17). There has been some movement towards such critiques of music, particularly within musicology, as evidenced by sessions at the 1988 American Musicological Society [AMS] conference addressing "Text and Narrative," "Feminist Scholarship and the Field of Musicology," and "Cultural and Aesthetic Issues" (Don & McCoy, 1988) and by the work of the Status of Women Committee of the AMS. Yet a parallel in music education does not exist. Some critiques relevant to music education, particularly of the social construction of music, have been undertaken, but these tend to be androcentric and not at all feminist (Frith, 1988; Shepherd, 1987; Vulliamy, 1980, 1984; Vulliamy & Lee, 1980, 1981).

This lack of feminist critique, this intractable silence, this corner where the world has yet to be split open (Rukeyser, 1973, p. 73) frustrates my voyage of exploration. So I have turned to other women studying music from a feminist perspective, and asked, "How do we find our Selves in this world?" We do not know. I remember Brossard's question to women writers:

Brossard:

"How then *to make sense collectively?*" (p. 112)

Narrator:

So far, in music, it appears that none of us has the answer, though I wonder if it is not The Answer we are looking for, but questions. If we look for questions we can create the patterns Frye suggests will open rather than close, generating many ideas rather than limiting us to The Answer.

For several of us the question has been put best by Elizabeth Wood, "We *must* question the bloody canon!" (personal communication, December 1988); for the canon defines music, divides it into categories, genres, historical periods, hierarchies, always in relation to Great Music. To question the Canon of Music means questioning the very structure of music itself: What is music? How do we define music? Why? Is music popular? elite? western? historical? contemporary? sound? Why do we separate ethnomusicology from musicology? music education from music? or the converse — Why do we hide music education in music? Why do we make non-western music invisible (inaudible) in musicology? What are the structures within which these categories originate? How are these definitions informed by our situation as gendered subjects within a political-cultural world? What happens to these definitions when we consider the interrelationship of race and class and gender?

The question "What is music?" may appear to be the same question when asked by the ethnomusicologist (Blacking, 1976; Merriam, 1964; Nettl, 1983) or the music educator (Reimer, 1989; Schafer, 1976) (both of whom inhabit the fringe of scholarship in the Canon of Music). But the feminist framing of "What is music?" places women at the centre of that inquiry. If I am. If I love. If I know. While it is difficult to say what this change towards a woman-centred perspective means, it is possible to suggest some possible forms the inquiry might take. Two suggestions borrowed from literature are that we:

> critique . . . phallocentrism in all the material and ideological forms it has taken, and . . . call for new representations of women's consciousness. It is not enough to uncover old heroines or imagine new ones . . . we need to examine the words, [the] syntax, the genres, the archaic and elitist attitudes toward language and representation that have limited women's self-knowledge and expression. . . . (Jones, 1985b, p. 374)

We could substitute "music" for "language" in this statement. In both cases, an aesthetic, as well as political, principle is involved.

Feminist critiques of the sociology of education, especially those which have developed nonsexist research methods (Eichler, 1988) provide many possibilities applicable to music, and particularly, music education. Feminist inquiry in music involves re-thinking and re-envisioning the musical culture of women. Catherine Stimpson (cited in Biklen & Shakeshaft, 1985) defines such new scholarship as concerned with ideas, facts, concepts and data about women and women's lives. She identifies three major goals: "to deconstruct error about women; . . . to add to the existing body of knowledge to compensate for the absence of women in the past; and to transform consciousness through such processes" (p. 47). Feminist inquiry in relation to music and music education is concerned with that transformation.

I read. I listen. I wonder. If I am. If I love. If I know. Some musicologists, moving towards what could be called, in traditional terms, an ethnographic or ethnomusicological viewpoint have begun this questioning of the Canon of Music. Elizabeth Wood no longer teaches "Women in Music," but "Music in Women's Lives." Wood makes use of this idea in another way. Her biography of Dame Ethyl Smyth departs from the usual format. She examines Smyth's operas (both her libretti and her scores) for insights and analogies to reveal patterns of her life not apparent from the "facts" alone. Jane Bowers' most recent work turns from women in western art music to women blues singers in Chicago to women and music cross-culturally. Susan McClary (1988) looks at the social construction of music, within the western art tradition, with a particular aim to identify aspects of female culture within that tradition. Ellen Koskoff (1989) considers the relationship of gender, music and society as a significant research category within ethnomusicology. Wonderful beginnings, yet, it often seems, so tentative. Almost hushed. Perhaps censured. Spinning.

Catherine Clément calls it vertigo, the force that drives Tosca over the parapet, leaping into the void, when she realizes that all that is left is her song, not her voice, but her song. In her introduction to Clément's *Opera,* McClary (1988) wonders if it would be leaping into the void for feminists to raise these questions against the Canon of Music. Later . . . after Tosca's leap, Clément sighs,

Clément:

"Nobody notices . . . Norma passes the silent torch of revolt to Carmen, and it falls into my hands, like a shuttle with which it is my turn to weave . . . way inside myself I shall keep the secret. And I shall be ready for the next encounter with my musical sisters." (p. 175)

Narrator:

Nicole Brossard describes "urban radicals"[2] rather than prima donnas. No longer is revolt a well-kept secret, rather that silent torch has become the combat writing of redefined words, including vertigo:

Brossard:

"Real I would be the other, the draining out, where I would make myself dizzy in the telling, where there would be no end of saying — I am a woman — (p. 44) . . . to see one's desire come *as far as possible,* that is, closer: to the very edge, right to the limits — where it might very well falter. Balance or vertigo (p.

70), . . . a shift in meaning going from excess to ecstasy, from circle to spiral, and from void to opening, as a solution for continuity." (p. 71)

Narrator:

Is this opening of the spiral where the next encounter with my musical sisters will be? Brossard describes it as

Brossard:

"the border between what's real and what's fictive, between what it seems possible to say, to write, but which often proves to be, at the moment of writing, unthinkable." (pp. 75-76)

Narrator:

That border distinguishes the urban radicals from their musical sisters. It is a long trek to the spiral opening from that musical world where opera is

Clément:

"the lament of woman. The only course open is death: that is opera's innermost finality." (p. 22)

Narrator:

The feminist voyageur seeks the border between real and fictive in order to discover urban radical musical sisters who sing in their own uncensored voices, no longer tentative and hushed. If I am. If I love. If I know.

Grumet suggests that the spiral border can be found.

Grumet:

"All that we need to decide, each day, when we are ready and the light is right, is where and when to draw the line." (p. 94)

Narrator:

But in music we have not yet arrived in that country. Just as the feminist musicologist adopts an ethnographic method, Clément notices,

Clément:

"Going to the opera is like an ethnologist taking a voyage to a strange land. . . . When I come home, I no longer recognize myself there; something has happened inside me that makes me wander, lost, for a long time." (p. 175)

Narrator:

I, too, wander, and wonder if this is the situation for woman in the Canon of Music? Perhaps Woman-in-Music wanders through a strange land, foreign to her Self, unaware that there is a border to be crossed, mixing the real and fictive to the point where she does not identify Woman, and cannot say, musically or otherwise, "I am a woman." Perhaps Woman-in-Music does not recognize herself in this ethnographic metaphor as always the observer, never an authentic participant or creator.

It appears that a woman writer may be in a more authentic expressive space than her musical sister on a voyage through the strange land of opera. Brossard speaks clearly about living on the very limits, crossing borders and passing through voids to reality. But Clément describes herself as lost, a keeper of secrets, and one who sees no way out. If we follow these two examples, Brossard's path is one of present and future life, whereas Clément's does not leave the past world of the fathers, foreseeing only the finality of death. On the other hand, a woman teaching may be located so that she occupies both the space of the writer's spiral opening and the prima donna's tragedy. Grumet identifies such a place in a teacher's possible ethnographic stance, specifically when identifying teaching as aesthetic experience:

Grumet:

"The art of teaching invites this inspection of its boundaries and territory, for if teaching is an aesthetic experience, it is also a form of labor and accommodation to bureaucracy. It is both subject to and extends social control. . . . (p. 78) Curriculum is . . . artifice. . . . None of us, neither teacher nor artist, dwells on one side of the line or the other. Even though aesthetic objects and aesthetic experience are spread out on the other side of the boundary from the places where money, supper, and trouble are made, the artist regularly passes back and forth between the actual and the possible, and we are, all of us, commuters." (p. 79)

Narrator:

Prima donnas, teachers, ethnomusicologists, commuters — moving in and out of a world we inhabit but wherein we do not live. A woman teaching music, Tosca teaching a song without a voice? No? Then, what? A woman teaching music . . . and the immediate image is a maternal figure seated at the piano surrounded by dozens of angelic faces. No? Then, it is the stern grandmother or spinster aunt who raps the knuckles of the young piano student. Of course these are stereotypes, perhaps archetypes. Life is different . . . perhaps. But perhaps, as Clément writes,

Clément:

"The story of women in the opera is no different from this true episode." (p. 178)

Narrator:

This true episode that retains silences in its telling. How do we tell true episodes within a context requiring silent archetypes?

Clément:

"The story of women in the opera is no different from this true episode. This is my story, no doubt. . . . Opera is the collection of these myths." (p. 178)

Narrator:

Grumet, too, refers to the myths and stories of teaching,

Grumet:

"Deprived of the opportunity to design structures of their own lives, their own work, many women, mothers and teachers, live through other people's stories." (p. 87)

Narrator:

Whereas opera collects the myths of women's episodes in music, the structure surrounding women teaching music perpetuates them. We live our lives through stories of our successful students who leave us for more prestigious male teachers and come back to tell us how we taught them more about music. We live our creative selves through the stories of the Great Composers. We live our lives through the women who succeed, the stars who simultaneously embody musical excellence and male-defined sexuality, while we are constantly mindful of those who failed — and became teachers. And, yes, we live our lives through the re-telling of the operatic myths to our students. I am concerned with the myths in which we, as women teaching music, participate — and with the myths we teach our students. Like Nicole Brossard,

Brossard:

"I have a score to settle with Knowledge because it terrorizes me from the moment it forces me to school, that is, forces me to learn more about the master's fantasies than about knowledge itself. And this takes a very long time to sort out. Now I select within knowledge, as though I were in a supermarket. I know the things I want." (p. 39)

Narrator:

The difference is that, unlike woman writers, woman musicians/music educators do not have a history of defining for ourselves the Knowledge we want within music. We, collectively and most likely individually, are as yet restrained from naming What We Want. Am I able to state aloud, and safely: If I am. If I know. If I love.

This is not unlike the situation Grumet describes in which women entered teaching to flee domesticity, only to find it reproduced in the schools:

Grumet:

"Women were not asked to create this moral leadership in either the home or school, but they were expected to be the medium through which [it was] communicated to the child. Their own passivity was to provide the model of obedience for the young to emulate. The self-abnegation and submission to universal principles of morality, decorum, and beauty constrained teachers . . . from developing a style of practice with which they were personally identified and for which they felt personally responsible. (p. 84) . . . The privatization of teaching repeats the exile of domesticity that has split public from private life and drained each domain of its vitality." (p. 93)

Narrator:

As women teaching music we have been expected to provide aesthetic leadership without creating it. The archetype/stereotype lady music teacher is a domestic model lacking vitality. In fact, one of her tasks has been to eliminate life from the music curriculum. Example: "Children should sing folk songs of their cultural heritage." But if the texts of such songs are too violent, too sexual, or just plain not nice enough, then it is up to the music teacher to rewrite the text to be more acceptable, more decorous. If the folk melody has characteristic turns or elisions, or is in an "uncommon" mode; if the intervals do not fall in expected positions; if the range is wide, then this melody must be modified to be singable by children. When music is in this way made anemic it can be no surprise that, after a point, children name music class as "dumb," "sissy," "not *real* music."

As women teaching music often we have been required to submit to standards of morality, decorum and beauty that may have more to do with the master's fantasies than our own best interests or those of our students. If we teach opera . . . Clément says:

Clément:

"Opera concerns women. No, there is no feminist version; no, there is no liberation. Quite the contrary: they suffer, they cry, they die. Singing and wasting your breath can be the same thing. (p. 11) . . . On the grand opera stage, you saw unhappiness and its opposite; you saw nothing of life, except the derision of figures who were thwarted, whose voices alone sung the truth. (p. 177) . . . That is indeed the world of opera. A great blaze of light and love, and death is the result. (p. 179) . . . The end of an opera is a work of mourning." (p. 174)

Narrator:

In "The Magic Flute," if we do not acknowledge the violent fight between the (metaphorically) divorced parents of Pamina, Zarastro and the Queen of the Night, that provides the good father with an apparent reason to kidnap and confine his daughter so she will not be influenced by her evil mother, is it possible that we are colluding with the idea that violence in families is acceptable? What would this mean to our students who have experienced similar situations in their own families? If we do not acknowledge this domestic conflict, insisting that the plot is but a convoluted tale revolving around serpents dropping from the sky, a silly flute-playing birdcatcher, odd rituals and other magic devices, what happens to our credibility when our students discover there was a divorce?

Another example: I was observing a secondary school music class. The teacher was introducing "The Rite of Spring." He described the scene: "This is ballet music, composed by Stravinsky, depicting a pagan celebration of spring. In this section, The Dance of the Young Adolescents, the young people are doing a frenzied dance around a virgin — she's dancing, too — as part of this spring celebration. At the end of the dancing the virgin is sacrificed to the gods." Immediately, the attitude, the body language, of the young women in that class changed ever so slightly, freezing, pulling inward, protecting from further violation, but they were silent. The young men were relaxed. One tipped his chair back on two legs, thrust his pelvis forward and said, " Sounds like quite a party." It makes no difference that in this particular situation, the teacher was a man; the same thing could have happened with a woman teacher. There is nothing uncommon about this standard, simplified explanation of "The Rite of Spring." The contradiction is that no matter that the musical content was excellent, another message, one of violation, was received by the women students. How do we, as women teaching music, mediate these situations arising within the curriculum? And if we do not address our role as mediator, is this not detrimental to us as well as to our students?

These examples are with programmatic music, music that has a reference to a text. Perhaps music-without-text is different? Clément thinks not:

Clément:

"Nothing is left but the music. Yes, finally, the music, like a transitional space; the music that is neither inside nor outside, but elsewhere surrounding you. The music where love and hatred can interact without vital risk, and where the light of passions burns and immediately goes out. Life is different, nothing in it happens that way." (p. 179)

Narrator:

Yet the reality is that much of the music we teach in the schools is of this programmatic genre. School structures do not encourage expressiveness as a pedagogical quality in teachers (Grumet, 1988), but that is what is required to teach untexted music. Programmatic music dominates the curriculum because it is easier to teach music from a referential viewpoint, using language, which is one of the accepted bases of schooling, to describe the nonverbal but sounding images of music. It requires much more time, commitment, musical sensitivity, and risk-taking to teach untexted music using metaphorical sound patterns rather than referential language. Therefore, it is through learning the myths of programmatic music that most students receive their education in the Canon of Music.

As women teaching music we need to, in the process of questioning the Canon of Music, discover our own musical myths and stories; operas that express vitality rather than *lasciatemi morir* (Clément, 1988). We need to draw the spiraling line in our own space and time, so close to the edge, where "I am a woman" can be composed. Like Grumet,

Grumet:

"... I call upon teachers to make a place for themselves where they can find the silence that will permit them to draw their experience and understanding into expression . . . [to] encircle aesthetic processes in general, suggesting that aesthetic experience is necessarily defined against the standard of daily experience, which it in some way contradicts or challenges . . . [to] root the aesthetic object in common experience. . . . I am arguing that we women must construct a special place for ourselves if our work as teachers is to achieve the clarity, communication, and insight of aesthetic practice — if it is, in short, to be research and not merely representation." (p. 88)

Narrator:

Keeping Grumet's words in mind, remember that Clément describes music as transitional space, an elsewhere surrounding. Add to these images of an encircling aesthetic, an elsewhere surrounding, that of Brossard's place/space as a foundation on which to build or a platform from which to leap. (Remember Tosca?) Brossard contrasts the "turning platform" with the void/non-space/hole that women pass through, embody, inhabit and that is equally useful as a foundation, a creating point.

Imagining forward (Brossard, 1988) from these metaphoric patterns, I wonder if the beginnings of our own musical myths, the incipient plans for those special places for such creation, may be found in our own classrooms at such times as we are struggling with our students to help them find their creative voices. I am thinking of an example in a grade 5/6 class I once taught. The students were writing a musical. It was their story, their songs. At first they were hesitant, not sure about taking the creative risk, not sure whether to trust my statement that this musical belonged to them, could be what they wanted to make it. The next stage, though wild with creative activity, still showed insecurity: "We're having too much fun. When is she going to stop us? What if the principal comes in?" Soon, the fun became serious fun, as students made critical decisions in the refinement of their work. After the public presentation several parents insisted that such a competent work could not have been written by the students themselves. But the fact that it was the students' production is precisely why it was so good — It was an authentic expression of their lives.

This may seem no different than any "creative activity." Certainly there is a history of this approach recorded in music education literature of the past twenty years. What will transform these experiences from activity into feminist myths is the woman teacher's realization of her own agency, of attending, of being present to both the aesthetic and political metaphors evolving in the artistic patterns created. Listen to Grumet:

Grumet:

". . . I believe that to adopt the stance of the artist is to challenge the taken-for-granted values and culture that one shares with others." (p. 81)

Narrator:

What needs to be emphasized in that story of the grade 5/6 musical is that while it was authentic expression of the students' lives, my role as the woman teaching music was not as an outsider to their world, the expert who imposed quality and standards. Neither did I give up my life selflessly to their needs. My ego was definitely involved, but not dependent on their success or failure. This was one of many interdependent ventures in that particular classroom. We were co-conspirators, doing what we were not supposed to do — the students were well aware of this, too — turning that deadly elementary Spring Festival into aesthetic experience.

Yet, that classroom musical experience did not quite become a new myth. It is remembered by many of us and may have had a significant effect on the creators/participants, but it was too isolated. Although that elementary musical was on the edge, as an aesthetic experience at a particular school, it did not quite cross the border into the space of composing "I am a woman." Those evolving aesthetic and political metaphors did not connect into a pattern, even while taken-for-granted values were questioned.

Grumet

"Because most of the people who teach our children in the public schools are women, we must ask whether there are particular conditions surrounding women's lives that will influence our capacity to take up and live out an aesthetic approach to our work in the classroom." (p. 81)

Narrator:

The act of conspiracy can be identified as being insubordinate within the particular conditions surrounding women's lives. Grumet is aware of the dangers of encouraging a feminist aesthetic, and realizes that in protecting our livelihood, it is possible to slip into familiar patterns that reinforce current structures — as, for instance, in the previous description of "The Rite of Spring" — rather than encourage authentic expression. She issues a caution:

Grumet:

"We must take care that in re-creating spaces that offer privacy we do not merely encourage the repetition of forms that have sequestered and hidden women's perceptions rather than revealed them. (p. 90). The danger is that a room of one's own[3] becomes a bunker. . . . Terrible vulnerability accompanies aesthetic practice. Where do we find the courage to reveal our work?" (p. 93)

Narrator:

Where do we find that courage to reveal, to revel in without fear of the cost,[4] to enjoy the privilege of naming That Which We Know? If I am. If I love. If I know. I think part of that courage can be found in the IF I pattern shared in the writing of Brossard, Clément and Grumet. Brossard identifies the pattern and plays with it most consciously:

Brossard:

"If I can find the lost stream, writing interests me. (p. 40) . . . I'll have to be in the fray. Rudely accosted, I must protest. I cry out, I dream, I want things to change. I write, therefore." (p. 37)

Narrator:

As with the earlier mentioned literary theory, it does not appear to me to be problematic to transfer the lost stream from literature to music. Brossard is examining the pattern of her existence as a creative woman, an urban radical. Her medium is writing. I want mine to be creating music . . . in the classroom. As I read Brossard, I put composing music in place of writing and I extend the pattern into a larger framework that leads me into greater understanding of the particular conditions surrounding women's lives, including my own, and towards the courage to reveal my work in the vulnerability of aesthetic practice. I hear a pattern of Brossard, Clément and Grumet intertwined. I imagine them speaking as if in conversation, perhaps about music:

Brossard:

". . . I write fragment because passing or instantaneous in the continuum." (p. 42)

Grumet:

". . . expressiveness has never been a quality of pedagogy encouraged in teachers . . . humanistic education . . . client-centered, self-abnegating facilitation of another's expression rather than dialogue. . . ." (p. 89)

Brossard:

". . . 'If I know ecstasy,' this is the fragment, writing the conditional have, inscribing greed, the me who searches in the pantry (not the medicine cabinet) for the ecstatic totality of all these desiring fragments. Euphoriture." (p. 42)

Clément:

"... Even today, if I love opera, it is because I know the charm and mending power of the way it beguiles me and puts me to sleep ... music mends and glues things back together. ..." (p. 180)

Brossard:

"If I know ecstasy, it's because something in my equilibrium is shaken, something of the role which enrolls me. I invert word order. ..." (p. 44)

Clément:

"... the hysterics stand back up. The great musical flow will not put them to sleep." (p. 180)

Brossard:

" "If I' allows for all ramifications. For remembering forward into the open and for sequencing. "It reminds us that everything is possible in the ardent vagueness. But, at the same time, always intercepted. It is lost and connects up with no reality (I know the depths when it is a question of inscribing on paper a discourse which reads by itself)." (p. 44)

Clément:

"... I do not know what this song will be". (p. 180)

Grumet:

"... If [I am] engaged in expressive work but find the symbols and content of expression that dominate [my] field, as well as the condition and relations of its work, are alien to [me], what do [I] do? This is the problem of women in educational theory ..." (p. 89)

Clément:

"I will have to slowly incorporate, without anyone's knowing, these dangerous objects, these women who fought so well, these sorceresses who from now on are part of my life. And at the same time that their music is inscribed in obsessive melodies, the ferment of swelling rebellion passes from them to me ..." (p. 175)

Brossard:

"'If I' is fictive, because I know that to tell of myself such as I am in a given environment, this is fragment ..." (p. 44)

Grumet:

"If I am a teacher, I rise early. . . .The point is that to be an artist is perpetually to negotiate the boundary that separates aesthetic from mundane experience. . . . I want to explore what it means to take up teaching as an art at this place and at this time." (p. 79)

Brossard:

". . . I cannot speak us without first knowing how to reply in I. 'If I know ecstasy,' I am transposed." (p. 40)

Clément:

"Just as you always stretch your arms when you leave the darkness, these women will always sing." (p. 181)

Narrator:

The perturbing sense of being a lost voyageur diminishes in the dizziness of this conversation. I hear myself joining in. If I am. If I know. If I love. No, this is not idle women's chatter, nor is it the shrieking of hysterics. It is not delirium, but the difficult work of discovering how we women can make musical sense collectively. This work calls for even greater exploration of our situations as gendered subjects within a political-cultural world, the creation of authentic representations of women's musical consciousness, and the examination of the musical syntax, the genres, the elitism toward music and its representation that have limited women's self-knowledge and expression. The greater exploration must involve women in all facets of music — composers, performers, technicians, theorists, historians, teachers, students — working musical patterns into metaphors of yet-to-be-named woman-sense so that we may articulate feminist theories of music and music education. It is only through expressive envisioning that we can create a musical paradigm structurally different from the Old Canon. Since much of this work happens in classrooms, as well as other learning/teaching situations, part of the revelation of these explorations will be found in the ways women teaching mediate music, as we experience it now and remembering into the future. We women in music, just as do the women writing as urban radicals, can take music spinning to the very edge, to the question of balance or vertigo, the dissolution of metaphoric pattern as we approach feminist theory, rather than keeping well-hidden deep inside ourselves.

As I wrote this paper it developed a form. The form has certain musical qualities, metaphorically, in its presentation — phrases, repetitions, accents, rests, motives, timbres, textures, development. If I were to represent it in score, the form would be some kind of moving spiral, returning to those IF I's on a new level as the composer spins its melodies around a void, spinning with ever greater intensity around a transitional space. I am most interested in those transitional spaces and voids. Transitional spaces and voids, as did this presentation, embody the silences in women's lives, even as we are those women who will always sing.

Epilogue

This play began with a prologue and in keeping with its own form, it ends with an epilogue.

This then is the introduction. I have other questions, too; rather shadows of question/answers. Some are so nebulous that I cannot say, speak or sing these shapes, patterns in/Forming that rush through my head, my body as wisps of melody, as borrowed phrases from the poets.

If I . . .
And now, as did Tosca,
leap into the void, but this time,
the vertigo rises not cosi fan tutte,
now,
as did Tosca, leap into the void,
not to her death, but this time,
not to my death
the vertigo rises,
leap into the void . . . transformed . . . fluid and ubiquitous . . .
urban radical . . .
If I am a teacher.
If I love music.
If I know ecstasy.

Notes

[1]The phrase, "if I know ecstasy," is Marlene Wildeman's translation of the French verb *jouir*. She says, "I would have gladly borrowed French *jouissance* and its verb *jouir*, if I had thought we anglophones could learn to take pleasure in these words, but instead I settled for 'ecstasy' as a rare, and reserved, but probable English equivalent" (Wildeman, in Brossard, 1988, p. 28).

[2]Brossard makes her "urban radicals" reference clear:

Who are these women who give me texts which make me think, a space I can take over and inhabit, a time for rebirth in each one? I call them urban radicals. Chance, the kind no throw of the dice will ever abolish, has it that they are lesbians, by their skin and by their writing. That is to say that they conceive of reality the way they envisage themselves, in the process of becoming. . . . (p. 80)

[3]Grumet is referring to Virginia Woolf's well-known essay, "A Room of One's Own." Even though this work is commonly known, I have found it helpful to make the reference clear when I have presented "Medusa's Aria" to an audience of musicians and music educators.

[4]These phrases, "courage to reveal, to revel in without fear of the cost," are versions of the English definition of *jouir*, that amazing verb translated as "to know ecstasy" by Marlene Wildeman (in Brossard, 1988).

References

Ammer, C. (1980). *Unsung: A history of women in American music.* Westport, CT: Greenwood Press.

Biklen, S.K., & Shakeshaft, C. (1985). The new scholarship on women. In S.S. Klein (Ed.), *Handbook for achieving sex equity through education* (pp. 44-52). Baltimore: John Hopkins University Press.

Blacking, J. (1976). *How musical is man?* Seattle: University of Washington.

Bowers, J. (1986, June). *Blues singer Estelle ("Mama") Yancey.* Paper presented at the Eighth Annual Convention of the National Women's Studies Association, Champaign-Urbana, Illinois.

Bowers, J. (1987). Foreword. In J. Briscoe (Ed.), *Historical anthology of music by women* (pp. ix-x). Bloomington: Indiana University Press.

Bowers, J., & Tick, J. (1986). *Women making music: The western art tradition, 1150-1950.* Chicago: University of Illinois Press.

Brossard, N. (1988). *The aerial letter* (M. Wildeman, Trans.). Toronto: The Women's Press. (Original work published 1985)

Clément, C. (1988). *Opera; or, The undoing of women* (B. Wing, Trans.). Minneapolis: University of Minnesota Press. (Original work published 1979)

Cohen, A. (Ed.). (1981). *International encyclopedia of women composers.* New York: R.R. Bowker.

Don, G., & McCoy, M. (Eds.). (1988). *Abstracts of papers read at the 42nd annual meeting of the American Musicological Society and the 11th annual meeting of the Society for Music Theory* (Baltimore, MD, 3-6 November). n.p.: A.M.S.

Eichler, M. (1988). *Nonsexist research methods.* Boston: Allen & Unwin.

Frith, S. (1988). *Music for pleasure.* London: Routledge & Kegan Paul.

Frye, M. (1989, March). *The possibility of feminist theory.* Lecture, Queen's University.

Grumet, M. (1988). *Bitter milk: Women and teaching.* Amherst: University of Massachusetts Press.

Jones, A.R. (1985a). Inscribing femininity: French theories of the feminine. In G. Greene & C. Kahn (Eds.), *Making a difference: feminist literary criticism* (pp. 80-112). New York: Methuen.

Jones, A.R. (1985b). Writing the body / L'ecriture féminine. In E. Showalter (Ed.), *The new feminist criticism: Essays on women, literature, and theory* (pp. 361-378). New York: Pantheon Books.

Kerman, J. (1985). *Contemplating music: Challenges to musicology.* Cambridge: Harvard University Press.

Koskoff, E. (Ed.). (1989). *Women and music in cross-cultural perspective.* Chicago: University of Illinois Press.

Lamb, R.K. (1989). Including women composers in music curricula: Development of creative strategies for the general music class, grades 5-8 (Doctoral dissertation, Columbia University Teachers College, 1987). *Dissertation Abstracts International, 48,* 2568-2569A.

LePage, J.W. (1980). *Women composers, conductors, and musicians of the twentieth century.* Metuchen, NJ: Scarecrow.

McClary, S. (1987). The blasphemy of talking politics during Bach year. In R. Leppert & S. McClary (Eds.), *Music and society: The politics of composition, performance, and reception* (pp. 13-62). Cambridge: Cambridge University Press.

McClary, S. (1988). Foreword the undoing of opera: Toward a feminist criticism of music. In C. Clément, *Opera; or, The undoing of women* (pp. ix-xviii). Minneapolis: University of Minnesota Press.

Merriam, A.P. (1964). *The anthropology of music.* Chicago: Northwestern University Press.

Nettl, B. (1983). *The study of ethnomusicology: Twenty-nine issues and concepts.* Urbana: University of Illinois Press.

Neuls-Bates, C. (Ed.). (1982). *Women in music: An anthology of source readings from the middle ages to the present.* New York: Harper & Row.

Reimer, B. (1989). *A philosophy of music education* (2nd ed.). Englewood Cliffs, NJ: Prentice-Hall.

Rukeyser, M. (1973). In Chester & Barba (Eds.), *Rising tides: Twentieth century American women poets.* New York: Washington Square Press.

Schafer, R.M. (1976). *Creative music education: a handbook for the modern music teacher.* New York: Schirmer Books.

Shepherd, J. (1987). Music and male hegemony. In R. Leppert & S. McClary (Eds.), *Music and society: The politics of composition, performance, and reception* (pp. 151-172). Cambridge: Cambridge University Press.

Vulliamy, G. (1980). Music as a case study in the "new sociology of education." In J. Shepherd, P. Virden, G. Vulliamy, & T. Wishart, *(Eds.) Whose music? A sociology of musical languages* (pp. 201-232). New Brunswick, NJ: Transaction Books.

Vulliamy, G. (1984). The application of a critical sociology to music education. *British Journal of Music Education, 1,* 247-266.

Vulliamy, G., & Lee, E. (1980). *Pop music in school* (2nd ed. rev.). Cambridge: Cambridge University Press.

Vulliamy, G., & Lee, E. (1981). *Pop, rock and ethnic music in school.* Cambridge: Cambridge University Press.

Wood, E. (1985, June). *Music in women's lives.* Paper presented at the Seventh Annual Convention of the National Women's Studies Association, Seattle, WA.

Wood, E. (1988). Foreword. In D. Jezic, *Women composers: The lost tradition found* (pp. xi-xiii). New York: The Feminist Press.

Zaimont, J.L., & Famera, K. (Eds.). (1981). *Contemporary concert music by women: A directory of composers and their music.* Westport, CT: Greenwood Press.

Part Four:

Beyond Schooling: Adult Education

and Training

Most texts on education do not include a section devoted to adults. Commentators persist in assuming that once people leave school they have finished their education. We all know that most of our real "education" takes place outside schools and throughout our lifetime. But even as adults, many people continue to pursue formal educational activities. In 1983, one in every five Canadians 17 and over took at least one course (Devereaux, 1985, p. 1). Over three million Canadians who were not already full-time students enrolled in organized educational activities — from job-related training to hobby classes.

Adult education and training are particularly important to women, as the Royal Commission on the Status of Women noted over twenty years ago:

> During the last ten years, a revolutionary change has taken place in education which promises greatly extended opportunities for women. Because of accelerating technological change, learning more than ever before is regarded as a continuing process throughout life. In the past, educational institutions, engrossed in the education of the young, were slow to acknowledge the potential as well as the special problem of adults, while today they are aware of the need to encompass and encourage mature students. Women who have been "only a housewife" and now see a new way of life and women and men whose jobs have been altered or eliminated are taking advantage of a second chance for education. (1970, pp. 187-188)

In 1983, 56% of adult learners were women; only 44% were men. Put differently, 21% of all Canadian women versus 17% of all Canadian men attended classes (Devereaux, 1985, p. 6).

The growth of adult student enrollment is perhaps nowhere more striking than at the colleges and universities. One way to look at this is to consider part-time enrollment, which is largely composed of "mature students." From 1970-71 to 1980-81, the proportion of part-time undergraduate students at Canadian universities grew from 52% of the full-time total to 64%. Moreover, the enrollment of women has far outpaced that of men. In 1970-71, women constituted only 43% of all part-time undergraduates. In 1980-81, they constituted 61% (Canadian Association for Adult Education/Institut canadien d'éducation des adultes [CAAE/ICEA], 1982, p. 10).

As soon as we begin to talk about "adult students," we face the difficulty of trying to decide who this includes. Even the age of an adult student is in dispute. A case in point is the different definitions used by two recent Canadian surveys. For Devereaux (1985), the adult learner is 17 and over; for the CAAE/ICEA (1982), he/she is 18 years and over. Educational institutions set different age limits. Some distinguish "mature students" as 25 and over (see, for example, Wilson & Lipenski, 1978). The CEGEPS (collèges d'enseignement général et professionnel) identify mature students as 21 years of age and over and having been out of school for two years (Association of Universities and Colleges of Canada, 1977).

Problems of identifying what is adult education are more complex when we try to determine what kinds of activities fall within adult education and what kinds can be genuinely called "educational." Some educators identify adult education as non-vocational whereas others identify it as any course, irrespective of content, taken by adults. In part because of the confusion of trying to decide what is vocational and non-vocational, adult educators are increasingly adopting the latter definition (Purvis, 1976, p. 14).

Adult education and training imply many different kinds of education, for many purposes, for many people. Students take courses offered by a wide range of organizations: school boards, community centres, community colleges, universities, prisons, employers and private organizations. The kinds of courses that adult students take also vary a great deal — credit, non-credit, part-time, full-time, correspondence. The difficulty of determining what is "adult education" is reflected in the plethora of terms used to describe it: continuing education, university extension, worker's education, lifelong learning (*éducation permanente*), non-formal education, recurrent education, popular education.

Adult education serves a variety of purposes, but it has had a long history of being concerned with inequality. This preoccupation has largely been confined, however, to class inequality. Most commentators see adult education as a second chance for those who are educationally and socially deprived (e.g., CAAE/ICEA, 1982; Kidd & Selman, 1978). More radically, some see it as education that is not constrained by the rigidities and political control of the regular school system (e.g., Freire, 1972). The adult education community's interest in the working class has not usually been extended to women. In their studies, adult educators have tended to ignore woman students, or even to be embarrassed by them since, it is assumed, they are bourgeois housewives, not members of the "working class." Only during the past decade or so have researchers begun to note the special problems posed by the relationship of adult education to women. If adult education can create a second chance, can it create one for women?

The relationship between adult education/training and women is complex; feminists have only begun to explore its implications. Feminists' main concern with adult education as with other educational sectors is to understand how power relations between women and men affect educational participation. More specifically, they seek to understand how gender has influenced access to programs, what impact adult education has on women, and what kinds of curriculum content and pedagogy women are exposed to.

Differential Access

Since the early 1970s, feminist researchers have focused on the question of women's and men's differential access to adult education (CAAE/ICEA, 1982; Canadian Congress for Learning Opportunities for Women [CCLOW], 1984; Jayaweera, 1979; McLaren, 1981; Royce, 1978; Scott,

1980; Tittle & Denker, 1980). Of primary concern is the *kind* of adult education to which women have access. In adult education, as elsewhere in society, a sexual division exists: women and men are distributed differently among the various kinds of courses that are offered. In hobby/craft/recreation courses, 80% of the students are women; in personal development/general interest courses, 66% are women; in academic courses, 56%; and in job-related courses, 39% (Devereaux, 1985, p. 25). In so-called "non-vocational" courses, women are the strong majority; in so-called "vocational" courses, they are the minority. In many ways, "vocational" and "non-vocational" courses constitute a dual system that falls largely along gender lines.

The designation of courses as either vocational or non-vocational is, however, quite arbitrary. Someone taking an "academic" or "personal interest" course may be preparing for a future vocation. Such courses may help to prepare women who have not been employed for several years to re-enter the workforce.

Women are less likely, nevertheless, to be in vocational courses, because they are less likely to be in jobs where employers will sponsor their attendance. Women's jobs have flat career lines and often offer less on-the-job education than do men's jobs (Wolf & Rosenfeld, 1978). Even when they are in vocational courses, women are less likely to have the fees paid by the employers. Devereaux (1985) found that 56% of men but only 44% of women in training have their courses paid for by their employers.

The level of female enrollment in national training programs is low and has declined since 1977-78. Women's share of places in General Industrial Training declined from 28% in 1977-78 to 24% in 1983-84, while their share of spaces in full-time institutional training dropped from 32% to 27%. These figures conceal the actual numbers — which have dropped even more sharply — of woman trainees. For instance, in industrial training, the numbers dropped from approximately 19,600 places in 1977-78 to about 8,200 in 1983-84 (Avebury Research and Consulting Limited, 1986, p. 41). In general, women constitute about one-quarter to one-third of those enrolled in these federally supported vocational training programs. The proportion of women in apprenticeship programs is much smaller. In 1983-84, only 3.8% of apprentices who began full-time courses under the institutional training program were women (Boothby, 1986, p. 17).

Within vocational training itself, gender segregation is strong. A major concern of feminists has been women's lack of participation in traditionally male domains such as construction and computing science. Pierson and Cohen (1984) examined three vocational training programs in Canada that were under federal legislation between 1937 and 1947. They concluded that the training possibilities for women were severely limited by conceptions of women's social role and fears of female competition for men's jobs. Notions of what is "normal" work for women remained surprisingly constant during and after the war experience.

Under the institutional training program in 1984-85, women made up, for example, 92.9% of the trainees in clerical occupations (Canada Employment and Immigration, 1986, Table 4.4, p. 72). In his study of women re-entering the labor force and training programs, Boothby (1986) summarizes such sexual divisions:

> Female and male participation in training programs differs greatly. Women are almost entirely absent from apprenticeships, one of the largest and most successful components of training programs. They are also underrepresented in the industrial training program. Under the Institutional training program, they form a high percentage of trainees in educational equivalency courses and general job-skill courses, and a relatively low percentage of those in skill training for specific occupations. Women train largely for typically female occupations, especially clerical occupations, and men for blue-collar occupations. The only blue-collar occupation for which large numbers of women train for is sewing machine operator. (p. 19)

To explain women's lack of access to "non-traditional" areas, studies have isolated many factors that work against women and that need to be rectified: inadequate training allowance (especially for those with children), low unemployment insurance benefits (since women earn lower wages on average than men), training in "surplus" occupations (those in which there is an excess supply of labor in local labor markets such as clerical work), scarcity of child care, lack of affirmative action strategies and the need for aggressive recruitment campaigns (Boothby, 1986; Buckland, 1985; CAAE/ICEA, 1982; CCLOW, 1984).

This emphasis on women's low participation rate in non-traditional training programs is important. Women do need greater access to male-dominated training and occupations. But this conclusion begs the question of what is happening in female-dominated occupations. Why are clerical workers, for example, so rarely sponsored by their employers to take courses? A further problem with research on access is that, as noted in Part Two, it places too much stress on women's own deficiencies. It suggests that all women need do to overcome their low status is to improve their personal characteristics and training.

The Impact of Education and Training on Women

Another important strand of feminist research since the early 1970s examines women's experiences as adult students — what it has meant to them and what they have gained. This research has looked at the psychological and social as well as the economic impact.

Many studies that examine the impact of educational experiences on adult women look at women enrolled in university and college programs, and measure psychological impact (Astin, 1976; Letchworth, 1970; Lovell, 1980; Tittle and Denker, 1980). In general, these studies find that most woman re-entrants want to change their lives but are not certain what they want. Many are dissatisfied with the kind of employment they have had, and/or have suffered from breakdowns of marriages, or shifts in their domestic responsibilities (e.g., children going to school or moving away from home). Many return with a sense of personal inadequacy, but with high hopes.

Researchers have also found that women's pursuit of studies is stressful not only psychologically but socially too (Lovell, 1980; Tittle & Denker, 1980). Family members (especially husbands) and friends may not support their endeavours and may even actively countermand them. Because of such stress, almost half of woman re-entrants may drop out of their program at least once (Scott, 1980, p. 17).

Despite such negative accounts, most studies suggest that women's adult educational experiences are positive, if not ideal. Some indicate that women may experience a sense of self-transformation akin to consciousness-raising (Lovell, 1980). A sense of self-transformation may be all the more striking for women from underprivileged backgrounds who are seeking actively, often desperately, to overcome past frustrations and structural obstacles (McLaren, 1987) and for women who through recent immigration have experienced a disrupted sense of self (Warren, 1990).

As a result of adult education experiences, women's self-perceptions may improve a great deal. However, their economical and occupational gains appear to be slight. As Wolpe (1980) stresses:

It is difficult not to fall into the trap of assuming that training schemes, even if they were geared for new types of employment, would be the panacea. If highly trained there is no guarantee that women would be employed. After all the unemployment rate is highest amongst women, and experience has shown that neither the demand for nor the form of women's labor is directly related to their level of training and skill. It is related to a complex set of factors; these include the wage structure, the labor movement as a whole, the nature of the division of labor, the power of the employers and so on. (p. 9)

The economic returns of education are lower for women than for men, as we pointed out in Part Two. This applies to adult education as much as to other forms of education. In her study, Lovell (1980) notes that upon completion of the program, the working-class male students were more likely to pursue higher education than the middle-class female students. Since women tend to enter low-status, feminized jobs, whatever their educational preparation, "equality of outcome" in the economic arena eludes their grasp (Tittle & Denker, 1980, p. 23). Moreover, McLaren (1985) found that as women increased their investment in education in the 1970s, the economic situation worsened. As a result, many students ended up if not unemployed, underemployed.

The concern about economic outcomes puts into sharp relief the point that without substantial reform in other institutions, many of the benefits of adult education and training cannot be realized.

Whose Knowledge and Whose Pedagogy?

For over a decade, the problem of access to adult education and the evaluation of women's experiences thus have claimed much of the attention of feminists who have examined adult education. A major problem of research on women's experiences as students, however, is that it often does not take into account the content and pedagogy of the course that the women take. Do they gain in confidence no matter how the course is taught? What difference would a woman-centred course make? More recently, researchers have begun to focus on the content and pedagogy of adult education courses, asking about the nature of the knowledge that is transmitted, how it is transmitted, and whom it serves. As Spender (1980) points out:

> When the aim is to provide women with exactly the same education as men there is an underlying assumption that the male way is the right way, and that one of the solutions to women's oppression lies in having women receive an equal share of the fruits of the ostensibly superior male educational diet. . . . Women have played virtually no part in determining the shape and form of education in our society. The models of education were firmly established and were within male control before women began their fight to enter educational institutions. Those models of education are still formulated and controlled by males. (p. 20)

Since so many adult students are women, Spender's observations are particularly important. As Hootsman (1980) notes: "Adult education is beginning to realize that although for years its participants have been predominantly female, the courses and programs have not adequately met women's needs and aspirations" (p. 79).

Women have been neglected in contemporary theory and practice of adult education (Thompson, 1983; Walker, 1982, n.d.). Walker (n.d.) finds some "spectacular blind spots" with reference to gender in the knowledge base of adult education and the assumptions that theorists make about adult development, adult learning, labor education and basic education. She finds that women are underrepresented or misrepresented, and writes:

> In education in general and in adult education too, the hierarchical structure of the discipline and the professional field both reflects and reproduces the general societal picture, with men in the top positions in the departments, associations and agencies; those institutions which control access to the profession, and to the knowledge base whereby it claims professional status as a field or discipline. This discrepancy between representation and control would seem to raise some important questions for a field such as adult education, with its philosophical commitment to education as a means to personal and social change. It raises questions about whose interests are being represented in adult education as it is currently structured, and opens up for examination the question of what an adult education might consist of if it truly represented the interests of a majority of its providers and participants. (p. 5)

Many feminists argue that adult education has the potential to be different (less patriarchal) than other forms of education (Hughes & Kennedy, 1985; Jean, 1984; Spender, 1980; Thompson, 1983). Its rhetoric, at least, is that it is flexible to meet student needs, that it emphasizes personal growth, and that it has non-hierarchical structures. However, for it to meet the interests of all the women it must serve, many changes will have to be made.

An important strategy must be for women to demand to be present where decisions are being made (Jean, 1984, p. 109). As Jean suggests, when feminists organize the education of adult women, they tend to develop a new type of education: less authoritarian, fairer and centred on learning rather than on teaching.

A feminist approach can make a difference. It can offset the imbalances of traditional curriculum, as Breault (1986) was able to do when she ran a Canadian Jobs Strategy Re-Entry program. It can build on women's strengths and interests and help them to feel more confident at the end of the course, not because conventional feminine roles were confirmed but because their resistance to them was encouraged (Thompson, 1983, p. 159). As Tom (1987) notes, however, when programs run by women for women are located within a labor market structure that promises few opportunities, the programs are riddled with contradictions. Such is also the case when women are involved in the decision-making and policy-formation processes of, for example, federally funded job-training programs (Butterwick & Witter, 1991).

Until women's participation in major social institutions is equal to that of men—is more than just token representation—it will continue to be contradictory. Women in all their diversity must be present where decisions are being made. Adult education will not meet the interests of all women until those of color, the working classes, lesbian orientation, and disablement have a direct say in how it is constructed.

Feminist analyses help us to understand not just women's and men's experiences within adult education and training, and not just the role of this educational sector in society. They also help us to see more fully how powerful social structures around such considerations as gender affect people's lives. Important as the family, compulsory schooling and wage labor are, other sectors like adult education and training also contribute to the formation and transformation of sexist and patriarchal societies.

The three contributors to this section on adult education and training explore distinct questions. Rockhill examines a group of women who desire to learn English but have little access to formal, or even informal instruction. Rockhill focuses on the contradictions involved in women's educational experiences — threat and desire, regulation and rebellion. In contrast to most studies that focus on such obstacles as insufficient institutional support, she looks unflinchingly at the ways in which the power relations between men and women, manifested through sexuality and violence, directly affect women's attitudes towards literacy and their participation in such programs. While Rockhill looks at the question of access and what it means to women, Jackson examines the question of content. She provides a critical analysis of "vocational knowledge" and how it has been defined by recent policy initiatives. In particular, she focuses on the new consensus, based on a reconstruction of the functional link between education and needs of the economy, concerning "skills" and "competence." Such a consensus, which harkens back to "Taylorism," is applied especially to occupational training in which women are predominant. Her work points to the ever-present problem of sexist and patriarchal curricula, and policy initiatives that support them. Such systematic bias is not something that is static or that has simply existed in the past; it emerges in new ways. In this context, Jackson's analysis is crucial.

Gaskell explores the dynamics of one clerical training program, asking what is taught and why. Moving inside the classroom, she raises the question of what counts as "skills" and how the value of skills is determined — for women, for the employer, or for the society at large. Underpinning her argument is the observation that women's skills have been discounted because women have not had the economic and political power to insist on their worth. To revalue women's work and women's skills is central to reorganizing the workplace and the educational system.

References

Association of Universities and Colleges of Canada. (1977). *The role of the university with respect to enrollments and career opportunities, admission policies, continuing education and community colleges* (A.U.C.C. Policy Studies, No. 1). Ottawa: A.U.C.C.

Astin, H.S. (1976). Continuing education and the development of adult women. *Counseling Psychologist, 6*(1), 55-59.

Avebury Research and Consulting Limited. (1986). *Decade of promise: An assessment of Canadian women's status in education, training and employment (1976-85)*. Toronto: Canadian Congress for Learning Opportunities for Women.

Boothby, D. (1986). *Women re-entering the labor force and training programs: Evidence from Canada*. Ottawa: Minister of Supply and Services.

Breault, L. (1986). Turning a male training model into a feminist one: Canadian Jobs Strategy re-entry. *Women's Education des Femmes, 5*(2), 14-17.

Buckland, L. (1985). *Education and training: Equal opportunities or barriers to employment? Research Studies of the Commission on Equality in Employment*. Ottawa: Minister of Supply and Services.

Butterwick, S., & Witter, S. (1991). *Gendered politics of Canadian labor market policy*. Unpublished paper.

Canada Employment and Immigration. (1986). *Annual statistical bulletin: National training Program (1984-85).* Ottawa: Author.

Canadian Association for Adult Education/Institut canadien d'éducation des adultes. (1982). *From the adult's point of view.* Toronto/Montreal: CAAE/ICEA.

Canadian Congress for Learning Opportunities for Women. (1984). *The National Training Act: Its impact on women.* Toronto: C.C.L.O.W.

Devereaux, M.S. (1985). One in every five: A survey of adult education in Canada. Ottawa: Minister of Supply and Services.

Freire, P. (1972). *Pedagogy of the oppressed.* Harmondsworth: Penguin.

Hootsman, H.M. (1980). Educational and employment opportunities for women: Main issues in adult education in Europe. *Convergence, 13*(1-2): 79-89.

Hughes, M., & Kennedy, M. (1980). Breaking out: Women in adult education. *Women's Studies International Forum, 6*(3), 261-269.

Hughes, M., & Kennedy, M. (1985). *New futures: Changing women's education.* London: Routledge and Kegan Paul.

Jayaweera. (1979). Programmes of non-formal education for women. *Convergence, 12*(3), 21-30.

Jean, M. (1984). Creating and communicating knowledge from a feminist perspective: The risks and challenges for women. In U.M. Franklin et al. (Eds.), *Knowledge reconsidered: A feminist overview.* Ottawa: Canadian Research Institute for the Advancement of Women.

Kidd, J.R., & Selman, G.R. (Eds.). (1978). *Coming of age: Canadian adult education in the 1960's.* Toronto: Canadian Association for Adult Education.

Letchworth, G.E. (1970). Women who return to college: An identity-integrity approach. *Journal of College Student Personnel, 11*(2), 103-106.

Lovell, A. (1980). Fresh horizons: The aspirations and problems of intending mature students. *Feminist Review, 6.*

McLaren, A.T. (1981). Women in adult education: The neglected majority. *International Journal of Women's Studies, 4*(2), 245-258.

McLaren, A.T. (1985). *Ambitions and realizations: Women in adult education.* London: Peter Owen.

McLaren, A.T. (1987). Rethinking "Femininity": Women in adult education. In J.S. Gaskell & A.T. McLaren (Eds.), *Women and education: A Canadian perspective* (pp. 333-350). Calgary: Detselig.

Pierson, R.R., & Cohen, M. (1984). Educating women for work: Government training programs for women before, during, and after World War II. In M.S. Cross & G.S. Kealey (Eds.), *Readings in Canadian Social History: Vol. 5. Modern Canada, 1930-1980's.* Toronto: McClelland and Stewart.

Purvis, J. (1976). The low status of adult education. *Educational Research, 19*(1), 13-24.

Royal Commission on the Status of Women. (1970). *Status of women in Canada.* Ottawa: Information Canada.

Royce, M.V. (1978). The common adventure of freedom. In J.R. Kidd & G.R. Selman (Eds.), *Coming of age: Canadian adult education in the 1960's.* Toronto: Canadian Association for Adult Education.

Scott, N.A. (1980). *Returning women students: A review of research and descriptive studies.* Washington, DC: National Association for Women Deans, Administrators, and Counselors.

Spender, D. (1980). Learning to create our own knowledge. *Convergence, 13*(1-2), 14-22.

Thompson, J. (1983). *Learning liberation: Women's responses to men's education.* London: Croom Helm.

Tittle, C.K., & Denker, E.R. (1980). *Returning women students in higher education: Defining policy issues.* New York: Praeger.

Tom, A.R. (1987). High hopes and small chances: Explaining conflict in a women's job training program. In J.S. Gaskell & A.T. McLaren (Eds.), *Women and education: A Canadian perspective* (pp. 371-388). Calgary: Detselig.

Walker, G. (1982). *Searching for the frame: A preliminary look at adult education, women and the work force.* Mimeograph. Toronto: O.I.S.E.

Walker, G.A. (n.d.). *Written with invisible ink: Women in the adult-education knowledge base (I).* Mimeograph. Ottawa: Carleton University.

Warren, C. (1990). *Female immigrants in technological training on the prairies: A search for self and community.* Unpublished manuscript.

Wilson, L., & Lipenski, B. (1978). A longitudinal study of mature students in credit programs. *Canadian Journal of University Continuing Education, 4,* 2.

Wolf, W., & Rosenfeld, R. (1978). Sex structure of occupations and job mobility. *Social Forces, 56*(3), 823-844.

Wolpe, A. (1980). Introduction to fresh horizons. *Feminist Review, 6.*

14
Literacy as Threat/Desire:
Longing to be SOMEBODY

Kathleen Rockhill

Education can be a highly charged and contradictory experience for women. Whether they actually attend programs or not, the "possibility" of participating — of "going to school" — carries with it images of hope and of fear. Women hope that education can deliver all it promises: that it will provide the means to a different life, a better life — a life in which they can be "somebody."

It is common today for education to be ideologically dressed as the pathway to a new kind of romance for women, the romance of a "career," a profession, a middle-class way of life; the image is one of a well-dressed woman doing "clean" work, important work. As such, it feeds her yearning, her desire, for a way out of the "working class" life she has known (Steedman, 1986). It is precisely because education holds out this promise for women that it also poses a threat to them in their everyday lives. This is especially true for women in heterosexual relationships when their men feel threatened by the images of power (independence and success) attached to education.

For women, education has been a primary site of regulation and of rebellion. The contradictory nature of education in women's lives was portrayed comically in the film, *Educating Rita.* In a rare depiction of how a woman actually *lived* returning to school, we see her turning away from her husband and the working class life she has known as she turns toward her male teacher to learn all that she has ever desired to be — a "lady" educated, cultured. Angered by her changes, Rita's husband burns her books. Much more tragic is the true story of Francine Hughes who, after years of suffering a nightmare of day-in and day-out brutality from her husband, seized upon education as her final site of resistance. Enraged at her for attending school, her husband did not stop at burning her books. Afterwards, Francine recalls, he continued to beat her:

> While he pounded on me, I slumped down, further and further, sinking into the corner. It was the loneliest moment of my life. It wouldn't matter how I yelled and screamed. Nobody would hear me; nobody would help me; nobody cared.
>
> Mickey said, "You dumb, mother-fucking whore, do you still think you're gonno go to school?" I felt my heart and my spirit break. "No, Mickey. I'm not gonna go to school." I'd lost. I was beaten, defeated, broken. He said, "Say it three times, a whore!" (McNulty, 1981:181)

Later that night, Francine finally broke out of his reign of terror by burning his and her house to the ground.

Although most of us can cite examples of women who have experienced male violence in connection with educational participation, we know little about how it is lived in women's lives. If violence is broadly defined to include non-physical forms, most women have experienced the threat that their having more education, or intelligence, or ideas of their own, poses for the people they know. In an intriguing study, Marian McMahon's (1986) work on the power of language suggests that, as a woman gains facility in a dominant language and uses it to express her ideas or experience, she is placed in a deeply contradictory bind: her "feminine" identity as a caretaker of others, as responsible for their sense of ego-strength, validity and authority, is disturbed, provoking the violence of those who feel themselves threatened or silenced by the power of her voice.

When violence is more narrowly defined to include male sabotage of educational efforts, whether through physical force or more subtle means, my guess is that a vast number of women are affected. Although systematic studies of women's experience of male resistance to (or support of) their educational efforts have not been undertaken, researchers are beginning to note the relationship (see Horsman, 1987; Ramdas, 1985; Thompson, 1983). As Ramdas stresses, "there must be a clear recognition of the role played by men in preventing women from going out of their homes and gaining access to equal opportunities" (p. 103). As she goes on to argue, women's participation in education must be considered in relation to the lack of control that they have over decision-making in their homes and communities, over money and property, over their bodies or biological processes, over religion, custom or tradition, as well as direct oppression by the men in their lives.

In order to look at how women's participation in education is embedded in the power dynamics between men and women, we need to look at how power operates in the concrete practices of everyday life: the direct opposition of men to women's participation in various forms of schooling; the general forms of male resistance to woman's participation in activities that may challenge her performance of traditional duties, as well as her gendered sexuality; the effect of male violence upon a woman who lives in the daily face of its threat, even if the violence is not explicitly directed against her participation in education programs. At its most fundamental, we need to ask how man's ownership of woman's labor and sexuality, her body and mind, affects her participation in education, and how education poses a threat to that ownership.

In the account that follows, I explore the ways in which education enters into the power relations between men and women. In particular, I look at how gender differences are constituted and constitutive of literacy practices in everyday life. I look at the relationship of literacy to sexuality and to violence, and to the public/private split between the words inhabited by men and women. My focus is upon how literacy is lived in the lives of Hispanic women who know little English. Although the study is based in the U.S., recent research on immigrant women in Canada suggest that this work has considerable relevance here (Das Gupta, 1986; Gannage, 1986; Ng, 1986; Roberts et al, 1987; Silvera, 1983; Skodra, 1987).

The analysis can draw upon a comparison between men and women, but the concentration upon the stories of women provides a basis for interpreting how gendered practices are integral to their understandings of their everyday lives.

Language, Literacy and Learning English

This study is based upon field work conducted in the West Side of Los Angeles from 1978 to 1982 (Rockhill, 1982). The location was chosen because of extensive local community contacts and because of the growing proportion (more than twenty-five percent) of Hispanics living there. While our focus was upon recent immigrants (most of whom are residing illegally in the country) who spoke little English, we interviewed other residents who spoke more English, as well as agency and community workers who were politically committed to working with the Hispanic community. The heart of this account is drawn from life-history interviews with approximately thirty-five Hispanic women, more than half of whom were recent immigrants. In addition to the life histories, we sought detailed descriptions of day-to-day interactions that led to the development of an inventory of situations in which the English language was encountered, and a description of how such situations were handled.

Without exception, the women we interviewed in this portion of the study were working-class, or lived at even more marginal levels of subsistence. Most had completed less than eight years of formal schooling. While the younger women tended to be more highly educated, only one had completed high school and been to university. Most were "economic refugees" from Mexico, and a few came from Guatemala, Columbia and Ecuador. We also interviewed more recent political refugees from San Salvador.

The "we" to whom I refer are my co-workers, university students, each of whom is fluent in Spanish and, in various ways, a participant in the local Hispanic community. Whether this effectively compensated for my being non-Hispanic and a very limited speaker of Spanish is difficult to answer. Certainly, it affected the way I worked and the questions I asked. My co-workers played an invaluable "translating role" and were themselves key informants, but the Hispanic women in the community with whom I could directly communicate provided me with my greatest sense of connection, as well as a sharp appreciation for the differences between my life and theirs. I will always regret not having been able to learn Spanish quickly enough to communicate, which painfully taught me how deeply our lives are structured by language *and* how difficult it is to learn, especially when one is absorbed in the multiple demands of daily life and opportunities for practice are limited.

"Illiteracy" is consistently conflated with language difference. Most of those branded as illiterate in the U.S. are not native speakers of English. In one of the first major studies to announce large numbers of adult "functional illiterates" in the U.S. (Adult Learning Project, 1975), 56 percent of those so classified were Spanish-surnamed. Official U.S. statistics suggest that Hispanic women are the largest single group categorized as "illiterate" (Hunter & Harman, 1979).

The people we interviewed do not directly talk about literacy. Instead they talk about not knowing English and being treated as though they are illiterate or stupid because of this. The women especially express feelings of shame, guilt and frustration at not being able to communicate in English. While both men and women stress the importance of knowing English — "it is of primordial importance" — at the same time they say that they get by OK without it. The general pattern is one of attending English classes soon after arrival and then stopping. If the couple is married, the wife goes with her husband and stops attending when he does. The men often complain about going to school in terms that suggest that they experience it to be demasculinizing: "I didn't like it," Luis explains, "because it made me feel nervous and it's a little embarrassing for a man to feel nervous, no?" In contrast, when the women talk of feeling confused, they tend to blame themselves for not understanding, explaining it in terms of being too preoc-cupied by family concerns to attend to the task of memorization. For example, Francita describes how her husband enjoyed listening to cassette tapes at night as a way of learning English, but she could not:

> . . . my head was with my children in El Salvador. I heard the cassettes and I didn't understand. I didn't understand anything. . . . I dedicated myself to think of my children. They hadn't written to me, what happened to them? Had they received the checks? All this, I couldn't dedicate myself to learning English.

All but the younger, more highly educated women stop going to classes, although the typical pattern is one of several attempts. Stopping is often precipitated by someone in the family getting sick, a change of work, or of living arrangements. They talk about worry, anxiety, too much on their minds, too much to do, feeling too old to concentrate and yet, express the hope that they will learn English: "God willing, I will learn one day," like a refrain, runs through their interviews. Gladys captures the sentiments of most:

> I am thinking of going to school within the next year. I went a few years ago, but I didn't continue because I had a problem with my eyes. Youth has more capacity to learn. But the mind of the old woman (she is forty-one) has more trouble with it. One thing or another, it's difficult to hold the reins of a house and family. And another thing to worry about work and whether there is going to be food and rent. So it appears to me that it is that, as well, the mind, and the words come in one time, but later I don't remember them.

But I think that, I am sure that I would learn it perfectly . . . you always regret it for not going to school, and for not learning. . . .

Whether married or the single head of a household, women are faced with the bulk of the work and emotional support necessary to maintain the family. These responsibilities are especially severe for immigrant women who must often live in combined families for several years after their arrival. In addition, the family they live with is typically that of their husband's parents. As Gannage points out in *Double Day; Double Bind* (1986), because the women must work a double day, there is no space in their lives to pursue actively potential paths of change. She notes that participation in union or educational activities is highly dependent upon knowing English, for which there is also no time.

The bind of the "double day" severely affects the women we interviewed. The issue of space — the lack of space for taking care of or developing oneself — is only partly due to the lack of time in the lives of working women; it is also because our lives are not allowed to take up space. That is to say, we have no space in part because we are seen and see ourselves as having no right to take up space, to put ourselves first, to say, "I want" or "I will." This frame of mind is structured by the day-in and day-out gendered ideological practices that construct us as totally responsible for the well-being of everyone else in the family *and* by the control of the men over our sexuality. In addition to the burdens of worry and double workloads borne by the Hispanic women we interviewed, their lives are structured so that they are confined, except for work or church, to the private sphere of the home. This confinement is a normal, taken-for-granted ritual embedded in the social and cultural practices of everyday life.

Furthermore, for some women, confinement is violently enforced by their husbands. Julia was so frightened of her husband that she spoke to us only once, on that occasion pouring out her story of imposed isolation:

> And there were three things that I wanted, like I wanted to eat: to know how to work, to know how to earn money, to understand what my children spoke in English and to know how to drive. These three things I wanted, like I wanted something to eat. He (husband) said, "No. The women here who work are just like any women and that these do this, here the women are like that, they start going out with others: I want my wife all for myself, not for other."

As was typical for the other women we interviewed, Julia's husband finally let her out of the home to work in order to supplement the family's income. In time, as she began to earn money, she felt strong enough to insist upon taking English classes, but she was terrified that he would make her stop.

As commentators talk about literacy they tend to decontextualize it from the lived realities of everyday life; they divide people into dichotomous categories, "the literate and the illiterate," "the motivated and the unmotivated," or "learners and non-learners." Both men's and women's experiences have been distorted by this ideological practice of violent abstraction. To attribute the experience of Gladys and the other women we interviewed to lack of motivation, to define them as illiterate, non-learners, is to do them a grave injustice.

To overcome this distortion, I have worked from a pluralistic conception of "literacies," looking at speaking, reading and writing practices in everyday life. But, I have also stayed with the symbolic conception of "literacy," and sought to understand what its meaning is in the lives of the women we interviewed. As the excerpt from Gladys' interview quoted in the foregoing reveals, there is a point at which taking classes is no longer conceptualized as learning to speak, read or write English, but as "going to school." It is in this transition, from thinking about acquiring specific literacies, to participation in a process of schooling or education, that literacy becomes symbolically associated with threat and desire.

Contextualizing literacy, breaking it down into literacy and language practices, looking for differences between the experiences of men and women, and seeking to understand how these are related to cultural as well as gender differences, has led me to see three ideas as important to explicating immigrant women's educational experiences. The first idea is that literacy is women's work but not women's right; the second idea is that the acquiring of English is regulated by material, cultural and sexist practices that limit women's access to the "public," confining them to the private sphere of the home; the third idea is that literacy is both threat and desire.

Literacy as Women's Work

By examining the women's everyday lives, we began to see that the women do most of the written work that involves English, whereas men do most of the spoken work. This is related to the confinement of women to the domestic sphere. Literacy becomes an extension of women's household work. This work, like the rest of housework and care for the family, is rendered invisible. Even the women are, by and large, not aware of the extent to which they handle written English as part of their daily chores and family responsibilities.

Women do most of the work of the household. In addition to domestic labor, they attend to most of the household business which involves the purchase of goods, as well as transactions around social services, public utilities, health care and the schooling of children. Most transactions requiring the use of forms are handled by the women. For example, while the husband typically goes to the bank, it is the wife who keeps track of the money. In a detailed inventory of English-language situations in everyday life, women report handling almost all of those which involve the use of the written word. For help, they turn to children, relatives or community workers. They turned to us repeatedly, asking us to assist in deciphering written forms, especially those related to monetary transactions. These transactions involved not only banking, but also employment, health care, major consumer purchases and home maintenance.

In contrast, when women enter the public domain where the English language is spoken, they do so in a variety of situations that do not arise on a regular basis. Shopping is the only exception, but to the extent possible, this is done in local markets where Spanish is spoken. In general, they do not experience frequent, repeated contact in linguistically similar situations, so they cannot learn to speak English through this work. If possible, they go with someone who can help them with English. Yet they do develop some facility in understanding written English, as we learned in the process of helping them fill out forms. We also came to appreciate that literacy is much more than a matter for "filling in the blanks." In a study of health care situations, I describe the complexity of the separate but interlocking social regulatory agencies with which women must be familiar in order to claim eligibility (Rockhill, 1984). Given the politically charged nature of their situations, it is not surprising that they depend upon trusted advocates, either friends or community workers, for assistance.

Our staff talked a lot about what we increasingly noticed as the invisibility of women's literacy in English. In most cases, when asked, wives say that their husbands know more English than they do. When couples are interviewed together, the man agrees that he knows more English. Sometimes further questioning reveals that the wife can read more, but often her greater facility with the written word is unacknowledged. This is not meant to imply that the women's literacy skills in English are good — only that they and their husbands perceive their literacy to be less than it is, and that the wives defer to their husbands as the one who is more competent. It is probably true in literacy situations involving language difference, where the dominant language is also the predominant spoken, official language, that facility with the spoken word has a greater presence than the written word. However, the wife's tendency to defer to the husband as the more proficient one also speaks to power issues between men and women.

My guess is that wives not only present their husbands as more competent, but believe that they are. In contrast with the men, most of the women say that they do not feel very confident in themselves, and talk of feeling ashamed. Several describe how their husbands "call them down," tell them they are stupid, illiterate, even whores; at the same time, they oppose their wives taking classes. Like other women we interviewed, Yolanda had studied English for awhile, but her new husband did not want her to continue her studies. She acquiesced saying, "OK, but one of us needs to study English. You go to school then." In time, he began to drink a lot and go around with other women. "I suffered a lot, many humiliations, too many offences. I remember that often he would tell me that I was illiterate."

Literacy is women's work, but not women's right. They do not experience their lives in terms of rights, but of responsibilities to their family and home. This is reflected in the form in which women tell their life stories.

Whereas the men present themselves as public figures, agents of their lives and the subjects of their histories through the experiences they recount, the women talk mostly about their families, the moves of their husbands, concerns for their children, hopes for their futures. The women prefer to learn English through classroom instruction; but the men, not the women, talk about their "right" to learn English. This is especially ironic since it is the men who are much more likely to learn English informally, through exposure to English language situations, whether at work or in other public arenas. In contrast, the women, who depend upon classes to learn the language, experience the greatest difficulties in attending.

The Public/Private Split

Individuals can learn a second language in two ways — either through informal, repeated contact with the spoken language or through formal instruction (Krashen, 1978; Schumann, 1978). Although typically some combination of the two forms is necessary, when one lacks opportunities for informal contact, formal instruction becomes more crucial. The primary reason women give for being unable to learn English is the lack of opportunities to practice. They want to attend classes in order to learn the language in part because they have fewer opportunities to practice spoken English than men have. This has a lot to do with the nature of the work available to them, and their confinement to the home.

Women talk of being afraid to speak in public, ashamed of not knowing English. Men stress the importance of talking, of making themselves understood by whatever means necessary. Men participate in and even control sectors of "the public" in a way that women cannot and do not. Because most public spaces are dominated by the English language, Hispanic men have demarcated spaces (e.g., clubs, restaurants, bars, sports, the neighborhood where they live) where they establish control and feel free to speak Spanish. Women tend to be excluded from these domains. There are no public places for Hispanic women to congregate. Potential exceptions are churches, parks, community centres or schools, but because these are riddled with all the problems of being in "the public," women meet male opposition, unless participation is in some way directly connected to family business.

Because they do not know enough English to feel that they can defend themselves, the women also express their fear of going out alone. In speaking about their fear, they describe their vulnerability to assault. They live in ghettos, in the heart of high-crime districts which stretch from one end of the city to the other. Like women everywhere, they feel themselves sexually preyed upon. Even if permitted to do so, they will not go out alone, especially not at night, not even to learn English. Moreover, since none of the women interviewed drives, they are dependent upon public transit — in Los Angeles, a very tedious and treacherous system to master even if fluent in English.

This public/private split is (re)constituted by the family. Not only must the women contend with the demands of the home but, because of sanctions against communication with others (Skodra, 1987), they must remain confined to the family as their primary site of interaction. The extended family provides an important source of support, but it is experienced as a highly contradictory support for married women, especially when ties with the husband's family dominate. Most husbands object to their wives going out and discourage them from learning how to drive except to perform the traditional work of women, or to earn money when it is essential to the family's survival. Confinement to the home is not unique to Hispanic women; a similar situation has been documented by research on different populations of immigrant women (Gannage, 1986; Skodra, 1987). As Gannage reports: "Many immigrant women rarely go out without being accompanied by their husbands. A night out with women friends or leisure activity independent from their husbands is unheard of" (p. 65).

Although most of the women have to work for the family to manage economically, the gendered structure of work is constitutive of and reconstitutes the public/private split. The work available to women tends to be an extension of their work at home and does not provide them with the opportunity to learn English in the same way that men can. This is a critical point. Not only do men have access to public spaces in a way that women do not, but this also means that there are some forms of work available to men through which they can learn English, and this is how most learn it. Work situations that involve contact with English-speaking people include construction, small restaurants, stores, and gardening. It is typical for a man to work with friends or relatives for a while who help them learn the ropes and the language, as well as assist them in acquiring loans for the relatively small amount of capital it takes to strike out on their own in these businesses. In Los Angeles, landscaping is especially popular; it requires little investment and is in demand, the year round, especially by the consumer-oriented, fun-loving gringo yuppies.

The range of work options open to women is much more limited. The choices narrow down to domestic or factory work. Unless a domestic worker happens upon a very unusual employer who helps her to learn English, she is confined to the home where she works and often lives in isolation, learning only the few English words that are specific to housework. In the factories, the possibility of learning English is even more bleak. As Ng and Estable (1986) point out, employment practices encourage the formation of "language ghettoes" which limit the possibilities of a woman's acquiring the official language even after years of working. there may be some forced interaction with the supervisor, but the language used on the floor — when it is possible to talk — is Spanish. In most forms of work, talk is restricted. Most of the day is spent in contact with a machine: "Also, as they say, something that doesn't help me out at all on my job is the fact that never do

I speak. Only sew, sew, sew. I don't have a chance to talk." So Gladys further elaborates upon her difficulty in learning English.

If a woman does manage to learn some English, she may be promoted to supervisor. As Westwood (1984) documents, this places her in a very uncomfortable position vis-à-vis her co-workers as she must enforce management policies. After promotion to supervisor, Clementina's boss wanted her to learn more English, but she resisted, feeling her separation from her friends and knowing that, no matter how much English she learned, there was no way for her to use it except to further the interests of management, alienating her even more from the women with whom she worked.

Ghettoization is brutally clinched by the heavy use of illegal labor — that is, the hiring of people without documents and paying them deplorably low wages. Also problematic is the quasi-legal status of people on temporary work permits. Lack of full legal status means constant fear of deportation for all. It would be a grave mistake to underestimate its effect for both men and women. With few work options, the responsibility of their children, and vulnerability to sexual abuse, the situation of women without documents is particularly severe. As Silvera's research (1983) reveals, this is especially true of domestic workers who are totally vulnerable to the whims of their employers. Consuelo describes being held captive at the age of fifteen: "her husband was one of those . . . um . . . he began to try to make me fall in love with him. . . ."

In their process of immigration, many of the single women we interviewed were sexually abused by men, sometimes under the guise of love, but often through overt violation. When they told their stories, they told them as hushed confidences. Bacilio does not have shame with which to contend. After telling of his sister's narrow escape from rape by three men, "cayotes," whom she paid to transport her across the border, he candidly adds: "you know, it is a lot of work and difficult for a woman to come up here from Mexico. It's very rare that a woman makes it up here without having been molested." Women who are in the country legally and not married are vulnerable in another way. Since marriage is one of the few ways to acquire legal status, men seek out women who will marry them. It is not uncommon for the man to be already married. One woman found out the night before she was to be married that her groom-to-be had a family in Mexico.

Literacy as Threat

When I began my research on literacy I asked nothing about sexuality. It quite amazes me that, despite this bias in my work, so many incidents were revealed — too many to ignore.

Maria's voice echoes in my mind. I don't know if I will ever forget her passionate cry; I know that I don't want to.

> I don't want to be a housekeeper all my life. I would like to be somebody, you know. . . . I would like to go out to talk to people, to work, to do

something interesting, to help somebody. It's terrible, because they say, "You are the woman. You have to stay in the home, you have to do dinner." You have to do *everything.*

Like Yolanda, Maria is one of the many women we interviewed whose husband would not permit her to go out of the house. Even before they were married, he had objected to her going to school, and she finally stopped going. When I interviewed her, she expressed her strong desire to study, to return to school, to do work that feels meaningful to her . . . to be *somebody.* Since her marriage and birth of a child, she has felt her husband change toward her, treating her more brutally, leaving her night after night to go out with his friends. Alone, isolated, she feels that she is no one. In a similar way, Yolanda describes how her husband changed after her marriage: "with the years, he began to see that I was absolutely alone, and he thought . . . why shouldn't I treat her this way?" At the time of the interviews, Maria was dreaming of running away to Mexico with her child, and Yolanda, already separated from her husband for several years, was working as a cleaning woman and returning to school in the hope of becoming a secretary.

Marriage, rather than education, is the "rite of passage" for the Latina. Marriage is the only way out of her parents' home; it is the only legitimate option for her to get out from under her father's control. With the exception of Clementina, who at the age of twenty-eight lived at home under the strict authority of her father and brothers, all the women we interviewed had been married. As Teresa, in her interview by Coles & Coles (1978), explains:

> Your whole life depends upon your husband. My aunt tells my cousins what kind of man to marry — someone who will take care of you and protect you. I have dreamt that I would someday meet a man who would have a lot of money, and he would have a big car, and we would drive away and live in a big house. Then I will have a happy life. But I won't meet a man like that. (p. 131)

In general, unless they are more highly educated, husbands are opposed to their wives taking classes or learning more than the rudiments of literacy in English. Once the acquisition of literacy moves beyond a question of basic survival skills, it carried with it the symbolic power of education. As such, it poses a threat to the power (im)balance in the family. Men want to feel in control; not only does this mean having more power than their wives, but controlling what they think and do. This is especially so when the man feels little or no power at work, or in the family as the "breadwinner," or in other social positions associated with masculinity. This may explain the large investment in the "macho act" of drinking. According to the women we interviewed, masculinity as domination is especially brutal in a culture where machismo reigns. The words of Maria echo the feelings of many: "I don't want a macho. I want a man."

Many of the women live with a great deal of violence in their daily lives. Alcoholism, or heavy drinking by their husbands, leaves them feeling desperate. It takes time for this underbelly of family violence to emerge.

After six interviews, Modesta broke down and sobbed: "He drinks a lot, he is very much like a man. Right now, things aren't going very well for us. He loves his children very much but he treats me badly. Very badly." As she told this story, she did so by way of explaining why her plans to return to school were continually aborted and unrealizable. Several other women related stories of being beaten; some left their homes, called the police or turned to the priest. Rosa related part of her story:

> It got to the point where he was drinking so much. He'd come home and try to beat up on all of us. My children were very small. I used to tell him, "You can do anything to me" — he'd get mad at me and beat me up — "but please don't touch the children. Leave them alone."

There are many more stories. Sometimes the violence is physical, sometimes more subtle. While it is true that not all the women talk of violence, it is also true that we asked very little about marital relationships — we did not even directly ask about her husband's attitude toward her going to school. These stories came out in the course of informal conversations between women about how literacy and English-language practices fit into the texture of their daily lives. It is the fact that I did not explicitly look for this information, and did not fully appreciate its significance when I heard it, that makes me aware of the importance of reconceptualizing how we think about literacy and educational participation where it involves women.

One reason why I have stayed away from including these incidents of violence in past accounts is that I do not want to feed into racist, class-biased stereotypes about "Mexicans." In time, I have begun to rebel against this privileging of race and class over sexual violence. I can no longer tolerate protecting men at the cost of continuing to silence women's violation.

While all women do not talk of violence, I want to stress that, under conditions of systematic sexism, we are oppressed through sexual practices that are enshrined as normal by the family, church, and other social institutions. While its form varies, violence toward women is not limited to a particular class or culture — and it has consequences that must be taken seriously if we really mean to address the question of woman's right to learn.

It saddens me greatly as I write this. I have lived in the face of male rage and violence. I have a feeling for what it means to live daily in the face of threat, never knowing what act will be interpreted as a transgression, an attack upon *male right* or power (Corrigan, 1986), setting off an explosion. You risk doing nothing to set off that rage and withdraw into the safety of a kind of death. The consequence is that you do not even consider the possibility of moving in what is perceived as a potentially threatening direction.

I am extremely privileged in comparison with the women I interviewed. I cannot help but think of how much more severely they are trapped if they live in a violent home situation. As the entry point to further education, literacy especially can be experienced as a threat that furthers withdrawal;

not only is there the continuing threat of violence at home with which to contend, but the lack of economic and social options for leaving. A husband does not have to oppose directly his wife's taking classes for the wife to censor herself and never allow the possibility. In situations where violence is part of daily life, and overwork already severe, it is almost impossible to find the energy to move in new directions, especially when these mean further upheaval and violence.

Literacy as Desire

Women are more likely to develop their English literacy skills once they are separated or divorced. Several of the women we interviewed had left their husbands and talked of changing their lives through education. For example, Patricia left the factory, explaining, "I know I am capable of doing something more than running a machine." Like the other, younger women we interviewed, she knows enough English so that she can see the possibility of finding a different kind of work. Youth, education and knowing some English tend to go together, as do the hope and desire for a better life. The influence of the women's movement in the dominant culture is an ingredient in the change in perspectives of some of the younger women. Undoubtedly, this is also a factor in male opposition as traditional gender divisions and sexual control is being resisted by women who want to do "something" with their lives. Maria expands upon her yearning "to be somebody";

> In the future, I would like to go to school . . . because I would like to have something more meaningful than a factory job. If I go to the school, I want to try to find some interesting job — you know — to learn how to get some more money doing something different because I need to be some other woman, you know. I don't want to be the same all the time.

Clearly, as a public space, school poses, for women, the possibility of contact with other women. Moreover, the school, and English, are both products of the dominant culture, as well as the passageway toward integration within it. English carries all of the power of the dominant language, as well as its cultural and social representations. To underline an obvious point, literacy is much more than a set of reading and writing skills. Literacy is a language and it is always about something. It cannot be separated from political processes that produce the content of the texts read, nor from the social situation in which readers relate to the texts. Literacy is a social practice, as well as a discursive and ideological practice, and it symbolizes becoming "educated." Just as education is embedded in sexist and racist regulatory practices of social control (Rockhill, 1987), it also produces and responds to the desire to change — to move out of one's class and cultural location, out of the confines of one's home — to become a lady, to be "some other woman," to do more fulfilling work, "to live a life," as one woman put it.

When women talk of literacy, they express feelings of desire. They have the desire to one day learn English, to go to school. Despite this desire, they do not think of literacy as a "right" for themselves, but for their husbands and their children. Acutely keen is their desire for their children to become educated.

Women do not put themselves first, but last, within the family. Even Elena, the highly educated, gifted woman we interviewed, now works as a domestic. Still, she explains how it is that she thinks of her life as a success:

> I consider myself to be a successful woman because I went to the school and they told me that my son was the best and that he likes to study. That is a triumph for me. And then, my husband says to me, "My work is going better and better." This is also a success for me.

Elena had to stop taking English classes because she could not find the time, with the combination of extensive family responsibilities and working as a domestic laborer six days a week. She accepts that she will never return to her profession, and devotes all her energies to providing a better life for her family.

As indicated, education symbolizes the hope for a better life, a different life, a way out of the working class into a world of middle class culture and lifestyle. The dream, for most women, is that they and/or their daughters can enter this world through secretarial work, nursing or teaching. For women whose only options are field, domestic, or factory work, the world of commercial and professional practice holds the hope of looking like and of being "somebody." This is what I think Maria means when she says, "I would like to be a somebody, you know."

Yolanda, working nights as a cleaning woman, talks of saving to send her daughters to finishing school and of providing them with a superior education so that:

> They have the way of getting a good job, without killing themselves, without having to work in the job that I have, which is not a . . . it's not a job which one can be ashamed of, but it's not a very clean job. Work is work, right? Because I work in this, I think that I am no less than others who work in offices, right? But if they have the way to work in an office, to have contact with people who have an education which is a bit higher than one has, then your children are going to improve.

Office work is clean work; it is also the way to meet a desirable partner for those who are unmarried. It is the home of dominant cultural images of femininity which depict slim, well-dressed, unmarried, beautiful, smiling women, working in offices. This image holds out the promise of marriage to a non-macho man and, as such, it poses a threat to the Hispanic male. Marriage is not questioned by the women we interviewed. Instead, the violence of marriage is explained in terms of machismo, not the institution itself and the power dynamic it constitutes.

The occupational structure of women's work is also significant to understanding the romanticization of office work. The primary way out of factories for women historically has been through employment in offices, teaching, nursing, or other forms of the "helping" professions. That these jobs are highly literacy dependent — that is, they demand highly developed literacy skills — is important to understanding the gendering of literacy. For women there has not been a middle level of work, where *some* capacity to speak, read and write in the dominant language is enough; instead these capacities have to be highly developed for movement into a more desirable kind of work. Except for the young and highly educated, the women we interviewed cannot learn enough English to move into the next stratum of occupations open to them.

While efforts to train women for work in the trades are noteworthy and potentially significant (Das Gupta, 1986), these initiatives will be problematic unless the issue of literacy as desire is addressed. The women who were interviewed do not want to be machinists; they want to be secretaries — and this work is being revolutionized by technology. If women are to turn to another kind of work, they have to see this as desirable, and this means that the dominant, sexualized and gendered images of desirable work for women have to change. It also means that proficiency in the English language cannot be used as a prerequisite to training, and that possibilities for learning English have to be better structured into the material and oppositional realities of women's lives. An obvious "solution" is to offer programs that teach "English in-the-workplace" but, unless other opportunities for schooling and education are also opened to immigrant women — unless the symbolic and ideological significance of literacy as schooling is addressed — the consequence will be to continue the class and ethnic biases of education.

Conclusion

This account suggests how gender difference is constituted and constitutive of literacy practices in everyday life. Even in something that appears as asexual as literacy, gender difference cannot be separated from domination through woman's sexuality. This is vividly portrayed by the public/private split between the worlds inhabited by men and women, the ways in which it is lived and enforced.

Under conditions of systematic sexism, gender means domination for women. Domination is economic and sexual. It is lived through our bodies, our family structures, our work, our cultural and educational practices, and the structure of the labor market.

Not to conceptualize themselves as having rights, to put themselves last, whether by choice or force, to take on the bulk of the responsibility for the family, is typical of the women we interviewed. In the case of physical violence, a woman bears it until it affects her children, rather than break up the family and break out of her enforced isolation.

Sexuality and literacy are connected. Woman's sexual domination is reproduced as literacy is lived through the gendered practices of the family and society. Literacy is integral to how our subjectivities are constructed so that these practices are taken to be natural and normal.

Women engage in literacy practices as part of the work of the family. When it becomes associated with education, literacy poses the potential of change and is experienced as both a threat and a desire. Thus, the anomaly that literacy is women's work but not women's right. And, the related anomaly that, in the "public" world of work, women who are not fluent in English are barred from access to the highly literacy-dependent work of women.

The images of desire associated with literacy and education are associated with images of the middle class, femininity and anglo ethnocentrism. These images pose a threat to traditional Hispanic family relations, especially when they challenge the male's experience of his masculinity. In these situations, the woman's participation in schooling can exacerbate violence. As such, it also poses a threat to women who do not want to put their families or themselves at risk.

To act seriously upon the principle of literacy or learning as a right — or even a possibility — for women, we must reconceptualize how we think about "the political" to include "the personal." Our educational work suffers from a splitting between the public and the private which reinforces the domination of women through gendered practices. While we have begun to look into reproductive practices, we are wary of acknowledging the centrality of family, religious, and other cultural forms, as well as sexual practices, to women's oppression. We act as though literacy is neutral, is some way apart from these forms, and so miss its charged dynamic for women. We must be willing to venture into the sensitive world of the supposedly private sphere; the sanctified realm of the family and church, the hidden realm of the sexual. The constitution of our subjectivity, and the ways in which literacy/learning/education enter into that constitution, also becomes a key political question.

References

Adult Performance Level Project (1975). *Adult functional competency: A summary.* Austin: University of Texas.

Coles, R., & Coles, H. (1978). *Women at crises: Lives of struggle and hope.* New York: Delacorte Press.

Corrigan, P. (1986). "Masculinity as right: Some thoughts on the geneology of 'rational violence'." Unpublished manuscript.

Das Gupta, T. (1986). *Learning from our history: Community development by immigrant women in Ontario, 1958-1986.* Toronto: Cross-Cultural Communication Centre.

Gannage, C. (1986). *Double day, double bind.* Toronto: Women's Press.

Horsman, Jenny (1990). *Something on my mind besides the everyday: Women and literacy.* Toronto: Women's Press.

Hunter, Carman St. J., & Harman, D. (1979). *Adult illiteracy in the United States.* New York: McGraw-Hill.

Krashen, S.D. (1978). "The monitor model for second-language acquisition." In R.C. Gringas, (Ed.) *Second language acquisition and foreign language teaching.* Arlington, Va.: Center for Applied Linguistics.

McMahon, M. (1986). "A circuitous quest: things that haunt me when I write." Unpublished manuscript.

McNulty, F. (1981). *The burning bed.* New York: Bantam.

Ng, R. (1981). "Immigrant women in Canada: A socially constructed category." *Resources for Feminist Research.*

Ng, R., & Estable, A. (1986). "Immigrant women in the labour force: Issues of social, economic and demographic concern." Unpublished manuscript presented to the Review Demography Directorate, Health and Welfare Canada.

Ramdas, L. (1985). "Illiteracy, women and development." *Adult education and development.* German Adult Education Association, No. 24.

Roberts, B., et al (1987). Looking for a greener future: Women workers in the Winnipeg garment industry. Toronto: New Hogtown Press.

Rockhill, K. (1982). "Language training by Latino immigrant workers: The sociocultural context." Unpublished report to National Institute of Education, Washington, D.C.

Rockhill, K. (1984) "Health crises in the lives of non-English-speaking Latino immigrants: Language legalities and trusted advocates." Unpublished manuscript.

Rockhill, K. (1987). "Gender, language and the politics of literacy." *British Journal of Sociology of Education.* 8(2), 153-167.

Schumann, J.H. (1978). "The acculturation model for second-language acquisition." In R.C. Gringas, (Ed.) *Second-language acquisition and foreign language teaching.* Arlington, Va.: Center for Applied Linguistics.

Silvera, M. (1983). *Silenced.* Toronto: Williams-Wallace.

Skodra, E. (1987). "A reinterpretation of southern European immigrant women: Everyday life experience." Toronto: OISE Ed.D. thesis draft.

Steedman, C. (1986). *Landscape for a good woman: A story of two lives.* London: Virago.

Thompson, J.L. (1983). *Learning liberation: Women's response to men's education.* London: Croom-Helm.

Westwood, S. (1984). *All day, every day: Factory and family in the making of women's lives.* London: Pluto Press.

15

Skill Training in Transition:
Implications for Women[1]

Nancy S. Jackson

Preface

The literature on work, skill and training has burgeoned since this article was written in the mid-1980s. The new literature reflects complex processes of rapid change in the nature of technology and its impact from sector to sector, in the character of women's work in many settings, and in our understanding of how concepts like "skill" are part of a social and political process. In a number of important ways, these developments have overtaken the analysis presented here; the same argument could not be written in 1990. However, there is one important way in which the relevance of this analysis is undiminished. That is, the existing infrastructure of education and training for work remains firmly rooted in the view of skills which is discussed here. Thus, the analysis presented can show us much of what is wrong with the way programs of education and training are conceptualized and administered. That this is true is a measure of obsolescence in our public institutions and an indicator of the importance for women of the clamor for reform to which this analysis is still meant to contribute.

Introduction

Over the last decade, women's groups in Canada at the national, provincial and local levels have fought long and hard to secure a fair deal for women in post-secondary education in general, and in college and institute-based programs of vocational/technical education and training in particular. The issue of access has dominated these efforts to date, because structural barriers to women in this sector (which includes a wide range of employment-oriented courses in both male and female dominated fields) have been blatantly discriminatory and have contributed to the continuing economic disadvantage and dependence of a majority of Canadian women.

However, in the last few years, changes have taken place in the vocational/technical sector that pose a different kind of threat to women's interests. The new threat lies not with the problem of access, but with the growing interest of policy makers in courses that service the short-term needs of employers. The design of instruction driven by this concern leads to problems within the learning environment itself. The conceptualization and organization of such instruction lead potentially, I will argue here, to impoverishment of the substance of vocational knowledge itself and to the separation of skills from the power and status of workers. While these developments are widespread in the arena of vocational and technical education and training, and affect both men and women, they should be of particular concern to feminists who see education and training as an important avenue for improving the economic status of women.

Although the issue of "skill training" has recently gained a good deal of public attention, North American academics have conventionally overlooked these "applied" programs, dismissing them as practical, instrumental, and therefore largely unproblematic from an educational point of view. This distinction between academically and vocationally oriented education produces some regrettable results. Strategically, it results in a dearth of critical investigation of the kinds of learning opportunities beyond public school which are accessible to the majority of the Canadian population, and on which women in particular rely heavily for entry to the labor market. Theoretically, the distinction perpetuates some very powerful but unexamined assumptions about the character of knowledge, skills and learning related to working life. These assumptions have been particularly damaging to our understanding of women's work and skills.

This paper will explore how concepts like "skill" and "competence" have been used by policy makers in the last decade to organize a new public consensus about the goals of education. I will argue that the interests of learners in general and women in particular are jeopardized by the current focus on the "requirements of industry" and the "needs" of the labor market, and that both a theoretical critique and political analysis are required to discern and defend women's interests in this context. This undertaking leads to some fundamental questions about the goals and objectives of current training policy in Canada.

Training Fever: Crisis and Solution

It has become commonplace to characterize the present decade as a period of educational crisis, and to locate the relation between education and work at the heart of the problem. As economic prosperity has faltered across the industrialized world, disrupting the fit between demand and supply of labor, aspects of educational provision have been widely identified as both a cause and a solution to the problem. Public schools have been charged with inefficiency and ineffectiveness in delivering the basic skills necessary to both social and employment situations. The post-secondary sector has been criticized for giving priority to the concept of individual opportunity rather than responding to the demands of the market for educated labor. Across North America and Western Europe there has been a resurgence of the view that the education system in its entirety should be understood in terms of its contribution to economic development and national prosperity (Carnegie Council, 1980; CEIC, 1983; Knave, 1984; OECD, 1983).

This general shift in the policy climate has led to a sharp reversal of the laissez-faire environment of educational expansion in the 1960s, and has brought increasing pressure to re-assert, indeed to reconstruct, a functional link between the educational apparatus and the needs of the economy (Avis, 1981; Finn, 1982; Gleeson, 1983). There has been a marked resurgence of the highly technocratic and instrumentalist view that the needs of industry can best be served by achieving a tighter definition of the "fit" between technical qualifications and the demands of the work process, and then by restructuring the educational system to match these specifications (Avis, 1981; Finn, 1982; Moore, 1983). In this context, post-secondary technical and vocational education has emerged as the centerpiece of both educational and labor market policy. Observers have referred to this as the dawn of a new mass education sector for the twenty-first century (see e.g., Gleeson, 1983).

Critics of these developments argue that educational policy is being used in the present context as the solution to problems that are essentially economic and political in origin (see Donald, 1979; Gleeson, 1983). They argue as well that the current emphasis on training amounts to a re-assertion of the work ethic as a means of social discipline in the face of declining real opportunities for work, particularly among youth (see Bates, 1984). These criticisms grow out of an ongoing theoretical debate about the relationship between social and technical relations in the educational enterprise, and reflect, in part, the current emphasis on social aspects of production relations, such as hierarchies of power and knowledge, discipline, and attitudes toward work (Avis, 1981; Gleeson & Mardle, 1980; Gorz, 1976; Hussain, 1976). Such criticisms, however, stop short of examining another aspect of the social character of the educational enterprise, the constitution of job knowledge itself. That is, education and training processes themselves are integral to the social construction of job knowledge, i.e., the process of determining what "counts" as legitimate job knowledge. This process of determination is highly consequential for employers and employees alike, and is integral to the politics of the work place as well as of the educational environment. This paper formulates, in a preliminary way, this constitutive process as a topic for examination.

Skills: The New Consensus

On both sides of the Atlantic, the concept of skill has become the lynch-pin of otherwise diverse strategies and objectives for change, orchestrating a broad public consensus about educational goals. It is important to notice that its usefulness in this regard depends upon what James Donald has called the "loose and baggy character" of the concept itself (1979:13; see also CCCS, 1981). "Skills" has become a metaphor for the total output of all our institutions of learning, and a standard by which they should be judged. "Skills" is used as measurement of accomplishment or of readiness for entry to almost any endeavor, be it private or public, economic or social. The list is familiar: basic skills, job skills, life skills . . . even "thinking skills" as seen in the title of an annual education conference in Cincinnati, Ohio.

As a curricular category the concept of skills is particularly useful because it appears to be "indifferent to contents. . . . an empty space into which a whole range of contents [can] be inserted" (Grahame, 1983:5). Because the concept of skill carries with it overtones of status representing whatever is knowledgeable, even scientific, it lends an aura of authority to whatever falls in its shadow. It also serves to indicate that the need for innovation in education is driven by economic circumstances, implying a common stake in the outcome. For all these reasons, the concept has become in the last decade a dominant form of popular understanding about the purpose and objectives of education (CCCS, 1981).

A number of critics have pointed out that the concept of skills has achieved a place at the pinnacle of educational rhetoric by appearing to neutralize what is at its root a fundamental conflict between capitalist imperatives and popular needs. Lenhardt (1981:213) captures the breadth of this critique in the following passage:

> . . . the concept of educational interests has been replaced by the concept of skill requirements, which is seen as being determined by economic growth or technological process. Both economic growth as well as technological progress are conceived of as having political relevance but being themselves of rather technical, "apolitical" nature. If the identification of educational interests and their transformation into educational policies is regarded as a technical problem rather than a matter of mediating conflicting social interests, then public democratic discourse with regard to educational matters is rendered meaningless.

Lenhardt argues that the concept of skills puts the discussion of educational objectives on apparently neutral territory. It invokes a realm of abstract necessity, where skill may stand in for imperatives that are qualitatively diverse and even contradictory.

Underneath this abstract consensus, however, lies a long history of struggle between employers and workers for control over the organization of work processes and over the supply and demand for qualified labor. On the employers' side, the need for skills has been subject to a particular time, place and stage of economic development, but never straightforwardly determined by technical or technological considerations. Instead, the demand for skills has always been mediated by social and political considerations relevant to the control of work (Edwards, 1979; Gordon et al., 1982; Noble, 1984), in which the technical factors are themselves embedded (Althusser, 1971; Gleeson & Mardle, 1980; Gorz, 1976). Central to these political considerations has been the interest of employers in minimizing their costs of labor, an interest which affects the determination of "need" in terms of the quantity and quality of education and training which are desirable from the employers' point of view (Blackburn & Mann, 1979; Finn, 1982;). Among workers and workers' organizations, the concept of skill has been an organizing device in the struggle for political, economic and social power, and control over educational measures has proved to be an important aspect of that struggle (see Barrett, 1980; Clement, 1981; Gaskell, 1983; More, 1980). It is important to keep in mind that these longstanding political divisions over the management of skill are the context in which the enterprise of vocational/technical education is embedded.

Since the mid-1970s, the use of the concept of skill to orchestrate decision-making about public policy in education has reached a new degree of sophistication. Educational planners and policy makers have turned their attention from the problem of "matching" demand and supply, to a concern for the way in which occupational skills are constituted, organized, and controlled in the context of learning. Historical forms of organization and control that invest skill within the purview of the worker, for which apprenticeships are the paradigm, have come to be seen as a limitation on the prerogative of employers to acquire, deploy and dispose of labor power according to their own interests. Previous concepts of craft mastery are being replaced by a different logic of skill in which the worker is in an employer-dependent role in a labor hierarchy (Blackburn & Mann, 1979). Such a shift gives the employer more control over the specification and utilization of knowledge and skills and thus greater flexibility in the deployment of labor power. Facilitating this flexibility has become a central objective in the reform of vocational education and training.

The Competency Solution

In this climate, the concept of competence has emerged as a guiding principle of vocational instruction. It has found favor among employers and educators alike because it promises to specify the content of skill (in any given area) for the purpose of its teaching and learning. It transforms the abstract claim of skill, as something that one possesses, into a more tractable form as something that one can do or perform. The latter form is seen to be superior for educational purposes inasmuch as it makes skill amenable to measurement, assessment and certification. The movement to use competence as the organizing principle of a variety of delivery systems in post-secondary education has reached bandwagon proportions (Spady, 1977). It is widely in use in the United States in two year and even four-year post secondary institutions, including some liberal arts programs (see Grant, 1979). It is the basis of curriculum used throughout Great Britain under both the Technician Education Council and the Business Education Council, established in the mid-1970s (see Cantor & Roberts, 1979). In Canada, competency systems are being introduced by provincial ministries across the country at the technical and applied programs level (Jackson, forthcoming). Commentators on this phenomenon point out that competency-based learning seems to be "ready-made" for the educational concerns of our time: cost-effectiveness, accountability, and specificity of outcomes (Gamson, 1979). As leading American proponents of the approach have phrased it, "stockholders in the enterprise of education are demanding better dividends than they have been receiving in recent decades" (Harris & Grede,

1977:253). The competency approach promises to eliminate what is super-ficial, to ensure quality of output, and to guarantee results by linking student performance to institutional accountability. The basic features of the approach that form the basis for these claims are described in the brief which follows.

Competency-based approaches to vocational/technical education specify very particular learning objectives and methods. First, they identify the employer as the primary consumer or end-user of occupational skills, and thus assign primary responsibility for defining learning objectives to employer groups within an occupational area. Commonly, these objectives are established in a controlled workshop setting under the direction of a curriculum specialist, and the product of the workshop process is called a skill profile. The skill profile is then passed on to educators for translation into educational plans and materials designed to meet the specified objectives. Secondly, competency-based approaches carefully specify the learning outcomes to be achieved in performative or behavioral rather than cognitive terms: hence the term "competency." The standard of accomplishment, and the basis of evaluation to which the instructional process is oriented, is the performance of specified, observable tasks, e.g., "to prepare ledger entries," "to transcribe dictated material," etc. The acquisition of these performance capabilities, rather than conceptual understandings of work tasks, is the legitimate object of the instructional process in the competency-based approach (Grant et al., 1979; Knaak, 1977; Parnell, 1978; Spady, 1980). This type of learning is widely accepted as appropriate for many vocational areas, and though even at the level of liberal arts instruction (see Ewan, 1979), though at that level it is subject to somewhat more debate and experimentation.

The concept of competence and the methods that have been introduced to education under its aegis are not new. Their history extends back to the turn of the century and the well-known work of the American Frederick W. Taylor ([1911] 1947) on scientific management and job analysis techniques (see Neumann, 1979; Tyler, 1975). Taylor made popular the basic techniques of job analysis adopted in competency-based systems, although he did not develop extensively the implications of this technique for education. The first large scale experiments with the educational applications of Taylor's ideas came in the United States with the onset of World War I and the resultant demand to train tens of thousands of trades people and technicians to support the war effort, both within the armed services and in the shipyards, munitions plants and other war industries. Leading vocational educators hired by the U.S. War Department to design training schemes brought with them the unmistakable influence of Taylorism (see for example, Allen, 1919; Dooley, 1919). The resulting war-time training programs were widely acclaimed and led to a number of post-war publications which, in turn, were highly influential in the wider educational community (see e.g., Chapman, 1921; Mann, 1922; Toops, 1921) . This accumulated experience of wartime training, combined with the work on scientific method in curriculum of the well-known educators Bobbit (1918) and Charters (1923), produced by the mid 1920s most of the salient features of competency-based education as it continues to be practiced to the present day (Newmann, 1979). In the 1920s these methods were hailed as measures for efficiency and economy in the educational sphere, and it is exactly these same ends that the competency approach has been called upon to serve in the 1970s and 80s.

In general, the competency approach shifts the practice in vocational/technical programs to more narrow, short-term, instrumental educational objectives. This is an integral part of the premise that competency programs are more flexible and responsive to the "needs" of industry than training programs have been in the past. This flexibility is accomplished by the replacement of lengthy and comprehensive programs and certifications with limited forms of training to levels specified by the employer to meet short-term goals. It involves treating knowledge and skills as incremental, i.e., subdivisible into component parts, and cumulative, so that they can be acquired over a lifetime in a pattern of recurrent work and schooling. This organization of learning is said to satisfy the needs of the worker for early access to the workforce, and to facilitate easy passage back and forth from work to training on a recurring basis throughout the adult working life. Thus the interests of all parties appear to be addressed.

Competency Criticized

The competency approach has also been the target of criticism on a number of grounds, and some of the leading criticisms are as old as the methods themselves. John Dewey's objections to vocationalism at the turn of the century foreshadow the most common criticisms of the competency approach to vocational instruction today. Dewey argued that narrow occupational instruction would "develop a machine-like skill in routine lines" but would sacrifice in the process those "qualities of alert observation and coherent and ingenious planning which make an occupation intellectually rewarding" ([1915] 1966:310). He further objected that to restrict the character of learning in the present would be to "injure the possibilities of present development and thereby to reduce the adequacy of preparation for a future right employment." He warned that such training was suited to "an autocratically managed society," where "a few do the planning and ordering, [while] the others follow directions and are deliberately confined to narrow prescribed channels of endeavor" ([1915] 1966:310).

Dewey's remarks were aimed at the practice of vocational instruction in the high school, at a time when vocational specialization of secondary education was being widely debated. Today, Dewey's concerns are echoed in more contemporary language in objections to the fragmentation and specialization of learning in the post-secondary sector. In Great Britain, critics of the use of competency-based curriculum in the Technician Education Council, the Business Education Council, and Manpower Services

Commission have claimed that its undue emphasis on behavioral objectives leads to a "prefabricated and encyclopaedic notion of knowledge," to the belief that "lists can represent the structure of knowledge," and to procedures that are shallow, quick and easy to put into effect. The approach, say the critics, tends to emphasize the learning of routine, unimportant, even trivial material, to inhibit valuable developments in the learning process (Cantor & Roberts, 1979:63-79), and to "block the development of elaborated knowledge or the formation of a coherent political consciousness" (Moore, 1983:30). In Canada, the competency approach has been criticized in a more philosophical vein for its reliance on behaviorist principles, with the charge that it suffers from "excessive reductionism" and failure to account for "intention and meaning" or the "motivational aspects of purposeful action" (Collins, 1983:177). Whatever the critical paradigm, the criticisms suggest that the competency approach stands in opposition to the traditional concepts of working knowledge which have been defended historically by the working class. It reduces the likelihood that education might provide "really useful knowledge" (Johnson, 1979), i.e., that which contributes to the workers' understandings of their own conditions. It raises instead the prospect of a form of schooling which "contributes to depriving the individual of autonomous control over the work process and his [sic] living conditions" (Lenhardt, 1981:200). It thus reduces the potential in education for collectivization of workers' knowledge and the political power which that brings, and increases the potential of the use of working knowledge to assert the interests of capital over those of workers.

Under scrutiny, the whole concept of competence, and the flexibility which it promises, can be seen to be deeply embedded in the employers' interests in labor power. The process of converting a work process into a skill profile of competencies to be mastered subsumes, and depends for its sense upon, the particular social forms in which work is organized in the workplace. But that larger work process itself is specifically excluded as an object of instruction. This form of learning has built into it the subordination of the worker to the employer, not as a matter of proper attitudes or discipline, but as a feature of the division of working knowledge itself. Thus, within the very terms of working knowledge is inscribed the social form of the division of labor which ties together workers and employers in the service of capital.

Through competency-based education, the particular form of the organization of working knowledge is transplanted from the workplace into the educational institutions as that form in which working knowledge will be disseminated, made available for learning. The focus on skills and competencies as the object of instruction largely obscures the developmental aspects of learning and knowledge related to work, how knowledge is modified and enhanced through practice, and how this gain may serve individual or collective welfare. It is a form of mastery in which emphasis on the knowing subject is replaced by a concern to produce an objectified form of knowing, i.e., performance, subject to external controls and measurement. Skill and its subset, competence, are thus educational objectives formulated as a matter of one's ability to service the employer (Grahame, 1983).

Locating Women's Interests

The obvious question to which we must return is why these developments in the world of skills training should be of particular interest to feminists. The answer is manifold. First, competency forms of training have the potential to be used to limit, rather than expand, women's access to opportunities at work. A brief historical example will be used here to illustrate this concern. Second, there is the possibility that the competency approach will be imposed on female dominated areas of training because of prejudicial stereotypes about women' work and skills, and that this development will erode the status and integrity of the fields themselves. Finally, there is evidence that the competency approach itself may be in contradiction with the kinds of knowledge that are in growing demand in the workplace. A brief discussion of changing clerical work processes will illuminate this concern. Each of these issues is explored in brief.

Women as Circumscribed Labor

As women, we are not strangers to political processes that obscure and devalue work and working knowledge. Women's work has been the victim of such practices for at least two centuries of industrialism. In the struggle of male (and mostly white) workers to preserve their power and stature in the workplace, as well as their dominance in the home, skill definitions have come to be saturated with gender (as well as racial) bias (Phillips & Taylor, 1980). We have learned that the result of having males define women's work and skills is definitions that routinely serve their interests and not ours. The outcome is no bargaining power, poor working conditions, low pay and a dead-end existence (Barrett, 1980; O'Donnell, 1984).

The educational developments examined briefly in this paper need to be understood as part of these long-standing political struggles, extending the battle over skill levels, power and pay from the workplace into the classroom. While the elaboration of competency approaches described here brings a greater level of sophistication to this struggle, the strategic role of education in organizing women's relative position in the workforce is far from new. Education and training have long been important not only because they serve as the gateway for entry to various kinds of work, or because they are a means to acquiring the technical know-how required to perform the job. They have been critical as well because they are part of the social and political processes through which status and power have come to be attached to various kinds of work and knowledge, and through which such stature has been routinely reserved for male workers (Barrett, 1980; Gaskell, 1983; Wickham, 1982).

Patterns of education and training in the twentieth century have channeled women into a narrow range of occupations in the service, clerical and public sectors, while creating barriers to entry in the vast majority of industrial occupations where males predominate. This process has ensured that women's experience and areas of knowledge were largely distinct from those of men, and has organized women's labor power as a separate and unequal entity in the labor market. The contribution of education and training policy to this type of occupational segregation has been widely recognized and has been the focus of much feminist advocacy. By contrast, less attention has been paid to how the programs in which women have been enrolled have systematically prepared them for a "circumscribed working life" (Pierson & Cohen, 1986:67) in either male or female dominated fields. Here the issue is not one of differentiating women's labor according to fields of knowledge and skill, but according to the scope and depth of the expertise that women can bring to bear on their work, and indeed on their employment futures.

The process of circumscription is demonstrated in the context of wartime employment for women by Pierson & Cohen (1986). Their research on the mobilization of women during World War II shows that the training women routinely received for the war industries was not designed to make them into skilled workers on a par with their male predecessors, but rather to employ them as short-term and limited workers at the bottom of the labor hierarchy. In some industries where plant conversions had to take place, production processes were specifically organized to create minute, monotonous operations that could be performed by inexperienced, temporary workers with a minimum of training, while preserving the more complex jobs for long-term employees. As the war progressed, and with it the shortage of labor, women were increasingly recruited into these positions at the bottom of the ranks of skilled workers. In hindsight, there is little question about the character and consequences of the training that was s provided in this context:

> Training provided for women under the War Emergency Training Programme was designed to fit them for a specific job for the duration of the war, not for a life-time career as an all-round skilled worker, much less a skilled mechanic who might compete with the men in the post-war job market. . . . (Pierson & Cohen, 1986:73)

Part of the importance of short-term, job specific training strategies during the war was the possibility of training workers only to the extent that served the immediate needs of their employers in the war industries or the armed services. While the normal length of courses under the War Emergency Training Program was set at three months, gradually shorter courses were introduced, particularly for women. Pierson & Cohen found that the majority of the training courses for women lasted from two to six weeks, and in many cases training was further reduced to a few days on the job. According to one source, the "general and theoretical" aspects of many trainings could be left out because the women had no "long term ambition" in the trades they were learning (Pierson & Cohen, 1986:76). Pierson and Cohen conclude that this training differential was one of several handicaps facing women who desired to continue in a non-traditional occupation at the end of the war.

In the 1980s in Canada as well as in other industrialized countries, women are not learning vocational skills to serve for "the duration of the war" but as the basis to support themselves and their children for the duration of their lives. Yet the forms of training available in an ever-widening number of programs in public institutions are precisely those, such as the competency-based approaches discussed above, that are conceived and developed out of an interest in short-term labor, whether in the context of war or the belief in rapid technological change. The question must be asked, by both men and women, whether by adopting such schemes we are importing not only a mechanism for efficiency, economy, and accountability in education and training, but also for the creation of disposable labor. The desirability of training for disposable labor is a matter for widespread public debate, as are questions about how such training might be organized, utilized and paid for.

Women as Stereotyped Labor

The second cause or concern among feminists about the popularity of the competency approach is, quite simply, that it will be imposed on female dominated fields of training, whereas it would be, indeed is being, seen as inappropriate in male dominated fields. A brief look at the program areas in which a competency approach has been implemented in British Columbia will illustrate this concern. On the one hand, such an approach is currently established in pre-apprenticeship or pre-trades level programs, selected programs for other equipment operators (e.g., steam shovel operator, dishwasher operator), and a number of special occupational programs for mentally or physically handicapped students. The bulk of these trainings are for male dominated occupations, and all, significantly, are distinguished by their focus on basic manual operations. On the other hand, the competency approach is being widely implemented in programs for white collar, female dominated occupations in the clerical, social and health care fields, such as early childhood education, human service work, general nursing, medical and dental assistance, and office administration. These programs address a considerable range of learning objectives in the manual, cognitive and affective realms. The contrast among these disparate areas of application is striking and disquieting. The source of this disquiet is evident in the following experience from my recent research in community colleges in B.C.

I have been studying the use of competency analysis as the basis for curriculum revision in clerical programs. In conversation with the Dean of applied programs at a college where I was doing field work, I asked about the choice of a competency approach in the clerical area. His answer was instructive:

> [Competency-based] training is appropriate for certain kinds of areas, but it's not a panacea by any stretch of the imagination . . . I don't think it would be unrealistic to move, for example, typing or word-processing to a certain level of competency approach. Because it's a highly physical type of thing, where you're not necessarily expecting someone to know how a word processing package is able to cut and paste, as long as it will, and you are able to manipulate it, and at a certain speed, and a certain level. That's what we are guaranteeing. (Jackson, 1988)

As a matter of record, the clerical programs in which the competency analysis was being introduced in this college at the time of our conversation encompassed all of the office administration programs in the business department. This included not only typing and word processing, but also legal secretarial, general secretarial, and bookkeeping programs and a more advanced program in office systems and records management. The populations in these programs are 99% female, including faculty and students. I did not pressure the Dean for a description of how the subject matter in these programs fit the criteria of "highly physical" proficiency that he had outlined, or for an explanation of how his criteria applied to the other social and health care programs at the college, in which I knew that competency-based approaches were already in use. At the same time, there were several programs in the business department that were male dominated and included some university transfer credits, for which the same type of competency analysis had been suggested by the administration. However, these proposals were met with substantial resistance among those faculty members who would be affected (predominantly male). When I asked these faculty members about their objections to the competency approach, one instructor summed up their concerns: "It was dreamed up by somebody with a small mind!" These same instructors did not object to the introduction of the competency approach in the clerical program areas.

These remarks are suggestive of familiar ways of thinking that routinely discount and discredit women's work and skills, and they draw our attention to the potential impact of such thinking in the arena of education and training policy. Obviously I mean to argue, in a preliminary sort of way, that competency approaches may be imposed on female dominated programs because of any number of reductive stereotypes about women's work and skills, and because they may not be effectively resisted. It is a corollary of Gamson's (1979) observations that the approach has been concentrated in low-status institutions in the United States. If selectively implemented in this way, the competency approach may contribute to the view that women's programs are low-skilled, and indeed have the effect of enshrining a deskilled version of the knowledge and skill base of women's occupations in the programs of instruction. In so doing, the competency approach has the potential to systematize, certify and thereby institutionalize a delimiting or degraded conception of working knowledge for women, rather than an expansive or developmental one.

Contradictions in Clerical Work

Aside from how current developments in competency education are judged on pedagogical, philosophical, or political grounds, there remain some troublesome issues from a purely instrumental perspective. They centre on the extent to which the competency approach is contradictory and dysfunctional in relation to developments in the workplace itself. This argument is germane to the situation of clerical workers in particular because they are faced with rapid transformations in office technology, the character and impact of which are topics of widespread debate.

In the last decade there has been abundant documentation of the negative impact of information technology on clerical work and workers in a wide variety of office and clerical work settings (e.g., Crompton & Reid, 1982; Glenn and Feldberg, 1979; Menzies, 1981). The introduction of large scale electronic systems in the 1970s led to the creation in many work places of large pools of relatively undifferentiated workers, commonly in data entry and word processing pools, performing relatively fragmented, routinized tasks in an isolated and increasingly controlled environment (see e.g., Crompton & Jones, 1984; Glenn & Feldber, 1979). This picture of the impact of microelectronics on clerical work is consistent with a tradition of labor process analysis that focuses on the fragmentation of skills in twentieth-century industrialism and the loss among workers of power and control over the work processes of which they are a part (Braverman, 1974; Noble, 1984, 1977; Shaiken, 1984). This is the development popularly known as "deskilling."

More recently, labor process researchers have become concerned about aspects of workplace organization which are hidden or disguised by the dominant "deskilling" framework. For example, emerging research evidence suggests that the impact of fifth generation micro-electronics on the skills of office workers is increasingly to polarize skills, creating a growing number of clerical positions which are professionalized, in contrast to those at the other end of the scale which are proletarianized (Adler, 1983; Appelbaum, 1985; U.S. Office of Technological Assessment, 1985). In meetings such as banks and insurance offices, researchers have found that many tasks formerly performed by professional or highly experienced workers, relying on their judgment and discretion, can be shifted downward to workers who execute the same functions with the aid of computerized systems of decision making. With the discretionary aspects of the work substantially reduced, the remaining job functions are designated as clerical. Such a reorganization accomplishes a "down-waging" of professional or semi-professional work, while it increases the level of complexity, abstraction and interpretation required in the performance of "clerical" duties. In the insurance industry, for instance, one result of this type of reorganization is that employers are more frequently hiring college graduates for clerical positions to ensure that the general literacy and problem-solving requirements of the jobs will be satisfied (Appelbaum, 1985).

Other researchers have found a similar pattern occurring in office settings in general. They report that integrated office systems distribute the burden of responsibility for the integrity of the work process across a broader range of workers and thus demand broader, rather than narrower, understanding of work processes (Bird, 1980). In this context, the need for general systems comprehension is becoming as aspect of "local mastery" and management, and analysis of information increasingly is becoming the basis of even basic office jobs (Adler, 1983; Bird, 1980; Gordon & Kimball, 1985). The same researchers also point out that those jobs that remain at the extreme pole of deskilling will be increasingly vulnerable to erosion through the introduction of voice-activated systems and optical character readers, as well as on-line entry and self-serve methods of recording transactions.

The educational implications of this vision of changes in clerical work are considerable and stand in stark contrast to the concept of manual proficiency invoked by the college dean quoted above. They cast doubt on the utility — for employers as well as employees — of training in focussed technical proficiency and a narrow understanding of clerical tasks. They point instead toward the need for a broad based approach to clerical education with an emphasis on the capacity for integration and synthesis of information. Movement in this direction is not likely in the current policy climate favoring short-term, specialized programs in the clerical field as well as in other areas of instruction in the community college system in Canada.

Conclusions and Implications

Widespread support for reforms of vocational education and training in Canada is a clear indication that the system of provision has come uncoupled from the interests it is called upon to serve: individual, industrial, social, and political. Our institutions of education and training have remained wedded to outdated pedagogic and occupational objectives, in a climate of continuing uncertainty about labor market demand, while the pressure to find training solutions to economic ills continues to build. Predictably, the solutions that appear to be within reach are themselves born of outmoded methods of thinking and contribute to the problems they are meant to solve. This conundrum is clearly articulated in a recent report from the Silicon Valley Research group in California who argue that the long-term viability of all forms of narrow technical expertise is called into question by the character of high technology. The authors predict that inasmuch as training institutions proceed within a narrow framework for skills development, they will do a poor job of providing employees with "effectively transferable skills" to cope with fluctuating demands, and will accomplish little more than providing a subsidy to firms by training temporary workers (Gordon & Kimball, 1985:97). On the contrary, Gordon & Kimball argue, programs of education and training should specifically avoid "over-commitment to relatively evanescent skills" in order to achieve their goals of adaptability and responsiveness to industrial needs (1985:106). This reasoning runs counter to the current wisdom and predominant practice in training policy in both Canada and the United States.

In this paper, I have argued that the competency approach to skill training falls precisely into the trap identified by the Silicon Valley Research Group. In the pursuit of flexibility and responsiveness to industry, it produces an organization of vocational training which fails to satisfy the legitimate needs of workers and addresses only the most short-sighted interests of employers. In particular, I have argued that the competency approach will not strengthen the position of women, individually or collectively, vis-à-vis long-term opportunities in the labor market, and that it may in fact serve to erode, rather than enhance the stature of women's job skills. In sum, competency-based training will not further the feminist agenda in education.

The compelling questions that follow from this analysis are not only about method and technique in vocational curriculum, but about the broad purposes and objectives of vocational education and training in Canada, and about the treatment of women in vocational policy. Are the current approaches to vocational/technical training designed to ensure the long-term employment of individuals in a highly demanding labor market and the long-term viability of technical expertise in a highly competitive international economy? Or are these policies designed to produce workers who should anticipate a "circumscribed" relation to the labor market and whose purchase on an employment future will be through a continuous recycling of disposable skills? Will workers in this category routinely include a high percentage of females with average levels of education, while the long term career prospects are reserved for individuals with a university degree? Is the primary utility of these particular policies their capacity to relieve short-term political problems: growing expenditures in the education and training sectors, immediate pressures of unemployment, fear of rising labor costs and faltering profit margins, etc.? If so, what is the responsibility of government to consider the long-term well-being of workers in general and women in particular in the search for solutions? Is there a concept of "flexibility" in training in which the servicing of employers' interests is not at the expense of workers' needs?

While competency-based approaches have had a pervasive influence on vocational/technical instruction in recent years, institutional training opportunities for women have been beset by other problems as well. Critics have repeatedly noted that the introduction by the federal government of the National Training Act in 1979 intensified the barriers to women's effective participation in a wide range of occupational training areas, and continued to channel women into training in low-paid and dead-end occupations. With the coming of the Canadian Job Strategy in 1985, critics have focused as well on the dilution of instruction through emphasis on work-site experience (a practice that benefits the employer in the short run without any assurance of continued employment for the trainee), and on the persistent lack of responsiveness of public educational institutions to the learning needs of under-educated women (Brown-Hicks & Avedon, 1986; CCLOW, 1986; Richardson, 1986). In other words, perhaps the time has come to re-assess whether women are gaining or losing ground in the training sector as a whole. In making that assessment, let us be wary that vocational relevance is not, as Carol O'Donnell has so aptly put it, "a euphemism for education on the cheap" (1984:170).

Notes
[1]Prepared for the Women and Education Conference, University of British Columbia, Vancouver, B.C., June 1986. This research has been supported by the Social Sciences and Humanities Research Council, Grant No. 410-85-356.

References

Adler, P. (1983). "Rethinking the skill requirements of new technology." Boston: Harvard Business School, Working Paper.

Allen, C.R. (1919). *The instructor, the man, and the job.* Philadelphia: Lippincott.

Althusser, L. (1971). "Ideology and ideological state apparatuses." *Lenin and philosophy and other essays.* New York: New Left Books.

Appelbaum, E.(1985). "Technology and work organization in the insurance industry." *I.L.R. Report,* 23, (1), 21-26.

Avis, J. (1981). "Social and technical relations: The case of further education." *British Journal of Sociology of Education,* (2), 2:149-161.

Barrett, M. (1980). *Women's oppression today: Problems in marxist feminist analysis.* London: Verso.

Bird, E. (1980). *Information technology in the office: The Impact on women's jobs.* London: Communications Studies and Planning Ltd.

Blackburn, R.M., & Mann, M.. (1979). *The Working Class in the labour market.* London: Macmillan.

Bobbit, J.F. (1918)). *The curriculum.* Boston: Houghton Mifflin.

Braverman, H. (1974). *Labor and monopoly capitalism.* New York: Monthly Review Press.

Brown-Hicks, J., & Avedon, L.. (1986). "Social movements as a means to empowerment: Why women must take control of their own learning." *Women's Education,* (4), 4:31-33.

Canada Employment and Immigration Commission (CEIC). (1983). *Learning a living in Canada: Report of the skill development leave task force.* Vol. 1. Ottawa: Supply and Services.

Canadian Congress for Learning Opportunities for Women (CCLOW). (1986). *Decade of promise: An assessment of Canadian women's status in education, training and employment, 1976-1985.* Toronto: Canadian Congress for Learning Opportunities for Women.

Cantor, L.M., & Roberts, I.F. (1979). *Further education today: A critical review.* London: Routledge and Kegan Paul.

Carnegie Council in Policy Studies in Higher Education. (1980). *Policy studies in higher education: A summary of reports and recommendations.* San Francisco: Jossey-Bass.

Castles, S., & Wustenberg, W. (1979). *The education of the future.* London: Pluto Press.

Centre for Contemporary Cultural Studies (CCCS). (1981). *Unpopular education.* London: Hutchinson.

Chapman, J.C. (1921). *Trade tests: The scientific measurement of trade proficiency.* New York: Holt, Rinehart and Winston.

Charters, W.W. (1923). *Curriculum construction.* New York: Macmillan.

Clement, W. (1981). *Hardrock mining.* Toronto: McClelland and Stewart.

Collins, M. (1983). "A critical analysis of competency-based systems," *Adult Education Forum.* 174-183.

Crompton, R., & Jones. G. (1984). *White-collar proletariat: Deskilling and gender in clerical work.* Philadelphia: Temple University Press.

Crompton, R., & Reid S. (1982) "The deskilling of clerical work." In S. Wood, (Ed). *The degradation of work.* London: Hutchinson, 1982.

Dewey, J. (1966). *Democracy and education.* New York: Free Press [1915].

Donald, J. (1979). "Green paper: Noise of crisis." *Screen Education,* 30, 13-49.

Dooley, C.R. (1919). *Final report of the national army training detachments.* Washington D.C.: War Department Committee on Education and Special Training.

Dwyer, R. (1977). "Workers' education, labor education, labor studies: An historical delineation." *Review of Educational Research,* 47, (1), (Winter) 179-207,

Economic Council of Canada. (1982). *In short supply: Jobs and skills in the 1980s.* Ottawa: Economic Council of Canada.

Edwards, R. (1979) *Contested terrain.* New York: Basic Books.

Elbow, P. (1979) "Trying to teach while thinking about the end," In G. Grant et al., (Eds.) *On competence.* San Francisco: Jossey-Bass.

Ewan, T. (1979). "Analyzing the impact of competence-based approaches on liberal education." In G. Grant et al, (Eds.) *On competence.* San Francisco: Jossey-Bass.

Finn, D. (1982). "Whose needs? Schooling and the 'needs' of industry." In T.L. Ree & P. Atkinson, (Eds.) *Youth unemployment and state intervention.* London: Routledge and Kegan Paul.

Gamson, Z. (1979). "Understanding the difficulties of implementing a competence-based curriculum," in G. Grant et al., (Eds.) *On competence,* San Francisco: Jossey-Bass, 1979.

Gaskell, J. (1983). "Conceptions of skill and the work of women," *Atlantis,* 8 (2), 11-26.

Gleeson, D., (Ed.) (1983). *Youth training and the search for work.* London: Routledge and Kegan Paul.

Gleeson, D., & Mardle, G. (1980). *Further education or training?* London: Routledge and Kegan Paul.

Glenn, E., & Feldberg, R.. (1979). "Proletarianizing clerical work: Technology and organizational control in the office." In A. Zimbalist, (Ed.) *Case studies on the labour process.* New York: Monthly Review Press.

Gordon, D.M., Edwards, R. & Reich, M. (1982) *Segmented work, divided workers.* Cambridge: Cambridge University Press.

Gordon, R., & Kimball, L.M. (1985) *High technology, employment and the challenges to education.* Santa Cruz: Silicon Valley Research Group.

Gorz, A., (Ed.) (1976). *The division of labour: The labour process and class struggle in modern capitalism.* Sussex: The Harvester Press Ltd.

Grahame, P.R. (1983). "Life skills autonomy and 'really useful knowledge': Notes toward a critique of skill" Paper presented at the Annual Meetings of the Canadian Sociology and Anthropology Association, Vancouver, June 1983.

Grant, G. et al., (Eds.) (1979). *On competence.* San Francisco: Jossey-Bass.

Harris, N.C., & Grede, J.F. (1977). *Career education in colleges.* San Francisco: Jossey-Bass.

Hussain, A. (1976). "The economy and educational system in capitalist societies." *Economy and Society,* 5, 4.

Jackson, N. (1988). Competence as good management practice: A study of curriculum reform in the community college. Ph.D. dissertation, University of British Columbia.

Johnson, R. (1979). "Really useful knowledge: Radical education and working class culture." In J. Clarke et al., (Eds.) *Working class culture.* London: Hutchinson.

Knaak, W.C. (1977). *Competency-based vocational education: A review.* Columbus, Ohio: Information Series No. 115, ERIC Clearinghouse on Career Education.

Lenhardt, G. (1981). "School and wage labour." *Economics and industrial democracy,* Vol. 2. London: Sage, 191-222.

MacDonald, L. (1985). "Training: For self-sufficiency or dependency?" *Women's Education,* 4, (1), 17-20.

Mann, C.R. (1922). "The technique of army training." *School and Society,* 15, 228-232.

Menzies, H. (1981). *Women and the chip. Case studies of the effects of informatics on employment in Canada.* Montreal: Institute for Research on Public Policy.

Moore, R. (1983). "Further education, pedagogy, and production." In D. Gleeson, (Ed.) *Youth training and the search for work pp. 14-31.* London: Routledge and Kegan Paul.

More, C. (1980). *Skill and the English working class.* London: Croom Helm.

Knave, G. (1984). "On the road to silicon valley? The changing relations between higher education and government in Western Europe." *European Journal of Education,* 19, (2), 111-129.

Neumann, W. (1979). "Educational responses to the concern for proficiency." In G. Grant et al., (Eds.) *On competence.* San Francisco: Jossey-Bass.

Noble, D. (1984). *Forces of production.* New York: Alfred A. Knopf.

Noble, D. (1977). *America by design.* New York: Oxford University Press.

O'Donnell, C. (1984). *The basis of the bargain: Gender, schooling and jobs.* Sydney: George Allen and Unwin.

Organization for Economic Cooperation and Development (OECD). (1983). *The future of vocational education and training.* Paris: OECD.

Parnell, D. (1978). *The case for competency-based education.* Phi Delta Kappa Educational Foundation.

Phillips, A., & Taylor, B. (1980). "Sex and skill: Notes toward a feminist economics." *Feminist Review,* 6, 79-88.

Pierson, R.R., & Cohen, M. (1986) "Government job-training programs for women 1937-1947." In R.R. Pierson (Ed.). *They're still women after all: The second world war and Canadian womanhood.* Toronto: McClelland and Stewart.

Richardson, K. (1986). "A women's training resource center," *Women's Education,* 4, (3), 27-33.

Shaiken, H. (1984). *Work transformed: Automation and labour in the computer age.* New York: Holt, Rinehart and Winston.

Spady, W.G. (1980). "The concept and implications of competency-based education," in R. Jaeger and C. Tittle, (Eds.) *Minimum competency achievement testing.* Berkeley: McCutchen.

Spady, W.G. (1977). "Competency-based education: A bandwagon in search of a definition." *Educational Researcher,* 6, (1), 7-14.

Taylor, F.W. (1947). *The principles of scientific management.* New York: W.W. Norton & Co., [1911].

Toops, H. (1921). *Trade tests in education.* New York: Teachers College Press, Columbia University.

Tyler, R. (1975). "Historical efforts to develop learning on a competency base." In W.R. O'Connell Jr. and W.E. Moosnaw, (Eds.) *A CBC undergraduate program.* Atlanta: Southern Regional Education Board.

United States, Office of Technological Assessment. (1985). *Automation of America's offices.* Washington D.C.: Government Printing Office.

Wickham, A. (1982). "The state and training programs for women." In E. Whitelegg et al, (Eds.) *The changing experience of women.* Oxford: Martin Robertson with the Open University Press.

16

The 'Art' of Managing Horses or the 'Skill' of Driving: Contesting the Meaning of Skill in Clerical Training

Jane Gaskell

Conceptions of skill are central to discussions of job training. Skill provides an explanation of why training matters: job training is supposed to develop skills workers will need at work; longer training programs develop more skills. Skill provides an explanation of the link between training and work: chances of getting a job are linked to the extent to which students have learned skills in training; employers prefer more skilled workers. Training programs become an institutional representation of skill, symbolizing skill, giving it a real material form. Training programs in turn regulate the supply of workers eligible for jobs, affecting the value of these workers in the marketplace.

The notion of skill is also central to relations of power in the workplace. "Skilled" is a category that gives status and importance to work in common parlance and in wage negotiations. Skill categories are ideological categories, used to justify and challenge existing hierarchies at work. Persons with more skill are seen to deserve respect and autonomy in their work. Those with little skill must be closely supervised and can be easily replaced. Thus a set of beliefs about skill and skill development are central to the legitimacy of the division of labor in industrialized societies.

But what counts as a skill? How do we recognize it? A skill is not, like a wage, something that can be simply identified and measured. Conflicting accounts of the skills involved in any job will be given by different people, at different times, for different purposes. What is noticed and valued depends on who is noticing and who is valuing.

Braverman (1974) gives a clear example of this process:

> In the circumstances of an earlier day, when a largely rural population learned the arts of managing horses as part of the process of growing up, while few as yet knew how to operate motorized vehicles, it might have made sense to characterize the former as part of the common heritage and thus no skill at all, while driving, as a learned ability, would have been thought of as a "skill." Today, it would be more proper to regard those who are able to drive vehicles as unskilled in that respect at least, while those who can care for, harness and manage a team of horses are certainly the possessors of a marked and uncommon ability. There is certainly little reason to suppose that the ability to drive a motor vehicle is more demanding,

requires longer training or habituation time, and thus represents a higher or intrinsically more rewarding skill. (p. 430)

Attributing skill levels to jobs involves drawing on common assumptions about how society works and what is important in it: the assumption that as technology gets more complex, jobs get more complex; the assumption that as education levels increase, the jobs workers do become more skilled; the assumption that everyone can drive a car. What we take to be a noteworthy skill that demands lengthy job training is fundamentally shaped by what is taken for granted in our society, what the social context is, and where and how, at any historical time and place, people learn to do something.

Positing a relationship between length of educational preparation and skill demands at work misrepresents the way educational requirements come into being. Braverman again points out that you cannot use increased educational levels as a measure of skill upgrading in the workforce.

> A complete picture of the functions and functioning of education in the United States and other capitalist countries would require a thorough historical study of the manner in which the present standards came into being, and how they were related, at each step of their formation, to the social forces of the society at large. But even a sketch of the recent period suffices to show that many causes, most of them bearing no direct relationship to the educational requirements of the job structure, have been at work. (p. 437)

Changes in labor legislation, in the unemployment rate, in state investment in educational institutions, and in employers' use of education as a screening device are among some of the important changes that have increased the educational levels of workers. None of these mean that the skill levels of jobs have changed.

Constructions of skill play an important part in the reproduction or transformation of social relations in the workplace. Some would argue that skill designations are nothing more than an expression of power relations. The more important, highly paid, powerful work is assumed to be more "skilled." We treat mental work as more skilled than manual work, justifying the power managers have over manual workers. Characteristics of powerful positions — autonomy, supervision of less powerful workers, making judgements for others — are what we count as higher order skills.

Power comes in many guises, and gender is one of them. Gender inequity at work is related to differences in the way skills are recognized and valued in jobs done by men compared to jobs done by women. As Barrett (1980) puts it, "Women have frequently failed to establish recognition of the skills required by their work, and have consequently been in a weak bargaining position in a divided and internally competitive work force . . . we need to know precisely how and why some groups of workers succeed in establishing definitions of their work as skilled" (p. 166). Skills in women's jobs are more likely to be taken for granted because women learn them privately, instead of in mandated educational programs. Skills women use have been seen as part of femininity, necessary for "women's work" but not credentialled or paid for.

In this paper I want to explore the social construction of skill in a job training program for a group of female Canadian clerical workers. To understand the debates about skill, one must explore both the structure of the program and the talk and intentions of instructors and students. I will argue that understandings of skill are contested, not given, changing, not fixed. They are contested within specific settings that both set limits on and make possible the debate. The specific debate that interests me here is related to the skills of clerical workers. Women's skills as clerical workers have not been highly valued. Assigning them value as skills worthy of respect and recognition in training programs is an enterprise that is both necessary and full of contradictions because of the very centrality of skill to training.

Skills and Secretarial Work in North America

The skills involved in secretarial work are not clearly agreed upon. Job definitions differ from employer to employer. Training requirements vary greatly, ranging from typing courses in high school to two-year courses at the community college. There are even B.A.s in secretarial science offered at some universities. The extreme variability in jobs and in training broadly labelled clerical or secretarial allows everyone to find some support for their notion of what the job entails.

Pringle (1988) notes that secretaries are defined more by who they are (women) and by their relation (helpmate and subordinate) to a boss than by what they do. The job is poorly paid for the education it requires and its importance to any organization. Blue-collar workers are systematically paid much more. Secretarial jobs are changing, because of the computer technology that has become common in offices, because unionization has increased rapidly, and because the women's movement has forced a rethinking about women's work. The fairly open and contested definition of secretarial work at the moment in North America provides an opportunity to look at the processes involved in the social construction of skill categories.

Disagreement about the skills involved in clerical work is illustrated by the debates that arose in Oregon when pay equity legislation forced government workers to evaluate these skills. As Acker (1989) comments,

> Men on the evaluation team saw clerical work in a much different light than did the women. According to the male image, much clerical work is typing and checking for accuracy. This is only a repetitive production job, in their estimation. Anyone with a high school education can type and write letters, they thought. Women evaluators, in contrast, saw these jobs as much more complex. Workers who primarily did typing had to edit and proof-read, rather than just check for errors. They needed to know how to choose the format and to construct new formats. Often typing was combined with receptionist work, and the pressure of completing reports and manuscripts combined with answering the telephone and responding to people at the

front desk required a cool head and the competence to do several things simultaneously. These were the arguments of the women evaluators. (p. 93)

What skills do secretarial/clerical jobs involve? There is no one answer, for the cultural assumptions, values and taken-for-granted reality of one group is contested by another. All people struggle to have their version of the world given legitimacy and power. What is clear is that women workers have had relatively little power to insist on their versions of their work.

In this paper I will explore some attempts by women to have secretarial work revalued within the context of job training. Both the limitations of the women's efforts and their importance in keeping open the issue of skill are noteworthy. Neither students nor instructors in this program find the answer to the question, "what do clerical workers need to know?" a simple one.

The Research Setting

The program that was studied for this research was funded by the Canadian government's "Job Entry" program. The program is one of the ways the state provides funding for women who are entering employment. Qualified instructors compete for contracts from Employment and Immigration Canada. Although much of the money goes to colleges, increasingly private contractors offer this program.

In the studied program, two instructors provided training for 26 weeks to 25 women. All the women were preparing for clerical jobs. The program paid the students a living allowance and some money for transportation and child care. The amount each student received was sometimes more than the women could expect to receive when, on the completion of the program, they got jobs as clerical workers.

The main parameters of the program were set by the state and they signalled the fact that little skill, and therefore little training, was seen as necessary for the jobs these students would get. The eligibility criteria set by the government did not include any educational prerequisites. The requirements were all related to demographic characteristics. Students had to be women, at least 25, eligible to work in Canada, with no experience in the labor market for the previous three years. A varying but defined percentage of the students had to be on welfare, and targets were set for the representation of Native women, women with disabilities, and visible minority women.

The length of the training was set at 26 weeks. There was one requirement that substantial time be spent "on site," that is, in the workplace, and another that "life skills" be included in the curriculum.

Twenty-six weeks is a short time to provide anything in the way of skills. The large amount of time "on site" suggests that the function of the program is to accustom and screen students, not to turn them into specialized and skilled workers. The requirement for teaching "life" skills builds in the assumption that students are deficient in some basic approaches to living.

Rob Moore (1983) makes this explicit in his analysis of why life skills and social skills are being introduced into vocational training in Britain:

> The voc-prep target group is non-academic, low achievers whose jobs have such a low skill content that they cannot provide the content for a curriculum. Consequently, it is necessary to discover alternative "needs" to provide both a rationale and a content for programmes. These needs are found in personal development and social skills. (p. 18)

The mode of evaluation of the program was set by the state. Placement rates, that is, the proportion of students who found employment at the end of the program, constituted the primary measure of success and the criterion used to decide whether the program would be re-funded. There was no independent measure of learning, no certificate or licensing exam or anything based in skill that signalled the successful completion of training. As the ultimate criterion of success for this program was placement rates, employers were in effect given the power to judge its adequacy.[1] From the point of view of the state, the program was about the most basic kind of employability, not about any specific skill development.

The instructors of the program, however, contested the notion that secretarial work demanded few skills and required little training. They had a long history of involvement in the women's movement. They wanted to challenge traditional definitions of women's work and women's experience, arguing that they were undervalued and deserved more respect.

As one instructor put it,

> "I've always been a feminist. My mother was a feminist, I was brought up as a feminist and I've always sort of thought that women are equal and can compete in any field. We try to give them [students] the general overall impression that women are perfectly as competent as men and try to . . . you know . . . to get them to feel that way about themselves. . . . Almost all if not maybe 100% of the speakers we bring in are women . . . they see them as role models."

The instructors believed in pay equity, discussed sexual harassment and realized that the demands of husbands and children for women's domestic labor constituted a major barrier to the equality of women at work. They thought the life skills component of the program treated significant skills that were too often overlooked, and they used this part of the program to discuss women's experiences at home and work seriously.

Instead of arguing that women should move into trades or blue-collar work, their version of feminism was to revalue clerical work. This, despite the fact that clerical jobs have wages that are so low that the instructors realized some women would be worse off financially when they got a clerical job than they were while they were enrolled in the job training. They argued that the office was becoming increasingly democratic and respectful of women, that employers were increasingly inclined to promote women out of entry-level clerical positions into responsible, even management jobs, and that even if this was not true for the workplace as a whole, it was true for the particular employers selected as hosts for the students in training. During interviews, instructors commented:

"To say that because secretarial work might have been demeaning at one time. . . . I don't feel that it is any more, that you shouldn't train women in that field. What other field is there? . . . I don't see it as any more demeaning than a lot of jobs that men do."

"I think employers have changed their attitudes immensely in the last 10 to 15 years. The women don't make the coffee any more . . . you know the idea that the secretary is a servant to the manager is rapidly disappearing . . . the attitude today is more that we are a team in the office and we are all working together and different people have different roles and the work that secretaries do now, a lot of it is really almost administration work for the management . . . gradually the line between the manager and the secretary is disappearing."

The instructors cared about the development of skills, and stated their objectives in these terms. They cared particularly about the development of confidence and a sense of self-worth. Their brochure outlined the purposes of the program as follows:

"The on-site [i.e., workplace] training should include a wide range of skills which the participant can master and which would be of value to many other potential employers. . . . The off-site [i.e., classroom] training is designed to develop skills which are highly valued in the business world. These include problem solving, decision making, planning and interpersonal skills, computer familiarity, typing, word processing and job search skills. . . . [I]t will assist each participant to achieve a manageable balance between home and work responsibilities which permits both roles to be maintained successfully."

The instructors negotiated the structure and content of the program, within the state guidelines. They had to balance their commitment to valuing women's work with their commitment to keep the program viable, that is, to place students and please employers. They contested and negotiated definitions of clerical work, but they had to encourage women to take jobs, even if the jobs were not "good" ones. The contradictions that emerged were many, and will be illustrated here by aspects of the program: the process of selection, the teaching of dress codes, and the construction of a resume.

The Process of Selection: Developing or Screening for Skill

The short time available for instruction in the program produced a contradiction for the instructors. If clerical jobs *did* require substantial skills, it was important to screen women before they entered the program to make sure they were capable of landing and keeping a job. On the other hand, full enrollment was important for the program's financial viability, and a commitment to women in need underlay the philosophy of the program. Which students should be admitted into the program?

The program had to be able to place students in jobs in order to survive. It needed to have good relations with employers in order to continue to find placements for the students, and it needed to satisfy the students by finding them jobs. "When they graduate their success is our success. We need an 81% placement rate. . . . We have to make sure they get hired."

But time was short. In 26 weeks there were severe limits on what could be taught, especially when few of those weeks involved instruction. The instructors began the program with two introductory weeks spent on orientation and "life skills." The students then spent 4 weeks in a secondary school classroom, taught by a retired high school business teacher, working on typing and computer skills. The remaining 20 weeks were divided between work placements and a couple of weeks back at the program office for discussion and counselling.

In the technical skills training component, it was clear that very little could be accomplished in four weeks, especially under conditions where the program was sharing equipment with the secondary school students. The students did spend time on typewriters upgrading their typing speed. They also learned Multi-Mate, a software program for personal computers that gave them an idea of what word processing was all about. No accounting, spread sheets or data base management programs, and no other word processing packages were taught. There was no dicta-typing, no shorthand, no basic grammar, spelling or arithmetic. The technical and academic skills taught were at a very introductory level.

Moreover, students who had a lot to learn used up a disproportionate share of resources, resources consisting of the instructors' time and money. "The lengths we go to! [counselling, charm school, psychiatrists, organizing day care]. . . . If I don't do it, they don't succeed and then I don't succeed. I'm in jeopardy of my contract if I don't succeed." The program needed students who already had skills, students who could use their time in the program to recognize, label, polish and feel confident in skills they already possessed.

On the other hand, there was some scarcity of applicants, produced by the mechanics of the timing of the funding, the state's requirements for eligibility, and the difficulties of advertising a small program in a city where many kinds of training programs are available. This encouraged the instructors to take any student who was eligible, whatever her skills and experience. Moreover, one of the major criticisms of job training has been that it serves those who are already employable, that it "creams off" the most able, investing scarce resources in them instead of in those who really need the training. A program committed to women's welfare would not write any women off. It would take risks on behalf of women who desperately wanted a way out of their poverty, their bad marriages, their depression.

The instructors felt that the skill demands of clerical jobs were such that they had to institute higher screening requirements than the state demanded.

This was not just an ideological commitment to reskilling clerical jobs. It was not just a bid to make the teaching and counselling easier. It was also an assessment of who could actually perform clerical and secretarial jobs at a level of competence that would not bring the program into disrepute. The instructors insisted on a screening interview, and made grade 12 (secondary school) completion a requirement. Applicants were preferred if they were emotionally secure, well dressed, used the English language correctly, and already had basic clerical skills, most importantly typing. A relatively high social status often helped. Some had university education, and some had wealthy husbands, as the needier students found out to their chagrin when they had get-togethers at these students' homes.

The instructors felt conflict over their selection decisions. "Our biggest dilemma is being tough enough . . . we think we can save their lives. We take them in." But they felt that 26 weeks was just not long enough to properly train women for clerical work, even while they recognized that there is no single length of time that is appropriate for all women. The variation in individuals' learning time could also lead to focussing on differences among women and construing the lack of learning as the students' problem. The instructors described some students as "too needy," "unplaceable," "not trainable" or "better off on income assistance." This rhetoric takes the length of the training program for granted and justifies a selection procedure that takes only the more able students while pointing to other students' inadequacies.

To take the length of their training as a sign of the skill of the women who graduated from this program would be very misleading. Instead of signalling that the women who graduated had few skills, the shortness of the training ensured that the program selected women who already had skills. The way instructors managed to insist on the skill of clerical work when confronted with government guidelines that did not allow much skill development was to screen students carefully. They did it with some ambivalence and with variable outcomes. But the social process they put in place shows why reifying length of training as an index of how much skill workers have is misleading, especially in the case of mature women who have learned much over the course of their lives, if informally. How much skill it does represent is a question of negotiation.

Teaching Dress Codes: Constructing and Valuing Life Skills

The instructors valued the time spent on "life skills" in the training program. Life skills covered a range of areas of instruction, from interview techniques to dealing with sexual harassment to managing a home when you also have a paid job. Government's mandating of life skills could suggest there are no "real" skills to teach, as Moore argues above, or that these women are so deficient in basic day-to-day competencies that they need very low-level education. But the instructors in this program argued that the skills labelled as life skills are ones that are important, difficult and too frequently taken for granted instead of taught. Far from seeing them as a need contrived to justify the training, they saw them as essential in allowing any woman to successfully negotiate entry into the labor market and deal with the politics of the office.

Learning about how to dress in the office was part of the "life skills" curriculum, and it illustrates some of the contradictions and the notions of skill that this program dealt with. The micropolitics of dress in the office expresses relations of power and gender and class. Modes of self-presentation and particularly dress have been central to statements about women's independence. The women's movement has been marked by rejection of traditional dress codes, from bloomers to bobbed hair to bras. As one of the instructors reminisced with one of the researchers, "When [we] were talking, I was reminded about when I wore shit-kicking boots and no bra. That was my statement in the women's movement."

The program had a required dress code to impress on students the seriousness of the enterprise — the fact that it was WORK, as the introductory brochure put it. "We won't let you wear jeans to class. There is a tendency when you're wearing jeans to act like you're wearing jeans. We're trying to change your image." Through the dress code, students were encouraged to actively construct themselves as "professionals."

There was a good deal of formal and informal discussion about dress. Just before students went to their work placements, what to wear was discussed in class and on the steps outside. The instructors' advice: "One of the safest things is a skirt and blouse. A suit is a big investment; you might be overdressed in a small company." "Reading the fashion pages in the newspaper is probably the worst thing you can do. You will need very classic clothes." Student: "An old sweater wouldn't be suitable, would it?" Instructor: "Dress it up. Use a scarf. If you use different scarves you can completely change your image." The students discussed how to wash clothes (does silk really need to go to the drycleaners?), where to buy clothes, and how much to spend on clothes.

A day-long session on dress was run by a consultant who had worked as a Status of Women officer, and struggled for women's rights. Clear rules were adduced. "Buy fake pearls that are knotted in-between the pearls and don't have too high a gloss." "Buy beige. It's boring as hell, but it goes with everything." But at the same time, the contextual discussion was fairly sophisticated. "Whatever I'll tell you today, someone else will tell you something else tomorrow." "It all comes down to the fact you'll have to figure out what your interviewer will be like." There are no simple rules. This is a complex process.

The discussion was interspersed with scientific findings: "Seventy-five percent of women from Harvard thought their appearance was important in getting a position," and direct advice: "Fake it till you make it. Dress like where you want to go, but never more than the boss." There was some critical analysis of the fashion industry: "There is a council that decides what colors we'll all be wearing," and practical, useful advice, "Always carry a bottle of clear nail polish and a sewing kit and nail file and a new pair of nylons"; "If you have a short neck, wear it knotted down here, [or] if you have big boobs, it will stick out." There were vocabulary lessons (Chanel suits, Spectator pumps) and discussions of Rubens' paintings of women and of the effect of AIDS on desirable body images (it makes plump more acceptable). The lesson was a wide-ranging one, calling on a variety of intellectual "skills."

The objective of the class was described as "to identify a professional look . . . the best things to wear to get ahead in business." Through looking at pictures of men and women, students were encouraged to critically examine the meanings of various styles of clothing, what clothes "say." "The jacket puts the woman at the top. Jacket is a mantel of authority. Men know it. They put it on when they see a client. A sweater is textured. It says touch me, it seems more friendly." As the class went on, each look was critiqued for how powerful it made the woman appear: "I think it's a very successful look"; "It says 'money'"; "Off-white or cream. Only the rich can afford to have them dry cleaned"; "Pearls are quite successful." This sometimes came close to a sociological discussion of the semiotics of dress.

They also discussed gender codes. Sexuality must be controlled, but cannot be denied. The instructor asked, "Is this a suitable look?" (showing a picture of a woman with open-toed shoes). Students replied in unison, "No." Instructor: "Why?" Students: "Men can't be responsible if they see toes hanging out." No-nos for women, as described on a sheet of paper handed out in class, include "no brassiere, no pantyhose or stockings, shoulder-length or longer hair, no make-up or too heavy make-up, dangling earrings or multiple earrings in one ear, unshaven legs and underarms." The discussion of dressing like or for men included the following comment: Student: "We don't want to look like men, but they are the ones that hire you. You need to understand them." The problems with dressing like a woman were that "there's nothing that will put you down in authority more quickly than a little pink sweater. You look like a housewife." Long hair is too "counter-culture" and yellow is "not a power color."

In this lesson are all the dilemmas of a feminist curriculum. The class affirms women's experience in a variety of ways. It communicates information about the office world in a code that women understand and are close to. The instructor is supportive and encouraging, trying to build the students' confidence: "When I came in I had the feeling I really didn't have to be here. You've put yourselves together well." The instructor encourages women to believe they can construct a new "image" of themselves, that they can define themselves in ways that will win respect.

But to dress to please employers and to get ahead is to fit into a world of men on their terms, and to fit into structures of authority that put the female employee at the bottom. To emphasize getting hired and getting ahead within these structures is to accept the legitimacy of them. At the end of the class, many of the students were arguing that the rules of dress were absurd and an imposition on their sense of themselves, their comfort and their rights to expression. The instructor was left with the dilemma of how to support this assertion of independence, while continuing to emphasize the necessity, indeed the point of the program, which is to have these women be acceptable to employers.

Student: "Sounds like we're dressing according to a man's code and feminizing it."

Instructor: "Well, I guess so. I guess we have to base it on a man's world."

Student: "But it's all so artificial."

Instructor: "But you have to get out with the enemy and infiltrate. I'm not saying you all have to wear what I've shown you . . . you find your own signature."

The program suggested women must get ahead to be valued, but that they are skilled and valuable, wherever they work. It suggested women should dress to impress those with power, but that those with power keep women down. It suggested clerical work is skilled and valuable, but that women need to move up into management if they want to be successful. It described employers as "the enemy" to be "infiltrated," but also as forward-looking and respectful of women.

In these classroom dialogues we can see the ways woman students are encouraged to construct themselves as clerical workers. The successful trainee is the one who is most able to construct herself in a "professional" image and to recognize, value and communicate her "skills." She will stick up for her rights, be confident and perform responsible work. This is an exhortatory discourse of possibility, about the value of clerical work and clerical workers. Job training is built on hope of transformation, of education, of change, and the discourse is a powerful one. But the construction of self does not take place in a social vacuum. A discourse of realism or "employability" also occurs in the classroom, and is even more pronounced in the work placements and in the past experience of these women. It says that clerical workers are at the "bottom," in unskilled and routine jobs. It says workers must learn to discern and conform to the hierarchies at work, where employers are on top, and where employers discriminate without much fear of reprisals. These messages are contradictory rather than coherent. They are the outcome of attempts to revalue skill within a program and a job market that is based on the assumption that clerical workers have little skill.

Doing Résumés: The Communication of Skill

In the class on preparing a résumé, the contest over what counts as a skill was most explicit. The instructors pointed out that the résumé is a way of communicating to employers what you can do, and that you must be careful to portray yourself as skilled, experienced and valuable. They advised their students on how to construct themselves as skilled workers. On a résumé a woman could decide what she counted as a skill. She could lay it out on her own terms. As the instructor explained, "We try to show that everything that they've been doing in their life, the things they are dismissing as just housewifely chores, are all really skills that they've learned and that they can help make a contribution in the business world." Skills that have been picked up informally, skills that were recognized in a screening interview but are not credentialled, skills that are taken for granted in the home can here be represented and given their actual worth for the labor market.

The process of preparing a résumé is a contest. It is a bid to have skills recognized. It may not work, but it is worth a try. And the process of having women name their own skills encourages them, as well as employers, to take the skills seriously.

In class the instructor explained, "We do skill right up front, not education but skill — that's a functional resume . . . we'll forget about chronological résumés here. In traditional application forms they want you to list your work starting from the most recent. It makes me freeze."

Student: "That's what Canada Employment wants you to do."

Instructor: "Well, we're going to trick them — assemble it so that the gaps don't show. . . . Because you have so many skills — look at all the ones you've got — I'm impressed. . . . Look at p. 15, we're going to use some of these words. They've been designed by experts — action words that people can hang on to . . . most words are 'ing' words. A résumé is not in past tense."

The words she refers to are words like "managing," "organizing," "analyzing."

Instructor: "With skills, what you list you don't have to be paid for . . . in a functional résumé your skills are what you've been paid for or not. You did the work, you had the skill. In the last group one woman ran her husband's trucking business for 25 years while her husband was out on the road. Never got a penny. But she had to do invoices, phoning, contracting. Doesn't matter if you've been paid or unpaid — doesn't connect with traditional paid employment."

The skills that the instructors particularly encouraged the women to recognize, value and write down were social skills. Many of these women had brought up children, managed to move from one country to another, helped their husbands, and made new friends. These involve skills that often do not count, that tend to be taken for granted as personality characteristics of women, rather than given their due as learned competencies. They are also skills that are valued less highly, at least in the entry-level labor market, than technical competencies.

Student: "What are interpersonal skills?"

Instructor: "Counselling, interviewing, dealing with people all day. A lot of secretarial work is interpersonal — handling complaints, conferences — handling people is distinct from technical. . . . Dealing with people is one of the hardest things to do. Those who go to management school — it's all people skills. The reason why women are doing well in the workplace is that they have good people skills. Don't forget the interpersonal — like handling complaints."

"Interpersonal skills — there are thousands of women who can type and use word processors but if they are being difficult or get in cliques — "

The value of technical skills was downplayed in relation to interpersonal skills, reflecting the relative lack of emphasis in the program on technical skills and the instructors' beliefs about the link between management and secretarial work. The most important qualities, students were told in one lesson, were to "1. Try to be polite to everyone. 2. Are you a team worker — so you pitch in, even though it may not be your regular job? 3. Attitude to learning. 4. Manners. 5. Being a compatible person. 6. Communication skills — oral, written, on the telephone. 7. Ability to work under pressure — able to work independently — listen for directions and proceed on your own — able to take the initiative — proofreading, versatility, decision making, time management."

As one instructor later said privately to the researchers, "What we try to do is give them entry-level skills to get them a job, and secondly, give them the self-confidence and maybe the ambition to feel that they can move ahead. . . . We tell the women this . . . that they have to start again at the bottom but they can work their way up much more quickly than they did as a young person because they've got maturity and experience and more common sense and better judgement and so on."

Later on, on the résumé, students were asked to list their past employment (though not in chronological order). The discussion of clerical categories pointed to the vagueness with which everyone defined the category, and the attempts of the instructors to define it as responsible and potentially managerial.

Student: "What's the difference between clerical and secretarial?"

Instructor: "Secretarial is higher level than clerical. My image is that it's someone doing work with one person rather than one person at large. Clerical — you're doing a lot that's the same as others."

Student: "The offices I've worked in, I did all of the secretarial and clerical work."

Instructor: "Separate the two — managing is a higher skill than typing. Don't be frightened by being office manager — biggest growth is in small business, not in large businesses. Small businesses always need office managers. That is a place where women are moving up faster."

Student: "I don't like the term 'girl Friday'; it's demeaning."

Instructor: [claps hands] "Alright, we've got a budding feminist. Give it some status and call it office manager. Give yourself the benefit of the doubt but if that doesn't feel good don't do it."

Student: "My boss never said I was office manager."

Instructor: "Did you hire or fire anyone?"

Student: "No."

Instructor: "Then you were more like a secretary. You weren't an office manager: they hire, fire, do budgets, supervise others."

Student: "My job was called S.T.II."

Instructor: "No abbreviations please on a résumé."

Student: "I still don't know what it stands for." [laughter]

Later in the class:

Student: "I wouldn't be happy with using 'secretary' or 'office manager' because I did everything — it was a one girl office. That office fell apart without me."

Instructor: "I have a list of classifications that I'll bring in but I don't have it here today."

Student: "How about General Office Supervisor?"

Instructor: "A supervisor usually manages others. Why don't you like secretary?"

Student: "Because it's too limiting. Office administrator?"

Instructor: "How about that? — office administrator — then you can say general office duties for printing and roofing company, etc. Don't list all your skills — they're on page 1, so put here what you didn't describe on page 1 . . . 'was responsible for all office duties.'"

The instructors encouraged women to see the construction of a résumé as a process of actively defining themselves. Information should be left out if it constructed the wrong image.

Student: "Sometimes you don't mention things."

Instructor: "Absolutely — that's why [other instructor] asked you to fill in the sheet with what you've done, what you like and don't like. So I don't put down I've sold encyclopedias."

Student: "People don't put negative things on — divorce, leaving employer."

They are encouraged to continue this process in the interview:

Student: "What if an employer asks your age?"

Instructor: "You can say . . . and smile . . . you were told in class 'B.C. human rights prohibits you from asking that. But I can assure you my health is good.' They know they are not supposed to ask that."

Other instructor: [smiling] "You'll turn all these women into feminists!"

In this class, employers were constructed as the enemy, though not in a very forceful way. Discrimination was described:

> Instructor: "If you think you'll get the same kind of salary your husband or even your son is getting, you will be surprised. The assumption is that men have a family to support, and women work for pin money. That is still the attitude of a lot of companies, especially when they are hiring part-time workers. Ontario is bringing in pay equity."
>
> Student: "Is there any effort to enforce pay levels?"
>
> Instructor: "No. But some companies are trying to get women into management . . . they are creeping up."

A balance had to be struck between recognition of women's inequality and encouraging women to believe that they could indeed make it in the work world, and do as well as a man. In a previous class, the instructors had brought in a woman from the ministry of labor who gave statistics on the wage gap between women and men, and indicated that the government could do relatively little to redress the balance. The class reacted with anger and frustration. The instructors called it "depressing." What in some contexts is a consciousness-raising activity — seeing differences in power and income clearly — became in this context a problem, undermining the instructors' optimism that women could better themselves through training.

By and large in the lesson on résumés, the students were encouraged to stand up for their rights in the face of employers who might well be a problem. The students were being encouraged to construct themselves as skilled "professionals." The instructors used the opportunity to reconstruct the women's own sense of themselves and their image of clerical and secretarial jobs. Notions of skill were contested, discussed, and changed. The contest was set up with employers portrayed as those that had to be "tricked" and convinced. Skill recognition here was a matter of struggle.

Conclusions

This paper began with the idea that skill is a key concept in understanding job training, and that "skilled" is a contested category. What counts as a skill is not clear. Are "life skills" or technical skills important? How important are interpersonal skills? How important is where they are learned and how they are credentialled? Answering these questions is not a technical matter; it is a judgement of value. Existing judgements made by employers must not be reified and treated as the only way one can conceive skill. These judgements must be debated and seen in the context from which they arose.

One particular form of reification was criticized by looking at the social processes involved in this program. The amount of time spent in a training program is not equivalent to the skill of the workers who graduate. The time available affects the amount that can be taught, but this in turn affects entry into the program as much as it affects outcomes from the program.

Versions of what skills count come into conflict even within the program. This clerical training program was committed to valuing the skills of women, but had to do so within structures set by the state and by employers. The program was ideologically feminist, but designed to prepare students for jobs that were firmly situated within a female segment of the labor market. The program was set up in such a way that the cost to the government had to be kept down, by keeping the length of the program down. And evaluation of the program was ultimately done by employers, both because they had to be convinced to take students on job placements and because they had to be convinced to hire graduates.

As a result, the program stressed skills, but could not teach or evaluate students to any significant extent in terms of their skills. It stressed rights for women, and democracy in the workplace, but it had to teach students to respect the existing power relations in the workplace, to ensure they were hired.

Classroom discussions offered students a way of constructing their work that was critical of existing social relations, of discriminatory employment practices and of the devaluation of women. Classroom discussion also impressed students with a discourse of "realism," one which said self-preservation entailed learning about and conforming very carefully to existing power structures, in all their gendered guises.

I have pointed to two conflicting discourses, one of hope and possibility and change, and one of realism and the necessity of being employable. The first is imbued with a feminist voice in this program and constructs clerical work as skilled and responsible. The second is structurally unavoidable, enforced by the state's evaluation criteria, the students' need for employment, the instructors' need to get the program funded, and the employers' criteria for evaluating female clerical workers.

Attempts to introduce a feminist consciousness into job training are contradicted by the overwhelming necessity to please employers. These instructors attempted to resolve the contradiction by presenting a view of employers as progressive. However, they and the students continue to recognize in ways large and small that overall, employers are not critics of the existing relations of production and do not highly value clerical skills.

The result, the content of this program, is best seen as a contest. The program does not impart skills preordained by the needs of employers, or of jobs, for these needs are always constructed and described by someone. The program is part of a social process that provides a credential signalling the skill of clerical workers and regulating entry to the job. But the actual content and meaning of the instruction is full of contradiction and is understood only in light of one's version of clerical work. If the work is considered important and complex, the training can be interpreted in this light. It teaches thinking in context, the analysis of social interaction, the ability to organize and manage and analyze. If the work is considered trivial, on the other hand, the training can be seen as lacking in content and depth. Only with the revaluing of clerical work can the first version of training prevail, and be elaborated in programs that develop and dignify women's work.

Note

[1]Under most market conditions employers' hiring rates would actually be determined by their need for labor, rather than by the availability of trained workers. This observation makes the state's assumption that placement rates actually measure the acceptability of a program's students incorrect. The requirement, and the requirement for long placements "on site," however, does serve as a very important way to give power to employers by forcing trainers to pay close attention to them.

References

Acker, J. (1989). *Doing comparable worth: Gender, class and pay equity.* Philadelphia: Temple University Press.

Barrett, M. (1980). *Women's oppression today: Problems in Marxist feminist analysis.* London: Verso Editions/NLB.

Braverman, H. (1974). *Labor and monopoly capitalism.* New York: Monthly Review Press.

Collins, R. (1979). *The credential society.* New York: Academic Press.

Maurice M., Sellier, F., & Silvestre, J.J. (1987). *The social foundations of industrial power.* Cambridge: MIT Press.

Moore, R. (1983). Further education, pedagogy and production. In D. Gleeson (Ed.), *Youth training and the search for work.* London: Routledge and Kegan Paul.

Pringle, R. (1988). *Secretaries talk.* London: Verso.

Future Directions

Though deep conceptual divisions remain, feminist theoretical writing about education manages to be constructively critical. Perhaps we are moving towards a synthesis of feminist educational approaches. Whatever their political orientation, all the contributors to this volume would like to see the educational system become less sexist. By challenging male-biased knowledge, we are attempting to make educational arrangements more favourable to girls and women. By challenging the privileging of gender, we begin to challenge privilege of all kinds. By incorporating women's concerns into our studies of education, we hope to redefine the boundaries of education, its pedagogy and knowledge. In a general sense, we are attempting to reshape education so that it may ultimately serve better the interests of both males and females.

As feminist scholars we aim our work at both academic and political ends. Like the founders of the social sciences, we do not see the academy as something separate from society (Bowles & Klein, 1983). We wish to reform as well as to inform. We believe that either directly or indirectly our research can provide the foundation for an action-oriented agenda to help public agencies eliminate gender-based imbalances in education (Kelly, 1984).

Canadian educational scholars and activists who want to promote gender equality work, however, in an inhospitable economic and political climate. The economy has reentered a recession in the early nineties. Employment growth over the last decade has been concentrated in low-status, part-time positions, most of which have been filled by women. The global restructuring of jobs sends much of the most dangerous and labor-intensive work to the Third World. Women's work is likely to suffer most of all.

"Restraint" budgets hit women particularly hard. In response to the economic crisis and financial deficits, governments have reduced expenditures on social programs. Women are more likely to be poor than are men (Gunderson & Muszynski, 1990). Women comprise the largest group needing social assistance, the largest group of government employees in education, health and social welfare, and the largest group requiring redress for systematic discrimination. Since education is a major area of expenditure it is especially vulnerable to public spending cuts. Such cuts cause difficulties directly for women raising their children, women teaching other people's children, and educational policies designed to rectify systematic discrimination against females. Within education, the cuts are too often directed specifically at areas where women are disproportionately located. As a result of the restraint package legislated by the British Columbia governement in July 1983, for example, colleges and other educational institutions reduced spending in women's studies courses, funding women's access coordinators, approving loans to part-time students (the majority of whom are women), and issuing grants (Bueckert, Renaud, & Stewart, n.d.).

At a time when governments do not perceive gender inequality as a problem, much less as a problem that they can or should solve, the role of feminist scholarship is especially crucial. As Sylvia Gold (1986), president of the Canadian Advisory Council on the Status of Women, asserts:

> The question here is not whether governments have an obligation to put forward policies which break down barriers in all facets of women's lives, including education. *They unquestionably do.* However, the women's movement must *define* the public policy issues, propose concrete policies that address them, and *push* for their implementation to ensure an improvement in the status of women in this country. The role of academics in the women's movement is crucial. (p. 10)

To understand the possibilities of transforming the Canadian educational system to reflect women's as well as men's concerns, we need to consider two questions. First, what kinds of changes in policies, pressure groups and resources have improved women's position in education. Second, what kinds of questions do researchers need to explore in the future so that educators, policy-makers and the general public can understand more fully how gender affects the educational process.

Since the late 1960s, several national milestones have marked improvements in opportunities for females in education as elsewhere. In 1970, the Royal Commission on the Status of Women made 167 recommendations to the government, several of which concerned education (e.g., elimination of sexual stereotyping in textbooks). In response to one recommendation, the government created the Canadian Advisory Council on the Status of Women in 1973. It monitors trends, conducts research, consults with women's groups and informs and advises government committees, task forces and officials on issues of concern to women. In the same year, the government established the Women's Program as a responsibility of the Secretary of State. The Program is the principal means by which the federal government funds women's voluntary organizations designed to improve the status of women. Since 1971, a minister has been responsible for the status of women; in 1976, a federal government department called Status of Women Canada was instituted to coordinate government activities in relation to women.

In 1978, the Canadian Human Rights Act came into effect. The Act contains a provision for equal pay for work of equal value, which applies to all federal public servants and employees of federal Crown Corporations and federally regulated private-sector companies. The Canadian Charter of Rights and Freedoms, part of Canada's constitution (1982), includes sections 15 and 28 (1985) which guarantee equality between women and men. The Employment Equity Act (Bill C-62), which came into effect in 1986, is aimed at removing employment barriers and promoting equality for women, native people, disabled persons and visible minorities. The legislation applies to all federally regulated companies and crown corporations with 100 or more employees. In response to this legislation, universities have begun to develop formal employment equity policies (Casey, 1987). The federal government has introduced gender targets into job training programs. Employment and Immigration Canada has designed policy initiatives to broaden the range of occupations for which women train. The Ministers Responsible for the Status of Women across the country in 1986 endorsed a framework for improving women's status in education that stressed encouraging women in non-traditional areas, and they assessed some progress in this strategy three years later (1989).

Legislative changes to improve women's position have also taken place at the provincial and municipal levels. These jurisdictions vary a great deal in the kinds of programs and policies they have established. At the provincial level, they range from "Women's Secretariats" that exist within specific ministries and provide local groups with discretionary grants, to Human Rights Commissions which receive complaints alleging sexual harassment. Pay equity legislation of different types has been passed in Manitoba, Ontario and Quebec.

Some ministries of education (provincial or territorial) have allowed high schools to develop distinct women's studies courses or to integrate women-related subjects into the pre-existing curriculum. Many colleges and universities have established women's studies courses or programs (Brodribb, 1983a; Eichler, 1990; Strong-Boag, 1983). Such courses differ from one another in how long they have been established, how secure they are within their institution, and how broad their coverage of subjects is. Some school boards and universities have developed policies and resources on issues like sexual harassment, pay equity, affirmative action and day care (Brodribb, 1983b; Canadian Education Association, 1988).

Many of these governmental and institutional initiatives have arisen as a response to the work of feminist pressure groups. Several groups have been particularly important in alerting the government to women's educational and training needs. CCLOW (the Canadian Congress for Learning Opportunities for Women), a national, non-profit women's organization established in 1979, actively promotes feminist principles in education and the empowerment of women. Its activities include research projects and policy papers, advocacy work, and a quarterly publication, *Women's Education des Femmes*. CRIAW (the Canadian Research Institute for the Advancement of Women), founded in 1976, and the Canadian Women's Studies Association, established in 1982, are dedicated to facilitating the work of feminist scholars and educators. The National Action Committee on the Status of Women, created in 1972, represents hundreds of Canadian women's groups. Its primary functions are to keep groups abreast of issues relevant to women (including education and training), and to lobby policy-makers.

Besides these national feminist groups, a myriad of other organizations have produced teaching resources, curriculum handbooks, media kits, videotapes and teachers' publications to combat sexism in education. These resources are designed to make girls and women more visible in the curriculum and to encourage students to consider a wider range of curriculum and job choices (for more details, see *Resources for Feminist Research, 12*(3) [1983]). Community and women's organizations offer a variety of bridging and skills-training programs for women. In Toronto alone, more than twenty such programs are available (Dance, 1985, p. 11).

Despite this flurry of activity, however, it is not at all clear that Canadian women are better off now than they were twenty years ago. Canadian women's progress may be a question of "now you see it, now you don't." What at first seems a victory for women, upon reflection may not be. The fact that the wage gap between women and men has declined, for instance, may have resulted from a drop in average male earnings, not from an increase in women's (Shifrin, 1987). As Doris Anderson quips, "We always get something, but not what we want" (cited in Nemiroff & Vander Voet, 1983, p. 8).

There are a variety of reasons why public policy may not be as effective as we would like in promoting women's progress. For most policy-makers and analysts, gender inequality is not a major problem. For example, Wilkinson's (1986) comprehensive survey of elementary and secondary education policy in Canada does not broach the question of gender inequality at all. Neither does the recent study by the Corporate Higher Education Forum entitled *To Be Our Best: Learning for the Future* (Downey, 1990), nor the Canadian Chamber of Commerce's *Focus 2000: Report of the Task Force on Education and Training* (1989). The Canadian Jobs Strategy, which was the new framework for vocational training developed by Employment and Immigration in 1985, emphasized private training and left little room for women's concerns for personal growth, for consciousness-raising, or for broadening general knowledge (Breault, 1986).

The political climate is ambivalent at best. Policies that promote women's interests coexist with actions — cutbacks, privatization — that don't. Policies that are brought in are often too weak to be very effective. The Employment Equity Act, for instance, insists only that, by 1988, employers covered by the legislation submit annual employment equity reports. The legislation does not require employers to implement employment equity measures or to establish goals and timetables. Moreover, there is no enforcement agency (Coates, 1985, p. 47).

Depending on the political and economical climate, new measures can have contradictory implications for women's status — that is, they may be both beneficial and harmful. The Canadian Charter could lead to gains for women, but the prospect of new gains seems distant when, to date, so much legal time has had to be spent protecting the gains women have already made.

Education is a particularly difficult area to change because of the different jurisdictions involved — federal, provincial, territorial — and because of the largely conservative nature of schooling. There is plenty of evidence to support the contention of Abella in her *Report of the Commission on Equality in Employment* (1984) that the movement of education is "glacially slow":

> Education has been the classic crutch upon which we lean in the hopes of coaxing change in prejudicial attitudes. But education is an unreliable agent, glacially slow in movement and impact, and often completely ineffective in the face of intractable views. It promises no immediate relief despite the immediacy of the injustice. (p. 8)

Though feminists examining education face daunting odds in their desire to improve the position of women, they have, as Nemiroff and Vander Voet (1983) put it, at least one decided advantage: "The state and its own resources have a jump on us in every category of operation . . . except perhaps commitment to women's causes" (p. 9). While the predominance of men in educational decision-making positions is a major obstacle to feminist reform, women's desire for change is sufficiently strong to permit some optimism about the likelihood of improving women's educational experiences. Hamilton (1985) is able, for example, to note optimistically the extent to which an oppositional current has been established by feminist politics and scholarship within academic disciplines:

> Feminists have indeed carried their protest into the university. . . . They have challenged not only the structure of the university, and the limited place of women within it, but also the very parameters of what constitutes knowledge, and many of the assumptions underlying the traditional academic disciplines. In simplest terms, the feminist slogan, borrowed from the New Left, that "the personal is political" not only legitimated new areas of research, but also probed their links with broader political, economic and social relations. (p. 3)

The growth of feminist research during the past two decades has been truly staggering and suggests that policy-makers may increasingly be unable to neglect women's issues.

Research Directions

Though all feminists who focus on education are concerned about gender inequality, their conclusions about how and why it occurs, and what should be done about it vary. Doing feminist research involves political assumptions, but also involves theoretical and methodological questions that go beyond the political realm. How should feminist research on education proceed? Where do we go from here, as researchers? Putting up signposts in these directions is a major function of the essays in this book.

By and large, the political assumptions that have informed feminist questions and theoretical frameworks have been taken from the liberal orientation that has dominated policy agendas. As Acker (1986) notes: "Virtually the only discourse admissible to public debate is the liberal-feminist equal opportunity one — with the accent on *opportunity* rather than *equal*" (pp. 9-10). In Canada, feminist researchers have exposed the prevalence of sexism in textbooks, the low rate of female access to male-dominated education and training, and unequal opportunities for female educators. They have called for new forms of curricula that add women in, career counselling that encourages females to consider non-traditional work, and hiring and promotion practices that do not discriminate against females.

Recent feminist theory offers new questions and paradigms for researchers, ones that open up exciting new possibilities for inquiry. With this new direction, researchers have moved from a demand that females catch up to males and that gender differences be eliminated to a celebration of the female experience and a demand that it be revalued. Research shows how our culture uses male experience as the norm and thereby denigrates female experience. Feminists have begun to utilize women's diverse experiences as a source for an alternative vision and alternative values. Women's culture, women's organizations and women's experiences are retrieved from the devaluation they receive in the hands of male-oriented researchers. This research begins a redressing of the balance that is sorely needed. By revaluing the female, we begin to understand how deeply gender affects our lives and why different strategies for change may be appropriate. Feminists call for schools to adapt to the interest of females, for curricula and pedagogy to reflect female ways of thinking and behaving, for a valuation of "traditional" female activities, courses and work.

Radical feminist insights pointing to the commonalities of women's experiences have been immeasurably useful for understanding gender. But socialist feminist theory has also helped to advance the debates on education. Socialist feminism argues that much feminist analysis is taken from the perspective of middle-class, western, white women. Radical feminism, they argue, is too prone to root women's experience in biology and to value it above men's experience. Radical feminism exaggerates the antagonistic relations between women and men, overemphasizes differences, and ignores the diversity of women's experiences. It distorts research and misdirects action, and makes women feel as alienated as did male scholarship. The gender categories celebrated by radical feminists — woman as nurturer, as comforter, as peacemaker — are traditional, historically and culturally specific constructions.

Instead we must examine the specificity of gender. A woman's class, race, culture, sexual orientation and age also influence what happens to her. A poor woman, a middle-class woman, a Native woman, a female child and an old woman all experience being female in different ways, ways that affect their desires, their aspirations, their education and their working lives. The effects of gender cannot be separated from the effects of other social conditions. People experience them all together. Feminists have called for an inclusion in research of the experiences of females of different classes, color, ethnic groups and so on. If schools are to be responsive to women's interests, they must recognize and accept diversity. Socialist feminists concerned about schooling have also called for changes in the economy and in the family. They argue that as long as most women are used as a cheap labor force, and are burdened with domestic responsibilities, improving their education will have little effect.

All feminists, regardless of their political stripe, are critical of male-biased knowledge. But once having launched this critique, the question of where it will take us in our pursuit of knowledge needs to be addressed. Some argue for female-centred knowledge, others for non-sexist knowledge. Female-centred knowledge establishes a distinct knowledge base — which may be called women's studies, feminist studies or feminology — derived from the female experience. It generates questions and answers by concentrating on women. It starts with the position of women and aims to reach a better understanding of the particularities of the female condition. A non-sexist mode of inquiry also requires female-centred knowledge, but seeks to integrate the concern for women into research questions so as to transform "malestream" knowledge. It aims to transform both the current male-centred and incipient female-centred approaches into something that is non-sexist (Eichler, 1987). This collection of essays is not only founded in a belief in the necessity for such an approach but is also presented as an attempt to discover whether it can be accomplished.

Some argue that a revaluation of the female implies a distinct methodology (Harding, 1987; Smith, 1987). Feminist research must not start from the knowledge of "experts" but from the standpoint of ordinary individuals. Female subjectivity becomes central to the generation of knowledge and a means to test its validity, and so exploratory and qualitative research is especially important. A different relationship between the researcher and subject is constructed. But as researchers we also have an obligation to examine patterns that are obscured in everyday life and to look at what accounts for women's experience of the world. Theorizing women's experience is necessary if we are to grasp the complexities of the social fabric.

To understand adequately the extent to which society, including education, is gendered, we need dramatic improvements in the gathering of statistical data, and in its analysis and dissemination. Documentation of the gender segregation of education, training, employment and income is either spotty, inconsistent, or non-existent. More systematic data is necessary in order to identify areas where women are excluded and to analyze the kinds of policy interventions most likely to be effective. If institutions are to be held accountable for improving women's position, administrators need the appropriate statistical data with which to monitor it. Quantitative research can be an important tool for women, revealing patterns of inequality, and exploring associations between social conditions and women's experience. We can use this data to generate knowledge so long as we do not forget to be "vigilantly suspicious" of the way it is used and of the categories it embodies.

Having a sound non-sexist methodology is indispensable to good educational research. So is having a sound theory. Feminists have had to rely on existing theories to help them develop their own language, concepts and propositions. They have had to deal with broad debates that arise from the theoretical traditions within which they work. A central debate of most contemporary theories regarding inequality concerns the importance of "structure" versus "agency" and evaluates the extent to which people are active agents able to respond to social structures. Feminist research has begun to expose the ways women have been oppressed by the structures of male-dominated society. It has shown how male-dominated cultures socialize males and females into rigid sex roles, how educational and economic systems channel women into low-status occupations, and how institutions of the family oppress women. Such research has been useful in pinpointing how women acquire a low social status. At the same time, much of this research has inadvertently denied women the possibility of making decisions, of responding to the conditions affecting them, of taking control of their lives. It has reinforced stereotypes of women's passivity, and provided little understanding of how women learn to survive and struggle within the power structures of society.

Feminist research needs to be contextualized, and to resolve the dilemma of "agency" versus "structure." Women are at the same time active agents struggling to control and change their lives, and constrained subjects shaped by social, cultural and economic structures. Women make choices, but the choices available are not of their own making. They become mothers, teachers, child care providers or whatever, not merely because of their biology or socialization, but because, within the given social context, it makes sense to do so. Research needs to present women as neither passive victims nor heroic superwomen who can remake the world as an act of will. The notion of contextualized action, always socially situated, always problematic, must guide and inform our research.

As this discussion suggests, in the space of only two decades, feminist researchers have accomplished a great deal. In the educational realm, they have revitalized old questions and developed new ones. Their work has only begun. The prospect of improving girls' and women's education in Canada, if daunting, is an exciting one.

References

Abella, Judge R.S. (1984). *Report of the Commission on Equality in Employment.* Ottawa: Minister of Supply and Services.

Acker, S. (1986). *What do feminists want —and what do they get —from education?* Paper presented at the Women and Education Conference, University of British Columbia, Vancouver, B.C.

Acker, S. (1987). Feminist theory and the study of gender and education. *International Review of Education, 33,* 419-435.

Armstrong, P. (1984). *Labor pains: Women's work in crisis.* Toronto: The Women's Press.

Arrowsmith, D. (1986). *Pay equity: Legislative framework and cases* (Research and Current Issues Series, No. 43). Kingston, ON: Queen's University, Industrial Relations Centre.

Bowles, G., & Klein, R.D. (Eds.). (1983). *Theories of women's studies.* London: Routledge and Kegan Paul.

Breault, L. (1986). Turning a male training model into a feminist one: Canadian jobs strategy re-entry. *Women's Education des Femmes, 5*(2), 14-17.

Brodribb, S. (1983a). Women's studies Canada 1983. *Resources for Feminist Research, 12*(3), 53-70.

Brodribb, S. (1983b). Canadian universities: A learning environment for women? *Resources for Feminist Research, 12*(3), 70-71.

Bueckert, L., Renaud, L., & Stewart, M.L. (n.d.). *Baseline report: Women's participation in B.C. colleges and institutes.* Ottawa, ON: Canadian Research Institute for the Advancement of Women.

Canadian Education Association. (1988). *Especially for women: Programs and services offered by school boards.* Toronto: CEA.

Canadian Chamber of Commerce. (1989). *Focus 2000 report of the Task Force on Education and Training.*

Casey, S. (1987). Still a long way to go. *CAUT Bulletin, 34*(5), 4.

Coates, M.L. (1985). *Employment equity: Issues, approaches and public policy framework* (Research and Current Issues Series, No. 44). Kingston, ON: Queen's University, Industrial Relations Centre.

Dance, T. (1985). Skills training for women. *Women's Education des Femmes, 3*(4), 11-13.

Downey, J. (1990). *To be our best: Learning for the future.* Ottawa: Corporate Higher Education Forum.

Eichler, M. (1987). The relationship between sexist, non-sexist, woman-centred and feminist research in the social sciences. In Greta Hofmann Nemiroff (Ed.), *Women and men: Interdisciplinary readings on gender.* Toronto: Fitzhenry and Whiteside.

Eichler, M. (1990). *Women's studies professors in Canada: A collective self-portrait.* Toronto: O.I.S.E. occasional papers.

Gold, S. (1986). *Government policies: Implications for women in education.* Paper presented to the Women and Education Conference, University of British Columbia, Vancouver, B.C.

Gunderson M., & Muszynski, L. (1990). *Women and labour market poverty.* Ottawa: Canadian Advisory Council on the Status of Women.

Hamilton, R. (1985). Feminists in the academy: Intellectuals or political subversives? *Queen's Quarterly, 92*(1), 3-20.

Harding S. (1987). *Feminism and methodology*. Bloomington: Indiana University Press.

Kelly, G. (1984). Women's access to education in the Third World: Myths and realities. In Sandra Acker (Ed.), *World yearbook of education 1984: Women and education*. London: Kogan Page.

Menzies, H. (1982). *Computers on the job*. Toronto: James Lorimer.

Ministers Responsible for the Status of Women. (1986). Toward a labour force stratagy: A framework for training for women. Vancouver, B.C., Nov. 20 and 21.

Ministers Responsible for the Status of Women. (1989). Towards a labour force strategy: A framework for training for women: An assessment. Nov. 9-10.

Nemiroff, G.H. & Vander Voet, S. McCrea. (1983). Feminist policy research: Does it affect government policy? *Women's Education des Femmes, 2*(2), 6-9.

Resources for Feminist Research, 12(3). (1983).

Shifrin, L. (1987, January 14). The progress of women: Now you see it, now you don't. *The Vancouver Sun*, p. B5.

Smith, D. (1987). *The everyday world as problematic: a feminist sociology*. Toronto: University of Toronto Press.

Strong-Boag, V. (1983). Mapping women's studies in Canada: Some signposts. *Journal of Educational Thought, 17*(2), 94-111.

Wilkinson, B.W. (1986). Elementary and secondary education policy in Canada: A survey. *Canadian Public Policy, 12*(4) 535-572.